Frommer's

Guatemala

3rd Edition

by Eliot Greenspan

WILEY

Wiley Publishing, Inc

Published by:

WILEY PUBLISHING, INC.

111 River St.

Hoboken, NJ 07030-5774

ISBN 978-0-470-88769-1 (paper); ISBN 978-1-118-02572-7 (ebk); ISBN 978-1-118-02573-4 (ebk);
ISBN 978-1-118-02574-1 (ebk)

Editor: Jessica Langan-Peck
Production Editor: Lindsay Conner
Cartographer: Andrew Murphy
Photo Editor: Richard H. Fox
Production by Wiley Indianapolis Composition Services

Front cover photo: Temple, Tikal, Guatemala © Aldo Pavan / AGE Fotostock, Inc.
Back cover photo: Santa Catalina Arch and Volcan de Agua Antigua Guatemala © Peter M. Wilson /
Alamy Images

For information on our other products and services or to obtain technical support, please contact our
Customer Care Department within the U.S. at 877/762-2974, outside the U.S. at 317/572-3993 or fax
317/572-4002.

Wiley also publishes its books in a variety of electronic formats. Some content that appears in print may
not be available in electronic formats.

Manufactured in the United States of America

5   4   3   2   1

CONTENTS

LIST OF MAPS

ABOUT THE AUTHOR

Eliot Greenspan is a poet, journalist, and travel writer who took his backpack and type-writer the length of Mesoamerica before settling in Costa Rica in 1992. Since then, he has worked steadily as a travel writer, freelance journalist, and translator, and has continued his travels in the region. He is the author of *Frommer's Belize, Frommer's Costa Rica, Frommer's Guatemala, Frommer's Ecuador, Costa Rica Day By Day* and *Costa Rica For Dummies,* as well as the Venezuela chapter in *Frommer's South America.*

HOW TO CONTACT US

In researching this book, we discovered many wonderful places—hotels, restaurants, shops, and more. We're sure you'll find others. Please tell us about them, so we can share the information with your fellow travelers in upcoming editions. If you were disappointed with a recommendation, we'd love to know that, too. Please write to:

Frommer's Guatemala, 3rd Edition
Wiley Publishing, Inc. • 111 River St. • Hoboken, NJ 07030-5774
frommersfeedback@wiley.com

AN ADDITIONAL NOTE

Please be advised that travel information is subject to change at any time—and this is especially true of prices. We therefore suggest that you write or call ahead for confirmation when making your travel plans. The authors, editors, and publisher cannot be held responsible for the experiences of readers while traveling. Your safety is important to us, however, so we encourage you to stay alert and be aware of your surroundings. Keep a close eye on cameras, purses, and wallets, all favorite targets of thieves and pickpockets.

FROMMER'S STAR RATINGS, ICONS & ABBREVIATIONS

Every hotel, restaurant, and attraction listing in this guide has been ranked for quality, value, service, amenities, and special features using a star-rating system. In country, state, and regional guides, we also rate towns and regions to help you narrow down your choices and budget your time accordingly. Hotels and restaurants are rated on a scale of zero (recommended) to three stars (exceptional). Attractions, shopping, nightlife, towns, and regions are rated according to the following scale: zero stars (recommended), one star (highly recommended), two stars (very highly recommended), and three stars (must-see).

In addition to the star-rating system, we also use seven feature icons that point you to the great deals, in-the-know advice, and unique experiences that separate travelers from tourists. Throughout the book, look for:

special finds—those places only insiders know about

fun facts—details that make travelers more informed and their trips more fun

kids—best bets for kids and advice for the whole family

special moments—those experiences that memories are made of

overrated—places or experiences not worth your time or money

insider tips—great ways to save time and money

great values—where to get the best deals

The following abbreviations are used for credit cards:

AE	American Express	DISC	Discover	V	Visa
DC	Diners Club	MC	MasterCard		

TRAVEL RESOURCES AT FROMMERS.COM

Frommer's travel resources don't end with this guide. Frommer's website, www.frommers.com, has travel information on more than 4,000 destinations. We update features regularly, giving you access to the most current trip-planning information and the best airfare, lodging, and car-rental bargains. You can also listen to podcasts, connect with other Frommers.com members through our active-reader forums, share your travel photos, read blogs from guidebook editors and fellow travelers, and much more.

THE BEST OF GUATEMALA

Guatemala's charms are as varied as the riotous colors woven into its famed fabrics. From the Maya ruins of Tikal and the colonial splendor of Antigua—both exquisitely preserved through the centuries—to the breathtaking natural beauty of Lake Atitlán and Semuc Champey, there is a range of destinations and attractions here to please just about any type of traveler. I've been visiting Guatemala for more than 25 years, and I continue to discover new places and have new experiences that add to my own personal "best of" list. Not every "best of" place or experience on this list will suit every traveler, but if you're looking for the best hotels or restaurants to fit a certain style, taste, or budget, or trying to figure out the must-see destinations for your trip, the lists below will help you narrow down your choices and fine-tune your itinerary.

THE best PURELY GUATEMALAN EXPERIENCES

o **Enjoying the Holy Week Festivities in Antigua:** Semana Santa, or Holy Week, is celebrated with both fervor and style in Antigua. In fact, the Holy Week celebrations are arguably the most beautiful and elaborate in all of the Americas, and rival even the most famous ones in Europe. Massive processions weave slowly through the cobblestone streets over painstakingly gorgeous *alfombras,* or carpets, made of fine colored sawdust and flower petals. The air is thick with incense smoke, and the small city is a spectacle for a solid week. See chapter 6.

o **Touring the Towns & Villages Around Lake Atitlán:** While Lake Atitlán is exceedingly beautiful in and of itself, the true charm of the lake is its ability to let you visit a half-dozen or more lakeshore towns via local water-taxi services. The water taxis run regular routes throughout the day, stopping at the villages of Santiago de Atitlán, San Pedro de la Laguna, San Marco, San Antonio Palopó, and more. You can hop on and off the taxis at your whim, and stay as long as you like before heading on to the next place or back home to your hotel. See chapter 7.

o **Paying Your Respects to Maximón:** A syncretic saint worshiped by Guatemala's Maya and Catholic alike, Maximón is the bad boy of the religious pantheon. Maximón apparently responds well to gifts, and has very specific tastes, so be sure to bring some rum or a cigar as an offering. Many towns across Guatemala have a carved idol of Maximón, or San Simon, although only a few really keep the practice of his daily worship

The Best of Guatemala

Gulf of Mexico

Caribbean Sea

MEXICO

BELIZE

HONDURAS

EL SALVADOR

NICARAGUA

Pacific Ocean

- Departmental Capital
- Ancient Ruins
- Major Airport

Laguna del Tigre

LAGUNA DEL TIGRE NATIONAL PARK

Paxbán

El Mirador

EL MIRADOR NATIONAL PARK

Dos Lagunas

Carmelita

TIKAL NATIONAL PARK

San Pedro

Paso Caballos

Tikal

Piedras Negras

Lacandón

El Naranjo

SIERRA DEL LACANDÓN NATIONAL PARK

Usumacinta

Laguna Perdida

Lago Petén Itzá

Flores

Santa Ana

San Francisco

PETÉN

La Libertad

CA-13

Pasión

Sayaxché

San Juan

El Ceibal

MEXICO

Machaquilá

Cancuén

Playa Grande

Rubelsanto

Chisec

Chiyú

Nentón

Barillas

HUEHUETENANGO

San Luis Ixcán

Soloma

QUICHÉ

ALTA VERAPAZ

Cahabón

Cuilco

Chajul

Cobán

Cahabón

Huehuetenango

Usparitán

Santa Cruz Verapaz

Polochic

CA-1

Canillá

Negro

SAN MARCOS

TOTONICAPÁN

Santa Cruz del Quiché

Rabinal

Salamá

BAJA VERAPAZ

Zacapa

San Marcos

Totonicapán

Chichicastenango

EL PROGRESO

Cabañás

Quetzaltenango

SOLOLÁ

Motagua

CA-9

Guastatoya

Chiquimula

QUETZALTENANGO

Lake Atitlán

Sololá

CHIMALTENANGO

GUATEMALA

Chimaltenango

GUATEMALA CITY

Jalapa

JALAPA

Takalik Abaj

Antigua

El Progreso

Retalhuleu

SACATEPÉQUEZ

Lago de Güija

Ocós

RETALHULEU

Mazatenango

SUCHITEPÉQUEZ

CA-9

Escuintla

El Progreso

JUTIAPA

Champerico

Samalá

Siquinalá

SANTA ROSA

Cuilapa

CA-1

Jutiapa

Tulate

Tiquisate

Masagua

CA-2

Valle Nuevo

Semillero

ESCUINTLA

Taxisco

Puerto San José

Paz

PACIFIC OCEAN

Tecojate

Sipacate

Iztapa

Monterrico

Las Lisas

THE BEST PURELY GUATEMALAN EXPERIENCES ☀

Enjoying the Holy Week Festivities in Antigua **19**

Touring the Towns and Villages
Around Lake Atitlán **18**

Paying Your Respects to Maximón **18**

Shopping at the Chichicastenango Market **13**

Studying Spanish and Staying
With a Local Family **15, 18, 19**

Watching the Sunrise From the Top
of a Pyramid in Tikal **2**

Cheering On Riders in the
"Drunken Horse Race" **12**

THE BEST OF NATURAL GUATEMALA 🍃

Lake Atitlán **18**

Semuc Champey **9**

Parque Nacional Laguna de Lachuá **10**

Volcán Santa María **16**

Nebaj & the Ixil Triangle **11**

El Petén **1**

Río Dulce **5**

Los Siete Altares **4**

Tortuguerio Monterrico **21**

THE BEST MAYA ARCHAEOLOGICAL SITES ▲

Tikal **2**

Yaxhá **3**

Copán **7**

Quiriguá **6**

Takalik Abaj **17**

THE BEST CHURCHES, CONVENTS & MONASTERIES 🏛

Catedral Metropolitana **20**

Iglesia San Francisco **20**

Convento de las Capuchinas **19**

Iglesia La Merced **19**

Iglesia de Santo Tomás **13**

Iglesia de San Andrés Xecul **14**

La Basilica **8**

alive. The towns with the most elaborate Maximón rituals and traditions include Santiago de Atitlán and Zunil. See chapters 7 and 8, respectively.

o **Shopping at the Chichicastenango Market:** Guatemala's Maya people are world famous for their incredible arts and crafts, which they sell predominantly at local and regional open-air markets. These markets are held in the central plazas of the country's towns and cities. The twice-weekly market in Chichicastenango is the largest and most famous of these open-air markets, with hundreds of stands selling everything from handicrafts and flowers to household goods and furniture. See p. 169.

o **Studying Spanish & Staying with a Local Family:** Studying Spanish in a foreign country is all the rage, and Guatemala is the perfect place to do it. In addition to the wonderful surroundings and bargain prices, the Guatemalan accent is one of the cleanest and easiest to master. All of Guatemala's major tourist destinations have Spanish schools, each of which offers the option of living with a local family while you study. See the various destination chapters, as well as chapter 3, for more information.

o **Watching the Sunrise from the Top of a Pyramid in Tikal:** A visit to Tikal is a remarkable experience on its own, but my favorite way to start a visit here is by catching the sunrise from the top of one of the pyramids. In addition to the ruins and the rising sun burning through the rainforest mist, the surrounding jungle comes to life with the cries of howler monkeys and the frenzied activity and calls of awakening birds. See chapter 9.

o **Cheering on Riders in the "Drunken Horse Race":** The tiny highland Maya town of Todos Santos Chuchumatán holds one of the equestrian world's oddest races every November 1. The town's "Drunken Horse Race" is a daylong event that involves equal parts drinking and racing. The last rider (who's highly intoxicated) left on his horse is declared the winner. Riders fall, and numerous riders and spectators end up lying in an unconscious stupor along the streets and walkways of the small town. It's hilarious, nerve-racking, and sad all at the same time. See chapter 8.

THE best OF NATURAL GUATEMALA

o **Lake Atitlán (Western Highlands):** Whether or not you agree with Aldous Huxley that Atitlán is the "most beautiful lake in the world," you would be hard-pressed to not be at least slightly impressed. Formed thousands of years ago in the crater of a massive volcano and surrounded today by several other towering volcanoes, Lake Atitlán is stunning. The road that circumnavigates much of the lake actually follows the rim of the extinct crater, and the views on the high end, and those from the lakeshore and the many boats plying its waters, are fabulous. See chapter 7.

o **Semuc Champey (Alta Verapaz):** Semuc Champey is a series of stepped waterfalls and pools that actually sit on top of a raging underground river in a narrow forested canyon. It's often described as the most beautiful spot in all of Guatemala, and in addition to swimming in the pools, there's great hiking here. The spots where the Cahabón River enters and then exits its underground tunnel are jaw-dropping in their power and fury. The surrounding area is also full of caves that are worth exploring. See p. 224.

o **Parque Nacional Laguna de Lachuá (Alta Verapaz):** The deep turquoise of Lake Lachuá may have you wondering whether you're staring at the Caribbean Sea. All around the lake, lush rainforests are home to an amazing array of tropical flora and fauna. See p. 224.

- **Volcán Santa María (Outside Quetzaltenango):** Not only is Volcán Santa María an imposing sight and exhilarating climb, the view from the summit peers down into the crater of its very active sister volcano, Santiaguito. It's about a 3- to 4-hour hike to the summit. Camping is allowed, and many enjoy spending the night up here, although it can get cold and windy. See chapter 8.

- **Nebaj & the Ixil Triangle (Northern Quiché Province):** This remote area was once ground zero in the government's oppressive civil war campaign against indigenous populations suspected of supporting leftist rebels. Today, it's the best place to go deep into the Guatemalan highlands for a glimpse into the country's timeless rural life and landscape. Numerous towns can be visited by hiking centuries-old dirt paths and trails. See chapter 8.

- **El Petén (Northeastern Guatemala):** The Petén province is a massive region comprised primarily of virgin tropical rainforest, and is home to many of the country's major archaeological sites and Maya ruins. The bird-watching is top-notch, and you can see a host of other species of tropical flora and fauna on a guided hike through one of the natural parks or nature reserves. See chapter 9.

- **Río Dulce (Lago Izabal Region):** The Río Dulce, or Sweet River, runs from a narrow opening at one end of Lago Izabal all the way down to the Caribbean Sea. Along the way it passes through lush tropical lowland rainforest, as well as one gorgeous narrow canyon. In addition, hot springs bubble from underground, creating hot pools where you can stop and soak. Boat trips between the villages of Fronteras and Livingston are popular. See chapter 11.

- **Los Siete Altares (Livingston):** The name of this place translates as "the Seven Altars." Each of these altars is, in fact, a beautiful jungle waterfall. The falls are set in a steady progression in a narrow forest canyon and fed by a gentle river. The final waterfall is the largest, with a deep pool for swimming. This spot was chosen as a location for the filming of an early "Tarzan" movie. See p. 246.

- **Tortuguerio Monterrico (Monterrico):** This turtle protection project is a great place to learn about the life cycle of giant sea turtles. If you're lucky enough to be here when the turtle eggs are hatching, you can take part in their weekly raffle, wherein participants are assigned a hatchling, and the quickest hatchling to the sea wins its sponsor a prize. If the turtle hatchlings aren't in season, you can still see iguanas and caimans and hike the nature trail. See p. 264.

THE best MAYA ARCHAEOLOGICAL SITES

- **Tikal (El Petén):** In my opinion, Tikal is the most impressive of all the ancient Maya ceremonial cities. Not only is the site massive and meticulously excavated and restored, it's set in the midst of a lush and lively tropical jungle. The peaks of several temples poke through the dense rainforest canopy, toucans and parrots fly about, and the loudest noise you'll hear is the guttural call of howler monkeys. In its heyday, the city probably covered as many as 65 sq. km (25 sq. miles) and supported a population of more than 100,000. See "Tikal" in chapter 9.

- **Yaxhá (El Petén):** This Classic-period Maya city was put on the map when CBS chose it as a site for its reality show *Survivor*. While little has been excavated, this remains the third-largest Maya ceremonial city in Guatemala, behind Tikal and El Mirador. See chapter 9.

o **Copán (Honduras):** It's not technically in Guatemala, but Copán is just a few quick miles over the Honduran border. A big and beautifully restored Maya city, Copán is renowned for its impressive quantity and variety of stone carvings, which can be seen on stelae, individual sculptures, architectural adornments, and one massive stairway of a major pyramid. The Museum of Maya Sculpture contains probably the best collection of original Maya ceremonial stone art in all of Meso-america. Back at the archaeological site, you can walk through some well-lit tunnels that reveal the Maya technique of building new temples over existing ones. See chapter 10.

o **Quiriguá (En Route to Puerto Barrios):** While overall this archaeological site is pretty small, it's home to an impressive collection of large carved stelae and stones. The tallest stela here is 10m (35 ft.) tall and weighs more than 65 tons. It's the tallest Maya stela yet discovered. Almost as interesting are the massive stones with complex hieroglyphic carvings. See p. 259.

o **Takalik Abaj (Northwest of Retalhuleu):** This little-known ruin is a hidden gem. Dating from the pre-Classic period, it's one of the oldest ceremonial and trade cities to be excavated in Guatemala. Perhaps its greatest claim to fame, however, is the fact that there's a lovely lodge located just off the grounds of the archaeological site, combining ecotourism and archaeological preservation in an interesting symbiosis. See p. 273.

THE best CHURCHES, CONVENTS & MONASTERIES

o **Catedral Metropolitana (Guatemala City):** It took a long time to build this church, some 86 years, but the elegant main cathedral of Guatemala City has stood the test of time and weathered the effects of some major earthquakes. Today, the most impressive aspect of this church is its facade, which is both big and bold. However, the interior holds a treasure-trove of religious art and icons. Fronting the Plaza Mayor, this is a great place to start any tour of downtown Guatemala City. See p. 99.

o **Iglesia San Francisco (Guatemala City):** This church isn't quite as old as other more famous Catholic churches in the country, but it has arguably the most impressive main altar—a massive work of carved wood that's almost 92m (302 ft.) tall. See p. 100.

o **Convento de las Capuchinas (Antigua):** Life was pretty difficult and austere for the nuns at this Capuchin convent, but today the grounds and buildings are some of the most pastoral and picturesque in all of Antigua. The large and sprawling complex was abandoned in the wake of the 1776 earthquake, but the damage was relatively minor. The view from the rooftop is not to be missed. See p. 127.

o **Iglesia La Merced (Antigua):** In a city awash in Catholic churches, convents, and monasteries, Iglesia La Merced reigns supreme. It's no small coincidence—nor small honor—that the principal procession of the Holy Week celebrations leaves from this church. The ornate baroque facade is painted bright yellow, with white trim, and the interior is full of art and sculptures. The ruins of the attached convent are also worth a visit. See p. 128.

o **Iglesia de Santo Tomás (Chichicastenango):** Dating back to 1540, this modest church serves simultaneously as a place for Catholic worship and ancient Maya rituals. The exterior steps, which possess a privileged perch over the town of Chichicastenango, are believed to represent the 18 months of the Maya calendar.

Today, these steps are constantly in use as an altar for Maya prayer and offerings. It was in the attached convent that the oldest known version of the Popol Vuh was discovered. See p. 170.

○ **Iglesia de San Andrés Xecul (Outside of Quetzaltenango):** The brilliantly painted ornate facade of this church, located in a small town in the Western Highlands, is easily the most psychedelic in the entire country. The facade features the prominent figures of jaguars mixed with religious iconography. Be sure to come in the afternoon, when the sun directly hits the church's front. See p. 181.

○ **La Basílica (Esquipulas):** This is the most famous religious site in Guatemala, and the only church in the country to earn the honor of being named a basilica. More than one million pilgrims from around the world come to the 1758 church to pay their respects to the famous statue, the *Black Christ.* See p. 230.

THE best OUTDOOR ADVENTURES

○ **Mountain Biking the Rural Back Roads:** The back roads and dirt paths of rural Guatemala are perfect for fat tire explorations. Whether you choose to take a ridge ride between small villages or a more technically challenging ascent or descent of a volcano, there is something for all ability levels. **Old Town Outfitters** (© **502/5399-0440;** www.adventureguatemala.com) is my favorite operator, and has excellent guides and equipment, and a wide range of tours and trips. See chapter 5.

○ **Climbing an Active Volcano:** Guatemala's mountainous terrain is predominantly volcanic, and many of these volcanoes are still active. There's nothing as primal as climbing the flanks of an active volcano or peering down into an erupting crater. Both of these experiences are possible on a climb to the summit of **Pacaya** volcano. Many tours take you close enough to actually feel the heat of fresh lava. Once Pacaya's whetted your appetite, there are numerous other volcanoes here to scale, including **Santa María, Tajumulco, Agua,** and **Acatenango.** See chapters 6 and 8, respectively.

○ **Swinging through the Treetops on a Canopy Tour:** Zip-trekking is becoming all the rage, and offers a different way to experience the rich wonders of the tropical rainforest. If you visit Tikal, don't miss the opportunity to take a trip with the **Canopy Tour Tikal** (© **502/7926-4270;** www.canopytikal.com; p. 201). Alternately, there's a canopy tour at the **Reserva Natural Atitlán** (© **502/7762-2565;** www.atitlanreserva.com; p. 144) just outside of Panajachel, and another new one at **Finca Filadelfia** (© **502/7728-0812;** www.filadelfiaresort.com; p. 131) just outside of Antigua.

○ **Exploring the Underworld:** Many of Guatemala's volcanic mountains are riddled with caves. The ancient Maya considered caves holy sites that served as passageways to the next world. The caves of **Lanquin** and **Candelaria** are popular tourist destinations, but my favorite cave adventure is a tour into the depths of **Kan' Ba.** This cave has a small river running through it, and the spelunking here is a mix of hiking, wading, and swimming. The entrance to the cave is a large opening where the river exits and forms a gentle jungle waterfall. See chapter 10.

○ **Rafting on the Cahabón River:** The Alta Verapaz region is rapidly becoming the center of Guatemala's growing adventure-tourism industry, and the raging rapids of the Cahabón River are part of the reason. After it exits the natural marvel of Semuc Champey, the Cahabón has both class III and class IV sections that are perfect for white-water rafting. Single-day adventures and multiday tours are available. Contact **Aventuras Turísticas** (© **502/7951-4213;** www.aventurasturisticas.com), or see chapter 10 for more details.

o **Landing a Marlin or Sailfish:** Although a relative newcomer to the world of international offshore game fishing, Guatemala is creating quite a buzz. The waters off Guatemala's Pacific coast are excellent for sportfishing year-round, and big game fish are being hauled in at a record pace. If you want to reel 'em in, contact **Parlama Sport Fishing** (© **502/5704-4254** or 7832-4332; www.parlama.com), or one of the dedicated fishing lodges located around Iztapa. See chapter 12.

THE best SHOPPING & MARKETS

o **Ron Zacapa Centenario:** While I spend a lot of time waxing poetic over the beauty and quality of Guatemala's arts and crafts, it's worth emphasizing how special this 23-year-old dark rum is. Whether you think you like rum or not, any aficionado of fine spirits should pick up a bottle of this amazingly smooth brew. See p. 31.

o **In Nola** (Guatemala City; © **502/2367-2424;** www.in-nola.com): This is the place in Guatemala City for textiles and just about any other arts-and-crafts item. The large store is beautifully laid out, service is excellent, and the prices are fair. You won't find the bargains you might be able to negotiate at the informal markets, but you won't be taken to the cleaners either. See p. 106.

o **Carlos Woods Arte Antiguo y Contemporáneo** (Guatemala City; © **502/2366-6883;** www.carloswoodsarte.com): This is the finest art gallery in Guatemala City, with an excellent variety of modern and historical works. The rooms here are well lit and beautifully designed, making a visit a pure pleasure whether or not you're looking to buy. See p. 106.

o **Nim Po't** (Antigua; © **502/7832-2681;** www.nimpot.com): A massive indoor space with a soaring ceiling houses this local craft and textile cooperative warehouse. Textiles, woodcarvings, and ceramic wares from across the country are available here. The quality varies greatly, but if you know what to look for, you can find some fine works without having to venture into the farther reaches of rural Guatemala. See p. 134.

o **Joyería del Angel** (Antigua; © **502/7832-3189;** www.delangel.com): Antigua has a glut of high-end jewelry stores selling locally produced wares. However, this shop has the most interesting and unique pieces that you'll ever see in one place in this town. It's worth checking their clearance rack, as they periodically try to update their stock. See p. 133.

o **Wer** (Antigua; © **502/7832-7161**): Give yourself some time to wander through the many rooms of art in this contemporary gallery, set up in the rambling space of a converted colonial-era home. More than 100 Guatemalan artists are represented here. See p. 132.

o **Santiago de Atitlán's Street Market** (Santiago de Atitlán; no phone): As soon as you step off the boat in Santiago de Atitlán, you'll see the line of stalls that head up the main street into town. In addition, Santiago's unique embroidered huipiles and pants, you'll find excellent carved masks and ceramic wares on sale here. See p. 158.

o **Chichicastenango's Market** (Chichicastenango; no phone): There's a reason this twice-weekly open-air market is so famous. The abundance and variety of wares for sale and the somewhat controlled frenzy of the entire operation are not to be missed. You may find better bargains and products around the country, but you'll never see so much in one place at one time. See p. 169.

- **San Francisco El Alto Market** (San Francisco El Alto; no phone): Local cognoscenti swear that the Friday market in San Francisco El Alto is even better than the one in Chichi. It's certainly a great market, and if you know what you're looking for, and how to bargain, you might even do better here than in Chichi. See p. 181.

- **Q'eqchi' Women's Craft Cooperative** (on the Río Dulce; no phone; www.aktenamit. org): The Caribbean lowlands are a particularly barren zone for die-hard shoppers. This small shop is the exception to the rule. You can only get to this humble cooperative by boat, but all of the tour operations in Livingston and Río Dulce stop here. See p. 249.

THE best HIGH-END HOTELS

- **Real InterContinental** (Zona 10, Guatemala City; ✆ 502/2413-4444; www. interconti.com): There are a host of high-end business-class hotels in Guatemala City, but this one tops them all in terms of rooms, amenities, facilities, location, and service. The InterContinental sits on a busy corner of the Zona Viva, with shops, restaurants, bars, and more just steps away in every direction. See p. 88.

- **Casa Santo Domingo** (Antigua; ✆ 502/7820-1220; www.casasantodomingo. com.gt): You can sometimes get lost on the extensive grounds of this fabulous hotel. In addition to the fine rooms, excellent service, and colonial-era ambience, this place features museum-quality collections of art and artifacts, as well as a large amphitheater. The whole complex sits on, and is integrated into, the ruins of an old convent. See p. 117.

- **Posada del Angel** (Antigua; ✆ 502/7832-0260; www.posadadelangel.com): With just five beautiful rooms, this place gives you intimacy with your luxury, and is consistently considered one of the top hotels in the entire country. I like the second-floor suite, with its own private rooftop terrace. See p. 119.

- **Palacio de Doña Leonor Boutique Hotel** (Antigua, Guatemala; ✆ 502/7832-2281; www.palaciodeleonor.com): Located in an old colonial mansion—just off Antigua's main plaza—that once belonged to Pedro de Alvarado's daughter, this plush and luxurious hotel also offers up all the modern conveniences you could ask for. The suites have massive flatscreen televisions and Jacuzzis, while the decor and ambience are decidedly colonial and decadent. See p. 118.

- **Mesón Panza Verde** (Antigua; ✆ 502/7832-2925; www.panzaverde.com): This elegant and artistic Antigua hotel has long been one of Guatemala's top options. The immaculately restored old building is loaded with artwork and interesting architectural details, and there's a wonderful, mazelike rooftop terrace with panoramic views. The restaurant (below) is one of the best in the country. See p. 122.

- **Hotel Atitlán** (Finca San Buenaventura, Panajachel; ✆ 502/7762-1441; www. hotelatitlan.com): This fabulous hotel is set on the shores of Lake Atitlán, with a stunning view of the lake and its surrounding volcanoes. Beautiful rooms, lush gardens, ample amenities, impeccable service, and a great restaurant make this a complete package. See p. 146.

- **Casa Palopó** (Carretera a San Antonio Palopó, Lake Atitlán; ✆ 502/7762-2270; www.casapalopo.com): Artwork and interesting design touches abound in this boutique hotel, which is perched high on a hillside overlooking Lake Atitlán. The vibe here is hip, intimate, refined, and romantic, and the place is perfect for couples. (Honeymooners should seriously consider it.) The restaurant is excellent. See p. 161.

- **Villas B'alam Ya** (Carretera a San Antonio Palopó, Lake Atitlán; ✆ 502/7762-2522; www.balamya.com): There are only four villas here, but each is private, unique, and very artistically decorated. Most are quite spacious, and all feature excellent views of the lake. See p. 161.

o **La Lancha Resort** (Lago Petén Itzá, Petén; ✆ **800/746-3743** in the U.S., or ✆/fax 502/7928-8331 in Guatemala; www.lalanchavillage.com): Set on a steep hillside overlooking the lake, this is the plushest hotel near Tikal. The rooms at this Francis Ford Coppola regional resort (he has two others in Belize) are decorated with style, featuring furniture and artwork from around the world. The food is also excellent, taking local cuisine as its inspiration and adding creative touches and refined twists. See p. 214.

o **Hotel Villa Caribe** (Livingston; ✆ **502/2223-5000** or 7947-0072; www.villasde guatemala.com): My favorite rooms here are the individual bungalows, which are what earns this hotel a spot in this exclusive group. These rooms have air-conditioning, cable television, and minibars, which the other rooms lack. However, every room here has a private balcony with a commanding view of the Río Dulce river mouth and the Caribbean Sea. See p. 249.

THE best BOUTIQUE & MIDRANGE HOTELS

o **Otelito Casa Santa Clara** (Zona 10, Guatemala City; ✆/fax **502/2339-1811**; www.otelito.com): With only 12 rooms, this exceedingly hip hotel stands out from all the large, high-rise, business-class monsters that dominate this downtown neighborhood. Each room is slightly different, but a sense of refined, minimalist design is felt in the decor throughout. In addition to the intimate setting and trendy vibe, they also have an excellent in-house fusion restaurant. See p. 89.

o **Casa Encantada** (Antigua; ✆ **502/7832-7903** or 866/837-8900 in the U.S. and Canada; www.casaencantada-antigua.com): This charming boutique hotel offers compact yet plush and luxurious rooms that rival some of the best in the city. The service is attentive and personable, and the rooftop terrace here is gorgeous. See p. 119.

o **Hotel Dos Mundos** (Panajachel; ✆ **502/7762-2078**; www.hoteldosmundos. com): The spacious rooms here are one of my top choices in Panajachel. Although the hotel is located right in the center of Calle Santander, the rooms are set back from the street in a quiet garden area, giving you easy access to all the action and peace and quiet at the same time. See p. 147.

o **Bambú Hotel & Restaurant** (Santiago de Atitlán; ✆ **502/7721-7332**; www.eco bambu.com): The two private lakefront bungalows are the best rooms in the house, and probably the best rooms in all of Santiago de Atitlán, so be sure to try and book one of these. Better still is that they're the same price as those in the larger building, which are set back from the water's edge. Even if you don't get one of the private bungalows, you'll be plenty happy at this excellent hotel. See p. 159.

o **Villa Santa Catarina** (Santa Catarina Palopó, Lake Atitlán; ✆ **502/7762-1291**; www.villasdeguatemala.com): This lakefront boutique hotel is one of the few options in the small and artistically blessed town of Santa Catarina Palopó. If you stay here, be sure to buy one of the distinctive local huipils. See p. 162.

o **Casa Mañen** (Quetzaltenango, Guatemala; ✆ **502/7765-0786**; www.comeseeit. com): This is my favorite hotel in Quetzaltenango. The rooms are all decorated with a range of local arts and craft works, the service is excellent, and the owners are very knowledgeable about the various local tour options. The large rooftop terrace offers wonderful panoramic views of the city. See p. 182.

- **Las Cumbres** (Zunil; ℂ **502/5399-0029;** www.lascumbres.com.gt): Built right on top of some steam vents fed by underground sulfur hot springs, some of the rooms here come with their own private natural steam bath. All of the rooms have a natural hot-spring-fed Jacuzzi, and there are other common steam baths and saunas for all to enjoy. Other amenities here include a squash court and small gym. See p. 183.

- **Casa Duranta** (Cobán; ℂ **502/7951-4188;** www.casaduranta.com): This small hotel offers up the most inviting and best equipped rooms in Cobán. Located just a few blocks from the bustling center of town, this place feels like a very calm and relaxing oasis. See p. 225.

- **Portal de la Fe** (Esquipulas; ℂ **502/7943-4124**): This should be the top choice for anyone coming to Esquipulas to pay their respects to the *Black Christ*. This hotel offers free Wi-Fi throughout, and is a definite step up from the other options around town in the same price range. See p. 232.

- **Hacienda San Lucas** (south of Copán Ruinas, Honduras; ℂ/fax **504/651-4495;** www.haciendasanlucas.com): This converted farm and ranch offers a sense of refinement and creative flare you won't find anywhere else in the Copán area. The hotel is set on a hillside across from and overlooking the Copán archaeological site. In addition, there's a secondary Maya site, Los Sapos, right on the grounds, as well as excellent hiking and horseback-riding trails. As if all this weren't enough, the restaurant is one of the best in Copán. See p. 240.

- **Catamaran Island Hotel** (Fronteras, Río Dulce; ℂ **502/7930-5494;** www.catamaranisland.com): Whenever I come to the Río Dulce area, I book one of this hotel's private bungalows built out over the water. I love sitting on my private balcony with a book, listening to the river lap against the support posts below me. At night, you'll usually be mingling with hotel guests and some itinerant cruising sailors who tie up at the hotel's dock or anchor just offshore. See p. 255.

- **Dos Mundos Pacific Resort** (Monterrico; ℂ/fax **502/7848-1407;** www.dosmundospacific.com): This beachfront resort gets my nod as the best and most comfortable of the lot in Guatemala. The individual bungalows are large and plush, the installations top-notch, and the setting lovely. See p. 265.

THE best BUDGET HOTELS

- **Xamanek Student Inn** (Zona 10, Guatemala City; ℂ **502/2360-8345;** www.mayaworld.net): This place offers true budget travelers a very respectable option in the heart of the Zona 10. There's a hostel-like vibe throughout this cozy converted home and common areas, and all the restaurants, bars, and bustle of Zona Viva are just outside its doors. See p. 90.

- **Posada Belén** (Zona 1, Guatemala City; ℂ **866/864-8283** in the U.S. and Canada, or 502/2253-6178 in Guatemala; www.posadabelen.com): You'll feel at home in this long-standing family-run hotel. The rooms are charming and beautifully done, and the converted home is filled with a wealth of art and Maya artifacts. Although it's near the heart of the city's colonial center, it's on a quiet street, away from the hustle and bustle. These folks have an excellent in-house tour operation. See p. 93.

- **Posada San Pedro** (Antigua; ℂ/fax **502/7832-3594;** www.posadasanpedro.net): A notable step up from most budget posadas in town, this cozy little hotel, has a mellow vibe, and an excellent rooftop terrace. They also have a separate annex on the north side of town. See p. 121.

o **Hotel Posada La Merced** (Antigua; ℂ **502/7832-3197** or 7832-3301; www. posadalamercedantigua.com): As the name implies, this popular hotel is just around the corner from beautiful La Merced church. The friendly and welcoming staff is a real plus. Those looking for longer stays can book the fully equipped apartments. Interior courtyard areas and a communal kitchen lend themselves to a friendly vibe. See p. 121.

o **Hotel Primavera** (Panajachel; ℂ **502/7762-2052;** www.primaveratitlan.com): I enjoy the neatly varnished wood and slightly European feel to this place. Some of the rooms feature large bay windows overlooking Calle Santander. If you land room no. 9, you're in for a real budget treat, as it comes with its own private stairway, entrance, and balcony. See p. 148.

o **Hotelito Sak'cari** (San Pedro La Laguna; ℂ **502/7721-8096** or 2475-1802; www. hotelsakcari.com): The rooms here lack something in the way of style and personality, but for a very reasonable price, you can enjoy the sunrise from a hammock stretched out on the veranda of one of the second-floor units. See p. 154.

o **La Casa del Mundo** (Jaibalito, Lake Atitlán; ℂ **502/5218-5332** or 5204-5558; www.lacasadelmundo.com): Set atop an isolated rocky outcropping jutting into Lake Atitlán, this hotel offers a few rooms with shared bathrooms that are a real steal (even the private bathrooms are a bargain), with stupendous views of the lake. A lakeside fire-heated Jacuzzi and several open-air terraces make this place really special. See p. 163.

o **Casa Doña Mercedes** (Quetzaltenango; ℂ **502/7765-4687** or 5687-3305; www. hostalcasadonamercedes.com): In a town with a glut of budget lodgings, this one stands out for its friendly service, immaculate rooms, and central location. See p. 183.

o **Hotel Santana** (Flores, Petén; ℂ/fax **502/7867-5123** or 7867-5193; www. santanapeten.com): This lakefront hotel is the best budget choice on the island of Flores. In fact, it might just be the best hotel on the island itself, regardless of price. All of the rooms come with private balconies with wonderful views. See p. 211.

o **La Casa de Don David Hotel** (El Remate, Petén; ℂ **502/7928-8469** or 5306-2190; www.lacasadedondavid.com): Located right on the shores of Lake Petén Itza, this well-tended hotel offers up clean and comfortable rooms and a wonderful, hostel-like vibe. The owners are very knowledgeable and helpful. See p. 216.

o **Hotel Alcazar Doña Victoria** (Cobán; ℂ **502/7952-1143;** www.hotelescoban. com): I love the rustic yet refined feel of the rooms in this beautiful colonial home. All of the rooms are different. Those on the second floor are my favorite, with high ceilings featuring exposed wood beams. Throughout the hotel there are eye-catching artistic touches. The owners have a couple other hotels in town, as well as the best adventure-tour operation in the region. See p. 226.

o **Yat B'alam** (Copán Ruinas, Honduras; **504/651-4338;** www.yatbalam.com): This little hotel has more style and class than any other option in Copán Ruinas, and at a great price to boot. See p. 241.

o **La Casa Rosada** (Livingston; ℂ **502/7947-0303;** www.hotelcasarosada.com): Set on the waterfront in Livingston, the individual bungalows feature cheerful design touches, with brightly painted furniture, architectural accents, and sea shell decorations. You'll have to use one of several communal bathrooms and showers, but these are just steps away and kept spotless. Moreover, the restaurant and in-house tour operation are great. See p. 251.

THE best RESTAURANTS

o **Tamarindos** (Zona 10, Guatemala City; © **502/2360-2815;** www.tamarindos. com.gt): This trendy Zona Viva restaurant has been wowing Guatemala City diners with eclectic fusion cooking for years. The menu is very long, and touches many bases, with culinary influences from Asia, Italy, and many places in between. Be sure to ask about daily specials, as this is where the chef really shines. See p. 95.

o **Zumo** (Zona 10, Guatemala City; © **502/2334-6316** or 2331-2895; www.zumo. com.gt): A newer entry on the scene, Chef Rodrigo Alvarado's creative fusion fare is as good tasting on the palate, as it is pleasing to the eye. And, the converted old home that houses this restaurant feels intimate, warm, and inviting. See p. 95.

o **Kacao** (Zona 10, Guatemala City; © **502/2237-4188** or 2377-4189): This popular restaurant takes Guatemalan cuisine and polishes it up a bit. The cooking is fairly traditional, with signature dishes from around the country, but the service, ambience, and presentation are far more refined than you'll find at almost any other place specializing in Chapin cuisine. Although they do a brisk lunch business, I prefer to come for dinner, when the thatch roof is illuminated by candles and other strategically placed lighting. See p. 95.

o **Ambia** (Zona 14, Guatemala City; © **502/2366-6890**): It's worth the effort to find this slightly out-of-the-way restaurant. The fusion cuisine is heavily influenced by a range of Asian styles, but you can also get hearty steaks and some delicious lamb. The ambience of the open-air dining is refined and elegant. See p. 98.

o **Mesón Panza Verde** (Antigua; © **502/7832-1745;** www.panzaverde.com): Don't come to Antigua without having a meal at Mesón Panza Verde. The Swiss chef ventures somewhat from his Continental roots, incorporating local ingredients into many of his dishes. The results are always superb. Tables are spread around various rooms, hallways, and open-air spaces in this elegant boutique hotel, and several nights a week there's live jazz to accompany your meal. See p. 118.

o **Bistrot 5** (Antigua; © **502/7832-5510;** www.bistrotcinq.com): Serving a mix of contemporary and traditional French bistro fare, this casually elegant spot is a great place for everything from a romantic dinner for two to a jovial gathering of a group of friends. See p. 123.

o **Hector's** (Antigua; © **502/7832-9867**): Located across the street from the lovely La Merced church, this bustling, intimate restaurant has taken this tiny town by storm. You'll have to come early to get a seat. The tiny kitchen here turns out some delicious food, and the ambience is cozy and convivial. See p. 124.

o **Hotel Atitlán** (Panajachel; © **502/7762-1441**): With a burning fireplace, wood furniture, and ornate table settings and decor, this is easily the most elegant and refined restaurant in or around Panajachel. When the weather is nice, you can grab one of the outdoor tables, which have a good view of the lake and volcanoes. Luckily, the cuisine and service here live up to the ambience and surroundings. The Sunday brunch is quite renowned. See p. 146.

o **Zoola** (San Pedro; © **502/5847-4857**): The service here is famously and, at times, painfully, slow, but it's always worth it. What's more, you can't beat the laid-back ambience and pillows-on-carpet seating that you get to enjoy while waiting. See p. 155.

o **Club Ven Acá** (Jaibalito; © **502/5051-4520;** www.clubvenaca.com): If you're staying around the lake, you'll definitely want to take a boat taxi to the private dock of this lakeside joint. The creative menu is varied and tasty, and if it's a nice day, you can spend some time lounging around their pool. See p. 164.

- **El Pasaje Mediterraneo** (Quetzaltenango; ✆ **502/5515-6724**): Located inside the popular Pasaje Enriquez complex, this restaurant serves up a tasty mix of tapas. You can either choose a table in the lively front passageway, or in a more secluded spot in one of the various dining rooms spread over several floors here. See p. 184.
- **La Luna** (Flores; ✆ **502/7867-5443**): If you find yourself in Flores, be sure to find your way to this restaurant. The eclectic decor varies from room to room, but like the food, it's consistently creative and tasteful. See p. 212.
- **Casa D'Acuña** (Cobán; ✆ **502/7951-0482**; www.casadeacuna.com): The beautiful garden courtyard setting is enough to earn it a place on this list, but the excellent chefs do their part as well. The long menu includes pizzas, pastas, and typical Mexican cuisine. Your best bet is to get a nice steak or fresh grilled fish. See p. 226.
- **Hacienda San Lucas** (south of Copán Ruinas on the road to Los Sapos ruins; ✆/fax **504/651-4495**): The house specialty is a fire-roasted chicken smothered in a spicy *adobo* sauce, which the owners claim is based on ancient Maya recipes. I can't imagine the Maya ate this well, but you certainly should. The open-air setting by lamplight is very romantic. See p. 240.
- **Bugamama** (Livingston; ✆ **502/7947-0891**; www.bugamama.org): You'd never know that this waterfront restaurant was a training school for local youth. The food, service, and setting are all excellent. Be sure to sample the *tapado,* a local seafood stew. See p. 251.
- **La Casa Rosada** (Livingston; ✆ **502/7947-0303**): On any given night, the regularly changing menu at this cozy restaurant might feature a Thai-influenced stir-fry or shrimp gumbo. However, I often end up ordering the local *tapado,* a seafood stew cooked in coconut milk, which is as good as any in the area. See p. 252.
- **Taberna El Pelícano** (Monterrico; ✆ **502/5584-2400**): The fresh grilled fish is always dependable at this beach restaurant, but they also have a large menu with some unexpected twists, including excellent pastas thanks to their Italian chef, and a rich goulash thanks to the European owner. See p. 267.

THE best OF GUATEMALAN NIGHTLIFE

- **La Bodeguita del Centro** (Guatemala City; ✆ **502/2230-2976**): This bohemian downtown bar has almost nightly programming that includes poetry readings, improvised theater pieces, and concerts of folk, jazz, and even hard-core punk. See p. 108.
- **Rattle 'N' Hum** (Guatemala City; ✆ **502/2366-6524**): If you're looking for a raucous and rowdy bar scene in Guatemala City, look no further. The beers are cold, the music is loud, and the crowd is young, restless, and ready to party. See p. 109.
- **Trovajazz** (Guatemala City; ✆ **502/2334-1241**; www.trovajazz.com): The compact pedestrian mall area of Cuatro Grados Norte is chock-full of clubs, bars, and discos, and this is consistently my favorite. There's live music most nights, and the ambience is relaxed and convivial. See p. 109.
- **Café No Sé** (Antigua; no phone; www.cafenose.com): This friendly boho-bar is my favorite haunt in Antigua. There's great tequila and mescal on hand—they import their own brews from neighboring Mexico—and there's often live music. See p. 135.
- **JP's Rumbar** (Antigua; ✆ **502/7882-4244**; www.rumbarantigua.com): Featuring down-home Cajun cuisine and almost nightly music, this new bar is a great place to meet locals and fellow travelers alike. See p. 136.

- **Circus Bar** (Panajachel; © **502/7762-2056**): This place is an institution in Panajachel, and for good reason. A "circus" theme dominates the decor, live music takes the stage most nights, and a friendly mix of locals, expatriates, and tourists populate the bar. See p. 150.

- **Buddha** (San Pedro; www.thebuddhaguatemala.com): In a small, party town with a plethora of bars, this place is consistently one of the most popular spots to spend an evening. There's a pool table, dart boards, board games, and poker tournaments, as well as nightly live music or DJs. See p. 156.

- **Salón Tecún** (Quetzaltenango; © **502/7761-2350**): While there are always plenty of people in the crowded interior of this popular Xela bar, the most happening scene is usually at the large picnic-style tables out front. In a university and language-school town with lots of clubs and bars, this is consistently the place to see and be seen. See p. 185.

- **Moonlight at Tikal** (Tikal; no phone): Standing atop of Temple IV under the full moon with nothing but the sound of crickets and howler monkeys remains one of my favorite after-dark memories of Guatemala. While this isn't officially open to the public, if you're staying at one of the hotels right outside the archaeological site at Tikal, you can sometimes receive permission to visit the site after dark. Be sure to ask your hotel if this is possible, and check on the current security situation. See p. 190.

- **Ubafu** (Livingston; no phone): The Garífuna people of Livingston are direct descendants of escaped African slaves, and this local bar swings nightly to the beat of ancient rhythms mixed with the modern forms of punta rock and reggae. Local bands beat out the rhythms on handmade drums and hollowed-out turtle shells. See p. 252.

THE best OF GUATEMALA ONLINE

- **http://lanic.utexas.edu/la/ca/guatemala:** Hosted by the University of Texas Latin American Studies Department, this site houses a vast collection of information about Guatemala.

- **www.visitguatemala.com:** This is the official site of the Guatemala Tourism Commission (INGUAT). The site is a bit clunky, but if you dig around, you can find some useful info.

- **http://guatemala.usembassy.gov:** This is the official site of the United States Embassy in Guatemala. It contains very useful contact information for U.S. citizens, and excellent general information and timely situational updates for everyone else.

- **www.revuemag.com:** This is an excellent English-language monthly magazine geared toward tourists and expatriates. The entire magazine, as well as past issues, is available online.

- **www.xelawho.com:** A slightly irreverent English-language magazine produced in Quetzaltenango and directed at the town's large population of foreign-language students, this site has honest reviews and a wealth of useful information.

GUATEMALA IN DEPTH

2

A millennium of Maya civilization, 3 centuries of Spanish colonial rule, and almost 4 decades of guerrilla war have left Guatemala's economy, politics, crafts, architecture, languages, and religions with one common trait: profound variety. Home to some 13 million people, Guatemala is the most populous country in Central America, and its residents are extremely diverse. However, Guatemala is also one of the poorest, least developed and violent countries in the region. Nearly 2 decades after the end of a long and brutal civil war, Guatemala seems perennially poised between starting along a rising path to prosperity, democracy, and justice, and taking a precipitous fall into chaos, crime, and continued impunity.

GUATEMALA TODAY

Long-lasting Maya and Spanish empires produced an ethnically, linguistically, and economically divided Guatemala. Around half of the population is *mestizo* (known as *ladino* in Guatemala), or mixed Spanish-Amerindian heritage. The other half belongs to one of 23 indigenous Maya groups, each with their own language and customs. The largest group is the Ki'che, who predominantly live around Lake Atitlán and in the western highlands, and make up around 10% of the country's population. Other Maya groups include the Cakchiquel, Tz'utujil, Mam, and Kekchi, and on the Caribbean coast live the Garífuna, descendants of former slaves and Carib Indians.

Racial tensions can be strong between these groups, especially between *ladinos* and the Maya in the cities, and between *ladinos* and Garífuna on the Caribbean coast. Subsurface religious tensions also exist between the vast-majority Catholic population and the more recent and fast-growing Evangelical Protestant movement, which draws its greatest support within indigenous communities.

The Guatemalan economy is still heavily agricultural, based on the production of sugar cane, coffee, and bananas, with tourism and manufacturing playing increasingly important roles.

Despite gradual economic growth since the 1996 peace agreement, the country's war-torn past continues to cast a long shadow on its economy and society. And there's been very little noticeable progress made towards building a better future. The gap between rich and poor is wide. Up to 80% of the population lives below the poverty line, some 54% of young children suffer from malnutrition, and crime continues to be a major problem, with an alarming spike in gang activity. Lawlessness pervades many parts of the country, and impunity reigns nationwide. Vigilante groups, frustrated at the lack of police presence, occasionally take justice into their own hands.

On November 4, 2007, Alvaro Colom of the center-left National Unity for Hope (UNE) party was elected president. However, his administration has had a rocky go of things, with little noticeable progress on the economic and security fronts, and several corruption scandals.

Today, Guatemala struggles to find it's footing on the road to recovery. But that road, like so many in the country, is bumpy, winding, and steep. Still, for those intrepid travelers who do visit, you will find a land of awe inspiring physical beauty; a heartfelt, humble and diverse peoples; an overabundance of color and craft works; and the almost perfectly preserved cities and streets of the ancient Maya and earliest Spanish settlers.

LOOKING BACK AT GUATEMALA

Early History

Before the arrival of the first Europeans, Guatemala was the land of the ancient Maya. Here, mathematicians came up with the concept of zero, astronomers developed a solar calendar accurate to a single day every 6,000 days, and scribes invented an 850-word hieroglyphic vocabulary that scholars consider the world's first advanced writing system. Some of this civilization's practices were less than civil: The Maya built extensive ball courts to play a game called "pok a tok," where the losing team could be executed.

Unlike the Incas of Peru, the Maya had no centralized ruler. Instead, the civilization consisted of a series of independent city-states, usually ruled by hereditary kings, often at war with one another. The most famous city-state is Tikal, in the northern Petén region, whose massive stone temples are the principal draw for tourists in Guatemala. In A.D. 562, Tikal was defeated in battle by the kingdom of Caracol, located in what is now the Cayo District of Western Belize. Other city-states inside contemporary Guatemala include Quiriguá, known for its detailed stelae, Kaminal Juyú near contemporary Guatemala City, Zaculeu, Iximché, Utatlán, and Petén Itzá.

Evidence of human presence in the Maya region dates as far back as the 10th millennium B.C. Maya history is often divided into several distinct periods: Archaic (10,000–2000 B.C.), Pre-Classic (2000 B.C.–A.D. 250), Classic (A.D. 250–900), and Post-Classic (900–1540). Within this timeline, the Classic period itself is often divided into Early, Middle, Late, and Terminal stages. At the height of development, as many as 10 million Maya may have inhabited what are now Guatemala, Belize, Mexico's Yucatán Peninsula, and parts of Honduras and El Salvador. No one knows for sure what led to the decline of the Classic Maya, but somewhere around A.D. 900, their society entered a severe and rapid decline. Famine, warfare, deforestation, and religious prophecy have all been cited as possible causes. See Jared Diamond's best-seller *Collapse* (Penguin, 2005) for more information.

Spanish Conquest

On his fourth and final voyage to the New World in 1502, Christopher Columbus sailed past the Caribbean coast of Guatemala on his way to Panama, but did not land. However, his oversight did not save the area from Spanish conquest.

The conquistador Pedro de Alvarado was sent by Hernán Cortés to Guatemala in 1523. He had roughly 120 cavalry troops, about 300 infantry men, and several hundred

THE MAYA calendar

While the standard Gregorian calendar is now in general use throughout Guatemala, some Maya communities and elders still rely on the ancient way of tracking time. In the Maya Calendar, each day has a hieroglyphic representation composed of numbers and pictographs, many of which can by found on stelae at most ancient Maya sites.

The Maya Calendar is actually a system of several calendars that can be combined in a number of sophisticated ways. The calendars and their accurate astronomical calculations predicting the cycles of the sun, moon, and Venus indicate the Maya had knowledge of mathematics and astronomy that was unknown to their old-world contemporaries.

The three main Maya calendar systems are known as the Tzolkin, Haab, and Long Count systems.

The Tzolkin calendar has 260 days, arrived at by multiplying 20 by 13. The numerical system was founded on a base 20 system (as opposed to our own base 10 system). Some think this came from the number of human fingers and toes, and that 13 symbolized the number of levels in the Upper World, where the gods lived. Another theory is that 260 days came from the approximate length of human pregnancy, and that midwives developed the calendar to coordinate with expected births. The Maya believed that each day of the Tzolkin had a character that influenced events. A priest read the calendar to predict a baby's future, and children were often named according to the day they were born.

The Haab was the Maya solar calendar made up of 18 months of 20 days each, plus a period of 5 unnamed days at the end of the year known as the Wayeb, which add up to a 365-day cycle. It was thought that if an event occurred one day during a specific Haab cycle, a similar event was likely to occur on that same day in the next Haab cycle.

The Long Count Calendar was used primarily by the priests and royalty. It tracked longer periods of time, and was based on the number of days since a mythical starting point (Aug 11, 3114 B.C.). The Long Count Calendar can be used to describe any date in the future.

In yet another layer of complexity, the Tzolkin combines with the Haab to form a synchronized cycle of 52 years, called the Calendar Round.

According to the Popol Vuh, the sacred Maya book of creation myths and predictions, we now live in the fourth world, the gods having failed in their first three creation attempts. It is believed that this age will end on December 21, 2012. While some New Age analysts have dire predictions for the date, more optimistic prognosticators foresee a day of positive human evolution. Hotels around Tikal and other major Maya ceremonial sites are already booking up for this date.

The Maya Calendar was so accurate it was adopted by other Mesoamerican societies, including the Aztecs and Toltecs.

indigenous slaves and mercenaries. In a ruthless campaign, Alvarado pitted different Maya tribes against each other, and then quickly turned on his unwitting accomplices. According to legend, when Alvarado killed the powerful Quiché king Tecún Umán at the Battle of Quetzaltenango in 1524, the quetzal (Guatemala's national bird) swooped down into the vast pools of blood and gained its red breast.

By 1525 Alvarado had completely subdued the western highlands, but the Spanish subsequently met with fierce resistance from many Maya tribes. Multiple invasions of the Petén failed, and the Kekchi in the central highlands held out as well.

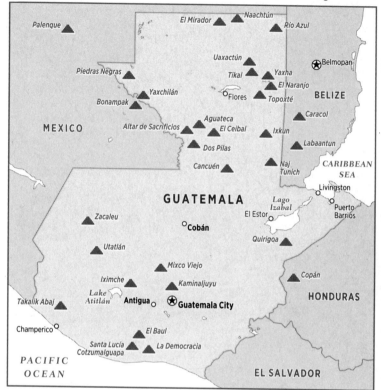

Unable to control the Kekchi by force, the military allowed a group of Franciscan friars under the leadership of Fray Bartolomé de las Casas to attempt the "humane" conversion of the tribe to Christianity. The friars succeeded, the population converted, and the area was given its Spanish name, "Verapaz" or "true peace." A human rights advocate until his death, Las Casas also successfully convinced the Spanish crown to pass the *New Laws* in 1542, awarding some basic protections to the *indígenas*.

Colonial Rule

During Spanish colonial rule, Guatemala was a Captaincy General, part of the Viceroyalty of New Spain. The Spanish established Guatemala's capital at Ciudad Vieja in 1527, but moved to what is now Antigua (then called Santiago de Guatemala) in 1543 after the old capital was buried in a wave of water and mud that cascaded down from the Volcán de Agua.

For 200 years, Antigua was the center of political and religious power of the entire "Audiencia de Guatemala," including the provinces of Costa Rica, Nicaragua, El Salvador, Honduras, and Chiapas in Mexico. After severe earthquakes ravaged Antigua in 1773, the crown decided to move the capital to safer ground. They chose the site of the ancient city of Kaminal Juyú, giving rise to Guatemala City.

In this colonial society, racial divisions were enshrined in law. *Peninsulares,* or Spanish-born Spaniards living in the New World, were at the top of the economic and political pyramid, followed by *criollos* (descendants of Spaniards born in the New World), *mestizos* (of mixed Spanish and Amerindian ancestry), *mulattos* (mixed Spanish and black), Amerindians, *zambos* (mixed Amerindian and black), and blacks. Individuals from the latter three groups were usually enslaved outright.

What's in a Name

Spanish conquistadors named the area Goathemala, based on an indigenous word meaning "land of many trees."

The Roman Catholic Church wielded enormous power, controlling vast plantations of sugar, wheat, and indigo run by forced indigenous labor. They used their wealth to construct some 80 churches, along with convents, schools, colleges, and hospitals.

There was great need for these hospitals: The diseases the Europeans brought decimated the Maya. By some estimates, nearly 90% of the Maya population was wiped out after Alvarado arrived. Those who survived his violent wrath fell rapidly to diseases such as plague, typhoid, and smallpox, to which they had no natural resistance.

Independence

Discontent with the exclusive rule of *peninsulares* reached a boiling point in the early 19th century, and a mood of reform swept across New Spain. Most of the fighting for independence took place in Mexico, where an unlikely coalition of conservatives and liberals eventually prevailed.

On September 15, 1821, Gabino Gainza, the captain general of Central America, signed the Act of Independence, breaking the region's ties with Spain. Although all of Central America initially remained part of Mexico—Mexico sent in troops to make sure that was the case—all Central American nations continue to celebrate their independence on September 15.

In 1823, an independent Central American Federation had taken shape. The Federation had a constitution modeled on that of the U.S. It abolished slavery, religious orders, and the death penalty, and instituted trial by jury, civil marriage, and a public school system.

By 1840, the Federation had dissolved in civil war, instigated by the conservative dictators who had seized power in most of the nations, such as Rafael Carrera, a charismatic 23-year-old swineherd-turned-highwayman who, in Guatemala in 1838, raised an army, seized control, declared Guatemala independent, and promptly reversed decades of liberal reforms. With the adoption of a constitution in 1851, Carrera officially became independent Guatemala's first president.

Banana Republic

Over the course of the next century, power generally continued to change hands by military rather than democratic means. Liberal reformers traded off with conservative reactionaries, but one entity saw its influence grow fairly consistently: the United Fruit Company.

United Fruit, nicknamed "El Pulpo" (the Octopus) for its sweeping influence, first arrived in Guatemala in 1901, when it purchased a small tract of land to grow bananas. The company built its own port, Puerto Barrios, and after being awarded a railway concession leading inland from the port, it had a virtual monopoly on long-distance transportation in the country. United Fruit's rise to prominence coincided with the successive and enduring dictatorships of Manuel José Estrada Cabrera and Jorge Ubico. Collectively, these two men ruled, with great deference to United Fruit Company, from 1898 to 1941.

"The Ten Years of Spring"

In 1941, a band of disgruntled military men, joined by students, labor leaders, and liberal political forces, overthrew Ubico and ushered in a period popularly referred to as "the Ten Years of Spring." Marked by moves to encourage free speech and liberal reforms, this time saw the election of Guatemala's first civilian president of modern times, Juan José Arévalo.

In 1951, Guatemala held its first-ever universal-suffrage election, bringing retired army colonel and political reformer Jacobo Arbenz to power. Confronting a vast gap between rich and poor, Arbenz fought for the passage of the 1952 Agrarian Reform Law, which redistributed thousands of acres of unproductive land to an estimated 100,000 peasant families. United Fruit was furious, having lost half its land. In 1954, the CIA, whose director sat on United Fruit's board, sponsored a coup d'état. Guatemala's new government, largely drawn from the ranks of its military, was flown into the capital aboard a U.S. Air Force plane.

Civil War & War Crimes

The new U.S.-sponsored regime eliminated the constitutional reforms of the previous decade, reinstituting rule by and for the *ladino* minority. In the early 1960s, a guerrilla war began between government forces and Marxist rebels, who drew their strength largely from indigenous communities and were headquartered in the highlands.

For the next 30 years, a succession of authoritarian rulers, nominally center-left or center-right, were brought to power by rigged elections or coups d'état. They largely followed the maxim of president and army colonel Arana Osorio, who said, "If it is necessary to turn the country into a cemetery in order to pacify it, I will not hesitate to do so." An estimated 200,000 people died or disappeared during the conflict, most of them indigenous. Death squads roamed the cities and highlands killing those suspected of rebel activity. Professors, students, union leaders, and priests were especially prone to attack.

In 1983, the Maya activist Rigoberta Menchú published *Me llamo Rigoberta Menchú y así me nació la conciencia* (translated into English as *I, Rigoberta*), an autobiographical tale of government massacres and the assassination of her own parents, who raised international awareness of the horrendous human rights situation in Guatemala. It won Menchú international acclaim, and in 1992, she was awarded the Nobel Prize for Peace. Some scholars later disputed factual claims made in the book, but the Nobel Committee has maintained its support for Menchú.

In August 1987, the five Central American presidents met in Esquipulas, Guatemala, to sign the Accords for Firm and Lasting Peace ("Paz firme y duradera"). The Accords called for free elections, national reconciliation commissions, and perhaps most revolutionary of all in the midst of the Cold War, the rejection of foreign interference in Central American affairs.

Following the recommendations of the 1987 accords, Guatemalan President Alvaro Arzú successfully negotiated a peace agreement with the URNG (as the united rebel factions were known) in December 1996. The agreement ended the 36-year-old civil war, with the government promising to support a Truth Commission led by the UN Mission to Guatemala, MINUGUA. The Constitution was also amended to allow for greater indigenous rights.

THE GARÍFUNA

Throughout the 18th century, escaped and shipwrecked slaves intermarried and blended in with the native Carib Indian populations on several islands in the Lesser Antilles, but predominantly on St. Vincent. The West Africans were a mixed lot, including members of the Fon, Yoruba, Ewe, and Nago tribes. Over the years, the West African and indigenous elements blended into a new people, known first as Black Caribs and today as Garífuna or Garinagu. The Garífuna have their own language, traditions, history, and rituals, all of which blend elements of the group's two primary cultural sources. African-style drumming with complex rhythmic patterns and call-and-response singing accompany ritual possession ceremonies spoken in a language whose entomological roots are predominantly Arawak.

The Black Caribs were fierce warriors and frequently fought the larger colonial powers to maintain their freedom and independence. In 1796, despite the celebrated leadership of Joseph Chatoyer, the Garífuna were soundly defeated by the British forces, who subsequently shipped several thousand of the survivors off to exile on the island of Roatán, in then–British Honduras. The Garífuna began migrating and eventually settled along the entire coast of what is present-day Honduras, Nicaragua, Guatemala, and Belize. For nearly 2 centuries now, the Garífuna have lived quiet lives of subsistence farming, fishing, and light trading with their neighbors, while steadfastly maintaining their language, heritage, and traditions.

From Paz Firme to the Present

Guatemala's security situation improved after the end of the war, but great challenges remained. First, the military still wielded significant power, and did its best to cover up its involvement in the atrocities of the war. In 1998, days after delivering a report on human rights that blamed 80% of the abuses on the military, Catholic Bishop Juan Geradi was bludgeoned to death in his home in Guatemala City. Government and judicial officials were too afraid of suffering the same fate to investigate the crime.

With low coffee prices fueling economic stagnation, the crime rate soared after the 1996 accords. Murder and armed theft were commonplace. The unemployed, many former soldiers, turned their machine guns to the lucrative profession of highway robbery, pulling over buses and trucks, especially in the Petén. Kidnappings became appallingly common.

Today, the economic and security situation in much of the country remains precarious. Violent gangs, or *maras*, are having a noticeable impact across Guatemala, particularly in poor urban areas, and drug trafficking and money laundering are major problems. The police force is overworked, underpaid, outmanned, and inexperienced. While, the judicial system is largely ineffective—it is estimated that between 80% and 90% of all crime goes unpunished.

THE LAY OF THE LAND

Guatemala sits at the top of the Central American isthmus, due south of Mexico's Yucatán Peninsula, between the Pacific Ocean and the Caribbean Sea. It covers an area of just more than 100,000 sq. km (40,000 sq. miles), slightly smaller than the state of Tennessee. It's bordered on the north by Mexico, on the east by Belize and the Caribbean Sea, on the southeast by Honduras and El Salvador, and on the southwest by the Pacific Ocean. Mountains cover nearly two-thirds of Guatemala, with the largest range being the **Cuchumatanes** in the northwest, really a southern extension of Mexico's Sierra Madre. South of the Cuchumatanes is **Volcán Tajumulco,** Guatemala's and Central America's highest point at nearly 4,200m (14,000 ft.). There are 32 other volcanoes in Guatemala, many of them active. Amid these mountains, Guatemala's landscape is coursed with caves, caverns, sinkholes, and underground rivers. Non-mountainous regions of the country include the narrow Pacific and Caribbean coastal plains, and a limestone plateau in the Petén, which is geographically part of the Yucatán.

Guatemala contains large expanses of lowland rainforest and highland pine forest. In an effort to combat the degradation of the rainforest brought about by widespread slash-and-burn agriculture, the Guatemalan government created the **Maya Biosphere Reserve** in the Petén Region in 1990. The reserve is the northernmost tropical forest in the Western Hemisphere and the largest contiguous tropical forest north of the Amazon, covering almost 800,000 hectares (2 million acres), or 10% of Guatemala's land area. The country is also home to rich **mangrove forest** on both the Pacific and Atlantic coasts. These saltwater-tolerant environments are major breeding and life-support grounds for a broad range of fauna.

Flora & Fauna

The diversity of Guatemala's wildlife is as striking as the diversity of its people. The country is home to more than 8,000 higher plant species, 250 species of mammals, and 800 species of birds. Wildly colored butterflies swarm around the Laguna de Lachuá, manatees have been spotted off the Caribbean coast, and jaguars prowl the forests of the Petén.

Revered by the ancient Maya and feared by most jungle dwellers, the jaguar is the largest New World cat, and can reach more than 6 feet in length and weigh more than 250 pounds. In addition to the jaguar, Guatemalan forests are home to four other wild cats—the puma, ocelot, margay, and jaguarundi—as well as such quintessential jungle dwellers as howler and spider monkeys, scarlet macaws, green iguanas, and boa constrictors.

The most famous resident of the Guatemalan rainforest, however, is the resplendent quetzal. Associated with the snake god Quetzalcoatl by Maya civilization, the national bird has a blood-red breast, almost electric-green feathers, and a tiny golden beak. The males of the species have tail feathers that can reach more than 2 feet in length. A good place to watch for them is in the **Biotopo del Quetzal** in the Verapaz highlands, though they can be quite difficult to spot. They are most active in the early morning.

Searching for Wildlife

Animals in the forest are predominantly nocturnal. When they are active in the daytime, they are usually elusive and on the watch for predators. Birds are easier to spot in clearings or secondary forests than they are in primary forests. Unless you have lots of experience in the Tropics, your best hope for enjoying a walk through the jungle or bird-watching excursion lies in employing a trained and knowledgeable guide.

Here are a few helpful hints:

o **Listen.** Pay attention to rustling in the leaves; whether it's monkeys above or pizotes on the ground, you're most likely to hear an animal before seeing one.

Shopping Tips

International laws prohibit trade in endangered wildlife, so don't buy any plants or animals, even if they're for sale. Do not buy any kind of sea-turtle products (including jewelry); wild birds; lizard, snake, or cat skins; corals; or orchids (except those grown commercially). No matter how unique, beautiful, insignificant, or inexpensive it might seem, your purchase will contribute to the further hunting of endangered species.

At most stores and shops, sales and import taxes have already been figured into the display price, and it is not normal to haggle. You can, however, bargain a price down (within reason) in more informal settings such as city markets.

o **Keep quiet.** Noise will scare off animals and prevent you from hearing their movements and calls.

o **Don't try too hard.** Soften your focus and allow your peripheral vision to take over. This way you can catch glimpses of motion and then focus in on the prey.

o **Bring your own binoculars.** It's a good idea to practice a little first to get the hang of them. It would be a shame to be fiddling around and staring into space while everyone else in your group "oohs" and "aahs" at the sight of a quetzal.

o **Dress appropriately.** You'll have a hard time focusing your binoculars if you're busy swatting mosquitoes. Light, long pants and long-sleeve shirts are your best bet. Comfortable hiking boots are a real boon, except where heavy rubber boots are necessary. Avoid loud colors; the better you blend in with your surroundings, the better your chances are of spotting wildlife.

o **Be patient.** The jungle isn't on a schedule; however, your best shot at seeing forest fauna is in the very early-morning and late-afternoon hours.

o **Read up.** Familiarize yourself with what you're most likely to see. A good all-around book to have is Les Beletsky's *Traveller's Wildlife Guide: Belize and Northern Guatemala.* Other relevant field guides include Thor Janson's *Maya Nature: An Introduction to the Ecosystems, Plants and Animals of the Mayan World,* and *Birds of Mexico and Central America.*

ART & ARCHITECTURE

Architecture

In Guatemala City, colonial buildings coexist with skyscrapers and tin-roofed slums. The Plaza Mayor, Catedral Metropolitana, and Palacio Nacional are all impressive colonial structures. You might call the architectural style of the Children's Museum "colonial" as well—that is, if you're referring to a lunar colony. Also check out the vermilion, neo-Gothic Iglesia Yurrita in Zona 4, which tips its hat to Catalan architect Antoni Gaudí.

Antigua is a fabulously preserved colonial city, and many of its colonial-era churches and buildings have fortunately survived several major earthquakes. Those that didn't fully survive still add to the city's ageless air of grandeur. The **Palacio del Noble Ayuntamiento** and the ruins of the **Convento de las Capuchinas** are two of its many highlights.

If you're looking for Classic monumental architecture in Guatemala, you're in luck. The creative Maya masons who constructed the stone pyramids built them to last—they've even survived the daily swarms of tourists who scamper all over them—though it's not clear how long they can endure an existence unprotected by guide ropes.

The most famous Maya ceremonial city in Guatemala is **Tikal.** With more than 3,000 mapped constructions to date and a score of impressive excavations and reconstructions, a visit here gives you the sense of visiting a vibrant ancient city. Smaller architectural marvels dot the country, including giant stone stelae at **Quiriguá,** and new sites are being discovered and excavated all the time. Those looking to see perhaps the finest example of Classic Maya hieroglyphics should head to neighboring Honduras and the ruins at **Copán,** where you'll find a staircase that holds the distinction of being the longest book written in stone.

Art

Guatemalan artists range from folk artists and artisans working in a variety of forms, materials, and traditions to modern painters, sculptors, and ceramicists producing beautiful representational and abstract works.

The best-known crafts are indigenous woven tapestries and clothing. Artisans use natural dyes extracted from the *clavel* and *heraño* flowers, then mix in the crushed bodies of mosquitoes to keep the colors from running. The fabrics are woven on huge looms or simple, portable back-strap looms. Traditional dress for women includes a *huipil* (blouse) and *corte* (skirt), often fastened to the waist with a rope belt. Women often also wear a *tocoyal,* or headdress. These can range from pieces of cloth to long, narrow ribbons wound in a tight spiral and adorned with tassels. Highly figured and embroidered men's shirts are called *trajes.*

Today, Maya textiles are displayed on the walls of hotels and restaurants. They are sold on the streets of cities, villages, and in souvenir shops (where you'll find dolls dressed in typical dress, purses, and other accessories made of the beautiful work). In your search, it's well worth a visit to a bustling market, such as those found in Guatemala City, Antigua, Chichicastenango, or Santiago Atitlán.

In recent years, mass-produced machine-woven fabrics have started appearing in markets. To spot a fake, look for gold or synthetic threads woven into the cloth, and for overly neat stitching on the back.

Note: Please show respect for the Maya culture and remember that only women wear *huipiles,* while many of the embroidered shirts and pants are meant specifically for men. While most Maya craftspeople are more than happy to see foreigners purchase their goods, for some indigenous people, seeing *gringos* walking the streets in native garb can be insulting—especially when women unknowingly wear traditional men's clothing, or vice versa. Use caution, and when in doubt, don't model your purchases in any but the most touristy towns or settings until you get home.

Other common handicrafts found in gift shops and markets across Guatemala include carved-wood masks and carved stone and jade.

Handicrafts are far from the only art in Guatemala. Mural painting is a growing form, especially works depicting emotional subjects. See the murals representing Guatemala's war-torn past and peaceful future in the church in **Rabinal** for an example.

If you're looking for modern art, various galleries in Guatemala City and Antigua carry a wide range of contemporary locally produced art; see chapters 5 and 6, respectively, for more information.

GUATEMALA IN BOOKS, FILM & MUSIC

Literature

Guatemala's literary tradition dates back to pre-Columbian Maya civilization, when Ki'che authors wrote the holy book **Popol Vuh.** The book traces the history of the Ki'che people beginning with their creation myth, linking the royal family with the gods in order to reaffirm its legitimacy. The book's exact age is unknown; the Spanish first recorded its existence in Chichicastenango in 1701. In 1972, the Popul Vuh was declared Guatemala's National Book. Several good translations into English exist, including Dennis Tedlock's ***Popol Vuh: The Definitive Edition of the Mayan Book of the Dawn of Life and the Glories of Gods and Kings*** ★★ and Allen J. Christenson's ***Popol Vuh: The Sacred Book of the Mayas.***

Apart from the Popol Vuh, Guatemala's most famous literary works come from the Nobel Prize–winning poet, playwright, and ambassador Miguel Angel Asturias. Considered one of the fathers of magical realism, Asturias authored such works as *El Señor Presidente* (1946), *Viento Fuerte* (1950), and *Hombres de Maíz* (1967). In **Men of Maize (Hombres de Maíz)** ★★★, which appears in translation, Asturias manages to integrate Guatemalan history, Maya mythology, and everyday life into a challenging and riveting prose style. Asturias's **The President (El Presidente)** is also a

---

THE WILD, WILD WORLD OF THE huipil

The most distinctive piece of traditional clothing found in Guatemala is the female blouse known as a *huipil*—a large shirt made of two rectangular pieces of heavy cloth, which are sewn together with no tailoring or shape other than a simple hole for the head (and often a slit along the centerline for breastfeeding). *Huipiles* are usually worn about waist length, but they are often significantly wider at the shoulders than the actual shoulders of the Maya women who wear them. *Huipiles* are traditionally woven on a simple back-strap loom, and feature intricate patterns and designs that may be a mix of loom technique and embroidery. These patterns and designs range from the entirely abstract to figurative, with people, animals, flowers, celestial bodies, and gods and goddesses all finding their way into the fabric of this distinctly Guatemalan art form.

One of the most fascinating aspects of the *huipil* is that dozens of villages have their own style of design: Nebaj in the Ixchil Triangle of villages in the Central Highlands is famous for its tight, intricate hand embroidery with figures of horses, birds, and people; the weavers from Chichicastenango embroider the neck, shoulder, and center of the chest areas with predominantly abstract designs; while those in San Lucas Toliman are known for their unique representational embroidery that resembles stick figures.

The *huipil* has been worn since long before the arrival of the Spaniards in the 16th century. However, it was the Spaniards who instituted the concept of specific village-related *huipil* styles to establish class and slave organizational structures. During the civil war of the last century, the army followed the conquistadors' lesson and used the *huipil* and other items of indigenous dress to identify people from villages thought to be sympathetic to the guerrilla cause.

very worthwhile read. A cultural center in Guatemala City bearing his name is home to chamber and open-air theaters, as well as a military museum and small art gallery. The **Miguel Angel Asturias Cultural Center** (✆ **502/2232-4041;** www. teatronacional.com.gt) is located at 24 Calle 3-81, Zona 1 (p. 99).

Probably the most internationally famous book to come out of Guatemala is *I, Rigoberta Menchú: An Indian Woman in Guatemala* ★, originally published in Spanish as *Me llamo Rigoberta Menchú y así me nació la conciencia,* an oral history of Menchú's revolutionary activities transcribed by the French anthropologist Elisabeth Burgos-Debray. This book and Menchú's subsequent efforts to draw international attention to the atrocities of the Guatemalan military regime won her the Nobel Peace Prize in 1992, a fitting honor on the 500th anniversary of Columbus's first transatlantic voyage.

Years later, Middlebury College anthropologist David Stoll stirred international controversy when he published **Rigoberta Menchú and the Story of All Poor Guatemalans,** which exposed inconsistencies in Menchú's story. Most pointedly, Stoll considers it unlikely that Menchú could have played a substantial leadership role in a peasant movement given the rigid patriarchy of that society. Menchú has since asserted that some events in the story were invented or embellished by the transcriber, Burgos-Debray. While the Nobel Committee and the international community as a whole have maintained their support for Menchú, you might want to pick up a copy of Stoll's book if only to get a murkier moral picture of that time of war.

Other Guatemalan authors to look out for, both in Spanish and occasionally in translation, include the wonderful short story writer Augusto Monterroso, as well as the poets Luis Cardoza y Arragon, Otto Rene Castillo, and Humberto Ak'Abal.

I find reading books about specific periods of Guatemalan history more enriching than a broad overview, but if you're looking for a sweeping narrative, try Greg Grandin's *The Blood of Guatemala: A History of Race and Nation.*

Immensely popular in its day was *Incidents of Travel in Central America, Chiapas and Yucatan* ★★★ (Volumes 1 and 2, originally published in 1841), a collection of descriptions of Maya sites by the American explorer and diplomat John Lloyd Stephens, featuring the illustrations of artist Frederick Catherwood.

For the strong of stomach, the Archdiocese of Guatemala's official report on the human rights abuses of the civil war, abridged and translated into English as *Guatemala: Never Again!,* is a powerful history. The report was explosive: Days after delivering it, Bishop Juan Gerardi was bludgeoned to death in his own garage in Guatemala City. It's filled with vivid analysis and testimonials from victims, blaming 80% of the atrocities on the Guatemalan military.

While guided tours and pamphlets available at Maya ruins provide a fair amount of information, those truly seeking an in-depth look at the ancient civilization will want to have some more detailed reference material handy when visiting the many ruins in Guatemala. *The Maya* ★, by Michael D. Coe, is a good primer on the history of this advanced and enigmatic culture. However, I find *A Forest of Kings: The Untold Story of the Ancient Maya* ★★ by David Freidel and Linda Schele to be a better read, which gives a better feel for what life was like in the Maya world. To delve into the intricacy and reasoning behind the Maya aesthetic legacy, check out Mary Ellen Miller's book, *Maya Art and Architecture.*

If you're looking for more contemporary works on the more contemporary Maya, *Scandals in the House of Birds* ★ by Nathaniel Tarn is a highly regarded, highly poetic ethnography of the Tz'utujil in Santiago de Atitlán.

There are a host of excellent books specifically about Tikal. ***Tikal: An Illustrated History of the Ancient Maya Capital,*** by John Montgomery, is a good place to start. ***The Lords of Tikal: Rulers of an Ancient Maya City,*** by Peter D. Harrison and others, is a similar option. Although it's out of print, you might want to try to find a copy of ***Tikal: Handbook of the Ancient Maya Ruins,*** by William R. Coe, written under the auspices of the University Museum of the University of Pennsylvania. Archaeologists from the university, working in conjunction with Guatemalan officials, did most of the excellent excavation work at Tikal from 1956 to 1969. Birders will want to have a copy of ***The Birds of Tikal: An Annotated Checklist*** by Randall A. Beavers, or ***The Birds of Tikal*** by Frank B. Smithe. The latter three books are hard to find, but you should be able to order used copies in the United States, and you can usually find copies of all of these in Flores or at Tikal.

If you're bringing along the little ones, or even if you're leaving them behind but want to share a bit of Maya culture with them, look for Pat Mora's beautifully illustrated book ***The Night the Moon Fell: a Maya Myth*** ★. Another good option is ***Guatemala ABCs*** ★ by Marcie Aboff, which is a cultural and historical primer written and illustrated for young children. Or, for a handy little picture book filled with photographs of Maya daily life, check out ***Hands of the Maya: Villagers at Work and Play*** by Rachel Crandell.

Finally, my favorite coffee table book to the country is ***Guatemala: A Journey Through the Land of the Maya*** ★★★, with stunning photography by Kraig Lieb, and insightful commentaries and essays by Michael Shapiro.

Music

In Guatemalan folk culture, both *mestizo* and Maya, the marimba is king. *Mestizo* forms reflect their Spanish roots with marimba bands and Spanish-language folk songs influenced by the mariachi and ranchero traditions. Maya music may also prominently feature flute and drum, as with the Ki'che and Cakchiquel, or violins and harps, as with the Kekchi.

If you're taken by the marimba and the sounds of traditional Guatemalan music, you can find a good selection of compilation discs at online music shops. I'd avoid the various vendors selling bootleg cassettes and CDs on the side of the road in Guatemala, since the quality can be sketchy, and the artists don't receive a dime. If you see a group you like while touring Guatemala, it is increasingly likely, though far from certain, that they will have a recording for sale.

Among the Garífuna along the Caribbean coast, you'll likely come across **punta** and **punta rock.** Punta is similar to many Afro-Caribbean and Afro-pop music forms, blending traditional rhythms and drumming patterns with modern electronic instruments. (Punta is usually more rootsy and acoustic than punta rock, which features electric guitars and keyboards.) Punta music is usually sung in the Garífuna dialect, though the latest incarnations feature lyrics in English and even Spanish. The Belize-based www.stonetreerecords.com and www.calabashmusic.com offer a good selection of punta records.

The king of contemporary Guatemalan music is **Ricardo Arjona,** a rocking songster and lyricist of the first order. Songs such as "Ella y El" ("She and He") and "Si el Norte Fuera el Sur" ("If North Were South") are smart works of social and political satire with very catchy melodies. Check out Arjona's ***12 Grandes Exitos*** (12 Greatest Hits, 2003) album. For a taste of quintessential '80s Guatemalan rock, look no further than the group **Alux Nahual** (www.aluxnahual.com) and their self-titled

> ### Men of Corn
>
> According to the Popol Vuh, humans originally came from corn, and therefore it has special significance in Maya culture. Corn not only plays a major role in the country's culinary tradition, it also lent its name to author Miguel Angel Asturias's 1967 Nobel Prize–winning masterpiece *Hombres de Maíz (Men of Corn)*.

1981 debut. Subsequent albums and tours helped establish the band as one of Guatemala's most famous and musically talented. The group officially broke up in 1999, but regrouped in 2006 to perform a benefit for victims of Hurricane Stan, and are currently doing sporadic performances and tours once again.

Discothèques still predominantly spin salsa and merengue, though **reggaetón** is starting to dominate. Reggaetón is a combination of hip-hop and Jamaican dance-hall reggae, whose firmest roots are in Panama, though the music was popularized in Puerto Rico. In tourist towns, you'll find a budding electronic music and DJ-driven dance scene.

In Antigua, you'll find the country's only live music club scene, with a mix of local and expatriate musicians playing everything from blues and jazz to Cuban son and contemporary folk.

On Screen

The Guatemalan film industry is still in its infancy. However, the country has had subtle appearances in mainstream American productions. If you need an excuse to watch *Star Wars* (Episode IV) again, look for Tikal in a cameo role as the Rebel Base (the "Massassi Outpost on the fourth moon of Yavin," for die-hard fans) toward the end of the movie. The 11th season of *Survivor* was also filmed at the Maya ruins of Yaxhá, and the tribes were named after ancient ceremonial cities. More recently, Andrzej Krakowski's *Looking for Palladin* (2009; www.palladinmovie.com), featuring Ben Gazzara and Talia Shire, was shot on location in Antigua. While going back a bit in time, *The New Adventures of Tarzan* (1935) was filmed in the rainforests of Guatemala, with the fabulous Atlantic coast waterfalls of Siete Altares (p. 246) playing a feature role.

GUATEMALAN FOOD & DRINK

With the exception of some regional specialties, the most common and prevalent aspects of Guatemalan cuisine are rather unimpressive. Guatemalan cuisine is similar to that of other Central American countries, relying heavily on black beans, white rice, and corn tortillas. Handmade tortillas, along with refried black beans, are usually served at almost every meal, as an accompaniment to some simply grilled meat or chicken. Very few vegetables are typically served at Guatemalan meals.

You will find excellent restaurants serving a wide range of international cuisines in Guatemala City, Antigua, and Panajachel. However, outside the capital and these major tourist destinations, your options get very limited very fast. In fact, many destinations are so small or remote that you have no choice but to eat in the hotel's dining room. Even at the more popular destinations, the only choices aside from the hotel dining rooms are often cheap local places or overpriced tourist traps serving indifferent meals.

If you're looking for cheap eats, you'll find them in little restaurants known as **comedores,** which are the equivalent of diners in the United States. At a *comedor,* you'll find a limited and very inexpensive menu featuring some simple steak and chicken dishes, accompanied by rice, refried beans, and fresh tortillas.

Guatemalans tend to eat three meals a day, in similar fashion and hours to North Americans. Breakfast tends to be served between 6:30 and 9am; lunch between noon and 2pm; and dinner between 6 and 10pm. Most meals and dining experiences are quite informal. In fact, there are only a few restaurants in the entire country that could be considered semiformal, and practically none require a jacket or tie (they'd be in the capital), although you can certainly wear them.

I have separated restaurant listings throughout this book into three price categories based on the average cost per person of a meal, including tax and service charge. The categories are **Expensive,** more than Q160; **Moderate,** Q80 to Q160; and **Inexpensive,** less than Q80. Keep in mind that the 12% IVA tax added onto all bills is not a service charge. A tip of at least 10% is expected. If the service was particularly good and attentive, you should probably leave a little extra.

Food

BREAKFAST   The typical breakfast in Guatemala is quite simple, usually anchored by some scrambled or fried eggs and accompanied by refried red or black beans and corn tortillas. If you order a *desayuno Chapin,* or Guatemalan breakfast, you'll also be served fresh fruit, a slice of local cheese, and some sautéed sweet plantains. Pancakes are often an option, though they might be oilier and crispier than the pancakes you're used to. Guatemalan coffee is world renowned, and you'll often get good strong coffee with your breakfast.

SANDWICHES & SNACKS   Guatemala's light menus show a heavy Mexican and American influence. Many simple eateries feature tacos, burritos, and tamales. *Empanadas,* small, deep-fried pastries stuffed with meat or potatoes, are ubiquitous. You can also get traditional sandwiches, often served on sliced white bread, as well as American-style burgers.

MEAT & POULTRY   Guatemalans eat a fair amount of meat and poultry. Chicken is the most popular, and in some remote places they'll serve it with the feet still attached. You might even get to pick the bird you'll be eating. Hunting iguanas for meat is illegal, but that does not mean it doesn't happen. *Note:* Do not order wild game unless you are certain it is farmed rather than hunted. Keep your eye out for *kac ik,* a savory turkey soup native to the Verapaz region. The dish is either served spicy or with chili on the side, and is spelled any number of ways on menus across the country.

SEAFOOD   Seafood is often available inland, though it's most plentiful and best on the coasts, especially the Atlantic coast, where shrimp, lobster, and a variety of fish are always on the menu. You're best off sticking to simple preparations, either grilled or fried.

If you're in a Garífuna region, don't miss the chance to try *tapado,* a fish stew or mixed seafood preparation served in a spicy coconut milk broth, often accompanied by mashed fried green plantains.

VEGETABLES   On the whole, you'll find vegetables surprisingly lacking in the meals you're served in Guatemala—usually nothing more than a little pile of shredded lettuce topped with a slice or two of tomato. Fresh garden salads are rare and hard to come by. Most restaurant meals are accompanied by a simple slaw of grated cabbage, a potato, or beet salad.

FRUITS   Guatemala has a wealth of delicious tropical fruits. The most common are bananas, mangoes, papayas, pineapples, and watermelons. Other fruits you might find include the *carambola* (star fruit) and the *guanabana* (soursop—a misleading name), whose white pulp makes for fabulous fruit shakes.

DESSERTS   Guatemala doesn't have a very extravagant or refined dessert culture. Flan, a sweet custard, comes in coconut and caramel flavors, and *tres leches* is a very sweet, runny cake that almost falls into the custard category.

Drink

BEVERAGES   Most major brands of soft drinks are available, as are fresh shakes (*licuados*) made with papaya, pineapple, mango, or my personal favorite, guanabana. Ask for them in milk (*en leche*) or water (*en agua pura*), and *sin hielo* (without ice) if you want to be extra sure you're not drinking tap water.

BEER, WINE & LIQUOR   The Cervecería Centroamericana's Gallo (Spanish for rooster) is the national beer of Guatemala. More than a mediocre lager, Gallo is a cultural force. Gallo T-shirts and other merchandise are everywhere. When Pope John Paul II came to Guatemala in 2002 to proclaim the first Central American saint, Gallo helped sponsor his visit. Other beers include Dorada and Moza, both produced from the same brewery as Gallo.

The region is not known for wine production, but some of the best rum in the world is distilled in Guatemala. Try the 23-year-old **Ron Zacapa Centenario** or the 12-year-old **Zaya Gran Reserva,** which have both won numerous awards and claim to be the best rum ever made.

PLANNING YOUR TRIP TO GUATEMALA

3

Guatemala is a land of many colors and cultures. Its many ruins attest to the architectural prowess of both the Maya and the Spanish conquistadors. A trip to Guatemala can focus on the art and culture, natural beauty, ancient archaeology, or a combination of the above. You can partake in adventure sports, spend some time brushing up on your Spanish, or lend a hand as a volunteer.

Some like to travel independently, while others are more comfortable booking a package tour. Guatemala is a country that's easier to navigate with a guide and organized transport for at least some legs of your trip. Whatever your interests or travel style, this chapter will provide you with all the tools and information necessary to plan and book your trip.

Guatemala sits at the northwestern tip of Central America. It's bordered by Mexico to the north, Belize and the Caribbean Sea to the east, Honduras and El Salvador to the southeast, and the Pacific Ocean to the southwest. The country covers an area of 100,000 sq. km (just more than 40,000 sq. miles), which is slightly smaller than the state of Tennessee. Almost two-thirds of the country is covered by mountains, most of which are volcanic. There are some 33 named volcanoes in Guatemala. Of these, quite a few are active, including Volcán Pacaya, Volcán Santiaguito, and Volcán Fuego.

Aside from a few major urban areas, the country is predominantly rural and densely populated. Most visitors stick close to a well-defined tourist trail that encompasses Guatemala City, Antigua, Lake Atitlán, and the Western Highlands, with a side trip to Tikal and the Petén. Those with more time, or a more adventurous spirit, are starting to explore the Atlantic Lowlands, Pacific coast, and the central region, which includes Las Verapaces and El Oriente.

For additional help in planning your trip and for more on-the-ground resources in Guatemala, please turn to "Fast Facts," on p. 277.

WHEN TO GO

The tourist high season runs December through March, coinciding with the winter months in most northern countries. It also coincides with Guatemala's dry season. Throughout this season, and especially around the Christmas and Easter holidays, hotels can be booked solid well in advance, so be sure to have a reservation, especially in the more popular tourist spots. Easter and Holy Week are major holidays in Guatemala and in Antigua specifically. Hotels in Antigua are booked solid as much as a year in advance.

In general, the best time of year to visit weather-wise is in December and January, when everything is still green from the rains, but the sky is clear. If you want to avoid the crowds, I recommend traveling during "shoulder" periods, near the end or beginning of the rainy season, when the weather is still pretty good. *Note:* Some of the country's rugged roads become downright impassable without four-wheel-drive during the rainy season (see below).

Climate

Guatemala is a tropical country and has distinct wet and dry seasons. However, some regions are rainy all year, and others are very dry and sunny for most of the year. Temperatures vary primarily with elevations, not with seasons: On the coasts it's hot all year, while up in the mountains and highlands, it can be quite cool at night and in the early morning, before the sun heats things up, any time of year. At the highest elevations (3,500–4,000m/11,500–13,120 ft.), frost is common.

Generally, the **rainy season** (or *invierno*, winter) is May through October, and the heaviest rain occurs in September and October. The **dry season** (or *verano*, summer) runs from November to April. Along the Pacific Coast, the dry season lasts several weeks longer than in other places. Even in the rainy season, days often start sunny, with rain falling in the afternoon and evening. On the Atlantic coast, the weather is less predictable, and you can get rain year-round, though this area gets less rain in July and August than the rest of the country. The rainforests of the Petén get the heaviest rainfall, and the rainy season here lasts at least until mid-November. The chart below is for Guatemala City, which has similar temperatures to Antigua, Lake Atitlán, and Chichicastenango. Conditions are different in the Petén, Central Highlands, and both the Atlantic and Pacific coasts.

Average Minimum/Maximum Temperature & Precipitation for Guatemala City

	JAN	FEB	MAR	APR	MAY	JUNE	JULY	AUG	SEPT	OCT	NOV	DEC
Min. Temp. (°F/°C)	54/12	54/12	57/14	57/14	61/16	61/16	61/16	61/16	61/16	61/16	57/14	55/13
Max. Temp. (°F/°C)	73/23	77/25	81/27	82/28	84/29	81/27	79/26	79/26	79/26	75/24	73/23	72/22
Precipitation (in.)	.30	.10	.50	1.20	6.00	10.80	8.00	7.80	9.10	6.80	.90	.30

Holidays

Because Guatemala is a predominantly Roman Catholic country, most of its holidays are church-related. The biggies are Christmas, New Year's, and Easter, which are all celebrated for several days. Keep in mind that Holy Week (Easter week) is a major holiday time in Guatemala. Government offices and banks are closed on official holidays, transportation services are reduced, and stores and markets might also close.

Official holidays in Guatemala include **January 1** (New Year's Day), Thursday and Friday of Holy Week, **June 30** (Armed Forces Day), **July 1** (Day of Celebration), **August 15** (Virgen de la Asunción), **September 15** (Independence Day), **October 20** (Commemoration of the 1944 Revolution), **November 1** (All Saints' Day), **December 24** and **25** (Christmas), and **December 31** (New Year's Eve).

Guatemala Calendar of Events

Most of the events listed here might better be considered a tradition, more than an event—there's not, for instance, a Virgen de la Asunción PR Committee that readily dispenses information. In many cases, I've given a more detailed description of the events listed below in the appropriate destination chapters throughout the book. Beyond that, your best bet for detailed information is to call the **Guatemalan Tourism Commission (INGUAT)** at ℂ **800/464-8281** in the U.S. or 1500 in Guatemala, or visit www.visitcguatemala.com. Alternatively, you can contact hotels where the event or festivities take place.

JANUARY

El Cristo Negro, Esquipulas. Pilgrims from across the world converge on the Basilica in this small city in El Oriente to pay their respects to the statue, the *Black Christ*. January 15.

APRIL

Holy Week. Religious processions are held in cities and towns throughout the country. Colorful carpets line the streets of Antigua in preparation for the processions, while in Quetzaltenango there's a live reenactment of the Passion and Crucifixion of Christ. Week before Easter.

JULY

La Fiesta Nacional Indígena de Guatemala, Cobán. This is one of Mesoamerica's greatest celebrations of Maya culture. The city of Cobán features a steady stream of street fairs, concerts, parades, and parties. This is celebrated for 2 solid weeks in late July, sometimes extending into early August.

AUGUST

Fiesta de la Virgen de la Asunción, celebrated countrywide. The Virgin of the Assumption is the patron saint of Guatemala City and, by extension, the entire nation. There are celebrations, parades, and small fairs across the country, but the largest celebrations are held in Guatemala City. August 15.

SEPTEMBER

Guatemala's Independence Day, celebrated all over the country. This is a national holiday. Major cities and most towns and villages have parades and public concerts. September 15.

NOVEMBER

Día de los Muertos (All Saints' Day), celebrated countrywide. The most famous celebration is the "drunken horse race" in the mountain town of Todos Santos. Guatemalans also fly giant, colorful kites to communicate with the dead in the village of Santiago Sacatepéquez. In the rest of the country, the celebrations may not be as elaborate or ritualized as in Mexico, but most Guatemalans take some time this day to remember the dead with flowers and trips to the cemeteries. November 1.

National Garífuna Day, Livingston. Although the official celebration day is November 26, the local Garífuna population in Livingston pulls out all the stops for a solid week of partying around the actual date. Garífuna from neighboring Honduras, Belize, and Nicaragua often come to help in the celebration. Garífuna food and dancing are available all over town. There are parades and street parties. November 26.

DECEMBER

Quema del Diablo (Burning the Devil), celebrated countrywide. Huge bonfires fill the streets throughout the country as trash, tires, old furniture, and effigies of Satan are burned in a symbolic ritual cleansing. December 7.

Fiesta de Santo Tomás, Chichicastenango. The patron saint of this highland city is celebrated with fireworks, parades, and a massive street fair. One of the highlights is the dance of the Palo Volador, or "flying pole," in which a team of acrobats dive from a high pole and are slowly lowered while spiraling outward, attached only by a rope to their ankles. The festivities build for several days leading up to the main festival day of December 21.

ENTRY REQUIREMENTS

Passports

Citizens of the United States, Canada, Great Britain, all European Union nations, Ireland, Australia, and New Zealand may visit Guatemala for a maximum of 90 days. A current passport, valid through your departure date, is required for entry into Guatemala. Driver's licenses and birth certificates are not valid travel documents. In some cases you may be asked to show an onward or return plane ticket.

Visas

It's possible to extend your tourist visa for an additional 90 days, but the process is slightly tedious. To do so, you must go to the **Immigration Office,** 6a Av. 3-11, Zona 4, Guatemala City (✆ **502/2411-2407**). The process involves presenting several authenticated documents and photocopies. Moreover, these documents will need a lawyer's stamp or a notarization from your embassy. Even though the official fee for an extension is just $15, the whole process can take as long as a week, and cost between $20 and $50.

If you need a visa or have other questions about Guatemala, you can contact any of the following Guatemalan embassies or consulates: in the **United States,** 2220 R St. NW, Washington, DC 20008 (✆ **202/745-4952**); in **Canada,** 130 Albert St., Ste. 1010, Ottawa, Ontario K1P 5G4 (✆ **613/233-7237**); and in **Great Britain,** 13 Fawcett St., London, England SW10 9HN (✆ **020/7351-3042**). There are no Guatemalan embassies in Australia or New Zealand, but you could try contacting the embassy in **Japan,** 38 Kowa Building 9F, no. 905, 4-12-24 Nishi Azabu, Tokyo 106-0031 (✆ **81/(03)3400-1830**) or **Taiwan,** 12 Lane 88, Chien Kuo North Road, Section1, Taipei (✆ **866/2-507-7043**).

It is advised to always have at least one or two consecutive blank pages in your passport to allow space for visas and stamps that need to appear together. It is also important to note when your passport expires. Many countries require your passport to have at least 6 months left before its expiration in order to allow you into the destination.

Customs

WHAT YOU CAN BRING INTO GUATEMALA

Visitors to Guatemala may bring any and all reasonable goods and belongings for personal use during their stay. Cameras, computers, and electronic equipment, as

---

Coming & Going

In 2006, Guatemala entered into an immigration and border control treaty with El Salvador, Honduras, and Nicaragua. This agreement, which allows free travel between the countries to all nationals of these signatory nations, creates a single 90-day entry visa for foreign visitors. What this means is that if you travel between these four countries, your total stay cannot exceed 90 days without seeking an extension from the immigration authorities in the country you are visiting as the 90-day period expires. If you want to "renew" your Guatemalan visa by exiting the country for 72 hours and then returning on a new tourist visa, it must be to a country not covered in this agreement.

well as fishing and diving gear for personal use, are permitted duty-free. Customs officials in Guatemala seldom check arriving tourists' luggage.

WHAT YOU CAN TAKE HOME FROM GUATEMALA

It is expressly illegal to take out any pre-Columbian artifact from Guatemala, whether you bought it, you discovered it, or it was given to you. Do not traffic in Maya artifacts.

For information on what you're allowed to bring home, contact one of the following agencies:

U.S. Citizens: U.S. Customs & Border Protection (CBP), 1300 Pennsylvania Ave., NW, Washington, DC 20229 (© **877/287-8667;** www.cbp.gov).

Canadian Citizens: Canada Border Services Agency, Ottawa, Ontario, K1A 0L8 (© **800/461-9999** in Canada, or 204/983-3500; www.cbsa-asfc.gc.ca).

U.K. Citizens: HM Customs & Excise, Crownhill Court, Tailyour Road, Plymouth, PL6 5BZ (© **0845/010-9000;** from outside the U.K., 020/8929-0152; www.hmce.gov.uk).

Australian Citizens: Australian Customs Service, Customs House, 5 Constitution Avenue, Canberra City, ACT 2601 (© **1300/363-263;** from outside Australia, 612/6275-6666; www.customs.gov.au).

New Zealand Citizens: New Zealand Customs, the Customhouse, 17–21 Whitmore St., Box 2218, Wellington, 6140 (© **04/473-6099** or 0800/428-786; www.customs.govt.nz).

Medical Requirements

No shots or inoculations are required to enter Guatemala. For more on medical concerns and recommendations, see "Staying Healthy," p. 44.

GETTING THERE & GETTING AROUND

Getting There

BY PLANE

Most international flights land at **La Aurora International Airport** (© **502/2321-0000** or 502/2260-6257; www.dgacguate.com; airport code GUA). A few international and regional airlines fly directly into **Flores Airport** (FRS) near Tikal. If you're only interested in visiting the Maya ruins at Tikal and touring the Petén, this is a good option. However, most visitors will want to fly in and out of Guatemala City.

To find out which airlines travel to Guatemala, please see "Airline & Rental Websites," p. 280.

Getting into Town from the Airport

You'll find various shuttle companies offering hotel transfers as you exit either the national or international terminal. These companies charge between Q30 and Q80 to any hotel in Guatemala City, and between Q50 and Q80 to Antigua. Many of the larger hotels also have regular complimentary airport shuttle buses.

If you don't want to wait for the shuttle to fill or sit through various stops before arriving at your hotel, there are always taxis lined up at the airport terminal exits. A taxi downtown will cost around Q40 to Q80. A taxi to Antigua should cost between Q200 and Q320. Expect to pay the higher rate, maybe even a little more, after dark.

Alamo, Avis, Budget, Dollar, Hertz, National, Tabarini, and **Thrifty** all have car-rental desks at the airport. See "Getting Around: By Car" below for more information.

BY BUS

Guatemala is connected to Mexico, Belize, El Salvador, and Honduras by regular bus service. If at all possible, it's worth the splurge for a deluxe or express bus. In terms of travel time and convenience, it's always better to get a direct bus rather than one that stops along the way—and you've got a better chance of getting a working restroom in a direct/express or deluxe bus. Some even have television sets showing video movies.

From Mexico, the principal border crossing is at La Mesilla, north of Huehuetenango. From Honduras, the main border crossing is at El Florido, on the route from Copán. From El Salvador, the main border crossing is at San Cristobal, along the Pan-American Highway. And from Belize, the main border crossing is at Melchor de Mencos, in the Petén district.

There are several bus lines with regular daily departures connecting the major capital cities of Central America. **Tica Bus Company** (© 502/2473-1639; www.ticabus.com) has buses running from Mexico all the way down to Panama, while **Pullmantur** (© 502/2367-4746; www.pullmantur.com) connects Guatemala with daily service to San Salvador, El Salvador, and Tegucigalpa, Honduras.

Do not arrive by bus at night if at all possible, as the bus terminals and surrounding areas are very dangerous at night. If you do, hop in a cab immediately after you arrive.

BY CAR

It's possible to travel to Guatemala by car, but it can be difficult. The drive from the United States involves crossing the entire country of Mexico from north to south. Driving can be problematic for a variety of reasons, including bad roads, limited services, crime, corrupt border crossings, and visa formalities. If you do decide to undertake this adventure, take the **Gulf Coast route** from the border crossing at Brownsville, Texas, because it involves traveling the fewest miles through Mexico.

Those planning to travel this route should try to find a copy of *Driving the Pan-Am Highway to Mexico and Central America,* by Audrey and Raymond Pritchard, which is out of print, but sometimes available online. There is also a wealth of information online at www.sanbornsinsurance.com and www.drivemeloco.com.

CAR DOCUMENTS You will need a current driver's license, as well as your vehicle's registration and the original title (no photocopies), to enter Guatemala.

CENTRAL AMERICAN AUTO INSURANCE Contact **Sanborn's Insurance Company** (© 800/222-0158 or 956/686-0711; www.sanbornsinsurance.com), which has agents at various border towns in the U.S. These folks have been servicing this niche for more than 50 years. They can supply you with trip insurance for Mexico and Guatemala (you won't be able to buy insurance after you've left the U.S.), driving tips, and an itinerary.

CAR SAFETY Be sure your car is in excellent working order. It's advisable not to drive at night because of the danger of being robbed by bandits.

Getting Around

SHUTTLES

For most of the major destinations, tourist shuttles or a private car and driver are your best means for getting around. There are a couple of major tourist shuttle services in

Guatemala, and almost every hotel tour desk and local tour agency can book you a ride to just about any major tourist destination in the country either on a regularly scheduled shuttle or with a private car and driver.

The main tourist shuttle company is **Atitrans ★** (② 502/7832-3371 24-hr. reservation number; www.atitrans.net) which offers both regularly scheduled departures to most of the major tourist destinations in the country, as well as private cars or vans with drivers. Or you can contact **Clark Tours,** 7a Av. 14-76, Zona 9, inside Clark Plaza (② 502/2412-4700; www.clarktours.com.gt); **Maya Expeditions,** 15a Calle "A" 14-07, Zona 10 (② 502/2363-4955; www.mayaexpeditions.com); **Turansa,** Carretera Roosevelt, Km 15, Zone 11, Super Centro Molino (② 502/2390-5757; www.turansa.com), or **Via Venture** (② 502/7832-2509; www.viaventure.com).

Shuttle rates from Guatemala City or Antigua to or from other major destinations run between Q80 and Q400 depending upon the destination. A private car or van with driver should cost between Q600 and Q1,600 per day, depending on the size and style of the vehicle and how many passengers are traveling.

BY BUS

This is by far the most economical way to get around Guatemala. Buses are inexpensive and go nearly everywhere in the country. There are two types: **Local buses** are the cheapest and slowest; they stop frequently and are generally very dilapidated. They also tend to be overcrowded, and you are much more likely to be the victim of a robbery on one of these. These buses are commonly referred to as **"chicken buses"** because the rural residents who depend on these buses often have chickens and other livestock as luggage. For all but the most adventurous types, I recommend you avoid these buses.

Express or **deluxe buses** run between Guatemala City and most beach towns and major cities; these tend to be newer units and much more comfortable. They also tend to be direct buses, thus much quicker. Most have working bathrooms, and some have televisions equipped with DVD players showing late-run movies.

Throughout the book, I've listed schedules and contact information for all the appropriate bus lines in the corresponding destination chapters.

BY CAR

In general, I don't recommend renting a car in Guatemala. The roads are often dangerous. Guatemalan drivers, particularly bus and truck drivers, have apparently no concern for human life, their own or anybody else's. A brutal Darwinian survival of the fittest reigns on Guatemala's roads. Passing on blind curves seems to be the national sport. Pedestrians, horses, dogs, and other obstacles seem to appear out of nowhere.

I highly recommend you avoid driving at night at all costs. While rare, there have been armed robberies of tourists and Guatemalans along the highways and back roads of Guatemala, particularly at night. Moreover, the inherent dangers of oncoming traffic and unseen obstacles are heightened at night.

Never leave anything of value in a car. Always try to park in a secure parking lot. If that's not possible, try to find a spot where some local kid or industrious worker will guard your car for a tip.

These caveats aren't meant to entirely scare you off from driving in Guatemala. Thousands of tourists rent cars here every year, and the large majority of them encounter no problems. Renting a car is a good option for independent exploring, and it does provide a lot more freedom and save a lot of time over bus travel. Just keep your wits about you.

Car Rental Tips

Although it's preferable to use the coverage provided by your home auto-insurance policy or credit card, check carefully to see if the coverage really holds in Guatemala. Many policies exclude 4WD vehicles and off-road driving—some of Guatemala can, in fact, be considered off-road. It's possible at some car-rental agencies to waive the insurance charges, but you'll have to pay all damages before leaving the country if you're in an accident. If you do take the insurance, you can expect a deductible of between $750 and $1,500. At some agencies, you can buy additional insurance to lower the deductible. To rent a car in Guatemala, you must be at least 21 years old and have a valid driver's license and a major credit card in your name. See "Getting Around" in chapter 5 for details on renting a car in Guatemala City. You can also rent cars in Antigua, Quetzaltenango, Panajachel, and in Santa Elena and Flores, near Tikal.

Note: It's sometimes cheaper to reserve a car in your home country rather than book when you arrive in Guatemala. If you know you'll be renting a car, it's always wise to reserve it well in advance for the high season because the rental fleet still can't match demand.

Among the agencies operating in Guatemala are **Alamo** (𝄯 502/2362-2701; www.alamo.com); **Avis** (𝄯 502/2324-9000; www.avis.com); **Budget** (𝄯 502/2232-7744; www.budgetguatemala.com.gt); **Dollar** (𝄯 502/2385-1301; www.dollar.com); **Hertz** (𝄯 502/2470-3737; www.hertz.com); **National,** 14a Calle 7-57, Zona 9 (𝄯 502/2362-3000; www.nationalcar.com); and **Thrifty** (𝄯 502/2379-8747; www.thrifty.com). **Tabarini** (𝄯 502/2331-2643; www.tabarini.com) is a good local company with offices at 2a Calle A 7-30, Zona 10, as well as at the airport.

Rates run between $40 and $120 per day, including unlimited mileage and full insurance.

GASOLINE   Gasoline, or *gasolina* in Spanish, is sold as *normal* and *premium*; both are unleaded. Premium is just higher octane. Diesel is available at almost every gas station as well. Most rental cars run on premium, but always ask your rental agent what type of gas your car takes. Gas stations are widely available along the highways, and in all major cities, towns, and tourist destinations. When going off to remote places, try to leave with a full tank of gas because gas stations can be harder to find. At press time, premium cost Q28 per gallon.

ROAD CONDITIONS   Most of the major highways in Guatemala are in pretty good shape. However, once you venture off the major highways, the situation deteriorates quickly and dramatically.

Again, the major highways and tourist destinations are generally well marked. Once you get off the beaten path, though, things change, and you may not encounter any signs or indications as you pass intersection after intersection.

RENTER'S INSURANCE   Even if you hold **your own car-insurance policy** at home, coverage doesn't always extend abroad. Be sure to find out whether you'll be covered in Belize, whether your policy extends to all persons who will be driving the rental car, how much liability is covered in case an outside party is injured in an accident, and whether the *type* of vehicle you are renting is included under your contract.

Most **major credit cards** provide some degree of coverage as well—provided that they were used to pay for the rental. Again, terms vary widely, so be sure to call your credit card company directly before you rent. Usually, if you are **uninsured** or are **driving abroad,** your credit card provides primary coverage as long as you decline the rental agency's insurance. This means that the credit card will cover damage or theft of a rental car for the full cost of the vehicle. If you already have insurance, your credit card will provide secondary coverage, which basically covers your deductible. *Credit cards will not cover liability* or the cost of injury to an outside party and/or damage to an outside party's vehicle.

MAPS   Car-rental agencies and the INGUAT information centers (see "Visitor Information," earlier in this chapter) at the airport and in downtown Guatemala City have adequate road maps. The most detailed map available is produced by **International Travel Maps** (www.itmb.com), which was updated in 2008 and is available online from the website listed, or from most major online book sellers.

DRIVING RULES   A current foreign driver's license is valid for the length of your 90-day tourist visa. Seat belts are required for the driver and front-seat passengers.

Official driving rules are often ignored. Drivers seldom use turn signals or obey posted speed limits. Transit police are a rarity, but they will bust you for speeding, so keep to the speed limit (usually 60–90kmph/37–56 mph) if you don't want to get pulled over. Never pay money directly to a police officer who stops you for any traffic violation. Speeding tickets can be charged to your credit card for up to a year after you leave the country if they are not paid before departure.

BREAKDOWNS   Be warned that emergency services, both vehicular and medical, are extremely limited once you leave Guatemala City, Antigua, or any of the major tourist destinations, and their availability is directly related to the remoteness of your location at the time of breakdown.

If you're involved in a breakdown or accident, you should contact Guatemala's roadside assistance force (PROVIAL; ✆ 502/2422-7878), which patrols most of the major highways in the country. Alternately, you can call the police at ✆ 110. Finally, you can also call **Asistur** (✆ 1500), and they should be able to provide an English-speaking operator and redirect your call to the appropriate agency.

If the police do show up, you've got a fifty-fifty chance of finding them helpful or downright antagonistic. Many officers are unsympathetic to the problems of what they perceive to be rich tourists running around in fancy cars with lots of expensive toys and trinkets. Many are looking for an easy bribe. Success and happy endings run about equal with horror stories.

If you don't speak Spanish, expect added difficulty in any emergency or stressful situation. Don't expect that rural (or urban) police officers, hospital personnel, service-station personnel, or mechanics will speak English.

If your car breaks down and you're unable to get well off the road, check to see whether there are reflecting triangles in the trunk. If there are, place them as a warning for approaching traffic, arranged in a wedge that starts at the shoulder about 30m (98 ft.) back and nudges gradually toward your car. If your car has no triangles, try to create a similar warning marker using a pile of leaves or branches. Finally, there have been some reports of folks being robbed by seemingly friendly good Samaritans who stop to give assistance. To add insult to injury, there have even been reports of organized gangs who puncture tires of rental cars at rest stops or busy intersections, only to follow them, offer assistance, and make off with belongings and valuables.

BY PLANE

Guatemala still doesn't have a very extensive network of commuter airlines. The only major destination regularly serviced by commuter traffic is Tikal. **TACA Regional Airline** (*©* **502/2470-8222;** www.taca.com) and **TAG Airlines ★** (*©* **502/2380-9401;** www.tag.com.gt) both have daily service to Tikal. See chapter 9 for more information.

Charter aircraft can sometimes be hired to travel to some of the more outlying destinations like Quetzaltenango and Puerto Barrios. If you have a big enough group, or big enough budget, and want to charter a plane, contact **Aero Ruta Maya** (*©* **502/2418-2700**) or **TAG Airlines** (*©* **502/2380-9401;** www.tag.com.gt).

MONEY & COSTS

THE VALUE OF THE QUETZAL VS. OTHER POPULAR CURRENCIES

Quetzal	US$	Can$	UK£	Euro (€)	Aus$	NZ$
1	$0.13	C$0.13	£0.08	€0.10	A$0.13	NZ$0.17

Frommer's lists exact prices in the local currency. The currency conversions quoted above were correct at press time. However, rates fluctuate, so before departing consult a currency exchange website such as **www.oanda.com/convert/classic** to check up-to-the-minute rates.

It's always advisable to bring money in a variety of forms on a vacation: a mix of cash, credit cards, debit cards, and, very occasionally, traveler's checks.

Currency

The unit of currency in Guatemala is the *quetzal.* In September 2010, there were approximately 8 *quetzales* to the American dollar, but because the *quetzal* does fluctuate, you can expect this rate to change.

The *quetzal* is theoretically divided into 100 **centavos.** However, because of their insignificant value, you will rarely see or have to handle *centavos.* If you do, there are coins in denominations of 1, 5, 10, 25, and 50 *centavos.* There are also 1 *quetzal* coins, which are quite common and handy.

There are paper notes in denominations of 1, 5, 10, 20, 50, 100 and 200 *quetzales.* This can be a bit of a problem for travelers, since the bill with the largest denomination is worth only around $25.

If your ATM card doesn't work and you need cash in a hurry, **Western Union** (*©* **502/2360-1737** in Guatemala; www.westernunion.com) has numerous offices around Guatemala City and in several major towns and cities around the country. It offers secure and rapid, money-wire and telegram service, although they charge a hefty commission for the service.

In this guide, you will find prices listed in both quetzales (the local currency) and U.S. dollars. As a general rule, with some rare exceptions, hotels throughout the country list their prices in U.S. dollars, or both, with the quetzal price pegged to the U.S. dollar. Many tour agencies, airlines and transportation services also follow this practice.

Restaurants almost uniformly list their prices in quetzales.

Throughout the book, I list the price in the currency you are most likely to find advertised or charged by the respective business. And while you can pay most hotel,

Small Change

When you change money, try to get some smaller bills and 1-*quetzal* coins. Petty cash will come in handy for tipping and public transportation. Even though the largest bill is not very valuable by Western standards, many taxi drivers and small shop owners have trouble making change for a 200 *quetzales* bill. Consider keeping the change separate from your larger bills so that it's readily accessible and you'll be less of a target for theft.

tour agency and transportation fees in U.S. dollars, this does not mean the foreign currency is universally accepted around the country. You will most certainly need to have quetzales to pay for most goods and services throughout the country.

EXCHANGING MONEY

You can change money at all banks in Guatemala. Most charge a very slight service fee. Given the fact that banks handle money exchanges, there are very few exchange houses in Guatemala, although you may run across one here or there. In general, there is little variation in the exchange rate offered at banks and exchange houses.

Hotels will often exchange money as well; there usually isn't much of a line, but they might shave a few *centavos* off the exchange rate. **Warning:** Be careful when leaving a bank. Criminals are often looking for foreigners who have just withdrawn or exchanged cash.

Most airport taxis, shuttles, and major hotels will accept dollars upon your arrival, so it's not absolutely essential to exchange money before traveling to Guatemala. There are two banks inside the airport terminal that will exchange dollars and major European currencies, and will cash traveler's checks. They are usually open for all arriving flights. However, if you arrive outside of this bank's hours, or want to avoid any delay at the airport bank or ATMs, you might consider exchanging at least some money—just enough to cover airport incidentals and transportation to your hotel—before you leave home (although you'll most likely get a lousy exchange rate and face some hefty fees). You can exchange money at your local American Express or Thomas Cook office or at your bank. American Express also dispenses traveler's checks and foreign currency via www.americanexpress.com or ℂ **800/807-6233,** but they'll charge a $15 order fee and additional shipping costs. American Express cardholders should dial ℂ **800/221-7282;** this number accepts collect calls, offers service in several foreign languages, and exempts Amex gold and platinum cardholders from the 1% fee.

ATMs

The easiest and best way to get cash away from home is from an ATM (automated teller machine). The **Cirrus** (ℂ **800/424-7787;** www.mastercard.com) and **PLUS** (ℂ **800/843-7587;** www.visa.com) networks span the globe; look at the back of your bank card to see which network you're on, then call or check online for ATM locations at your destination. Be sure you know your personal identification number (PIN) and daily withdrawal limit before you depart. **Note:** Remember that many banks impose a fee every time you use a card at another bank's ATM, and that fee can be higher for international transactions (up to $5 or more) than for domestic ones (where they're rarely more than $2). In addition, the bank from which you withdraw cash may charge its own fee. For international withdrawal fees, be sure to ask your bank.

ATMs are fairly common throughout Guatemala, particularly in Guatemala City and Antigua, and at most major tourist destinations around the country. You'll find them at almost all banks and most shopping centers. Still, make sure you have some cash at the start of your trip; never let yourself run totally out of spending money, and definitely stock up on funds before heading to any of the more remote destinations in the country. Outside the more popular destinations, it's still best to think of your ATM card as a backup measure, because machines are not nearly as readily available or dependable as you might be accustomed to, and you might encounter compatibility problems.

Note: While many of Guatemala's ATMs will work fine with five- and six-digit PINs, some will only accept four-digit PINs. Before traveling, it's wise to change your PIN to avoid any unexpected hassles in getting access to quick cash.

Credit Cards

All major credit cards are accepted in Guatemala, although MasterCard and Visa will give you the greatest coverage, while American Express and Diners Club are slightly less widely used and accepted.

WHAT THINGS COST IN GUATEMALA	QUETZAL	US$
Taxi from the airport to Guatemala City	40.00–80.00	5.00–10.00
Shuttle from airport to downtown Guatemala City	30.00–80.00	3.75–10.00
Local taxi ride	25.00–50.00	3.15–6.25
Shuttle from Guatemala City to Antigua	50.00–80.00	6.25–10.00
Round-trip flight between Guatemala City and Tikal/Flores	2,400–3,840.00	300.00–480.00
Double room, expensive	800.00–1,200.00	100.00–150.00
Double room, moderate	400.00–800.00	50.00–100.00
Double room, inexpensive	160.00–400.00	20.00–50.00
Dinner for one without wine, expensive	240.00	30.00
Dinner for one without wine, moderate	120.00	15.00
Dinner for one, inexpensive	64.00	8.00
Bottle of Gallo beer	15.00–30.00	1.90–3.75
Bottle of Coca-Cola	5.00–15.00	0.65–1.90
Cup of coffeet	5.00–8.00	0.65–1.00
Gallon of premium gas	28.00	3.50
Admission to most museums	10.00–30.00	1.25–3.75
Admission to Tikal National Park	150.00	18.75
Exit tax	240.00	30.00

Because credit card purchases are dependent upon phone verifications, some hotels and restaurants in more remote destinations do not accept them. Moreover, some add on a 5% to 10% surcharge for credit card payments. Always check in advance if you're heading to a more remote corner of Guatemala.

To report a lost or stolen **American Express** card from inside Guatemala, you can call ☎ **336/393-1111** collect in the U.S.; for **MasterCard,** ☎ **1800/999-1480,** or call ☎ **636/722-7111** collect in the U.S.; for **Visa,** ☎ **1800/999-0115,** or call ☎ **410/581-9994** collect in the U.S.; and for **Diners Club,** call ☎ **502/2338-6801,** or call collect to ☎ **303/799-1504.**

When you contact your bank or issuing company, it might be able to wire you a cash advance off your credit card immediately; in many places, it can deliver an emergency credit card in 1 or 2 days. Odds are that if your wallet is gone, the police won't be able to recover it for you, but your credit card company or insurer might require a police report number, so file a police report anyway (after you cancel your credit cards).

STAYING HEALTHY

Staying healthy on a trip to Guatemala is predominantly a matter of being cautious about what you eat and drink, and using common sense. Know your physical limits, and don't overexert yourself. Respect the tropical sun and protect yourself from it. Limit your exposure to the sun, especially during the first few days of your trip and, thereafter, from 11am to 2pm. Use a sunscreen with a high protection factor, and apply it liberally. Remember that children need more protection than adults do. I recommend buying and drinking bottled water or soft drinks everywhere you travel in Guatemala. Those wishing to really stay on the side of caution should avoid any drinks with ice in them, as well as any raw fruits or vegetables that may have been washed in unsafe water. In general, fruits and vegetables that are peeled—bananas, oranges, avocados—are safe. The sections below deal with specific health concerns in Guatemala.

BEFORE YOU GO

No specific vaccines are required for traveling to Guatemala. That said, many doctors recommend vaccines for hepatitis A and B, as well as up-to-date booster shots for tetanus.

Your existing health plan might provide the coverage you need, but double-check; you might want to buy **travel medical insurance** instead. (See "Insurance" under "Fast Facts" in chapter 13.) Bring your insurance ID card with you when you travel.

If you suffer from a chronic illness, consult your doctor before your departure. For conditions like epilepsy, diabetes, or heart problems, wear a **MedicAlert identification tag** (☎ **888/633-4298;** www.medicalert.org), which will immediately alert doctors to your condition and give them access to your records through MedicAlert's 24-hour hot line.

Pack **prescription medications** in your carry-on luggage, and carry prescription medications in their original containers, with pharmacy labels—otherwise they won't make it through airport security. Also bring along copies of your prescriptions in case you lose your pills or run out. Carry the generic name of prescription medicines, in case a local pharmacist is unfamiliar with the brand name. Don't forget an extra pair of contact lenses or prescription glasses.

Dear Visa, I'm Off to Tikal!

Some credit card companies recommend that you notify them of any impending trip abroad so that they don't become suspicious of foreign transactions and block your charges. If you don't call your credit card company in advance, you can still call the card's toll-free emergency number if a charge is refused—provided you remember to carry the phone number with you. Perhaps the most important lesson here is to carry more than one card so you have a backup.

If you worry about getting sick away from home, consider purchasing **medical travel insurance** and carry your ID card in your purse or wallet. In most cases, your existing health plan will provide the coverage you need.

GENERAL AVAILABILITY OF HEALTHCARE

Guatemala's public healthcare system is overburdened, under-funded, and outdated. Throughout the book, I've listed the nearest public hospital and, when available, private hospital or clinic. Still, when you're in Guatemala, your hotel or local embassy will be your best source of information and aid in finding emergency care or a doctor who speaks English. Most state-run hospitals and walk-in clinics around the country have emergency rooms that can treat most conditions. However, I highly recommend that you seek out a specialist recommended by your hotel or embassy if your condition is not life-threatening and can wait for treatment until you reach one of them.

COMMON AILMENTS

TROPICAL ILLNESSES   Your chance of contracting any serious tropical disease in Guatemala is slim, especially if you stick to the well-worn tourist destinations. However, malaria and dengue fever both exist in Guatemala, so it's a good idea to know what they are.

Malaria is found in rural areas across the country, particularly in the lowlands on both coasts and in the Petén. There is little to no chance of contracting malaria in Guatemala City or Antigua. Malaria prophylaxes are available, but several have side effects, and others are of questionable effectiveness. Consult your doctor regarding what is currently considered the best preventive treatment for malaria. Be sure to ask whether a recommended drug will cause you hypersensitivity to the sun. Because malaria-carrying mosquitoes usually come out at night, you should do as much as possible to avoid being bitten after dark. If you are in a malarial area, wear long pants and long sleeves, use insect repellent, and either sleep under a mosquito net or burn mosquito coils (similar to incense, but with a pesticide).

Of greater concern is **dengue fever,** which has been spreading throughout Latin America since the mid-1990s. Dengue fever is similar to malaria, and is spread by an aggressive daytime mosquito. This mosquito actually seems to prefer populated areas, and dengue has occurred throughout the country. Dengue is also known as "bone-break fever" because it is usually accompanied by severe body aches. The first infection with dengue fever will make you very sick but should cause no serious damage. However, a second infection with a different strain of the dengue virus can lead to internal hemorrhaging and could be life-threatening.

Many people are convinced that taking B-complex vitamins daily will help prevent mosquitoes from biting you. I don't think the American Medical Association has endorsed this idea yet, but I've run across it in enough places to think that there might be something to it.

If you develop a high fever accompanied by severe body aches, nausea, diarrhea, or vomiting during or shortly after a visit to Guatemala, consult a physician as soon as possible.

AMOEBAS, PARASITES, DIARRHEA & OTHER INTESTINAL WOES

Guatemala suffers from periodic outbreaks of **cholera,** a severe intestinal disease whose symptoms include severe diarrhea and vomiting. However, these outbreaks usually occur in predominantly rural and very impoverished areas. Your chances of contracting cholera while you're in Guatemala are very slight.

Other food and waterborne illnesses can mimic the symptoms of cholera and are far more common. These range from simple traveler's diarrhea to salmonella. Even though you've been careful to buy bottled water, order your *licuado en leche* (fruit shakes made with milk rather than water), and drink your soft drink warm (without ice cubes—which are made from water, after all), you still might encounter some intestinal difficulties. Most of this is just due to tender northern stomachs coming into contact with slightly more aggressive Latin American intestinal flora. In extreme cases of diarrhea or intestinal discomfort, it's worth taking a stool sample to a lab for analysis. The results will usually pinpoint the amoebic or parasitic culprit, which can then be readily treated with available over-the-counter medicines.

Except in the most established and hygienic of restaurants, it's also advisable to avoid ceviche, a raw seafood salad, especially if it has any shellfish in it. It could be home to any number of bacterial critters.

In the event you experience any intestinal woe, staying well hydrated is the most important step. Be sure to drink plenty of bottled water, as well as some electrolyte-enhanced sports drinks, if possible.

RIPTIDES Most of Guatemala's Pacific coast beaches have riptides: strong currents that can drag swimmers out to sea. A riptide occurs when water that has been dumped on the shore by strong waves forms a channel back out to open water. These channels have strong currents. If you get caught in a riptide, you can't escape the current by swimming toward shore; it's like trying to swim upstream in a river. To break free of the current, swim parallel to shore and use the energy of the waves to help you get back to the beach.

BEES, SNAKES & BUGS Although Guatemala has Africanized bees (the notorious "killer bees" of fact and fable), scorpions, spiders, and several species of venomous snakes, your chances of being bitten are minimal, especially if you refrain from sticking your hands into hives or under rocks in the forest. If you know that you're allergic to bee stings, consult your doctor before traveling.

Snake sightings, much less snakebites, are very rare. Moreover, the majority of snakes in Guatemala are nonpoisonous. If you do encounter a snake, stay calm, don't make any sudden movements, and don't try to handle it. As recommended above, avoid sticking your hand under rocks, branches, and fallen trees.

Scorpions, black widow spiders, tarantulas, bullet ants, and other biting insects can all be found in Guatemala. In general, they are not nearly the danger or nuisance most visitors fear. Watch where you stick your hands, and shake out your clothes and shoes before putting them on to avoid any unpleasant and painful surprises.

What to Do If You Get Sick Away from Home

Your hotel will be your best resource if you fall ill while traveling in Guatemala. Most hotels will be able to refer you to a local doctor, clinic, or hospital.

For travel abroad, you may have to pay all medical costs up front and be reimbursed later. Medicare and Medicaid do not provide coverage for medical costs outside the U.S. Before leaving home, find out what medical services your health insurance covers. To protect yourself, consider buying medical travel insurance (see "Insurance," in the "Fast Facts" section of chapter 13).

Very few health insurance plans pay for medical evacuation back to the U.S. (which can cost $10,000 and up). A number of companies offer medical evacuation services anywhere in the world. If you're ever hospitalized more than 150 miles from home, **MedjetAssist** (℃ 800/527-7478; www.medjetassistance.com) will pick you up and fly you to the hospital of your choice virtually anywhere in the world in a medically equipped and staffed aircraft 24 hours day, 7 days a week. Annual memberships are $225 individual, $350 family; you can also purchase short-term memberships.

I list **additional emergency numbers** in the "Fast Facts" section of chapter 13 as well as in the "Fast Facts" sections of the chapters on major towns and tourist destinations.

Safety

Guatemala is a violent country, with gross levels of civil injustice, extreme economic hardship, and frequent public unrest and protests. Guatemala still bears the wounds and ongoing effects of its brutal 30-year civil war. This is only exacerbated by ongoing political corruption and the deep infiltration by organized criminal gangs and narcotics traffickers into the political, police, and judicial systems. Still, most of this crime and violence is internal. Most of the popular tourist areas have a strong security presence. A specialized branch of the police force, POLITUR, exists specifically to deal with tourists and crimes against tourists. All that said, robberies and pickpocketing are the greatest problem facing most tourists in Guatemala. Crowded markets, public buses, and busy urban areas are the prime haunts of criminals and pickpockets. Never carry a lot of cash or wear very valuable jewelry. Men should avoid having wallets in your back pockets, and women should keep tight grips on your purses. (Keep it tucked under your arm.) Be sure not to leave valuables unattended or unlocked in your hotel room.

Rental cars generally stick out, and are easily spotted by thieves. Don't ever leave anything of value in a car parked on the street, not even for a moment. Also be wary of solicitous strangers who stop to help you change a tire or bring you to a service station. Although most are truly good Samaritans, there have been reports of thieves preying on roadside breakdowns. Public intercity buses are also frequent targets of stealthy thieves. Never check your bags into the hold of a bus if you can avoid it. If this can't be avoided, when the bus makes a stop, keep your eye on what leaves the hold. If you put your bags in an overhead rack, be sure you can see the bags at all times. Try not to fall asleep. For more information on car and road safety, see "Getting Around: By Car," earlier in this chapter.

Political gatherings to protest current economic and social conditions are not uncommon. The most common form that will affect any tourist is road and highway blockades. There's really little you can do to avoid this; however, a fair amount of patience and some compassion will ease the bother and lower your stress levels. Many of these protests and blockades are announced in advance in the newspapers. If you have an important flight or connection, and you have a long ride to the airport, ask your hotel to check on any alerts, and be sure to leave plenty of time for your drive to the airport.

SPECIALIZED TRAVEL RESOURCES

In addition to the destination-specific resources listed below, please visit Frommers.com for additional specialized travel resources.

LGBT Travelers

Guatemala is a largely Catholic, socially conservative Central American nation, and in general terms the nation is considerably homophobic. Public displays of same-sex affection are rare, and violence against prominent gay and lesbian activists is not unheard of. For these reasons, the local gay and lesbian communities are pretty discreet. For good, comprehensive information on the current situation for gay men, check out the site **Gay Guatemala** (www.gayguatemala.com), which appears in both English and Spanish. Information on the lesbian scene, and specifically lesbian clubs and bars, is much harder to come by. While Guatemala City has something of a gay and lesbian scene, and several bars and clubs cater to this clientele (see "the Gay & Lesbian Scene" in chapter 5), the situation gets radically worse outside of the capital. The more touristy and cosmopolitan destinations of Antigua, Panajachel, and Quetzaltenango can be considered somewhat gay and lesbian friendly; however, the overall reality is rather challenging for gays and lesbians travelers and locals alike in Guatemala.

The **International Gay and Lesbian Travel Association** (IGLTA; © 954/630-1637; www.iglta.org) is the trade association for the gay and lesbian travel industry, and offers an online directory of gay- and lesbian-friendly travel businesses and tour operators.

Travelers with Disabilities

Although Guatemala does have a law mandating Integral Attention to Persons with Disabilities, and a few non-governmental organizations are addressing the needs of the country's disabled population, there are relatively few handicapped-accessible buildings or vehicles in the country. In most cities, sidewalks are narrow, crowded, and uneven. Few hotels offer wheelchair-accessible accommodations, and there are no public buses thus equipped. In short, it can be difficult for a person with disabilities to get around Guatemala. Still, most disabilities shouldn't stop anyone from traveling. There are more options and resources out there than ever before.

Senior Travel

Although it's not common policy in Guatemala to offer senior discounts, don't be shy about asking for one anyway. You never know. Always carry some kind of identification, such as a driver's license, that shows your date of birth, especially if you've kept your youthful glow.

Many reliable agencies and organizations target the 50-plus market. Two such companies offering periodic trips to Guatemala are **Elderhostel,** currently being rebranded as "Road Scholar," (© **800/454-5768;** www.roadscholar.org), which arranges worldwide study programs for those ages 50 and older, and **ElderTreks** (© **800/741-7956** in the U.S. and Canada; 0808-234-1714 in the United Kingdom; or 416/558-5000 from anywhere else; www.eldertreks.com), which offers small-group tours to off-the-beaten-path or adventure-travel locations, restricted to travelers 50 and older.

Family Travel

To locate accommodations, restaurants, and attractions that are particularly kid-friendly, refer to the "Kids" icons throughout this guide.

Hotels in Guatemala often give discounts for children 11 and under and children under 3 or 4 are usually allowed to stay for free. Discounts for children and the cutoff ages vary according to the hotel, but in general, don't assume that your kids can stay in your room for free.

Hotels offering regular, dependable babysitting service are few and far between. If you'll need a babysitter, make sure that your hotel offers the service, and be sure to ask whether the babysitters are bilingual. In many cases, they are not. This is usually not a problem with infants and toddlers, but it can cause problems with older children.

All children, no matter how young, will need a valid passport to enter Guatemala. By law, minors 17 and under need no special permission to enter or leave Guatemala. However, I recommend that adults traveling with children who are not your own carry documented permission from the parent or guardian of record.

Women Travelers

For lack of better phrasing, Guatemala is a typically "macho" Latin American nation. Misogyny and violence against women are part of the social fabric. Women should be careful walking alone at night throughout the country. More and more hotels are ratcheting up security measures for women traveling alone on business or for pleasure. Some are even offering secure "women only" floors, with the added perk of spa services.

Student Travel

Check out the **International Student Travel Confederation (ISTC)** (www.istc. org) website for comprehensive travel services information and details on how to get an **International Student Identity Card (ISIC),** which qualifies students for substantial savings on rail passes, plane tickets, entrance fees, and more. It also provides students with basic health and life insurance and a 24-hour helpline. The card is valid for a maximum of 18 months. You can apply for the card online or in person at **STA Travel** (© **800/781-4040** in North America; © 132-782 in Australia;

C 0871/230-0040 in the U.K.; www.statravel.com), the biggest student travel agency in the world; check out the website to locate STA Travel offices worldwide.

Although you won't find any discounts at the national parks, most museums and other attractions around Guatemala do offer discounts for students. It always pays to ask.

Single Travelers

Many people prefer traveling alone. Unfortunately, the solo traveler is often forced to pay a premium price for the privilege of sleeping alone. On package vacations, single travelers are often hit with a "single supplement" to the base price. To avoid it, you can agree to room with other single travelers on the trip, or you can find a compatible roommate before you go from one of the many roommate locator agencies.

GAP Adventures ★★ (*C* **800/708-7761** in the U.S. and Canada, or 416/260-0999; www.gapadventures.com) is an adventure tour company with a good range of regular and varied tours in Guatemala. As a policy, they do not charge a single supplement and will try to pair a single traveler with a compatible roommate.

SUSTAINABLE TOURISM

Despite its geographic and ecological similarities to Costa Rica and neighboring Belize, Guatemala is not a popular or developed ecotourism destination. Some of the small hotels, isolated nature lodges, and tour operators around the country are making efforts to implement sustainable and responsible tourism practices, but they are in the minority, and nationwide there is very little cultural or political awareness or will to deal with environmental conservation and sustainable practices. Unfortunately given the overall dire economic and social conditions nationwide, this is understandable.

In 2010, Guatemala was ranked near the bottom for countries in the Americas in the Environmental Performance Index (EPI; http://epi.yale.edu). Massive deforestation throughout much of the highlands has lead to devastating mudslides and erosion during the rainy season.

To date there is no overall organizational structure or classification system to rate, train and assist local hotels, restaurants and tourism operators in sustainable tourism practices. The Rainforest Alliance is actively working in the field here, and their web site: **www.sustainabletrip.org** is in its early stages, but is promising.

Recycling is very rare in Guatemala. You can occasionally find separate bins for plastics, glass, and paper on town and city streets, at national parks, and at the country's more sustainable hotels and restaurants. This is a very nascent phenomenon, but I hope it will begin to grow and spread. Your hotel will be your best bet for finding a place to deposit recyclable waste, especially if you choose a hotel that has instituted sustainable practices.

While sustainable tourism options are expanding in Guatemala, organic and sustainably grown fruits and vegetables (as well as coffee) are just beginning to become available. Very few restaurants feature organic produce, although hopefully that will change in the near future.

Several of the tour operators listed in the "Top Tours & Excursions" in chapter 5 (p. 110) have trips specifically geared towards ecotourists. You might also focus on specific hotels and lodges that have an ecotourism bent or have implemented sustainable practices, such as those I recommend in the box below.

Volunteer travel has become increasingly popular among those who want to venture beyond the standard group-tour experience to learn languages, interact with locals, and make a positive difference while on vacation. Volunteer travel usually doesn't require special skills—just a willingness to work hard—and programs vary in length from a few days to a number of weeks. Some programs provide free housing and food, but many require volunteers to pay for travel expenses, which can add up quickly. For specific information on volunteer options in Guatemala, see "Volunteer & Working Trips," later on in this chapter.

Also, see "The Lay of the Land" in chapter 2 for additional information on the various ecosystems and geographical highlights you'll find around the country.

SPECIAL INTEREST & ESCORTED TRIPS

Active, Adventure & Theme Tours

There are plenty of options for active, adventure, or theme vacations to Guatemala. Popular themes and activities include bird-watching, Maya archaeology, cave explorations, and mountain biking. In many cases, you may want to add on a specific theme tour or partake in some adventure activity as an a la carte option within the broader

---

sustainable BUSINESSES IN GUATEMALA

Following is a selection of hotels, restaurants, tour operators and attractions that I feel are making real efforts to implement sustainable and responsible practices. Throughout the book, highlighted hotels, as well as restaurants and other businesses that pay more than mere lip service to sustainability.

GUATEMALA CITY:
Hotel Princess (p. 90)
Posada Belén Museum Inn (p. 93)

ANTIGUA:
Valhalla Macadamia Nut Farm (p. 131)
Via Venture (p. 58)

LAKE ATITLAN:
Reserva Natural Atitlán (p. 144)
Laguna Lodge (p. 163)

WESTERN HIGHLANDS:
Guías Ixiles (p. 175)
Quetzal Trekkers (p. 179)
Unicornio Azul (p. 187)

TIKAL & THE PETÉN:
Hotel Petén Espléndido (p. 210)
Café Arqueológico Yaxhá (p. 212)
Hotel Gringo Perdido (p.215)
La Casa de Don David Hotel (p. 216)
Martsam Travel (p. 214)

CENTRAL GUATEMALA:
X'kape Kob'an (p. 227)
Biotopo del Quetzal (p. 228)
Ram Tzul (p. 229)
Casa K'inich (p. 238)
Hacienda San Lucas (p. 240)

IZABAL & THE ATLANTIC LOWLANDS:
Finca Tatin (p. 250)
Bugamama (p. 251)
Hacienda Tijax (p. 255)

PACIFIC COAST:
Tortuguerio Monterrico (p. 264)
Takalik Maya Lodge (p. 273)

GENERAL RESOURCES FOR green TRAVEL

In addition to the recommendations and resources for Guatemala listed above, the following websites provide valuable wide-ranging information on sustainable travel. For a list of even more sustainable resources, as well as tips and explanations on how to travel greener, visit www.frommers.com/planning.

○ **Responsible Travel** (www. responsibletravel.com) is a great source of sustainable travel ideas; the site is run by a spokesperson for ethical tourism in the travel industry. **Sustainable Travel International** (www. sustainabletravelinternational.org) promotes ethical tourism practices, and manages an extensive directory of sustainable properties and tour operators around the world.

○ **Carbonfund** (www.carbonfund. org), **TerraPass** (www.terrapass.

org), and **Cool Climate** (http:// coolclimate.berkeley.edu) provide info on "carbon offsetting," or offsetting the greenhouse gas emitted during flights.

○ **Greenhotels** (www.greenhotels. com) recommends green-rated member hotels around the world that fulfill the company's stringent environmental requirements. **Environmentally Friendly Hotels** (www.environmentallyfriendly hotels.com) offers more green accommodation ratings.

○ **Volunteer International** (www. volunteerinternational.org) has a list of questions to help you determine the intentions and the nature of a volunteer program. For general info on volunteer travel, visit **www.volunteerabroad. org** and **www.idealist.org**.

scope of your trip to Guatemala. However, some of you may want to build your entire itinerary around a specific theme or activity. The agencies listed below specialize in adventure tourism or specialized activities, as indicated. In addition to the agencies and operators listed below, most of the package and escort tour operators listed further down also offer a selection of themed specialty tours or adventure options.

GENERAL ADVENTURE TOUR & SPECIAL-INTEREST TOUR OPERATORS

○ **Adrenalina Tours ★** (© 502/7761-4509 or 5308-1489; www.adrenalinatours. com). Not for pregnant women or those with heart conditions. With offices in Xela, Antigua, Panajachel, Huehue, and San Marcos, this Guatemalan-based company specializes in strenuous hikes and volcano climbs—one is rated "dangerous due to toxic gases." They also offer 4WD off-road tours, with a vehicle, driver, and multilingual guide, for around $150 per day, among their many options.

○ **Adventure Life** (© 800/344-6118 in the U.S. and Canada; www.adventure-life.com) has several different trips, including biking, kayaking, and trekking; visiting villages and ruins; or Easter Week in Antigua. Prices range from 6 days for around $950 to 11 days for around $2,615 per person. Airfare not included.

○ **AdventureSmith Explorations** (© 877/620-2875 or 530/583-1775 in the U.S. and Canada; www.adventuresmithexplorations.com) offers several different trips, with experiences running the gamut from rafting and cave exploration to Maya ruins and markets. Some include Belize, southern Mexico, or the Copán ruins in

Honduras. Five days cost around $850; 9 days around $1,500 per person, not including airfare.

○ **Bike Hike Adventures** (© **888/805-0061** in the U.S. and Canada, or 604/731-2442; www.bikehike.com) is a Vancouver-based company specializing in multiday, multi-adventure tours for small groups. Their 8-day tour will have you hiking, mountain biking, sea kayaking, and tree-canopy exploring. You'll visit Guatemala City, Antigua, Chichicastenango, the Volcán Pacaya, Lake Atitlán, and Tikal. They'll let you design your own trip, too. The cost for their 8-day adventure is around $1,999 per person, not including airfare.

○ **CA Tours** ★ (© **44/132-983-6309** in the U.K., or 502/7832-9638 in Guatemala; www.catours.co.uk). If motorcycles are your thing, this is your trip. They offer a range of tours, from one-day tours around the Pacaya volcano or Lake Atitlan for around $100 per person per day, to 10 days coast to coast ride for $2,100 per person; airfare not included. You can use the motorcycle they supply, or pick from several other models and pay extra for rental. They will also customize a tour for you.

○ **GAP Adventures** ★★ (© **800/708-7761** in the U.S. and Canada, or 416/260-0999; www.gapadventures.com) is a major international adventure and educational tour operator with a full plate of theme tours to Guatemala. Options include hardcore adventure activities, language-learning trips, and stints doing volunteer work. Their prices vary according to the trip and activity, but are very competitive.

○ **Maya Expeditions** (© **502/2363-4955;** www.mayaexpeditions.com) are pioneers in adventure and ecotourism in Guatemala. They offer dozens of tour, activity, and theme options, including Maya archaeology, river rafting, and weaving. They also offer relaxing day tours. They use knowledgeable local guides and bring in academic experts. Contact them for prices.

Language Learning

Guatemala is a major destination for folks looking to learn or brush up on some Spanish. You can find courses of varying length and intensity, as well as many that include cultural activities and day excursions. Some of the schools have reciprocal relationships with U.S. universities so, in some cases, you can even arrange for college credit. Most Spanish schools can arrange for homestays with a local Guatemalan family for a total-immersion experience. These homestays include a private room and either two or three meals daily taken with the family. Most of the schools integrate excursions and cultural programs into their curriculum. Classes are often small, or even one-on-one, and can last anywhere from 2 to 8 hours a day. Listed below are some of the larger and more established Spanish-language schools, with approximate costs. The majority are located either in Antigua or Quetzaltenango, and to a lesser extent around Lake Atitlán. But there are Spanish-language schools in such far-flung corners of the country as Monterrico and the Petén. Contact the schools for the most current price information.

Guatemalan Spanish is considered one of the most pure, in terms of clarity and pronunciation, in the Americas. Compared to the Spanish spoken in other Latin American countries, Guatemalan Spanish tends to be more clearly enunciated and slightly slower. This is one of the reasons language schools are so popular throughout Guatemala.

Quetzaltenango has the greatest concentration of language schools, followed in short order by Antigua. In broad strokes, the programs in Quetzaltenango are less expensive. In Antigua, you'll pay a slight premium for living and learning in arguably the hippest and most desirable city in the country. That said, in reality, the price difference is often negligible. I personally recommend you decide where you want to spend your time and what kind of side trips and extracurricular adventures you might want to enjoy, and choose by location.

o **Academia de Español Guatemala** ★, 7a Calle Oriente, #63, Antigua (✆ **502/7832-5057;** www.acad.conexion.com), offers group and one-on-one classes. Their main facility features a lovely garden, with its own swimming pool, as well as free Internet and Wi-Fi connections. A 1-week program including 4 hours of private instruction per day costs just $100, with a week-long homestay costing an extra $75.

o **Celas Maya Spanish School,** 6a Calle 14-55, Zona 1, Quetzaltenango (✆ **502/7761-4342;** www.celasmaya.edu.gt), offers intensive Spanish and Ki'che Mayan language classes. One of the larger and more popular schools in Xela, these folks charge between $185 to $215 per week, for 5 hours daily of one-on-one instruction, including a homestay with a local family.

o **Centro Lingüístico Maya** ★, 5a Calle Poniente, #20, Antigua (✆ **502/7832-0656;** www.clmaya.com), offers weeklong programs with 4 to 7 hours of private instruction per day. The 4-hour-per-day week runs $140, with the homestay costing an extra $80 per week.

o **Eco Escuela de Español** ★, San Andrés, El Petén (✆ **502/5940-1235;** www.ecoescuelaespanol.org), is a community-based language school program in a small village on the shore of Lake Petén Itzá. The program costs just $150 per week, including lodging and three meals daily with a local family, as well as 4 hours of daily class time, usually one-on-one.

o **Escuela de Español San José el Viejo** ★★, 5a Av. Sur, #34, Antigua (✆ **502/7832-3028;** www.sanjoseelviejo.com), is one of the few institutions with its own rooms. Rates here for a week of 4-hour daily classes run $85. While their onsite rooms run $220 to $490 for a full week, double occupancy.

o **Jardín de América Spanish School** ★, Calle 14 de Febrero, Panajachel (✆ **502/7762-2637;** www.jardindeamerica.com), is located in downtown Panajachel, just a few blocks from the shores of Lake Atitlán. Their homestay program places students with predominantly local Maya families for an interesting cultural experience. A weeklong program with 4 hours of private instruction daily and homestay costs $170.

o **Proyecto Lingüístico Quezalteco** ★, 5a Calle 2-40, Zona 1, Quetzaltenango (✆ **502/7765-2140;** www.plqe.org), is a very well run school that integrates an understanding of Guatemala's social and political context into their learning experience. They actually have two campuses, one in downtown Xela and another in a more rural, mountain setting. A weeklong program, including 5 hours of daily private instruction and a homestay, costs $200.

o **San Pedro Spanish School,** San Pedro La Laguna, Lake Atitlán (✆ **502/5715-4604;** www.sanpedrospanishschool.com), is an excellent little school that even offers classes in the Tz'utujil Mayan dialect. Rates run $150 per week for 4 hours of classes per day and a homestay with a local family.

o **Ulew Tinimit Spanish School** ★, 4a Calle 15-23, Zona 1 (✆ **502/7763-0516;** www.spanishguatemala.org), is one of the better Xela language schools. These folks also offer classes in Ki'che and Mam Mayan dialects. A 1-week program with 5 hours of class instruction daily and a homestay costs $150.

Other Academic Trips & Learning Vacations

○ **Art Workshops in Guatemala** (℃ 612/825-0747 in the U.S. and Canada; www.artguat.org). This group offers many creative opportunities, including nearly every genre of writing, plastic arts, and even yoga. While there are opportunities to try your hand at Maya weaving, that class watches the real experts at work and visits the markets where their works are sold. Ten-day tours run around $1,795–$1,995 per person, plus airfare, depending on workshop.

○ **Jim Cline Photo Tours** (℃ 877/350-1314 in the U.S. and Canada; www.jim cline.com) is guided by a professional photographer who teaches participants to see Guatemala through the camera lens. The 10-day "Living Maya" tour, limited to nine people, focuses on colonial architecture, colorful markets, small villages, the natural beauty of Lake Atitlán, and the Maya people. Cost is around $3,575 per person, plus airfare.

Volunteer & Working Trips

If you want to lend a hand while in Guatemala, you have several options. **Habitat for Humanity International** (℃ 502/7763-5308 in Guatemala; www.habitat guate.org) has several chapters in Guatemala and sometimes runs organized Global Village programs here. Their Global Village trips are large, group-escorted trips that include work on a Habitat for Humanity building project, as well as other cultural and educational experiences. The costs range from $1,200–$2,000, not including airfare, for a 9- to 14-day program.

In Antigua, I recommend checking in with **Proyecto Mosaico** ★, 3a Av. Norte, #3 (℃/fax **502/5817-6660;** www.promosaico.org) a German-funded non-governmental organization that helps arrange a wide array of volunteer opportunities around Central America.

If you have educational, medical or tourism skills and want to work with the Q'eqchi' Maya in the remote rainforests of the Rio Dulce region, contact **Ak'Teneamit** (℃ **502/2254-1560;** www.aktenamit.org). These folks prefer a 6-month commitment, but will work with you to find an appropriate volunteer position.

Alternatively, up in the Western Highlands around Quetzaltenango, you can check in with **Entre Mundos** (℃ 502/7761-2179; www.entremundos.org), which functions as a bridge between a host of non-governmental organizations and community projects. They specifically work to connect foreign volunteers with appropriate community, social, health, and educational projects.

Packages for the Independent Traveler

Before you start your search for the lowest airfare, you may want to consider booking your flight as part of a travel package. Package tours are not the same thing as escorted tours. Package tours are simply a way to buy the airfare, accommodations, and other elements of your trip (such as car rentals, airport transfers, and sometimes even activities) at the same time and often at discounted prices—kind of like one-stop shopping. Packages are sold in bulk to tour operators—who resell them to the public at a cost that often undercuts standard rates.

Before you book your package through a tour company, remember that with a few phone calls and e-mails, you can often organize the same thing on your own without having to pay the sometimes hefty service fee. This book contains all the information and resources you need to design and book a wonderful trip, tailored to your particular interests and budget. Moreover, package vacations are minor industry in Guatemala and do not offer the kinds of amazing bargains as those to Cancún or the Caribbean. In fact, many come with hidden charges and costs, so shop carefully.

Your best bet is often to do it yourself or to go with a Guatemalan-based specialist; many of these companies emphasize adventure travel or ecotourism and can put together a complete custom itinerary for you. For a complete listing of tour companies servicing Guatemala, see "Recommended Package & Escorted Tour Operators" and "General Adventure Tour & Special-Interest Tour Operators" in this chapter.

Package tours can vary by leaps and bounds. Some offer a better class of hotels than others. Some offer the same hotels for lower prices. Some offer flights on scheduled airlines, while others book charters. Some limit your choice of accommodations and travel days. You are often required to make a large payment upfront. On the plus side, packages can save you money, offering group prices but allowing for independent travel. Some even let you add on a few guided excursions or escorted day trips (also at prices lower than if you booked them yourself) without booking an entirely escorted tour.

Before you invest in a package tour, get some answers. Ask about the **accommodations choices** and prices for each. Then look up the hotels' reviews in a Frommer's guide and check their rates online for your specific dates of travel. You'll also want to find out what **type of room** you get. If you need a certain type of room, ask for it; don't take whatever is thrown your way. Request a nonsmoking room, a quiet room, a room with a view, or whatever you fancy.

For more information on package tours and specific providers, and for tips on booking your trip, see Frommers.com. Travel packages are also listed in the travel section of your local Sunday newspaper. Or check ads in the national travel magazines such as *Budget Travel Magazine, Travel + Leisure, National Geographic Traveler,* and *Condé Nast Traveler.*

Escorted General-Interest Tours

Escorted tours are structured group tours with a group leader. The price usually includes everything from airfare, hotels, and meals to tours, admission costs, and local transportation.

Despite the fact that escorted tours require big deposits and predetermine hotels, restaurants, and itineraries, many people derive security and peace of mind from the structure they offer. Escorted tours—whether they're navigated by bus, motorcoach, train, or boat—let travelers sit back and enjoy the trip without having to drive or worry about details. They take you to the maximum number of sights in the minimum amount of time with the least amount of hassle. They're particularly convenient for people with limited mobility and can be a great way to make new friends.

Escorted tours are also a good bet in Guatemala, since safety and the conditions of internal travel can be daunting for many independent travelers

On the downside, you'll have little opportunity for serendipitous interactions with locals. The tours can be jampacked with activities, leaving little room for individual sightseeing, whim, or adventure—plus they also often focus on the heavily visited sites, so you miss out on many a lesser-known gem.

For more information on escorted general-interest tours, including questions to ask before booking your trip, see www.frommers.com.

Before you invest in a package deal or an escorted tour:

o Always ask about the **cancellation policy.** Can you get your money back? Is a deposit required?

o Request a complete **schedule.** (Escorted tours only)

o Ask about the **size** and demographics of the group. (Escorted tours only)

o Discuss what is included in the **price** (transportation, meals, tips, airport transfers, and the like). (Escorted tours only)

o Finally, look for **hidden expenses.** Ask whether airport departure fees and taxes, for example, are included in the total cost—they rarely are.

Recommended Package & Escorted Tour Operators

NORTH AMERICAN–BASED TOUR OPERATORS

These agencies and operators specialize in well-organized and coordinated tours that cover your entire stay. Many travelers prefer to have everything arranged and confirmed before arriving in Guatemala, and this is a good idea for first-timers.

o **Caravan Tours** (© 800/227-2826 in the U.S. and Canada, or 312/321-9800; www.caravantours.com). If you don't mind sharing your vacation with up to 45 fellow travelers, and a slight cattle-car feel to the whole operation, this is a great value. See six places (Guatemala City, Antigua, Lake Atitlán) in 11 days for around $1,000 per person. Airfare not included.

o **Overseas Adventure Travel** ★★ (© 800/493-6824; www.oattravel.com) offers good-value natural history and "soft adventure" itineraries, with optional add-on excursions. Tours are limited to 16 people. The "Route of the Maya" 14-day package includes 8 days in Guatemala, and also visits Copán in Honduras and ruins in Belize. Around $2,395 per person including round-trip airfare from Miami or Houston.

U.K.-BASED TOUR OPERATORS

o **Imaginative Traveller** (© 44/147-366-7337; www.imaginative-traveller.com) is a good-value operator specializing in budget student, group, and family travel. Their offerings focus on the larger Maya world, and usually combine trips to Guatemala with time spent in parts of southern Mexico and Belize. They offer a variety of different itineraries ranging from 1-day trips to a 46-day excursion. Rates vary widely, according to the length of the tour, but are very reasonable.

o **Journey Latin America** ★ (© 44/208-747-8315; www.journeylatinamerica.co.uk) is a large British operator specializing in Latin American travel. They offer a range of escorted tours around Latin America, with some that spend much of the time in Guatemala. They also design custom itineraries, and often have excellent deals on airfare.

GUATEMALAN TOUR OPERATORS

Because many U.S.-based companies subcontract portions of their tours to established Guatemalan companies, some travelers like to set up their tours directly with these companies, thereby cutting out the middleman. While that means these packages are often less expensive than those offered by U.S. companies, it doesn't mean they're cheap. You still pay for the convenience of having all your arrangements handled for you.

Scores of tour agencies in Guatemala City, Antigua, and the other major tourist destinations offer a plethora of sightseeing and adventure options. These agencies, and the tour desks at most hotels, can arrange everything from tours of the Maya ruins to village market shopping sprees. While it's generally quite easy to arrange most of these popular tours and adventures at the spur of the moment during your vacation, some are offered only when there are enough interested people or on set dates. If you have a specialized tour or activity in mind, it pays to contact the hotel you will be staying at or a few of the companies listed here before you leave home to find out what they might be doing when you arrive.

- **Clark Tours** (© **502/2412-4700**; www.clarktours.com.gt) has been operating for more than 70 years in Guatemala, making it the oldest tour company in the country. They have several offices and are the official representatives of American Express in Guatemala. They offer many tours, including an afternoon in Antigua for around $30 per person; 2- to 4-day archaeology trips starting at around $400 per person; and the 15-day Guatemalan highlights tour that takes in all of the country's major tourist destinations, including Antigua, Lake Atitlán, Chichicastenango, Rio Dulce Tikal, and Copán, Honduras for around $2,000 per person.

- **Martsam Tour and Travel** ★★ (© **866/832-2776** in the U.S. and Canada, or 502/7867-5093 in Guatemala; www.martsam.com) based on the island of Flores, these guys are hands down the best operators for Tikal and the Petén, although they also have an office in Antigua and can book tours for the entire country.

- **Via Venture** ★★ (© **502/7832-2509**; www.viaventure.com). This well-run operation specializes in custom-designed itineraries using the finest high-end hotels in the country, as well as an excellent team of guides and ground transport services. They are also particularly strong in the area of adventure tourism and theme vacations. The tour operator has an extensive and well thought out sustainable tourism policy (http://www.viaventure.com/sustainable_tourism_policy.htm). In addition to Guatemala, these folks run trips and combined itineraries into Belize and Honduras.

STAYING CONNECTED

Telephones

Guatemala has a fairly extensive telephone network reaching most of the country. However, cellphones are far more common and readily available than land lines.

Pay phones are very rare these days. However, calling cards for both cellphones and land lines are widely available at general stores and pharmacies all over the country.

Most hotels will let you send and receive faxes for a fee; however, their phone charges tend to be high so I recommend getting a calling card.

There are no area codes inside Guatemala.

To call Guatemala from abroad:

1. Dial the international access code: 011 from the U.S. and Canada; 00 from the U.K., Ireland, or New Zealand; or 0011 from Australia.
2. Dial the country code 502.
3. Dial the 8-digit number.

To make a call inside Guatemala: Simply dial the eight-digit number.

To place a call from your home country to Guatemala: Dial the international access code (011 in the U.S. and Canada, 0011 in Australia, 0170 in New Zealand, 00 in the U.K.), plus the country code (502), followed by the eight-digit number.

To place a direct international call from Guatemala: Dial the international access code (00), plus the country code of the place you are dialing, plus the area code and the local number.

For directory assistance: Call ℭ **2333-1524;** for an international operator and directory assistance, call ℭ **147-120** from any landline.

Mobile Phones

All of Guatemala's cellphone networks are GSM. If your cellphone is on a GSM system, and you have a world-capable multiband phone such as many Sony Ericsson, Motorola, or Samsung models, you can make and receive calls across civilized areas around much of the globe, from Andorra to Uganda. Just call your wireless operator and ask for "international roaming" to be activated on your account. Unfortunately, per-minute charges can be high—usually $1.50 to $4 in Guatemala.

In Guatemala, there are several competing cellphone companies and networks. The main companies are **Claro** (ℭ **502/2420-1414;** www.claro.com.gt), which is a division of Telgua, the national telephone company; **Movistar** (ℭ **502/2379-1960;** www.movistar.com.gt), a division of the international firm Telefonica; and **Tigo** (ℭ **502/2428-0000;** www.tigo.com.gt). All of these companies sell prepaid GSM chips that can be used in any unlocked tri- and quad-band GSM cellphone. Most companies charge around a Q25 to Q50 activation fee, and this usually includes a few *quetzales* worth of talk time. All have numerous outlets across the country, in most major cities and tourist destinations, including La Aurora International Airport. Moreover, all of these outlets and shops all over the country sell activated new phones for as little as Q100, and this also usually includes a few *quetzales* worth of talk time. The ready access to activated new phones at such low prices makes renting a phone unnecessary. Once your minutes run out, prepaid calling cards are widely available, and come in denominations from Q10 to Q200.

Voice-Over Internet Protocol (VoIP)

If you have Web access while traveling, consider a broadband-based telephone service (in technical terms, **Voice-over Internet protocol,** or **VoIP**) such as Skype (www.skype.com) or Vonage (www.vonage.com), which allow you to make free international calls from your laptop or in a cybercafe. Neither service requires the people you're calling to also have that service (though there are fees if they do not). Check the websites for details.

Even if you don't have your own Skype or Vonage account, Internet cafes in most major tourist destinations in Guatemala usually offer the option of making international calls over their VoIP connections. Rates range anywhere from 5¢ to $1 per minute.

Internet & E-Mail

WITHOUT YOUR OWN COMPUTER

Cybercafes can be found all over Guatemala, especially in the more popular tourist destinations. Heck, there are even cybercafes in remote areas like Livingston and Monterrico.

Aside from formal cybercafes, many **hotels** have at least one computer with Internet access. However, I recommend you avoid **hotel business centers** unless you're willing to pay exorbitant rates.

WITH YOUR OWN COMPUTER

More and more hotels, resorts, cafes, and retailers around Guatemala are offering high-speed Wi-Fi access, either free or for a small fee. Throughout the book, I list which hotels provide free, or for a fee, Wi-Fi and high-speed Ethernet access.

In Antigua and Guatemala City (especially in the Zona Viva), you'll find a range of hotels, restaurants, and cafes that offer free Wi-Fi connections. Wherever possible, I've listed this in the hotel or restaurant descriptions throughout the book. To a lesser extent, you will find Wi-Fi connections becoming available around Lake Atitlán, Quetzaltenango, Flores, and Santa Elena, and even in some of the more remote destinations around the country.

Guatemala uses standard U.S.-style two- and three-prong electric outlets with 110-volt AC current, and standard U.S.-style phone jacks. Wherever you go, bring a **connection kit** of the right power and phone adapters, a spare phone cord, and a spare Ethernet network cable—or find out whether your hotel supplies them to guests.

TIPS ON ACCOMMODATIONS

With the exception of a few large business-class hotels clustered in Guatemala City's Zona Viva, Guatemala has no truly large-scale resorts or hotels. What the country does have is a wealth of intimate and interesting **small-to-midsize hotels** and **resorts.** Most of these are quite comfortable and very reasonably priced by most international standards. A few very classy luxury boutique hotels are scattered around the country, and are found with relative abundance in Antigua and around Lake Atitlán. Real budget travelers will find a glut of very acceptable and very inexpensive options all across the country. **Warning:** Budget-oriented lodgings often feature shared bathrooms and either cold-water showers or showers heated by electrical heat-coil units mounted at the shower head. These are affectionately known as "suicide showers." If your hotel has one, do not try to adjust it while the water is running. Unless specifically noted, all the rooms I've listed in this guide have private bathrooms.

A hotel is sometimes called a *posada* in Guatemala. As a general rule, a *posada* is a smaller, more humble, and less luxurious option than a hotel. However, there are some very serious exceptions to this rule, particularly in Antigua, where some of the finest accommodations are called *posadas*.

In general, prices drop dramatically outside of Guatemala City and the more popular destinations like Antigua, Lake Atitlán, and Tikal. In fact, outside of these destinations, you'll find very few hotel options charging more than $75 per night for a double, even for the swankiest room in town.

If you're traveling on a budget and staying in some of the less expensive hotels, one item you're likely to want to bring with you is a towel. Your hotel might not provide one at all, and even if it does, it might be awfully thin.

Note: Air-conditioning is not necessarily a given in many midscale hotels and even some upscale joints. In general, this is not a problem. Cooler nights and a well-placed ceiling fan are often more than enough to keep things pleasant, unless I mention otherwise in the hotel reviews.

Autohotels

One type of hotel you may run across, especially in Guatemala City, is an *autohotel*. *Autohotels* are not self-service affairs—except for the most desperate. They are, however, semi-discreet operations used mainly for romantic liaisons. Most *autohotels* feature rooms with two-car garages with doors or curtains so that nosy spouses or private eyes cannot see the license plates. *Autohotels* rent out by the hour, and are usually not of very much interest to the average tourist.

Throughout this book, I've separated hotel listings into several broad categories: **Very Expensive,** more than $150 for a double; **Expensive,** $101 to $150; **Moderate,** $50 to $100; and **Inexpensive,** under $50 double. *Unless otherwise noted, rates given in this book do not include the 12% IVA and 10% hotel tax.* These taxes will add considerably to the cost of your room, so do factor them in.

Frommer's uses a zero- to three-star rating system. This star system is a relative system, and not necessarily on a par with standard industry star-rating systems. A truly special bed-and-breakfast, run with style and aplomb, may get two or three stars, even though the rooms do not have televisions or air-conditioning. Meanwhile, a large resort with a host of modern amenities may receive one or no stars. Every hotel listed is in some way recommended. This book is selective, and I've done my best to list the best options in each price range and each region, while weeding out the hotels you should not even bother with.

For tips on surfing for hotel deals online, visit www.frommers.com.

SUGGESTED GUATEMALA ITINERARIES

From the natural beauty of Lake Atitlán and the country's colorful markets to the perfectly preserved architecture of Antigua and Tikal to the thundering drums and dances of the Garífuna people, there's something for everyone in Guatemala.

By far the safest and most convenient way to get around Guatemala is by small tourist shuttles and minivans. Several major shuttle companies and local tour agencies offer daily transfers between the country's major destinations. **Atitrans** (© **502/7832-3371** for 24-hr. reservation number; www.atitrans.net) and **Turansa** (© **502/2390-5757**; www.turansa.com) are the best and most extensive shuttle services. Most fares run between Q80 and Q320 one-way. Alternatively, you can take the local bus lines, particularly those that offer deluxe or luxury-class service. Despite the deluxe and luxury designations, this is a very economical means of travel, with one-way fares averaging between Q30 and Q80. The only major destination in Guatemala served by regular commuter airline service is Tikal. Those in a time crunch should fly, but if you have the time, you might consider traveling to Tikal by land, stopping in Cobán, Copán, and Lago Izabal along the way.

The following itineraries are designed to show you the best the country has to offer, with specific routes depending on your interests and travel companions. You can follow them to the letter or use them as an outline or basic guideline, mixing and matching destinations, activities, and attractions from the rest of this book.

The Regions in Brief

Guatemala City Set on a high, broad plateau and surrounded by volcanic peaks, Guatemala City is the largest city in the country, and the only one with a contemporary, modern feel to it. That said, with a population of more than three million, the city is overwhelmingly a sprawling, congested, confusing, and polluted urban mess. Guatemala City has a small but vibrant arts-and-nightlife scene, as well as some of the finest hotels and restaurants in the country. The city sits at an elevation of 1,469m (4,897 ft.) above sea level, and enjoys moderate temperatures year-round. Home to the country's principal international airport and bus connections to every corner of the country, Guatemala City serves as a de facto transportation hub for most, if not all, visitors.

Antigua This small, picturesque colonial city lies just 40km (25 miles) southwest of Guatemala City. In fact, for a couple hundred years, it was the nation's capital, until a series of devastating earthquakes and mudslides forced its evacuation. Like its neighbor and the current capital, Antigua is also set in a valley surrounded by towering volcanic mountain peaks. However, the Antigua valley is much, much smaller. The entire colonial city is little more than 10 blocks by 10 blocks, with a touch of modern urban sprawl around the edges. The city is one of the most well-preserved examples of a colonial city in the Americas. The colonial core of Antigua is a living museum, with rough cobblestone streets and restored colonial-era buildings, mixed in with a few newer constructions that maintain the colonial style and feel. Combined with this living museum are a host of actual museums, and ruined and restored examples of grand churches, convents, and monasteries. From Antigua, the **Agua** and **Fuego volcanoes** are clearly visible.

Lake Atitlán Lake Atitlán is technically part of the Western Highlands, but for the purposes of this book, and in the minds of most travelers, it is a world unto itself. Lake Atitlán is a beautiful mountain lake that is actually the filled-in crater of a massive volcano. It's hard to imagine this, since today, several more volcanoes rise from around the shores and tower over the lake. More than 16km (10 miles) across at its widest point, Lake Atitlán has a series of small villages and a few major towns lining its shores. While roads connect all of these towns (in many cases they are rough dirt and gravel), the main means of transportation between the various towns and villages is by boat and boat taxi. The main town and gateway to Lake Atitlán is **Panajachel,** which sits on the northern shore of the lake. Other major towns include **Santa Catarina Palopó** and **San Antonio Palopó** to the east of Panajachel, and **Santiago de**

Atitlán and **San Pedro La Laguna** across the lake to the south.

The Western Highlands The area to the west and northwest of Guatemala City is widely referred to as the Western Highlands, or Altiplano (the "Highlands" in Spanish). This is the heart of Guatemala's rural Maya population. Following the collapse of the major Maya empires of the Petén and lowland coastal regions, many fled in small groups and family units to Altiplano. Today, the Western Highlands are populated with a dense patchwork of small, rural farming communities spread around the rough, steep, mountainous region. The towns and cities of **Chichicastenango, Quetzaltenango,** and **Huehuetenango** serve as central market and commercial centers for the smaller surrounding communities. The Western Highlands are home to Guatemala's greatest artisans, and are the best place in the country to purchase a wide array of arts, crafts, carvings, and textile products. Perhaps the most famous place to buy these goods is the **twice-weekly market** held in Chichicastenango. Those looking for a taste of the real rural Maya Altiplano should visit the village of **Nebaj** and the surrounding area, known as the **Ixil Triangle.**

The Petén The Petén, or El Petén, is Guatemala's largest and least populated province. It occupies the entire northeastern section of the country, and borders Mexico to the north and Belize to the east. It's an area of lush primary tropical rainforest, within which lies an immense natural wealth of flora and fauna, as well as many of Mesoamerica's most amazing archaeological treasures. In 1990, the government of Guatemala officially established the **Maya Biosphere Reserve,** a tract of 1 million hectares (2.5 million acres) that includes most of the Petén province. Moreover, the Maya Biosphere Reserve adjoins the neighboring **Calakmul Biosphere Reserve** in Mexico and the **Río Bravo Conservation Area** in Belize, comprising a joint protected area of more than 2 million hectares (5 million acres).

The only major population centers of note in El Petén are the sister cities of Santa Elena and Flores. In addition to the world-renowned ruins of **Tikal,** visitors to the Petén can visit the archaeological sites of **Yaxhá, El Ceibal, El Mirador,** and **Uaxactún,** to name just a few.

Central Guatemala   The central section of Guatemala comprises the general area east of Guatemala City, before the Atlantic Lowlands. This is the country's most up-and-coming tourist destination, and includes the **Alta Verapaz** and **Baja Verapaz** regions, as well as **El Oriente,** or the "East." Just over the border in Honduras lie the fabulous Maya ruins of **Copán,** which are often included as a stop on a more complex itinerary through Guatemala. **Las Verapaces** (the plural for the combined Alta Verapaz and Baja Verapaz) is a rich highland region with numerous opportunities to go whitewater rafting or cave exploring. It's also home to several of Guatemala's most stunning natural areas, including the pools and waterfalls of **Semuc Champey** and the turquoise splendor of **Lake Lachuá.**

To the south and east of Las Verapaces lies El Oriente. Most visitors come here to visit the town of **Esquipulas.** Housed in the impressive Basílica of Esquipulas is the famous statue, the *Black Christ.* Believed to have magical, curative, and wish-giving powers, the church and its Christ attract more than one million pilgrims a year.

Atlantic Lowlands   The common name for this region is a gross misnomer—Guatemala actually borders the Caribbean Sea. However, most Guatemalan maps, books, and tourist information sources refer to this region as the Atlantic coast or Atlantic lowlands, and the highway is officially known as La Carretera al Atlántico (the Atlantic Hwy.). That quibble aside, this is a beautiful and often neglected part of the country. The region really begins around **Lago Izabal,** the largest freshwater lake in the country. From Lago Izabal, the **Río Dulce (Sweet**

River) runs gently down to the sea. Along the way it passes through rich primary forests, several nature reserves, and beautiful steep-walled canyons.

Another primary attraction on the Caribbean coast is the small Garífuna village of **Livingston.** The Garífuna are a unique race born of the intermarriage between escaped slaves and Carib Indians. Livingston, which is known as La Buga in the local Garífuna language, is only accessible by boat. The rainforests around Livingston are great for bird-watching and wildlife-viewing.

Located just off the Atlantic Highway are the Maya ruins of **Quiriguá,** which contain some wonderful examples of carved monumental stelae and massive carved stone rocks.

Pacific Slope   Below the mountain chains that run the length of Guatemala, from Mexico down to El Salvador, the land gently slopes off and flattens out before meeting the Pacific Ocean. This is a hot and steamy agricultural region with large sugar-cane, pineapple, and banana plantations. Spread throughout this agricultural land are several lesser-known Maya and pre-Maya ruins. Of these, **Takalik Abaj** and **Finca El Baúl** are worth a visit by anyone truly interested in ancient Mesoamerican archaeology. In general, the beaches of Guatemala's Pacific coast have dark sand, rough surf, and little development. Given the length of this coastline, there are few developed beach destinations and resorts. If you expect the same kind of beach experience offered throughout the Caribbean, or even the rest of Central America and Mexico, you will be disappointed. The most popular beach town on the Pacific coast is **Monterrico,** which has a handful of small hotels and resorts. The nearby port towns of **Puerto Quetzal, Iztapa,** and **Puerto San José** have garnered well-deserved reputations as top-notch **sportfishing** centers, with excellent opportunities to land marlin, sailfish, and other deep-sea game fish just offshore.

GUATEMALA IN 1 WEEK

One week will allow you enough time to visit (and actually enjoy) four of Guatemala's prime destinations. This itinerary takes you to the best of Guatemala, and includes a colonial city, a breathtaking natural wonder, an extensive traditional market, and spectacular ancient Maya ruins. Not bad for 1 week.

Day 1 Antigua

Once you arrive in Guatemala, head straight to Antigua, check into your hotel, and hit the streets. Get familiar with the city by starting out at **Plaza Mayor ★★** (p. 100) in the center of town. Have a sunset cocktail at the **Sky Bar** at **Café Sky** (p. 125), and end the night with dinner at **Hector's ★★★** (p. 124).

Day 2 The Colonial Core

Start your morning by visiting the major attractions around the city's colonial core. There are almost too many sights to see, and it may be hard to choose. Your best bet is to sign up for a walking tour with **Antigua Tours ★★** (p. 125). Many of their tours are led by longtime resident and well-known author Elizabeth Bell.

Spend the afternoon shopping at Antigua's fabulous shops, galleries, and local markets.

Don't miss the opportunity to have dinner, and perhaps listen to a little jazz, at **Mesón Panza Verde ★★★** (p. 118). Toast your second night in the city with a lively mix of locals, expats, and tourists at **Café No Sé ★★★** (p. 135).

Day 3 Lake Atitlán ★★★

Since this is a relatively tight itinerary, I recommend you stay in or around **Panajachel ★** (p. 139). Spend the day walking around town, and be sure to visit the **Museo Lacustre Atitlán ★** (p. 144). For a good hike through some beautiful foliage, head to the **Reserva Natural Atitlán ★★** (p. 144). Splurge for dinner with a meal at **Hotel Atitlán ★★★** (p. 146).

Day 4 Around the Lake

Set aside the whole day to visit some of the other cities and towns around Lake Atitlán. Sign up for an organized tour, or head down to the docks and climb aboard one of the public boat taxis. You won't have time to visit the more than half-dozen towns and villages around the lake, but you must visit **Santiago de Atitlán ★★** (p. 156). After that, and as time allows, I recommend a stop in **San Pedro La Laguna ★** (p. 150), followed by a late afternoon drink and meal at **Club Ven Acá ★★** (p. 164).

Day 5 Chichicastenango

Take a day trip to the **market in Chichicastenango ★★★** (p. 169). Chichicastenango, or Chichi, is a little more than an hour's drive from Panajachel, and all of the local tour agencies and hotel tour desks in Panajachel can arrange a

Guatemala in 1 Week

Guatemala in 1 Week map showing numbered itinerary stops:
1. Antigua
2. Lake Atitlán
3. Chichicastenango
4. Tikal

guided tour or simple transfer. Even if you come here just to shop, be sure to take some time to visit the **Iglesia de Santo Tomás ★★★** (p. 170) and the **Museo de las Máscaras Ceremoniales ★** (p. 170).

You'll get back to Panajachel with plenty of time to enjoy the evening. Head to the **Sunset Café** (p. 150) for a namesake cocktail, and then walk a little way up Calle Santander to **El Bistro ★** (p. 149) for dinner. End your evening with a drink at the **Circus Bar ★★** (p. 150).

Note: Chichicastenango's market is only open on Thursday and Sunday. Feel free to swap this day of the itinerary with any of the other 2 days around Lake Atitlán to match the market day schedule.

Days 6 & 7 Tikal ★★★

In my opinion, **Tikal ★★★** (p. 190) is the most impressive ancient Maya city in all of Mesoamerica. You'll probably have to leave Panajachel at an ungodly hour to catch your flight to Tikal, but it'll be worth it. I suggest spending 1 night in the Tikal area, and true Maya buffs will want to stay at one of the hotels right at the archaeological site, which will allow you extra hours to explore. Those with a more passing interest will be better off staying in Flores or at one of the hotels on the lake.

Early international flights from Aurora International Airport in Guatemala City are hard to catch if you're flying from Tikal the same date, so you may have to adjust your itinerary to allow an overnight in either Antigua or Guatemala City before your flight home.

GUATEMALA IN 2 WEEKS

If you've got 2 weeks, you'll be able to hit all the highlights mentioned above, as well as some other less traveled destinations, including the Caribbean coast and Lago Izabal. You'll also be able to spend some time in Guatemala City, which has wonderful museums, restaurants, and nightlife.

Days 1 & 2 Guatemala City

For this itinerary, I recommend booking a hotel in Zona 10, also known as **Zona Viva.** Once you've set your bags down, spend the afternoon at the side-by-side museums **Museo Ixchel del Traje Indígena ★★** (p. 102) and **Museo Popol Vuh ★** (p. 102). The first deals almost entirely with the history, manufacturing, and artistry of traditional Guatemalan Maya textiles, while the latter provides a concise yet broad overview of Maya history.

Make dinner reservations at **Kacao ★★** (p. 95), and spend the rest of the evening walking around Zona Viva, one of the city's few safe neighborhoods, ducking into any bar or nightclub that strikes your fancy.

Begin Day 2 in Guatemala City's colonial center, or Zona 1. Start at **Plaza Mayor ★** (p. 100), referred to by some locals as "the center of all Guatemala," and make your way to the **Catedral Metropolitana ★★** (p. 99) and the **Palacio Nacional ★** (p. 100). Take a break on a bench in one of the open-air plazas, and do some people-watching.

For dinner, reserve a table at **Tamarindos ★★★** (p. 95), my favorite restaurant in the city. After dinner, you'll want to explore the cafes, pubs, bars, and discos in **Cuatro Grados Norte** (p. 94), a hip section of Zona 4.

Days 3, 4 & 5

For these days, follow the itinerary for the same 3 days in "Guatemala in 1 Week," above, beginning at Lake Atitlán and visiting Chichicastenango on market day.

Days 6 & 7 Cobán & Alta Verapaz

On your way to Cobán and the Alta Verapaz, be sure to stop at the **Biotopo del Quetzal ★** (p. 228). Spend a couple hours hiking there and marveling at the richness of the tropical cloud forest. If you're very lucky, you may even spot a resplendent quetzal, the national bird of Guatemala.

Spend the afternoon in the small mountain city of Cobán. Visit the **Príncipe Maya Museum ★★** (p. 220), and stop at the **Hotel La Posada ★** (p. 226) for a break, some coffee, and a view of the town's main plaza.

Wake up early the next morning, and head for **Semuc Champey ★★★** (p. 224), a stunning series of pools and waterfalls located about 2 hours out of

Guatemala in 2 Weeks

town. Stop at the small town of **Lanquin,** but bypass the caves until later in the day. After you're done with Semuc Champey, try the eerie and exciting cave tour at **Kan' Ba ★★** (p. 223). If you've still got the energy, head back towards Cobán and stop at the **caves at Lanquin** (p. 223) right around sunset, to watch the amazing spectacle of thousands of bats exiting the cave for their evening meal.

Days 8 & 9 Lago Izabal

From Cobán, head to **Lago Izabal ★★** (p. 252) and the rough-and-tumble town of Fronteras. Get a cabin over the water at the **Catamaran Island Hotel ★** (p. 255). In the afternoon, take a boat tour to **Castillo de San Felipe ★** (p. 254), and then go for dinner at the **Restaurante Río Bravo ★**, which is also built out over the water. On the following day, take a **day tour down the Río Dulce to Livingston ★★** (p. 244). The boat ride in each direction is stunning. In Livingston, you'll want to wander the few streets of this small Garífuna town. For lunch, order a plate of the local specialty, *tapado,* a seafood soup made with coconut milk, at **Bugamama ★★** (p. 251). Though time is short, I also recommend hiring a boat in Livingston for a trip to **Los Siete Altares** ★★ (p. 246), a beautiful series of jungle waterfalls.

Days 10 & 11 Tikal ★★★

Follow the outline for days 6 and 7 in "Guatemala in 1 Week," above.

Days 12, 13 & 14 Antigua ★★★

You'll finish up in **Antigua** (p. 112), Guatemala's most picturesque and enjoyable city. Follow the outline for "Antigua in 3 Days," below.

GUATEMALA FOR FAMILIES

Guatemala's not the typical family destination, but if your kids are inquisitive and adventurous, there's plenty here to keep them occupied and interested. Locals are quite friendly and accommodating to children, and you'll even find a few hotels or attractions specifically geared toward families. This 10-day itinerary is designed for families with athletic and adventurous kids.

Day 1 Antigua ★★★

Arrive and head straight to **Antigua** (p. 112). Check into your hotel, and spend the afternoon walking the rugged cobblestone streets and getting to know this colonial-era city. Teenage boys will get a kick out of the central fountain on the **Plaza Mayor** ★★ (p. 100). In the afternoon, head up to the **Cerro de la Cruz** ★ (p. 127) for a beautiful panoramic view of Antigua and the volcanoes that surround it. Parents might want to steal some time for shopping or a romantic dinner. Many hotels in Antigua have, or can arrange for, babysitters.

Day 2 Volcán Pacaya

Venture 1½ hours outside of Antigua to the active **Volcán Pacaya** ★★ (p. 136). The climb is strenuous, but in the end you'll be treated to an otherworldly scene of volcanic smoke, ash, and fresh molten lava. The descent can include some "ash skiing," which will appeal to any skateboarders or snowboarders in your group.

Day 3 Quetzaltenango

Drive north to the bustling city of **Quetzaltenango** ★ (p. 176). After settling into your hotel, use the afternoon to visit the small town of **San Andrés Xecul** (p. 181) and its church. The church is painted in a dizzying mass of bold primary colors, and the intricate facade is not to be missed. After marveling at the main church, head uphill to the town's smaller church, where you're likely to see locals praying in a vacant lot and cemetery just next to the church.

Day 4 Around Quetzaltenango

Active families will want to spend this day climbing **Volcán Santa María** ★★ (p. 180). At 3,677m (12,256 ft.), this is a long and challenging climb, but the view from the top is impressive. I especially like staring down into the crater of Santa María's very active sister volcano **Santiaguito.** Less athletic families might opt to visit the **Laguna de Chicabal** ★ (p. 181), a pretty lake formed

Guatemala for Families

1. Antigua
2. Volcán Pacaya
3. Quetzaltenango
4. Xocomil and Xetulul
5. Cobán
6. Semuc Champey
7. Lago Izabal/ Río Dulce
8. Livingston
9. Guatemala City

inside the crater of an extinct volcano. Real laid-back families can opt to soak in the sulfur hot springs at **Las Fuentes Georginas** ★ (p. 180).

Day 5 Time for a Theme Park

Take a day trip from Quetzaltenango to the side-by-side water and theme park attractions of **Xocomil** ★★ (p. 274) and **Xetulul** ★ (p. 274). Make sure your kids don't focus on comparing this to Disney World or Six Flags. Instead, have them relish in the fact that they're in Guatemala and have a chance to interact with local kids. If I had to pick, I would choose the Xocomil water park, though you can easily visit both in 1 day. Both feature plenty of modern rides and attractions, including those with an ancient Maya theme and design.

Day 6 Cobán

Guatemala's Alta Verapaz region is a beautiful area of wild forests, raging rivers, and extensive cave networks. The drive here will take up much of your day, but be sure to stop at the **Biotopo del Quetzal** ★ (p. 228) on the way. Spend a couple hours hiking and see if your kids can spot a resplendent quetzal, the national bird of Guatemala.

Day 7 Semuc Champey ★★★

Semuc Champey ★★★ (p. 224) is often described as the most beautiful spot in Guatemala, and I agree. To get here, sign up for a tour from Cobán. After you're done with Semuc Champey, try the cave tour at **Kan' Ba** ★★ (p. 223). At the end of the cave tour, be sure to ask for an inner tube, and float down the Cahabón River to Hostal Las Marias, where you can have lunch. Time your day so that you can visit the **caves at Lanquin** (p. 223) in the late afternoon, when thousands of bats exit the cave mouth to feed.

Day 8 Río Dulce

From Cobán, head to the town of Fronteras on the Río Dulce. Kids will love staying in an over-water cabin at the **Catamaran Island Hotel** ★ (p. 255). If you can drag the kids away from the pool, take an afternoon boat tour to **Castillo de San Felipe** ★ (p. 254), where they can imagine themselves pirates storming the castle.

Day 9 Livingston

In the early morning take a boat down the Río Dulce to Livingston. The boat ride is beautiful. In Livingston, check into the **Hotel Villa Caribe** ★★ (p. 249), which has a lovely setting overlooking the ocean and the best pool on Guatemala's Caribbean coast. Spend the day on a guided hike to **Los Siete Altares** ★★ (p. 246) with a local Garífuna guide. The tour should take you through town and then on a brief dugout canoe ride through some mangroves, leaving you on the beach a few miles from the waterfalls. (You can hike here.) Active kids will enjoy jumping off the top of the tallest waterfall here, but parents should use discretion in deciding if they think it's safe for their child. For dinner, reserve a table at the Hotel Villa Caribe, which features a nightly presentation of Garífuna drumming and dancing.

Day 10 Fly Home

You'll have to take a very early boat out of Livingston, but you should have plenty of time to get from Livingston to Guatemala City in time for your return flight home.

MAYA RUINS HIGHLIGHTS TOUR

Guatemala occupies the heart of the ancient Maya world, which spreads into southern Mexico, present-day Belize, and parts of Honduras and El Salvador. This 12-day itinerary will take you to most of the major Maya sites covered in this book, including Copán in Honduras. The best way to undertake this trip is to hire a private car and driver. If you really want to do this right, and time and money are of no concern, be sure to book a multi-day trip out of El Petén to **El Mirador** ★★ (p. 209), a massive, Classic Maya site still in the early stages of excavation. See "Getting There & Getting Around" in chapter 3 for further information.

Maya Highlights

Ancient Ruins

0 — 40 mi
0 — 40 km

Gulf of Mexico
Caribbean Sea
MEXICO
BELIZE
HONDURAS
EL SALVADOR
NICARAGUA
Pacific Ocean

El Mirador
Río Azul
Carmelita
Belize City
Piedras Negras
Lacandón
San Pedro
Tikal
Belize
Belmopan
Yaxhá
Flores
Melchor de Mencos
BELIZE
MEXICO
Usumacintla
Sayaxché
El Ceibal
Ixkun
Poptún
San Luis
CARIBBEAN SEA
Cancuén
Livingston
Barillas
Chisec
El Golfete
Río Dulce
Puerto Barrios
Soloma
Cobán
Cahabón
El Estor
Lago Izabal
Los Amates
Motagua
Huehuetenango
Santa Cruz Verapaz
Negro
Salamá
Quiriguá
HONDURAS
Santa Cruz del Quiché
Zacapa
Copán
Chichicastenango
Motagua
Guastatoya
Quetzaltenango
Lake Atitlán
Jalapa
Takalik Abaj
Retalhuleu
Antigua
Guatemala City
Ocós
Mazatenango
Champerico
Escuintla
Cuilapa
Jutiapa
Tulate
Semillero
Iztapa
Paz
Tecojate
Monterrico
EL SALVADOR
PACIFIC OCEAN
Sipacate
Puerto San José

Pan-American Hwy
Lacantún
Cuilco

1. Guatemala City
2. Takalik Abaj
3. Copán
4. Chiminos Island Lodge
5. Tikal
6. Yaxhá

Day 1 Guatemala City

Once you've settled in, head to the **Museo Popol Vuh ★** (p. 102), followed by the **Museo Nacional de Etnología y Arqueología ★★** (p. 103). These two downtown museums will give you a good introduction to the overall history and extant findings of Guatemala's ancient Maya. In the afternoon, visit **Parque Arqueológico Kaminaljuyú** (p. 101), the ruins of a pre-Classic city located on the outskirts of current-day Guatemala City.

Days 2 & 3 Takalik Abaj ★★

From Guatemala City, journey to another pre-Classic site, **Takalik Abaj ★★** (p. 273). A great part of the charm of visiting these ruins is the chance to stay on-site at the lovely **Takalik Maya Lodge ★** (p. 273). Takalik Abaj has some interesting features you won't find at other ruins on this route, including a T-shaped ball court and *barrigón*, or "fat-bellied," sculptures.

Days 4 & 5 Copán ★★★

From Takalik Abaj, a long drive and border crossing stand between you and the fabulous Classic-era ruins of **Copán ★★** (p. 233). Next to Tikal, Copán is my favorite Maya archaeological site. It's somewhat less extensive, and fewer plazas and pyramids have been excavated, but Copán features some of the most ornate and best preserved examples of Maya architectural and historical sculpture to be found. The **Museum of Maya Sculpture** (p. 235) is worth a visit in and of itself. You'll also want to be sure to tour the **Rosalia and Jaguar Tunnels** (p. 237).

Day 6 En Route to Chiminos Island Lodge

From Copán you'll be driving to **Chiminos Island Lodge** ★★ (p. 209). You'll have to leave your car and driver in the town of **Sayaxché,** where you'll pick up a boat to this lovely isolated lodge. On your way from Copán, take a minor detour to the small Maya ruins at **Quiriguá** (p. 259). Quiriguá features several massive carved stelae. The tallest (here and in the Maya world) is more than 10m (35 ft.) tall, and weighs more than 65 tons. Quiriguá also has several massive stones, which have been carved into the zoomorphic shapes of frogs, serpents, turtles, and mythical beasts, and covered with hieroglyphs.

Days 7 & 8 Lesser-Known Ruins

Chiminos Island Lodge makes a great base for exploring several lesser-known Maya ruins, including **El Ceibal** ★ (p. 208), **Aguateca** (p. 209), and **Petexbatún** (p. 209). All of these can be visited on organized tours available through the lodge.

Days 9 & 10 Tikal

By now you're ready to visit **Tikal** ★★★ (p. 190), which I consider the most impressive of all the Maya archaeological sites in Mesoamerica. If you're using this itinerary, you'll want to stay at the **Jungle Lodge** ★ (p. 201), which is located just outside the entrance to the archaeological site, and is as close as you can get without pitching a tent inside the ancient city. See chapter 9 for a detailed walking tour of the Tikal ruins.

Days 11 & 12 Ruins Around Tikal

You can either stay at the Jungle Lodge or move to one of the hotels in Flores or on the shores of Lake Petén Itzá. Whichever you choose, you should still stick around this region and explore the other ruins around Tikal, including **Yaxhá** ★★ (p. 208), where one season of the reality series *Survivor* was shot. Other sites worth exploring include **Nakum** (p. 208), **Uaxactún** (p. 209), and **El Zotz** ★ (p. 207).

ANTIGUA IN 3 DAYS

Diminutive Antigua is one of the finest colonial cities in all of the Americas. Its rough cobblestone streets feature a dense mix of old colonial buildings, impressive Catholic churches, and various monasteries and convents. A good portion of these lie in ruins due to the many earthquakes and natural disasters that have plagued the area and led to Antigua's forced evacuation in 1777. If you're like me, you'll fall under the spell of this enchanting city, and 3 days will seem like too little time to fully enjoy its many charms. Still, the itinerary below will give you a good dose of some of the best Antigua has to offer.

① Plaza Mayor
② La Fonda de la Calle Real
③ Reilly's
④ Café Condesa
⑤ Café Sky
⑥ Hector's
⑦ Casa de Artes
⑧ Joyería del Angel
⑨ Textura
⑩ Nim Po't
⑪ Mercado de Artesanías y
    Campañia de Jesús
⑫ Mensón Panza Verde
⑬ Café No Sé

Day 1 Getting Acquainted

After arriving at your hotel, spend the rest of the day getting your bearings by starting out at the **Plaza Mayor ★★** (p. 100), the center of the city and its principal reference point, and then strolling around Antigua's colonial core.

In the late afternoon, grab a taxi and head to the **Cerro de la Cruz ★** (p. 127), where you'll get a great panoramic view of the city as the sun sets behind the outlying volcanoes.

For dinner, sample some traditional Guatemalan cuisine at **La Fonda de la Calle Real ★** (p. 124), and then stroll around the Plaza Mayor, or head to **Reilly's ★** (p. 136) for a nightcap.

Day 2 Walking Around

Take a morning walking tour with **Antigua Tours ★★** (p. 125). These tours are highly informative and take you to most of the prime attractions in Antigua. The company has excellent guides, and many of their tours are led by longtime resident and well-known author Elizabeth Bell.

Use the afternoon to hit any of the major sites or attractions you feel you've missed or need more time to fully explore. If you find yourself around the Plaza Mayor and wanting a coffee break, duck into the **Café Condesa** (p. 124).

Have a sunset cocktail at the **Sky Bar** at **Café Sky ★** (p. 125) and dinner at **Hector's ★★** (p. 124) a bustling bistro, with excellent food and service.

Day 3 Active Pursuits

It's time to get a little active, so sign up to climb **Volcán Pacaya ★★** (p. 136). This is an exciting and energetic climb, but it's also accessible to most people in reasonably good shape. If you do the morning tour, you should be back in Antigua by 1pm.

Save the afternoon to do some shopping. Be sure to visit **Casa de Artes ★** (p. 133), **Joyería del Angel ★★** (p. 133), and **Textura ★★** (p. 135). If you're looking for bargains, try **Nim Po't ★★★** (p. 134) and the **Mercado de Artesanías y Compañía de Jesús ★** (p. 134).

For your final dinner, pull out all the stops and reserve a table (possibly accompanied by some jazz) at the **Mesón Panza Verde ★★★** (p. 118). Wind up your last night at **Café No Sé ★★★**, where you'll find a lively mix of locals, expats, and travelers (p. 135).

GUATEMALA CITY

G uatemala City is the country's capital and largest city. In fact, with a population of some three million, it's the largest city in Central America.

Guatemala City was founded as the country's third capital in 1776, following the destruction of two earlier attempts by natural disasters—earthquakes and mudslides. Christened with the unwieldy name of La Nueva Guatemala de La Asunción de la Valle de la Ermita by Spain's King Charles III, it's most commonly known by its simple abbreviation, **Guate.** Long before the Spaniards moved their capital here, this was the site of the pre-Classic Maya city of Kaminaljuyú, whose ruins you can still visit. The city is set on a broad plateau at an elevation of 1,468m (4,897 ft.) above sea level, and is surrounded by mountains and volcanoes on all sides.

Despite its well-deserved reputation as a violent and dangerous place, Guatemala City has plenty to offer travelers. The principal commercial and tourist zones are full of fine hotels and excellent restaurants, and the nightlife found in Zona Viva and Cuatro Grados Norte is the best in the country. The city also boasts theaters, art galleries, and several worthwhile museums.

5

ORIENTATION

Arriving

BY PLANE

All flights into Guatemala City land at **La Aurora International Airport** (𝄞 **502/2321-0000** or 502/2260-6257; www.dgacguate.com; airport code GUA), which is located in Zona 13 on the edge of the city center and about 25km (16 miles) from Antigua. See chapter 13 for details about airlines that service Guatemala City.

There is an **INGUAT** (Guatemalan Tourism Commission; www.visit guatemala.com) information booth inside the airport, which is open to meet all arriving flights.

There are a couple of banks inside the airport that will exchange dollars and some European currencies, and cash traveler's checks. They are usually open whenever there are arriving or departing flights. There's also an ATM near the baggage claim area.

You'll find various shuttle companies offering hotel transfers as you exit either the national or international terminal. These companies charge

Guatemalan addresses may look confusing, but they're actually easy to understand. All addresses are written beginning with the *avenida* or *calle* that the building, business, or house is on, followed by the nearest cross street and actual building number, written out as a two-number hyphen combination. This is then followed by the zone. For example, the INGUAT Office on 7a Av. 1-17, Zona 4 is located at no. 17, on Avenida 7, near the cross street of 1a Calle in Zona 4. Be very careful, first and foremost, that you're in the correct zone. 7a Av. 1-17, Zona 4; and 7a Av. 1-17, Zona 10, are two radically different addresses.

between Q30 and Q80 to any hotel in Guatemala City, and between Q50 and Q80 to Antigua. Many of the larger hotels also have regular complimentary airport shuttle buses, which are best to reserve in advance.

If you don't want to wait for the shuttle to fill or sit through various stops before arriving at your hotel, there are always taxis lined up at the airport terminal exits. A taxi downtown will cost around Q40 to Q80.

Avis, Budget, Hertz, National, Tabarini, and **Thrifty** all have car-rental desks at the airport. See "Getting Around: By Car" below, for more information.

BY BUS

Guatemala's bus system is a chaotic mess. Scores of independent companies provide service to just about every nook and cranny in the country. However, there is little rhyme or reason to their terminal locations. If you arrive in town by bus, you may end up at the large and hectic main bus terminal and market area in Zona 4, or at any number of private terminals around the city, often in Zona 1. It's always easy to find a taxi near any of the bus terminals, and I recommend taking one to your final destination in the city, which should cost Q40 to Q80.

Warning: Guatemalan buses are often the targets of crime, both violent and nonviolent. Do not arrive by bus at night if at all possible, as the bus terminals and surrounding areas are very dangerous at night. If you do, hop in a cab immediately after you arrive.

BY CAR

Unless you're already familiar with the city, arriving by car can be a confusing and challenging endeavor. Prepare for gridlock and a general disregard for anything resembling common courtesy. The road in from Antigua and the Western Highlands turns into Calzada Roosevelt, which becomes the Bulevar Liberación as it heads toward Zona 10. If you're heading to Zona 1, take the Anillo Periférico to the northeast soon after entering the urban sprawl.

The road from the Pacific Coast (CA-9) enters Guatemala City from the southwest and turns into Calzada Raul Aguilar Batreó as it heads toward downtown. On the other side, CA-9 enters the city from the northeast, bringing in traffic from the Atlantic Coast, El Oriente, and Las Verapaces.

Visitor Information

The **Guatemalan Tourism Commission** (**INGUAT**; ✆ **502/2421-2800;** www.visitguatemala.com) has its main offices at 7a Av. 1-17, Zona 4. This office is open Monday through Friday from 8am until 4pm, and can provide maps and brochures.

Guatemala City

Museo Nacional
de Historia Natural

Museo Nacional de
Etnoigía y Arqueología

7a Avenida

6a Avenida

5a Avenida

Diagonal 3

Museo de
los Niños

Museo Nacional
de Arte Moderno

Parque
La Aurora

Mercado de
Artesanías

1a Calle

Zoo

Boulevard Aeropuerto

Diagonal 12 (Boulevard Liberación)

Avenida la Castellana

La Aurora
International
Airport

1a Avenida

ZONE 9

2a Avenida

Parque
Centro
América

ZONE 13

14a Calle

13a Calle

12a Calle

11a Calle

10a Calle

8a Calle

3a Avenida

4a Avenida

6a Calle

5a Calle

6a Avenida

5a Avenida

18a Calle

7a Avenida

6a Avenida

6a Avenida

Plazuela
España

Synagogue &
Einstein Institute

6a Avenida A

Obelisk

Avenida la Reforma

7a Avenida

Los Próceres
Shopping
Mall

1a Avenida

11a Calle

10a Calle

9a Calle

ZONE 10

16a Calle

15a Calle

14a Calle

13a Calle

12a Calle

11a Calle

2a Avenida

3a Avenida

4a Avenida

U. S. Embassy

10a Calle

9a Calle

8a Calle

Avenida la Reforma

6a Calle

2a Avenida

3a Calle A

6e Avenida

5a Avenida

4a Calle

6a Avenida

7a Avenida

13a Calle

Diagonal 6

ZONE 15

4a Calle

3a Calle A

8a Avenida

Universidad
Francisco
Marroquín

Museo Ixchel del
Traje Indígena

Museo Popol Vuh

0   200 m
0   200 yds

More useful for tourists is the booth that they maintain at the airport (© **502/2260-6320**), which offers a similar selection of information. They can also make a call for you if you need a hotel or car-rental reservation. This booth is allegedly open for all incoming flights, but may be closed if your flight is very early or late, or generally too much outside of normal business hours. To get tourist assistance and information from anywhere within Guatemala, dial © **1500.**

Hotel concierges, tour desks, and local travel agencies are another good source of information. There are scores of tour agencies around Guatemala City. I recommend **Clark Tours,** 7a Av. 14-76, Zona 9, inside Clark Plaza (© **502/2412-4700;** www.clarktours.com.gt); **Maya Expeditions,** 15a Calle "A" 14-07, Zona 10 (© **502/2363-4955;** www.mayaexpeditions.com) and **Turansa,** Carretera Roosevelt, Km 15, Zona 11, Super Centro Molino (© **502/2390-5757;** www.turansa.com).

City Layout

Guatemala City is divided into 21 zones or *"zonas."* The *zonas* are numbered sequentially in a spiral pattern beginning with Zona 1, the most central and oldest zone in the city. In general, the city is laid out on a standard grid, with *avenidas* (avenues) running roughly north-south, and *calles* (streets) running east-west. Of the 21 zones, below are those that you're likely to visit, as they hold the majority of the city's hotels, restaurants, and major attractions.

The Neighborhoods in Brief

Zona 1 This is the most central and oldest section of the city, home to the Plaza Mayor, Metropolitan Cathedral, and National Theater, as well as many budget hotels, stores, and restaurants. Several buildings date back to the capital's founding in 1775, when a *mudéjar* (Moorish) architectural style was so fashionable and uniform that the only thing that distinguished one private home from another was the size. Unfortunately, other aspects of the urban environment can overshadow the neighborhood's charms. Traffic noise and exhaust fumes flood the crowded streets and avenues. Be very cautious when exploring this area and avoid going out at night, as petty theft and even gun violence are common.

Zona 4 Just south of Zona 1, this area was once known as the Cantón de Exposición, as its center was the Guatemala Pavilion from the 1890 Paris World's Fair. A touch of Paris still remains: the Torre del Reformador, a smaller version of the Eiffel Tower built in 1935 to commemorate the progressive administration of President Justo Rufino Barrios (1873–85). Travelers will want to be aware of the central INGUAT office here, housed in the Civic Center along with the Bank of Guatemala, the Supreme Court of Justice, and other government buildings. Nearby, the compact Cuatro Grados Norte is a pedestrian-friendly and safe section of bars, restaurants, shops, and discos. The sprawling, chaotic second-class bus terminal is in this zone as well.

Zonas 9 & 10 These ritzy zones straddle the Avenida La Reforma in the southern part of the city center, with Zona 9 to the west and Zona 10 to the east. The streets are lined with trees and gardens, embassies and eateries, luxury hotels and shops. Zona 10 is also known as the "Zona Viva" because of its abundance of hotels, restaurants, and bars. The streets in Zona 10 are relatively safe, and the area has a hopping nightlife. More than just a playground for the well-heeled, Zona 10 is also home to the Museo Ixchel del Traje Indígena, Botanical Garden, and Popol Vuh Museum, with its notable collection of pre-Columbian pottery.

Zona 13 The airport, several museums, and the Aurora Zoo are all in Zona 13, southwest of Zona 9. It's a pleasant place to spend an afternoon or a night if you have an early morning flight from La Aurora airport. The hotels in Zona 9 and Zona 10 are also quite close to the airport.

GETTING AROUND

Note: Guatemala City has an extensive network of metropolitan buses, but a vast number of assaults take place on them at all times of day and night. I highly recommend you take a taxi instead.

By Taxi

Taxis are plentiful and relatively inexpensive, and while they're supposed to use meters, many don't. It's always best to ask before taking off whether it will be a metered ride, and if not, to negotiate the price in advance. A ride anywhere in the city should cost between Q20 and Q80.

If you need to call a cab, ask your hotel or try **Taxi Amarillo Express** (© 502/2470-1515; www.amarilloexpress.com), **Taxi Blanco y Azul** (© 502/2440-8789), **Taxis 2000** (© 502/2433-9984), or **Taxis Las Amaericas** (© 502/2362-0583). Taxi Amarillo Express cabs all use meters.

On Foot

Guatemala City is not very conducive to exploring by foot. The city is spread out, and many of the major attractions are far from one another. Plus street crime is a problem. It's relatively safe to walk around zonas 1, 4, 9, 10, and 13 by day. However, with few exceptions, you should never walk around Guatemala City at night. Those few exceptions include the most developed parts of Zona 10, or the Zona Viva; and the hip, strip of bars and restaurants in Zona 4, known as Cuatro Grados Norte.

By Car

Driving in Guatemala City falls somewhere between a headache and a nightmare. There is little need to navigate Guatemala City in a car. I highly recommend you take taxis and leave the driving to others. If you do find yourself driving around Guatemala City, go slow, as pedestrians and vehicles can appear out of nowhere.

If you want to rent a car, the following all have airport locations, and some also have offices in downtown or at major hotels: **Alamo** (© 502/2362-2701; www.alamo.com); **Avis** (© 502/2324-9000; www.avis.com); **Budget** (© 502/2232-7744; www.budgetguatemala.com.gt); **Dollar** (© 502/2385-1301; www.dollar.com); **Hertz** (© 502/2470-3737; www.hertz.com); **National,** 14a Calle 7-57, Zona 9 (© 502/2362-3000; www.nationalcar.com); and **Thrifty** (© 502/2379-8747;

 He's Gone to Zona 20

Though there is no actual Zona 20, you may hear locals refer to it. In a bit of local gallows humor, when someone dies in Guatemala City, they say, *"Se fue para la zona 20,"* which translates to "He's gone to Zona 20."

> ### 💬 Killer Tomatoes
>
> Guatemala's urban buses are the popular stamping ground for armed robbers and muggers. They are also largely driven by aggressive and carefree drivers whose homicidal tendencies might be better served in the armed forces. These factors, along with the fact that they are painted a deep red, have led local residents to dub them *"los tomates asesinos,"* or "the killer tomatoes."

www.thrifty.com). **Tabarini** (ⓒ **502/2331-2643;** www.tabarini.com) is a good local company with offices at 2a Calle A 7-30, Zona 10, as well as at the airport.

Rates run between Q320 and Q960 per day, including unlimited mileage and full insurance.

[FastFACTS] GUATEMALA CITY

Airport See "Arriving," above.

American Express
Clark Tours (ⓒ **502/2412-4700;** www.clarktours.com.gt) is the representative of American Express Travel Services in Guatemala. Their main offices are in Guatemala City at Clark Plaza, 7a Av. 14-76, Zona 9. They also have a desk at the downtown Westin hotel. To report lost or stolen Amex traveler's checks within Guatemala, dial ⓒ **800/327-1267,** or call ⓒ **336/393-1111** collect in the U.S.

Babysitters Hotels offering regular, dependable babysitting service are few and far between. If you need a babysitter, make sure that your hotel offers this service, and be sure to ask whether the babysitters are bilingual. In many cases, they are not. This is usually not a problem with infants and toddlers, but it can cause problems with older children. Babysitters

charge between Q15 and Q40 per hour.

Banks You'll have no trouble finding a bank in Guatemala City. Numerous bank branches can be found all over zonas 1, 4, 9, 10, and 13. Banks are usually open Monday through Friday from 9am to 4pm, although many have begun to offer extended hours. The most widespread banks include **Banrural** (www.banrural.com), **Banco G&T** (www.gytcontinental.com.gt), **Banco Uno** (www.bancouno.com.gt), **Banco de Guatemala** (www.banguat.gob.gt), and **Banco Industrial** (www.bi.com.gt).

Bookstores Bibliophiles might be disappointed in Guatemala City. You'd be better off purchasing any specific reading material, for pleasure or research, before your trip. The best bookstore in the city for tourists is **Sophos** ★★, 4a Av. 12-59, Plaza Fontabella, Zona 10 (ⓒ **502/2419-7070;** www.sophosenlinea.com),

which also has a lovely coffee shop attached. **Gémenis Bookstore,** 3a Av. 17-05, Zona 14 (ⓒ **502/2366-1031**); and **Vista Hermosa Book Shop,** 2a Calle 18-50, Zona 15 (ⓒ **502/2369-1003**), also carry books in English.

Camera Repair Some outlets of **Quick Photo** (ⓒ **502/2368-0488;** www.quickphotoonline.com) and **Fuji Film** (ⓒ **502/2420-3900;** www.fujifilm.com.gt) have technicians on hand, and carry a limited range of replacement and repair parts. Be sure to call first, to see if they can help your particular situation.

Car Rentals See "Getting Around: By Car" above.

Cellphones There are several competing cellphone companies in Guatemala that have numerous outlets across the city, including at the airport. All sell prepaid GSM chips that can be used in any unlocked tri-band GSM cellphone. Moreover, all sell activated new phones for as little as Q100. Storefronts at the airport, and at many hotels around the city, will also rent out cellphones, however, given how inexpensively you can buy a new activated phone, I don't think this is a worthwhile option anymore.

Calling cards, for both cellphones and land lines, are widely available at general stores and pharmacies all over the country.

Your best bet for making international calls is to head to any Internet cafe with an international calling option. These cafes have connections to Skype, Net2Phone, or some other VoIP service. International calls made this way can range anywhere from 5¢ to $1 per minute. If you have your own Skype or similar account, you just need to find an Internet cafe that provides a computer with a headset.

Currency Exchange All banks will exchange money for a small service charge. Many of the hotels, restaurants, and shops in Guatemala City will also accept U.S. dollars and euros, though many give less than advantageous exchange rates.

Dentists Call your embassy, which will have a list of recommended dentists, or ask your hotel. Alternately, you can try **Centro Dental de Especialistas,** 20a Calle 11-17, Zona 10 (📞 **502/2385-7777;** www.centrodental.com.gt).

Doctors Contact your embassy for information on doctors in Guatemala City, or see "Hospitals," below.

Drugstores A drugstore or pharmacy is called a *farmacia* in Spanish. In Guatemala, they are also sometimes called *droguería*. There are scores of pharmacies around Guatemala City, and most major hotels have one attached or nearby. Ask your hotel, or call **Farmacias Meykos** (📞 **502/2422-2422**) or **Farmacias Fayco** (📞 **502/2368-0898;** www.farmaciasfayco.com), both have numerous outlets around the city and offer 24-hour delivery service for a small fee.

Embassies & Consulates See "Fast Facts" in chapter 13.

Emergencies In case of any emergency, dial 📞 **1500** from anywhere in Guatemala. This will connect you to **Asistur,** which will have a bilingual operator, who in turn can put you in contact with the police, fire department, or ambulance service, as necessary. Alternately, you can dial 📞 **110** for the National Police; and 📞 **125** for the Red Cross (Cruz Roja, in Spanish). Moreover, 📞 **911** works as an emergency number from most phones in Guatemala.

Express Mail Services Most hotels can arrange for express mail pickup, or you can contact **DHL,** 12a Calle 5-12, Zona 10 (📞 **502/2379-1111;** www.dhl.com), and **Fed Ex,** 14a Calle 3-51, Zona 10 (📞 **1801/00FEDEX;** www.fedex.com).

Eyeglasses An eyeglass store is called *óptica* in Spanish. There are many around Guatemala City, but your best bet is to ask your hotel. If you need to see an optometrist, contact **Visión Integral,** 2a Av. 9-03, Zona 9 (📞 **502/2334-2301;** www.visionintegral.com.gt).

Hospitals Hospital Centro Médico, 6a Av. 3-47, Zona 10 (📞 **502/2279-4949;** www.centromedico.com.gt), is an excellent private hospital, with English-speaking doctors on staff. Alternately, the **Hospital General San Juan de Dios,** 1a Avenida and 10a Calle, Zona 1 (📞 **502/2220-8396**), is the biggest and best equipped public hospital in the city.

Internet Access A good number of hotels and restaurants around town provide free wireless access. Internet cafes are very common in Guatemala City. Rates run between Q4 and Q12 per hour.

Laundry & Dry Cleaning Most folks rely on their hotel's laundry and dry-cleaning services, although these can be expensive. You can also try **Lavanderia El Siglo** (📞 **502/2366-4789;** www.lavanderiaelsiglo.com) or **Lavandería Interdry,** 18a Calle 11-12, Zona 1 (📞 **502/2251-4063**) or 5a Calle 3-28, Zona 9 (📞 **502/2339-2111**).

Maps INGUAT (📞 **502/2421-2800;** www.visitguatemala.com) will provide you with a pretty acceptable map that has the entire country on one side and Guatemala City and Antigua on the other. The map is free, and you can pick one up at their booth at the airport or by visiting their downtown office at 7a Av. 1-17, Zona 4. You can also buy good detailed maps in most gift shops and at **Sophos ★★**, 4a Av. 12-59, Plaza Fontabella, Zona 10 (℃ **502/ 2419-7070;** www.sophos enlinea.com).

Newspapers & Magazines *La Prensa Libre* is the country's most highly regarded daily newspaper, with an outstanding investigative reporting staff. The lower-brow *Nuestro Diario* has the highest circulation. There are several other daily papers, including *Siglo XXI.* There are currently no English-language newspapers. The free, monthly *Revue Magazine* (www.revuemag. com) is the most valuable locally produced information source, with museum, art gallery, and theater listings. It's widely available at hotels and other tourist haunts around the country.

Police In case of an emergency, dial ℃ **1500** from anywhere in Guatemala. This will connect you to a bilingual operator at Asistur who can put you in contact with the police, fire department, or ambulance service. Dial ℃ **110** or **120** for the **National Police,** and ℃ **125** for the **Red Cross** (**Cruz Roja,** in Spanish). As in the U.S., ℃ **911** works as an emergency number from most phones in Guatemala.

Post Office A post office is called *correo* in Spanish.

The main **post office,** 7a Av. 12-11, Zona 1 (℃ **502/ 2232-6101**), is a beautiful building. It costs around Q7 to send a letter to the U.S. or Europe. Postcards to the same destinations cost Q5.

Restrooms There are few public restrooms available around town. Most hotels and restaurants will let travelers use their facilities, although they are happiest if you are a paying client.

Safety Safety is a serious issue in Guatemala. In Guatemala City, I highly recommend that you stick to the most affluent and touristy sections of town highlighted in this book. Basic common sense and street smarts are to be employed. Don't wear flashy jewelry or wave wads of cash around. Be aware of your surroundings, and avoid any people and places that make you feel uncomfortable. Basically, it is unwise to walk almost anywhere except the most secure and heavily trafficked tourist zones after dark. Rental cars generally stick out and are easily spotted by thieves, who know that such cars are likely to be full of expensive camera equipment, money, and other valuables. Don't ever leave anything of value in an unattended parked car.

Taxes There is a $30 tax that must be paid upon departure. This is often included in your airline ticket price. Be sure to check in advance. If not, you will have to pay the fee in cash at the

airport. There is an additional airport security fee of Q20.

A 12% IVA (value added) tax is tacked on to the purchase of all goods and services. An additional 10% tax, on top of the 12% IVA, is added to all hotel rooms and lodgings.

Taxis See "Getting Around," above.

Time Zone Guatemala is 6 hours behind Greenwich Mean Time, which is equivalent to Central Standard Time in the United States. Daylight saving time is observed by setting clocks ahead 1 hour from the last Sunday in March to the last Sunday in October.

Useful Telephone Numbers For directory assistance, call ℃ **2333-1524;** for an international operator and directory assistance, call ℃ **147-120;** while for local operator assistance, dial ℃ **147-110.** To make a direct international call, dial ℃ 00 + the country code + the area code + the phone number. To get the current time, dial ℃ **333-1526.**

Water Drink only bottled water within Guatemala City and be especially careful to do so when traveling outside the capital, as waterborne diseases are very common in this country.

Weather The weather in Guatemala City is mild year-round, with an average daytime temperature of around 70°F (21°C), and a rainy season May through October. For more details, see "When to Go" in chapter 3.

adoptions IN GUATEMALA

For years adoptions of Guatemalan-born children, particularly by Americans, was a major phenomenon. Many of the high-end hotels in Guatemala City have whole floors dedicated to serving adoptive parents as they go through the process.

Guatemala was an attractive choice for international adoption for a number of reasons. There had traditionally been few restrictions on who can adopt in Guatemala, the wait time was relatively short, prospective parents were required to spend relatively little time in-country, and Guatemala is a lot closer to the U.S. than countries in Asia or Africa, where adoptions by foreign nationals are also common.

However, on January 1, 2008, Guatemala signed the Hague Adoption Convention, hoping to curtail corruption in the process and reduce the number of abducted or "baby-farmed" infants entering the process. Tragically, child trafficking in Guatemala is a reality. Both abductions and baby-farming, where poor peasant women and girls are encouraged to have children for a small fee, have been uncovered.

At press time, all new adoptions of Guatemalan-born children were on hold and the country's newly established National Council for Adoptions (CAN) was working its way through a backlog of previously initiated cases, while trying to establish criteria and processes that would meet the requirements of the Hague Adoption Convention. In 2008, there were 4,727 adoptions granted to foreign parents. That number dropped to just 756 in 2009. Most of the adopted children are infants under 1 year of age. To date, the U.S. Citizenship and Immigration Services is not processing I-800A petitions for prospective parents, as the State Department has not yet determined that Guatemala has gotten its act together enough.

Prospective parents can find a wealth of information online. The U.S. State Department's page on the subject (www.adoption.state.gov/country/guatemala.html) is a good place to start. You could also contact the **Guatemalan Embassy** in your home country.

WHERE TO STAY

There are tons of good hotel options in Guatemala City, with something to fit any budget. Most visitors choose to stay in the ritzier and safer side-by-side neighborhoods of zonas 9 and 10, which I highly recommend. Budget travelers and those seeking a heavy dose of the city's colonial center gravitate to Zona 1, but keep in mind that you need to be very careful about walking around this neighborhood at night.

Zonas 9 & 10

These side-by-side zones contain the greatest concentration of hotels, restaurants, bars, and shops in the city, and heavy police presence makes them relatively safe for strolling and exploring on foot. Most of the hotels here are high-end business-class affairs, but there are actually options to fit most budgets. This area, particularly Zona 10, is often referred to as Zona Viva, or the "Alive Zone," because of all the dining and nightlife options.

Zonas 9, 10, 13 & Environs

ACCOMMODATIONS ■
Barceló Guatemala City **7**
Best Western Stofella **22**
Biltmore Express **9**
Hotel Ciudad Vieja **30**
Holiday Inn **17**
Hotel Princess **8**
Hotel San Carlos **28**
La Casa Grande **29**
Otelito Casa Santa Clara **25**
Radisson Hotel & Suites **23**
Real InterContinental **12**
Westin Camino Real **13**
Xamanek Student Inn **19**

DINING ◆
Carpaccio **14**
Casa Chapina **15**
Clio's **21**
Frida's **11**
Hacienda Real **10**
Kacao **16**
Panadería San Martin **18**
Pecorino **26**
Sushi-Itto **21**
Tamarindos **27**
Tapas y Cañas **20**
Tre Fratelli **21**
Zumo **24**

ATTRACTIONS ●
Aurora Zoo **6**
Jardín Botánico **33**
Mercado de Artesanías **5**
Museo de Arte Moderno **4**
Museo de los Niños **2**
Museo Ixchel del
  Traje Indígena **31**
Museo Nacional de Etnología
  y Arqueología **3**
Museo Nacional de
  Historia Natural **1**
Museo Popol Vuh **32**

ZONE 4

1a Calle

Torre del Reformador

2a Calle

3a Calle

4a Calle

5a Calle

6a Calle

Parque Centro América

6a Avenida

7a Avenida

8a Calle

1a Avenida

2a Avenida

3a Avenida

4a Avenida

5a Avenida

6a Avenida-A

10a Calle

ZONE 9

11a Calle

12a Calle

Plazuela España

13a Calle

Synagogue & Einstein Institute **8**

4a Avenida

2a Calle

5a Avenida

3a Calle

6a Avenida

4a Calle

5a Calle

Diagonal 12 (Boulevard Liberación)

14a Calle

5a Avenida-A

6a Avenida

6a Avenida-A

7a Avenida

7

6

Parque La Aurora

7a Avenida

Museo Nacional de
Etnolgía y Arqueología

3

4

Museo Nacional
de Arte Moderno

5

Mercado de
Artesanías

ZONE 13

*La Aurora
International
Airport*

18a Calle

Museo Nacional de
Historia Natural

1

2

Museo de
los Niños

Jardín Botánico
1a Calle

ZONE 5

Campo de Marte

10a Avenida

2a Calle

Boulevard Vista Hermosa

3a Calle

2a Calle A

3a Calle

Avenida la Reforma

3a Calle A

3a Calle A

6a Avenida

4a Calle

2a Avenida

32

Museo Popol Vuh

31

6a Calle

Museo Ixchel del Traje Indígena

7a Calle

4a Calle

Universidad Francisco Marroquín

U.S. Embassy

4a Avenida

5a Avenida

8a Calle

30

9a Calle

ZONE 15

29
28

3a Avenida

9a Calle

9a Calle

10a Calle

10a Calle

7a Calle

1a Avenida

2a Avenida

4a Avenida

11a Calle

27

26

Diagonal 6

11a Calle

25

12a Calle

21

24

22

ZONE 10

23

19

6a Avenida

17

18

13a Calle

13a Calle

15
16

12

20

14

13

14a Calle

11

7a Avenida

Avenida la Reforma

9

10

15a Calle

5a Avenida

8a Avenida

9a Avenida

10a Avenida

11a Avenida

12a Avenida

16a Calle

Diagonal 6

Los Próceres Shopping Mall

Obelisk

18a Calle

0   200 m
0   200 yds

VERY EXPENSIVE

In addition to the places listed below, the **Barceló Guatemala City ★★**, 7a Av. 15-45, Zona 9 (**✆ 800/227-2356** in the U.S. and Canada, or 502/2378-4000; www. barceloguatemalacity.com), is another excellent high-end hotel, though I think the similar-class hotels listed below are better located.

Real InterContinental ★★★ This is my favorite of the high-end, business-class hotels in the city. The rooms, facilities, and service are a notch above the competition. Rooms are spacious and in great condition, and all are carpeted and feature firm beds and flatscreen televisions. Business rooms come with a fully equipped workstation that features a combination fax machine, scanner, and copier, as well as an ergonomic chair and an in-room coffeemaker. Rooms on the InterClub floors have separate check-in desks, butler services, and a private lounge with regularly replenished snacks, free continental breakfast, and daily complimentary cocktail hour. There's an attractive pool area with a large Jacuzzi nearby. The hotel is situated on a busy corner in the Zona Viva, with scores of good restaurants, bars, and shops just steps away.

14a Calle 2-51, Zona 10. **✆ 502/2413-4444.** Fax 502/2413-4445. www.interconti.com. 239 units. $110–$180 double; $230–$300 junior suite. AE, DISC, MC, V. Free valet parking. **Amenities:** 2 restaurants; 2 bars; babysitting; well-equipped gym and spa; Jacuzzi; pool; room service; smoke-free rooms. *In room:* A/C, TV, hair dryer, minibar, Wi-Fi.

Westin Camino Real ★★ ☺ This long-standing and popular Zona 10 hotel has aged well. The Grand Lobby, while not huge, features stately marble floors and a beautiful domed ceiling with intricate stained-glass work. The rooms are all up to Westin's corporate standards, with their trademark "Heavenly Sleep" beds and fancy shower heads. Standard rooms come with either one king-size or two queen-size beds. Because the hotel is built in an arc, rooms on the east side are slightly larger. The junior suites have separate sitting rooms and 29-inch flatscreen televisions. The sixth floor is dedicated to families, particularly those with small children or those visiting Guatemala to finalize adoptions. The executive floors have a few more business perks, including in-room fax machines and a small TV in the bathroom. The large pool is the best hotel pool in the city. The hotel has a free airport shuttle, free Wi-Fi in the lobby, and high-speed Internet connections, by cable or wireless, are available in every room for a fee.

14a Calle and Av. La Reforma, Zona 10. **✆ 800/228-3000** in the U.S. and Canada, or 502/2333-3000 in Guatemala. Fax 502/2337-4313. www.westin.com. 274 units. $149–$290 double; $209-$350 suite. AE, DC, MC, V. Free parking. **Amenities:** 2 restaurants; 2 bars; lounge; 24-hr. casino; babysitting; concierge; 3 pools; room service; smoke-free rooms; well-equipped spa; indoor squash court; lit outdoor tennis court. *In room:* A/C, TV, hair dryer, minibar, Wi-Fi.

EXPENSIVE

In addition to the hotels listed below, the **Holiday Inn,** 1a Av. 13-22, Zona 10 (**✆ 502/2421-0000;** www.holidayinn.com), is a good option.

Biltmore Express This business-class hotel has acceptable rooms and professional service. The rooms are all carpeted and come with either one king-size or two double beds. I think it's worth the splurge for one of their "Parlor Suites," which are much larger and come with a kitchenette and larger bathroom. The best features here are the location and the fact that this hotel is connected to the Westin Camino Real. For $10 per day, guests at the Biltmore Express can use the pool, gym, tennis court, squash court, and spa at the Westin. This hotel also has a free airport shuttle. There are Ethernet connections in all the rooms offering broadband access for another $10 per day.

15a Calle 0-31, Zona 10. © **502/2410-5000.** Fax 502/2410-5005. www.biltmoreexpress.com.gt. 116 units. $120 double; $150 parlor suite. Rates include continental breakfast. AE, DC, MC, V. Free parking. **Amenities:** Restaurant; bar; room service; smoke-free rooms. *In room:* A/C, TV, hair dryer.

Otelito Casa Santa Clara ★

This small, boutique hotel is the most stylish option in the zone. Each room is distinct, but all feature minimalist decor and subdued tones. Most have one or two queen-size beds, and either wood or tile floors. The bathrooms all feature marble floors and showers with thick seamless glass walls and doors. I like the "Pistachio" and "Mandarina" rooms, which are second-floor units toward the back of the building. The suite here comes with a Jacuzzi tub and separate sitting room. The hotel's elegant restaurant sits in a high-roofed atrium area just off the reception, and serves an excellent breakfast and changing seasonal dinner menu. Neighboring clubs and discos are loud on weekends and their thumping beats can be a problem in some rooms here.

12a Calle 4-51, Zona 10. ©/fax **502/2339-1811.** www.otelito.com. 12 units. $140 double; $200 suite. AE, DC, MC, V. Free valet parking. **Amenities:** Restaurant; bar; room service; free Wi-Fi. *In room:* A/C, TV, hair dryer, minibar.

Radisson Hotel & Suites ★★

This is another excellent and well-located business-class hotel in Zona 10. The rooms are all large and well appointed, with contemporary decor and all the amenities you might expect. All rooms should really be classified as suites, or at the very least junior suites. Each has a large sitting area, dry bar, and kitchenette. The rooms also come with DVD players, and the hotel has an extensive library of titles available for rental. Free Wi-Fi is available in public areas and in most of the rooms, and Ethernet connections are available in all rooms for a small fee. The service here is excellent. Separate floors are reserved for single women travelers, families, or those involved in the adoption process. There's a small sushi bar and restaurant just off the lobby, in addition to their more typical restaurant serving international fare.

1a Av. 12-46, Zona 10. © **800/333-3333** in the U.S. and Canada, or 502/2421-5151 in Guatemala. Fax 502/2332-9772. www.radisson.com. 115 units. $90–$150 double. AE, DC, MC, V. Free parking. **Amenities:** 2 restaurants; bar; babysitting; small gym; Jacuzzi; room service; sauna; smoke-free rooms; free Wi-Fi. *In room:* A/C, TV/DVD, hair dryer, kitchenette, minibar.

MODERATE

Best Western Stofella ★ 🗡

This centrally located hotel is everything you might expect from a popular chain. The rooms are well appointed and well equipped, it's located on a quiet street, just a block away from the bustling Zona Viva, and the price is right. In fact, if you book on the Internet, you can often get an excellent deal. Service is attentive and accommodating, and a host of restaurants, bars, and shops are within easy walking distance.

2a Av. 12-28, Zona 10. © **800/780-7234** in the U.S. and Canada, or 502/2410-8600 in Guatemala. Fax 502/2331-0823. www.stofella.com. 70 units $55–$68 double. AE, DISC, MC, V. Free parking. **Amenities:** Restaurant; bar; tiny gym; Jacuzzi; room service. *In room:* A/C, TV, hair dryer; Wi-Fi.

Hotel Ciudad Vieja

Originally a budget hotel, this place upgraded their rooms and grounds, and upped their prices a bit. It's still a good deal, and located in the heart of the Zona Viva. The rooms are of good size, with comfortable beds and tasteful decorations. Perhaps the best thing this hotel has going for it is its large garden area. The more informal restaurant here is located in a lovely courtyard, in a large glass atrium. The intimate bar, with its low vaulted ceiling, is a popular meeting place for guests.

8a Calle 3-67, Zona 10. ✆ **502/2331-9104.** www.hotelciudadvieja.com. 26 units. $69 double. Rates include full breakfast and complimentary airport shuttle. AE, DC, MC, V. Free parking. **Amenities:** 2 restaurants; bar; smoke-free rooms. *In room:* TV, free Wi-Fi.

Hotel Princess ★ 🐾   This cozy hotel is well located and offers many of the perks and amenities of the fancier business-class hotels in the area for much less. The lobby features flowering vines and open interior space that soars up five stories to a glass atrium ceiling. The rooms are outfitted in what they call "English-style decor," with a dark stained-wood headboard above the bed and an elegant wood armoire. Rooms come with either one king-size bed or two doubles. Most have large, 27-inch televisions. Twelve of the rooms have balconies, and I recommend you request one of these if possible. The corner units are the largest rooms, with bigger bedrooms, though I'd opt for the balcony over the extra space if given the choice. This hotel strives to reduce dependence on non-renewable energy sources, and use environmentally-friendly cleaning materials, and is working towards the Rainforest Alliance's "Sustainable Trip" certification.

13a Calle 7-65, Zona 9. ✆ **502/2423-0909.** Fax 502/2334-4546. www.hotelesprincess.com. 103 units. $75–$90 double; $100–$120 suite. AE, DC, MC, V. Free parking. **Amenities:** Restaurant; bar; small exercise room; small pool; room service; sauna; smoke-free rooms; free Wi-Fi. *In room:* A/C, TV, hair dryer.

Hotel San Carlos 🛏   Located right on the busy Avenida La Reforma, this charming three-story hotel features a Tudor exterior that's a little out of place in this Central American country. The British influence is apparent in the rooms, which feature antique furniture or knockoffs. My favorite rooms have plenty of space and varnished wood floors. This place is very similar in feel to La Casa Grande (below), but trumps it in terms of amenities and comfort. The San Carlos has a small lap pool in a pretty garden area.

Av. La Reforma 7-89, Zona 10. ✆ **502/2247-3000.** Fax 502/2247-3050. www.hsancarlos.com. 23 units. $90 double; $125–$175 suite. Rates include full breakfast and complimentary airport transfers. AE, DC, MC, V. Free parking. **Amenities:** Restaurant; bar; lounge; pool; room service; free Wi-Fi. *In room:* TV, hair dryer.

La Casa Grande   This small boutique hotel harkens back to an earlier time. With whitewashed walls and a red-clay tile roof, this two-story building is an anomaly in an area of high-rise glass and steel buildings. Rooms feature antique tile floors and Victorian-style furnishings and decor. Even though the main building is set back from the street, the rooms closest to the street can be noisy. The hotel is very close to the United States embassy, and historically has catered to American families involved in adoption proceedings. La Casa Grande has several pleasant courtyard and interior sitting areas.

Av. La Reforma 7-57, Zona 10. ✆/fax **502/2332-0914.** www.casagrande-gua.com. 28 units. $75–$100 double. Rates include taxes. AE, DISC, MC, V. Free parking. **Amenities:** Restaurant; bar; room service. *In room:* TV, hair dryer, minibar.

INEXPENSIVE
Xamanek Student Inn 🛏   With the opening of this cozy place, backpackers and budget travelers finally have an excellent option in the heart of the Zona Viva. Rooms are spread over two floors of this centrally located converted home. There's a small

garden area, large common areas, lending library, complimentary Internet-equipped computer, and TV lounge area. All of the rooms are immaculate, and the two with private bathrooms are a real steal. The hotel has no restaurant, but does serve breakfast daily, as well as snacks and drinks throughout the day.

13 Calle 3-57, Zona 10. © **502/2360-8345.** www.mayaworld.net. 7 units, 2 with private bathroom $35 double with private bathroom; $14 per person, shared bathroom. Rates include continental breakfast and taxes. No credit cards. **Amenities:** Lounge. *In room:* No phone.

Zona 1

This is the heart of the downtown colonial core of Guatemala City, and is often referred to as the "Old Town," or "Old City." The area is convenient for visiting many of the city's colonial-era attractions, and is full of hotels. You'll definitely get more bang for your buck down here as well. However, this is a busy part of town, and tourists are often targeted for pickpocketing and petty crime. Be particularly careful after dark, when I recommend you take a taxi, even for short trips.

MODERATE

Hotel Royal Palace   This is the most atmospheric option in the Old Town. From the crystal chandeliers in the grand lobby to the well-maintained rooms, this classic hotel maintains all the charm and ambience of a bygone era. The rooms are large and stylish, some with carpeting and others with antique tile floors. My favorite rooms are those with balconies overlooking the street, where you can watch the daily parade from the comfort of your own room. (The trade-off for this great people-watching is more street noise.) The sparsely equipped gym is a bit of an embarrassment, but the cedar sauna is quite inviting.

6a Av. 12-66, Zona 1. © **502/2416-4400.** Fax 502/2416-4314. www.hotelroyalpalace.com. 76 units. $55 double; $65 junior suite. Rates include full breakfast. AE, DISC, MC, V. Free parking. **Amenities:** Restaurant; bar; concierge; gym; room service; sauna. *In room:* TV, hair dryer.

INEXPENSIVE

In addition to the places listed below, **Hotel Spring,** 8a Av. 12-65, Zona 1 (© **502/2230-2858;** www.hotelspring.com), and **Hotel Ajau** (© **502/2232-0488;** hotelajau@hotmail.com), 8a Av. 15-62, Zona 1, are two other good budget options.

Chalet Suizo   This popular budget hotel is clean and safe, but is lacking in charm and style. Rooms are spotless but very basic, with bare walls and virtually non-existent decor. Each floor shares a broad interior veranda with various sitting areas, and the hotel has a nice central courtyard garden, which makes this a great place to meet fellow travelers. The rooms with private bathrooms also come with televisions, which the more basic, shared-bath rooms lack.

7 Calle 14-34, Zona 1. © **502/2251-3786.** Fax 502/2232-0429. www.english.hotelchaletsuizo.com. 30 units, 15 with private bathroom. $21 double with shared bathroom; $31 double with private bathroom. AE, MC, V. Free parking. **Amenities:** Restaurant, room service; free Wi-Fi. *In room:* No phone.

Hotel Colonial   The exterior and interior public areas of this hotel are extremely charming. I especially like the interior central courtyard, with its fountain and wrought-iron furniture. The rooms are fairly simple and plain, and some could use updating and maintenance. Still, for the price, this is a good budget option in the heart of downtown. Most of the rooms have two or three twin beds, and either varnished wood or antique tile floors. The more expensive rooms have more space. My

Zona 1

3a Calle
3a Avenida
4a Avenida
5a Avenida
6a Avenida
6a Avenida A
7a Avenida
8a Avenida
9a Avenida
10a Avenida
10a Avenida A
11a Avenida
12e Avenida
13a Avenida

3a Calle
4a Calle
5a Calle
6a Calle
7a Calle
8a Calle
9a Calle
10a Calle
11a Calle
12a Calle
12a Calle A
13a Calle
14a Calle
15a Calle
16a Calle
17a Calle
18a Calle
19a Calle
20a Calle
23a Calle

Palacio Presidencial
Museo de la Semana Santa
Palacio Nacional
National Library
Parque Centenario
Plaza Major
Catedral Metropolitana
Santa Rosa
Iglesia La Merced
El Carmen
MUSAC
San Miguel de Capuchinas
Santo Domingo
Museo Nacional de la Historia
Casa MIMA
Teatro al Aire Libre
El Fuerte San José
Teatro Nacional

0   200 m
0   200 yds

Guatemala City — ZONE 6 — MAP AREA
ZONE 1
ZONE 4
ZONE 9
ZONE 10
ZONE 16
ZONE 12
ZONE 13

ACCOMMODATIONS ■
Chalet Suizo **13**
Hotel Ajau **15**
Hotel Colonial **14**
Hotel Royal Palace **9**
Hotel Spring **10**
Posada Belén **12**

DINING ◆
Arrin Cuan **1**
Restaurante & Bar Europa **7**
Restaurante Altuna **8**

ATTRACTIONS ●
Catedral Metropolitana **4**
Centro Cultural Miguel
  Ángel Asturias **16**
Iglesia La Merced **5**
Iglesia San Francisco **11**
Museo Nacional
  de la Historia **6**
Palacio Nacional **2**
Plaza Mayor **3**

favorites are the second-floor units with small balconies overlooking 7a Avenida. The restaurant serves simple and acceptable Guatemalan and international fare.

7a Av. 14-19, Zona 1. ⓒ **502/2232-6722** or 2232-2955. Fax 502/2232-8671. www.hotelcolonial.net. 42 units. $18–$30 double. Rates include taxes. MC, V. Free parking. **Amenities:** Restaurant; smoke-free rooms. *In room:* TV, no phone.

Posada Belén Museum Inn ★ 📷 If you're looking for a charming, family-run bed-and-breakfast at a very reasonable price, this should be your first choice in Zona 1. In fact, it's my top budget choice in the whole city. The converted colonial-era home that houses this hotel was built in 1873, and features a lush and beautiful interior garden. Rooms are decorated with rustic wood furniture, checkerboard tile floors, washed walls, and local arts and crafts. Hot water here is supplied by solar panels, a nice touch. The hotel is set on a short, lightly transited street, so its rooms are quieter than many of the other downtown options. This place advertises itself as a "museum," and has an extensive collection of Maya artifacts and colonial-era art and carvings. The owners and their in-house guides and drivers are very friendly, knowledgeable, and professional.

13a Calle A10-30, Zona 1. ⓒ **866/864-8283** in the U.S. and Canada, or 502/2253-6178 in Guatemala. Fax 502/2251-3478. www.posadabelen.com. 11 units. $49 double. AE, DC, DISC, MC, V. Free parking. **Amenities:** Restaurant; lounge; room service; Wi-Fi. *In room:* No phone.

Zona 11

While not generally mentioned in the typical list of tourist-recommended neighborhoods, Zona 11 is home to the Grand Tikal Futura, a major, modern high-rise hotel. This hotel is located right at the point where the highway to and from Antigua and the Western Highlands enters the downtown area. There are no shops or eateries within walking distance, but if you're planning on renting a car, it's convenient to stay here and have it delivered to the hotel. When you head out, simply turn right as you exit the hotel, and you'll be on Calzada Roosevelt, which soon turns into CA-1.

EXPENSIVE

Grand Tikal Futura ★★ Originally built and run as a Grand Hyatt, this hotel features a soaring atrium lobby hung heavy with flowing vines. From the outside, the architecture is meant to suggest the shape of the pyramids at its namesake archaeological site, although I never quite get that impression. The rooms are all very comfortable and up to luxury standards, with lots of space, plenty of shiny marble in the bathroom, and all the modern amenities you could want. The rooms on the higher floors command fabulous views. The gym and spa are perhaps the best of any hotel in the city, with a lovely indoor pool and a large, well-equipped workout area with separate locker rooms. The hotel is connected to a large mall, with a food court, movie theaters, and scores of shops. The hotel features a good Thai restaurant and popular bar, and also provides a free airport shuttle.

Calzada Roosevelt 22-43, Zona 11. ⓒ **502/2410-0800.** Fax 502/2440-4050. www.grandtikalfutura. com.gt. 205 units. $110–$130 double; $150–$600 suite; $700 presidential suite. Rates include complementary airport shuttle. AE, DISC, MC, V. Free parking. **Amenities:** 2 restaurants; bar; lounge; babysitting; well-equipped gym and spa; Jacuzzi; indoor pool; room service; smoke-free rooms; 2 squash courts; 2 outdoor lit tennis courts. *In room:* A/C, TV, hair dryer, Wi-Fi.

Zona 13 (Near the Airport)

There are a couple of hotel choices right near the airport. However, given the fact that hotels in zonas 9 and 10 are less than 10 minutes away from the airport by taxi, this is a very limited advantage and minor consideration. You'll enjoy much better access to restaurants, bars, and shopping if you stay at any of the hotels listed above. However, these are two good options if you really need to be close to the airport.

MODERATE

Crowne Plaza 🏷 If you have your heart set on finding a modern, business-class hotel right near the airport, look no further. In fact, this is your only option in this category. The Crowne Plaza is everything you could want, especially if you're only staying here before or just after a flight. It's also a good value. Rooms are in good shape, and many have excellent views of the surrounding mountains and volcanoes. The gym and spa are modern and well equipped, and for those looking for less health-conscious entertainment, there's a casino attached to the hotel.

Av. Las Ameritas 9-08, Zona 13. ℂ **502/2422-5050.** Fax 502/2422-5001. www.crowneplaza.com. 183 units. $80–$95 double; $152 executive level or junior suite; $170–$255 suite. AE, DISC, MC, V. Free parking. **Amenities:** Restaurant; bar; lounge; babysitting; casino; well-equipped gym and spa; Jacuzzi; midsize outdoor pool; room service; smoke-free rooms. *In room:* A/C, TV, minifridge, free Wi-Fi.

INEXPENSIVE

Dos Lunas Guest House 🏷 This budget hotel is somewhere between a hostel and a cozy bed-and-breakfast. Rooms are simple and very well maintained, and the shared bathrooms are kept spotless. The one room with its own bathroom is very nice, and has a queen-size bed with a carved-wood headboard. There are a couple of small interior gardens and two common lounge areas with cable television. In addition to free Wi-Fi throughout, free Internet access is available on some shared computers, and the hotel provides free airport transfers.

21a Calle 10-92, Zona 13. ℂ **502/2261-4248** or 2261-4337. www.hoteldoslunas.com. 6 units, 1 with private bathroom. $14 per person shared bathroom; $36 double. Rates include full breakfast, complimentary airport transfers, and taxes. MC, V. Free parking. **Amenities:** Restaurant. *In room:* No phone, free Wi-Fi.

WHERE TO DINE

Guatemala City has some excellent restaurants. As with the hotels, the best and most varied selection of restaurants is to be found in zonas 9 and 10. Likewise, there are some good restaurants in Zona 1, particularly for lunch, as the area can be a little sketchy at night. Another exception is the 2-square-block pedestrian mall area of Zona 4 known as **Cuatro Grados Norte,** which is full of bars, restaurants, shops, and art galleries.

For those with problems adjusting to the local flavor, you'll find no shortage of fast-food chains, including **McDonald's, Burger King, Pizza Hut, Wendy's, Quiznos,** and **KFC.** If you want to sample a local version, try the fried chicken at **Pollo Campero.**

Zonas 9 & 10

In addition to the places listed below, the restaurant at the boutique hotel **Otelito Casa Santa Clara,** 12a Calle 4-51, Zona 10 (ℂ **502/2339-1811**), is an excellent, upscale fusion spot with many local fans. For French food, try **Clio's,** 4a Avenida 12-59, Plaza Fontabella, Zona 10 (ℂ **502/2336-6948;** www.cliosbistro.com), and for sushi try **Sushi-Itto,** 4a Av. 16-01, Zona 10 (ℂ **502/2368-0181;** www.sushi-itto.com.gt). Refined Italian food can be found at **Pecorino,** 11a Calle 3-36, Zona 10 (ℂ **502/2360-3035;** www.ristorantepecorino.com). And for excellent

Continental fare served up in an elegant, yet relaxed, open-air garden setting, **Carpaccio,** 14a Calle 0-25, Zona 10 (✆ **502/2368-0690**), is a good bet.

VERY EXPENSIVE

Jake's ★★ INTERNATIONAL/FUSION This long-standing and very popular restaurant is perennially—and still—one of the top spots in Guatemala City. Like Tamarindos (below), this place features a long menu with a wide range of dishes culled from various world cuisines, but the vibe and execution are a bit more conservative. You can get a straight Caesar or Caprese salad, as well as any number of pasta plates. Steaks are of excellent cut and perfectly prepared. Service is semi-formal and very attentive. The "tablecloths" are blank sheets of white paper, and there's a cup of crayons on every table. There's a cool bar off the front of the operation. Jake's also has an extensive and reasonably priced wine list.

17a Calle 10-40, Zona 10. ✆ **502/2368-0351.** Reservations recommended. Main courses Q80–Q240. AE, DC, MC, V. Mon–Sat noon–3pm and 7–10:30pm; Sun noon–4pm.

Tamarindos ★★★ INTERNATIONAL/FUSION This place offers a perfect blend of creative and artful cooking, accompanied by attentive service and a very attractive ambience. Inside, there are several different dining rooms, each with its own decor. All feature subdued lighting combined with a minimalist modern aesthetic. The menu is long and eclectic, running the gamut from steak with a chili poblano sauce to moo shu duck. Italy and Asia are the dominant culinary influences, with everything from sushi to risotto. Be sure to try the appetizer of homemade ravioli stuffed with pear and ricotta cheese, served over a bed of caramelized onions with a red cherry and balsamic vinegar sauce. Save room for dessert; their molten *bomba de chocolate* (chocolate bomb) is superb, as is the Chai tea bread pudding.

11a Calle 2-19A, Zona 10. ✆ **502/2360-2815.** www.tamarindos.com.gt. Reservations recommended. Main courses Q68–Q282. AE, DC, MC, V. Mon–Sat 12:30–4pm and 7:30–10:30pm.

Zumo ★★★ INTERNATIONAL/FUSION Chef Rodrigo Alvarado is a shining, young light on the local culinary scene. This elegant restaurant rambles through several rooms and a covered open-air, interior courtyard of a converted old home. Small groups should be sure to reserve the private wine cellar dining room. The dishes feature artistic presentations and taste as good as they look. I recommend starting off with the seared scallops served on a bed of sweet potato "capellini" with basil oil and a blackberry sauce, or the parmesan crusted calamari rings. For a main dish, try either shrimp, fish, or steak with the excellent house chipotle sauce. And be sure to save room for the pumpkin crème brulée for dessert. Zumo features an excellent and very fairly priced wine list.

1a Avenida 12-16, Zona 10. ✆ **502/2334-6316** or 2331-2895. www.zumo.com.gt. Reservations recommended. Main courses Q79–Q189. AE, MC, V. Mon–Fri noon–3:30pm and 7–10:30pm; Sat 7–10:30pm.

EXPENSIVE

Kacao ★★ 🎋 GUATEMALAN This is *the* place to come for traditional Guatemalan cooking prepared and presented with style and flare. Various regional specialties include *pepian,* chicken in a pumpkin seed and tomato sauce from the Western Highlands, and *tapado,* spicy Caribbean seafood soup in coconut milk. The silky black-bean soup is finished off in a clay bowl and baked in the oven. There are a host of steak, poultry, and seafood options. For dessert, try the fried apple rings served with a vanilla-rum sauce. The restaurant decor is as traditional as the menu. Waiters wear traditional Maya garb, and the tablecloths are old *huipiles*. Service can be a tad slow, but it's worth the wait.

2a Av. 13-44, Zona 10. ⓒ **502/2237-4188** or 2377-4189. Reservations recommended. Main courses Q44–Q176. AE, DC, MC, V. Daily noon–4pm and 6–11pm.

MODERATE

Casa Chapina ★ GUATEMALAN   While nowhere near as formal or fancy as Kacao, this is another good option for traditional Guatemalan cooking. The first thing you'll notice is the open area where local women are hand-making fresh tortillas on steel *comales* over open flames. The rest of the space features high ceilings, wood furniture, and various wall hangings of traditional Guatemalan textiles. Unfortunately, there are also a couple of TVs showing sporting events or whatever the staff wants to watch when there's no game on. I find this distracting. However, the mood is quickly restored when wandering mariachi groups come through to play you a song or two tableside for a few *quetzales*. The menu is heavy on steak and grilled chicken dishes. Every meal is served with three different sauces, two of which are fairly spicy. Be sure to ask for some of those fresh tortillas, or you may be served some mediocre garlic bread.

1a Av. 13-42, Zona 10. ⓒ **502/2337-0143** or 2368-0663. Main courses Q52–Q112. AE, DC, MC, V. Daily 7am–11pm.

Frida's 🍴 MEXICAN   While I find the Mexican fare here pretty average, I do enjoy the convivial atmosphere and lively crowds that fill this popular joint. I usually order nachos and other appetizers to accompany the delicious, but slightly sweet, margaritas. If hungrier, I opt for the *enchiladas de mole poblana,* corn tortillas stuffed with shredded chicken and topped with a spicy, chocolate-based sauce. The tortilla soup is also very good. The decor features reproductions of artwork by the restaurant's namesake, the late Mexican artist Frida Kahlo. These folks also have a separate outlet in Antigua.

3a Av. 14-60, Zona 10. ⓒ **502/2367-1611.** www.lasfridas.com. Reservations recommended. Main courses Q64–Q106. AE, DC, MC, V. Daily noon–1am.

Hacienda Real ★★ STEAKHOUSE   This is one of the city's busiest steakhouses, and their success has allowed them to open several branches around town (with franchises in Panama and El Salvador, as well). The interior of this massive Zona 10 outlet is quite atmospheric, with heavy wooden tables and chairs, several dining rooms, and ample open-air veranda seating. Antique wood-cart wheels lean against the walls, and an abundance of ferns and potted plants are spread about. The plain grilled steaks are superb. You have your choice of a wide range of cuts, cooked to order, or both locally raised and imported beef. If you want more flavor, order the *lomito pimienta,* which comes with a green pepper sauce.

5a Av. 14-67, Zona 10. ⓒ **502/2380-8383.** www.hacienda-real.com. Reservations recommended. Main courses Q75–Q150. AE, DC, MC, V. Daily noon–10:30pm.

Tapas y Cañas ★ SPANISH   Head to Altuna (see below) if you want traditional Spanish fare and ambience, but come here if you're looking for a more modern interpretation of Spain's classic cooking, and a livelier bar scene. Sure you can still get some pretty traditional tapas and main dishes, but they are served up on fancy white plates, with artistic arrangements and ornamental dustings of ground peppers and herbs. You'll also find dishes that take their cue from other cuisines, like the tangy barbecued lamb chops. The main dining room has a modern feel, with clean lines, dim lighting, and linen covered tables, while the exposed brick wall, red tile floors, and wood-beam ceilings hark back to an earlier era.

13a Calle 7-78, Zona 10. ℭ **502/2388-2727.** www.tapasycanas.com. Reservations recommended. Tapas Q30–Q80; main courses Q65–Q115. AE, DC, MC, V. Daily noon–11pm.

Tre Fratelli ITALIAN   This popular chain, with branches across Central America, California and Texas, serves respectable northern Italian fare with a slight American flare. With eight restaurants spread across Guatemala, and several around the city, their most popular outlet is the new two story affair in the Zona Viva's Plaza Fontabella. I like to start things off with their Cinque Domande salad, which features mixed lettuce, Gorgonzola cheese, almonds, and a delicious balsamic vinegar dressing. For a main, I recommend the Bistecca Inferno, a thick cut of meat with a spicy brandy-cream sauce. There's also a wide selection of pastas, and several good pizzas cooked in a wood-fired oven. The portions here are pretty hefty, so come with an appetite.

4a Avenida 12-59, Plaza Fontabella, Zona 10. ℭ **502/2366-3164.** www.trefratelli.com. Reservations recommended. Pizzas Q45–Q65; pastas Q65–Q100; main courses Q75–Q130. AE, DC, MC, V. Daily noon–11pm.

INEXPENSIVE

Panadería San Martin 🍴 COFFEE SHOP/BAKERY   Set on a busy corner in the heart of the Zona Viva, this place is extremely popular and busy throughout the day. Folks come here for breakfast, lunch, or a coffee break, and the San Martin handles them all well. Breakfasts are excellent, and you can't beat the lunch special of soup alongside a half-sandwich and a half-salad for Q50. These folks have a bakery on premises, and a wide selection of sweets and gourmet coffees. The indoor seating is a bit too sterile for me, with its high-backed booths and Formica tables. I prefer to grab a seat in the shady outdoor patio or on the front veranda.

13a Calle 1-62, Zona 10. ℭ **502/2420-9916.** www.sanmartinbakery.com. Reservations not accepted. Main courses Q30–Q48. AE, DC, MC, V. Daily 6am–8:30pm.

Zona 1

MODERATE

Restaurante Altuna ★ SPANISH   The old-world charm of this Spanish restaurant fits perfectly with the architecture and Spanish colonial history of Zona 1. This place is light on tapas, but has a long list of main dishes. There's excellent paella, of course, but I also recommend squid in its own ink, as well as the *bacalao a la Vizcaina*, which uses imported cod in a tasty medley of tomatoes, peppers, and garlic. In addition, fish and shrimp come in a score of different preparations. Terrestrial fare includes a delicious rabbit stew and several steak options. Service is relatively formal and reserved, but very professional. This place has a large, reasonable wine list. There's a second branch of Altuna in the trendy Zona Viva at 10a Calle 0-45, Zona 10 (ℭ **502/2332-6576**).

5a Av. 12-31, Zona 1. ℭ **502/2251-7185** or 2253-6743. www.restaurantealtuna.com. Reservations recommended. Main courses Q62–Q192. AE, DC, MC, V. Daily noon–10pm.

INEXPENSIVE

Arrin Cuan ★ ☺ GUATEMALAN   This is my favorite restaurant in Zona 1. The rambling old building that houses the classic Guatemalan eatery is a quiet retreat in this busy area. The main dining room features wood tables crammed around the edges of a small interior garden. Hanging ferns and potted plants liven everything up. The menu is heavy on Guatemalan classics, with such regional dishes as *kac ik*, a filling turkey soup from the Alta Verapaz. If you want to sample something really exotic, order the *tepezquintle*, a large rodent served grilled over hot charcoal. This place has a children's play area, and plenty of free parking in a guarded lot across the street. A marimba band plays most days during lunch and dinner.

5a Av. 3-27, Zona 1. ✆ **502/2238-0242.** www.arrincuan.com. Main courses Q50-Q80. AE, DC, MC, V. Daily 7am-10pm.

Restaurante & Bar Europa 🎁 AMERICAN/INTERNATIONAL   For more than a decade this has been *the* hangout for American expatriates, Peace Corps workers, and assorted travelers. You can get excellent burgers and club sandwiches, as well as spicy, thick chili and a wide range of bar and comfort food. Breakfasts are huge, and this might be the only place in Guatemala to get good hash browns in the morning. The bar will always have a sports game on, and the place gets hopping during any playoff season.

11a Calle 5-16, Zona 1. ✆ **502/2253-4929.** Main courses Q40-Q95. AE, DC, MC, V. Mon-Sat 8am-1am.

Zona 4
INEXPENSIVE

L'Osteria ★ ☺ ITALIAN/PIZZA   This is my favorite restaurant in the Cuatro Grados Norte area. The menu is fairly limited, with not much more than a range of pasta dishes and thin-crust pizzas. Still, they do both of these well, and the setting is very pleasant. The pizzas are cooked in a wood-burning brick oven, and the pasta portions are large. For a change, you could get the eggplant parmigiana or some hearty minestrone soup. The ambience is casual and homey. On sunny afternoons, I like to grab one of the outdoor tables underneath the hanging vines on the large front patio, which offers a great view of the pedestrian traffic outside the restaurant's iron fence. This is a great option for families, especially on Sundays, when a magician or a story-teller usually performs in the afternoon.

Ruta 2, 4-75, Zona 4. ✆ **502/2379-8719.** Main courses Q70-Q115. AE, DC, MC, V. Tues-Thurs 11am-3pm and 6-10:30pm; Fri-Sat 11am-3pm and 6pm-midnight; Sun 11am-9pm.

Zona 14
EXPENSIVE

Ambia ★★★ 🎁 INTERNATIONAL/FUSION   This slightly hard-to-find restaurant is worth the effort. It's set on the grounds of a small complex of shops, most of which specialize in high-end kitchen design, wine, foodstuffs, and kitchen wares. The main dining area is outdoors on a large stone patio under a soaring roof, or out in the open under canvas umbrellas. A few additional tables are set on a covered veranda overlooking this patio, and there's another quiet room for more intimate occasions. The menu and wine list are both huge and inviting. They call what they do "New Age," though I liken it to the fusion cuisine you'll find most places. The menu features a fair number of vegetarian items, and there's a heavy Asian influence throughout.

10a Av. 5-49, Zona 14. ✆ **502/2366-6890.** Reservations recommended. Main courses Q65-Q235. AE, MC, V. Mon-Sat noon-3pm and 7-10:30pm.

WHAT TO SEE & DO

While it's certainly easy to visit all of these attractions on your own by taxi, many travelers like the convenience and built-in guide offered by organized city tours. **Clark Tours,** 7a Av. 14-76, Zona 9, inside Clark Plaza (© **502/2412-4700;** www. clarktours.com.gt), offers several different city tours. Most of these combine a tour around the principal attractions of Zona 1 and the colonial core, with stops at the **Museo Popul Vuh,** the **Museo Ixchel del Traje Indígena,** and one of the city's large markets.

Zona 1

Catedral Metropolitana (Metropolitan Cathedral) ★★
This stately, blue-domed, earthquake-resistant cathedral was completed in 1868 after 86 years of construction. The neoclassical structure inspires both austerity and awe, with its stone floors, colonial paintings, lofty arches, and bursts of gold at its altars. Perhaps the cathedral's most striking feature is the entrance, which is supported by 12 pillars, each of which is inscribed with the names of hundreds of Guatemalans who died or "disappeared" during the civil war. The interior is large and filled with religious icons, carvings, and artworks. You can tour the cathedral in about 20 minutes.

8a Calle and 7a Av., Zona 1. No phone. Free admission. Daily 8am–8pm.

Centro Cultural Miguel Angel Asturias (Miguel Angel Asturias Cultural Center) ★
Set on a hill overlooking downtown and named for Guatemala's most renowned literary figure, this complex houses the National Theater, a chamber theater, and an open-air theater within a modernist structure that almost looks like an ocean liner. Built originally in 1827 among the ruins of the San José military fortress, the complex has grown and was officially inaugurated in 1978. Among the theaters and galleries, you can find a variety of reasonably priced shows and exhibitions, ranging from plays by Guatemalan authors and Shakespeare in Spanish to marimba concerts and ballet. The view from the top is beautiful. This complex also contains a military museum, a small art gallery, conference rooms, and three cafeterias.

24a Calle 3-81, Centro Cívico, Zona 1. © **502/2232-4041.** www.teatronacional.com.gt. Free admission. Daily 8am–6pm. Various theater, dance, and concert performances take place at night. Ticket prices vary.

Cerro del Carmen
The name of this spot translates to "Carmen Hill," and it's a beautiful perch from which to take in the view of Guatemala City below. Adorning the hilltop is a Carmelite hermitage, which was left close to ruins by the 1976 earthquake. However, this hermitage does possess a beautiful silver embossed image of the Virgin of Carmen that dates back to the early 1600s. Be careful when visiting this area, and definitely do not come here after dark.

1a Av. and 1a Calle A, Zona 1. No phone. Free admission. Daily 24 hr.

Iglesia La Merced (La Merced Church) ★
Not to be confused with its more famous sister church of the same name in Antigua, this lovely baroque-style building has one of the most ornate facades of any Catholic church in Guatemala City. The interior is quite stunning as well, and features an extensive collection of religious art, sculpture, and relics. Originally built and administered by the order of La Merced, it was taken over by the Jesuits in the early 19th century.

5a Calle and 11a Av., Zona 1. © **502/2232-0631.** Free admission. Daily 6am–6pm.

Iglesia San Francisco (San Francisco Church) ★★ The namesake Franciscan order built this baroque church in the early 19th century. The main altar is an impressive piece of work, at almost 92m (302 ft.) tall and 12m (40 ft.) wide. The church is famous for its woodcarvings, which include its main altar and a couple of beautiful pieces donated by King Charles V of Spain.

13a Calle and 6a Av., Zona 1. 🕐 **502/2232-6325.** Free admission. Daily 6am–5pm.

Museo Nacional de la Historia (National History Museum) This modest history museum is located in a beautiful old building that once housed the National Property Registry. The museum contains a collection of paintings and historical artifacts displayed in a maze of rooms spread out over three floors. The collection dates mostly from the 18th and 19th centuries and relates primarily to past governments, presidents, and other important historical figures. One room is a re-creation of former President Jorge Ubico's living room. The museum is a bit unimaginative and provincial in my opinion, but it merits a half-hour visit as you walk around Zona 1.

9a Calle 9-70, Zona 1. 🕐 **502/2253-6149.** www.portalmuseosguatemala.net. Admission Q40. Mon–Fri 9am–4pm; Sat–Sun 9am–12:30pm and 2:30–4pm.

Museo Numismático (Numismatic Museum) Coin and bill collectors will want to stop by this museum, which is largely the initiative of the Banco de Guatemala. In addition to a broad collection of the country's currency throughout the ages, which ranges from shells, obsidian, and cacao beans to more modern pieces of coinage and paper money, the museum also features a few early instruments for fashioning coins and a hefty ingot of gold dating back to the colonial era.

Plazoleta del Banco de Guatemala (Bank of Guatemala Plaza), Centro Cívico, Zona 1. 🕐 **502/2429-6000.** www.banguat.gob.gt. Free admission. Mon–Fri 9am–5pm.

Palacio Nacional (National Palace) ★ The grand *palacio*, the Plaza Mayor's most ornate building, once housed the nation's executive branch. It was built by prison laborers under the order of President Jorge Ubico, and was completed in 1943. Many of the 350 rooms are off-limits to the public, but those that *are* open are definitely impressive. Above the Sala de Recepción hangs a sizeable Bohemian crystal chandelier, on which brass and golden *quetzales* perch. A second chandelier, this one of solid 18-karat gold, adorns the Sala de Banquetes. In 1980, a car bomb shattered the stained-glass windows on the second floor, which ironically had depicted the "10 Virtues of a Good Nation." Like the nation's virtues themselves, most of the windows have been reconstructed. There's a permanent collection of fine art, as well as several rotating gallery spaces. Free 45-minute tours are offered throughout the day. The highlight of the tour is often a stop at the Presidential Balcony, where you can imagine yourself addressing the nation.

6a Calle, btw. 6a Av. and 7a Av., Zona 1. 🕐 **502/2253-0748.** Free admission. Daily 9am–noon and 2–5pm.

Plaza Mayor ★ Called the "center of all Guatemala," the Plaza Mayor brings together the great powers of Guatemalan society: the government, the church, the army, and the people. It consists of two large plazas, the Parque del Centenario with its central fountain, and the Plaza de las Armas, intended as a military parade ground. The Plaza Mayor was first laid out and designed in 1778, just 2 years after the city was founded. The impressive buildings surrounding the plaza include the Catedral Metropolitana, the Palacio Nacional, and the National Library. Next to the Guatemalan flag in front of the Palacio Nacional burns an Eternal Flame dedicated to the "anonymous heroes of peace." Crowds gather here to celebrate holidays, protest, and sell their goods. The makeshift market here is busiest on Sundays, when vendors offer a wide variety of crafts at reasonable prices, though you might be able to find better deals in the small towns along Lake Atitlán or in Quetzaltenango. While the Plaza Mayor and its surrounding buildings still exude a strong air of colonial charm, I find the placement of a Wendy's franchise right on the corner by the Catedral Metropolitana a little off-putting.

Btw. 6a Calle and 8a Calle, and btw. 5a Av. and 7a Av., Zona 1. No phone. Free admission. Daily 24 hr.

Zona 2

Mapa en Relieve (Relief Map) ☺ While I find this attraction a bit cheesy, and the off-scale accentuation of the mountains a bit disconcerting, it's still a great way to get a feel for the lay of the land, and kids love it. What's more awe-inspiring is that this map, constructed in 1905, was done far before the existence of resources such as Google Earth and satellite imaging. Its designer, Francisco Vela, did an impressive job, even if the mountains and volcanoes do come across a bit too tall and pointy. The open-air map shows the country's major mountains, volcanoes, rivers, lakes, and railways. Despite its age, this attraction has weathered the years well. The map is massive, covering an area of some 40×80m (130×260 ft.), and an observation tower gives you a good view. The map isn't in a particularly safe neighborhood, so it's best to come and go by taxi. Allow about 30 minutes to take in this exhibit.

Parque Minerva, Av. Simeón Cañas, Zona 4. ✆ **502/2254-1114.** www.mapaenrelieve.org. Admission Q15. Daily 9am–5pm.

Zona 4

Iglesia Yurrita 🏠 This is not your run-of-the-mill colonial *iglesia*. This captivating structure, with an ornate blood-red tower and stonemasonry, was built in 1929 by the Yurrita family. The architecture shows a mix of styles from neo-Gothic to baroque. Many people think it could be the work of Antoni Gaudí, the famous Spanish architect. The interior colors and artwork are almost as spectacular as the exterior. Look for the painted glass window made to look like the daytime sky. This church is also known as La Capilla de Nuestra Señora de las Angustias (the Chapel of Our Lady of Anguish). You can tour the church in about 15 to 20 minutes, so come in a taxi and have the driver wait for you.

Ruta 6 and Vía 8, Calle Mariscal Cruz, Zona 4. ✆ **502/2312-5143.** Free admission. Daily 8am–6pm.

Zona 7

Parque Arqueológico Kaminaljuyú (Kaminaljuyú Archaeological Park) This was a major pre-Classic Maya city that seemed to have both ceremonial and trade functions. As early as A.D. 100, there were more than 200 structures here. The hieroglyphics discovered here predated those from other major Maya sites, and helped push back the first proven examples of Maya literacy. Most of the ruins remain buried, but the bases of a few pyramids and some tombs have been excavated. One of the more striking features of visiting this site is the fact that it exists in the midst of Guatemala City's major urban sprawl. Still, most of the best artifacts and carvings uncovered here are housed at the **National Museum of Ethnology and Archaeology** (see below). Allow about an hour to visit this site.

12a Av. 11-65, Zona 7. ✆ **502/2322-5571.** Admission Q30. Mon–Sat 8am–4pm.

Zona 10

Zona 10 is also commonly referred to as Zona Viva, though only the small section of Zona 10 with the greatest concentration of hotels, restaurants, and shops falls under this category. Its western boundary is defined by the broad, tree-lined Avenida La Reforma; to the west of the avenue lies Zona 9. Avenida La Reforma was modeled after the Champs Elysées in Paris. At the southern end of the avenue is the Plaza Obelisco, which is a broad rotunda at the center of which sits a tall obelisk and the eternal flame of Guatemala.

Jardín Botánico (Botanical Garden)   Guatemala City's almost 18,000-sq.-m (200,000-sq.-ft.) Botanical Garden was the first in Central America and is the only one in the country. It displays more than 1,400 varieties of local and exotic plants, including many endangered species. All exhibits are labeled with their common name in Spanish and their scientific name in Latin. The gardens are quite beautiful and extensive, and provide a welcome respite from the smog, traffic, and commotion of downtown Guatemala City.

Calle Mariscal Cruz 1-56, Zona 10. ℂ **502/2334-7662.** Admission Q15. Mon–Fri 8:30am–3:30pm; Sat 8am–noon.

Museo Ixchel del Traje Indígena (Ixchel Museum of Indigenous Dress) ★★
Ixchel was the Maya goddess of fertility and weaving, and she certainly inspired artistic talent in her people. A collection of textiles from approximately 120 indigenous communities is on display here, providing a good introduction to and history of the crafts travelers are likely to see on their journey across the country. The museum also has two permanent exhibitions of paintings: 61 watercolors of Maya traditional dress from the collection of Carmen de Pettersen, and 48 oil paintings of the Cakchiquel artist Andrés Curruchiche. Three 13-minute videos are shown by request on the second floor. I recommend you ask to see the one on traditional fabrics before you tour the museum. Allow about an hour to visit the museum, a little more if you watch all the videos. It's located on the tranquil campus of a small university, making it a nice place to bring a picnic lunch.

Universidad Francisco Marroquín, end of 6a Calle, Zona 10. ℂ **502/2331-3622.** Admission Q40. Mon–Fri 9am–5pm; Sat 9am–1pm.

Museo Popol Vuh ★   Named for the most famous Maya holy text, this museum houses an impressive collection of pre-Columbian art, spread through some six or seven small rooms. It's adjacent to the **Museo Ixchel** (see above) on the campus of the Universidad Francisco Marroquín. The collection includes stone sculpture, multicolored pottery, incense holders, and even funeral pyres. Don't miss the huge "Lord Bat" sculpture. There's also an area featuring colonial art, along with other folklore such as traditional dance masks and clothing. The museum offers special events, public lectures, and courses on everything from Maya cuisine to Egyptology. It should take you about 1 hour to tour this museum.

Universidad Francisco Marroquín, end of 6a Calle, Zona 10. ℂ **502/2361-2301.** www.popolvuh.ufm. edu. Admission Q35, Q15 students, Q10 children 2–12. Mon–Fri 9am–5pm; Sat 9am–1pm.

Zona 13

This is a modern and well-maintained part of the city, which includes the airport, several prominent museums, and the city's zoo. Any trip to the attractions in this *zona* should also include a stop at the **Mercado de Artesanías** (**Artisans' Market;** see "Shopping" below).

Aurora Zoo ★ ☺ Small by world standards but surprisingly well maintained and attended, the Aurora Zoo is a nice spot to pose for pictures with the wild Guatemalan animals you might not have seen on your journey through the country. Dating back to 1924, the zoo has one of the most impressive collections of animal life in Central America, and features giraffes, hippos, water buffaloes, leopards, and lions. Education, conservation, and rehabilitation are the zoo's mission, and they carry it out well. The park is divided into four sections: the African savanna, the Tropics, Asia, and the petting zoo. Various lectures and programs for children are held daily.

Boulevard Juan Pablo II, Zona 13. (✆ **502/2475-0894.** www.aurorazoo.org.gt. Admission Q20 adults, Q10 children 2-12. Tues–Sun 9am–5pm.

Museo de Arte Moderno (Museum of Modern Art) If you're looking for cutting-edge Guatemalan modern art (modern meaning 1800 to the present), a visit here is a must. Avant-garde paintings, caricatures, photographs, sculptures, and other objects fill the halls of this almost-colonial building. Exhibitions include works of national and international artists, mostly Latin Americans. The layout of the building is confusing, but getting lost can result in some interesting sightseeing.

5a Calle and 7a Av., Finca La Aurora, Local 6, Zona 13. (✆ **502/2472-0467.** Admission Q10. Tues–Fri 9am–4pm; Sat–Sun 9am–12:30pm and 2–4pm.

Museo de los Niños (Children's Museum) ★ ☺ The museum sets out to secure the future of Guatemala by educating its children—and if it were left up to the building's architects, it's clear that the future would take place on the moon. The lunar-colonial structure houses a wide variety of exhibits for the young and young at heart. If you have a few hours to spare in Guatemala City, let your inner child enjoy the gigantic game of Operation, or ride a bicycle with a skeleton attached to a neighboring bicycle to demonstrate bone movement. Other exhibits, such as the centrifugal force simulator and the static electricity generator, don't *appear* to be 100% harmless to children, but don't worry, they're safe. This place is very close to the zoo, making these two attractions a good combination outing for families with children.

5a Calle 10-00, Finca La Aurora, Zona 13. (✆ **502/2475-5076.** www.museodelosninos.com.gt. Admission Q35. Tues–Fri 8:30am–noon and 1–4:30pm; Sat–Sun 9:30am–1:30pm and 2:30–6pm.

Museo Nacional de Etnología y Arqueología (National Museum of Ethnology and Archaeology) ★★ This museum houses the most important collection of Maya archaeological artifacts in the country. It traces indigenous history over the centuries and through the present day, using several hundred Maya artifacts to tell the story. (Unfortunately, the only written descriptions are in Spanish.) Exhibits include a room dedicated to Maya technology (paper, and ceramic, shell, and bone tools), as well as a display of indigenous clothing. The highlight of the collection is the jade exhibit, with earrings, bracelets, masks, and an impressive scale model of Tikal. It should take you about an hour to 90 minutes to take everything in.

6a Calle and 7a Av., Finca La Aurora, Local 5, Zona 13. (✆ **502/2475-4010.** www.munae.gob.gt. Admission Q60. Tues–Fri 9am–4pm; Sat 9am–noon and 1:30–4pm.

Museo Nacional de Historia Natural (National Museum of Natural History) The museum's founder, Professor Jorge Ibarra, ran the place from its inception in

1950 until 1996, and his name was actually added to the full official name of the museum. It's divided into 20 areas, from the Origin of the Universe to an area dedicated to us mammals. While this incarnation of a popular museum is not as extensive as others in major cities around the world, you won't find a room honoring the "Poc" species of duck, an animal native only to Guatemala and close to extinction, anywhere else. Accompanying the museum is a library of books on ecology meant for children. *Note:* The exhibit explanations are only in Spanish.

6a Calle 7-30, Finca La Aurora, Zona 13. ⓒ **502/2472-0468.** Admission Q15. Tues–Fri 9am–4pm; Sat–Sun 9am–noon and 2–4pm.

OUTDOOR ACTIVITIES

Guatemala City is a hectic, somewhat dangerous, congested urban center, and not a particularly inviting place to pursue most outdoor activities. If you want to exercise or get out into nature, you're best off leaving the city.

BIKING   Though you can forget about riding a bicycle in Guatemala City, several tour companies organize mountain biking trips in the hills, mountains, and volcanoes just outside the city. Contact **Old Town Outfitters ★★** (ⓒ 502/5399-0440; www.bikeguatemala.com), which is based in Antigua and can arrange transportation for you to join any of their daily mountain bike rides. See chapter 6 for more information.

GOLF   Guatemala is not known for its golf, but there are actually several good golf courses close to the city. All of the courses are private or country clubs, but most will usually let outside guests play with advance notice. If you plan on going to Guatemala to play golf, contact the courses below in advance to arrange some playing time. Alternatively, many of the higher-end business hotels in Guatemala City have relationships with one or more of the courses, and can usually arrange tee-times. Greens fees are relatively inexpensive, running between Q320 and Q800.

The **Mayan Golf Club** (ⓒ 502/6685-5800; www.mayangolfclub.com) is located 10km (6 miles) from the airport. This 18-hole course offers excellent views of the Pacaya and Agua volcanoes, as well as Lake Amatitlán. Another good option is the **Hacienda Nueva Country Club** (ⓒ 502/6628-1000; www.haciendanueva.com), a beautiful course located about 20km (12 miles) outside of downtown at Km 25 of Ruta Nacional 18 on the road to Mataquescuintla. The **Alta Vista Golf & Tennis Club** (ⓒ 502/6641-5058; www.altavistagolf.com.gt) has the most challenging course in the country. This place is located just beyond the Hacienda Nueva Country Club at Km 26.5 of Ruta Nacional 18 on the road to Mataquescuintla.

JOGGING   As is the case with biking, Guatemala City is not very amenable to jogging. There are no public parks or outdoor spaces I can recommend as safe and secure for a foreigner to go jogging, and the busy streets of the secure Zona 10 district are not suitable. If you want to run, try the **Grand Tikal Futura** (ⓒ 502/2410-0800; www.grandtikalfutura.com.gt), which has a small outdoor jogging track.

SPAS & GYMS   You can certainly burn some calories or get a pampering massage while in Guatemala City. Most of the high-end business hotels in town have some sort of spa or exercise room, which vary widely in terms of quantity and quality. The best-equipped hotel spas I've found include those at the **Real InterContinental** (ⓒ 502/2413-4444; www.interconti.com), the **Westin Camino Real** (ⓒ 502/2333-3000; www.westin.com), and the **Grand Tikal Futura** (ⓒ 502/2410-0800; www.grandtikalfutura.com.gt).

SWIMMING The tropical daytime heat makes a cooling dip quite inviting. Several of the higher-end hotels in Guatemala City have pools, but none of them will let outside guests use their facilities, even for a fee. If you really want to have access to a swimming pool, check the listing information under "Where to Stay," earlier in this chapter, and make sure you choose a hotel with a swimming pool.

TENNIS The **Westin Camino Real** (✆ 502/2333-3000; www.westin.com) and the **Grand Tikal Futura** (✆ 502/2410-0800; www.grandtikalfutura.com.gt) are the only downtown hotels with tennis courts. If you're a die-hard tennis player and must play while in town, you should stay at one of these hotels. There are no other public facilities open to tourists downtown. Alternatively, you can contact any of the golf and country clubs listed above; all of these have multiple tennis courts, and will allow outside guests to play with advance reservations.

SHOPPING

In many respects, Guatemala City is a great place for shopping, particularly if you're interested in Guatemalan arts and crafts. While it's much more fun and culturally interesting to visit one of the traditional markets, like that in Chichicastenango or Santiago Atitlán, you can find just about anything made and sold throughout Guatemala on sale in the city. Moreover, you can find these arts and crafts in large, expansive markets, as well as in small, boutique shops. **Note:** It is illegal to export any pre-Columbian artifacts out of Guatemala.

The Shopping Scene

There are two main markets in Guatemala City, the **Mercado Central,** or Central Market, in Zona 1, and **Mercado de Artesanías (Artisans' Market),** in Zona 13. Both are massive and stocked with a wide range of arts, crafts, textiles, and souvenirs available throughout the country. Aside from these, the greatest concentration of shops can be found in the Zona Viva. These shops tend to be higher-end, and you'll often pay a premium price for the same goods available at the markets. However, the markets are often flooded with low-quality items, which are often weeded out from the offerings at the higher-end shops.

In addition to the Mercado Central, Guatemalans love to shop for bargains along 6a Avenida in Zona 1. This busy city street is crammed with makeshift stands and kiosks selling everything from bootleg CDs and DVDs to housewares and clothing. However, be careful; this is a busy and crowded area, and pickpockets feast on tourists.

Middle- and upper-class Guatemalans tend to shop in modern malls. Some of the malls in Guatemala City include **Centro Comercial Miraflores,** Calzada Roosevelt, Zona 11; **Centro Comercial Tikal Futura,** Calzada Roosevelt, Zona 11; and **Gran Cento Comercial Los Próceres,** 16a Calle, Zona 10, all of which could rival those in other parts of the world.

Shopping A to Z
ANTIQUES
Antigüedades lo de Víctor 🎁 This downtown shop, which occupies a colonial-era home, has everything antique, from knickknacks to large pieces of furniture. If you can't find anything to your liking, check other shops on this street, as there are several antiques dealers here. 12a Calle 3-39, Zona 1. ✆ **502/2232-7276.**

ART

Carlos Woods Arte Antiguo y Contemporáneo ★★   After several generations of focusing on antiques and classic artwork, this family-run gallery has moved into a larger space and added contemporary works to their repertoire. The lighting, architecture, and well-thought-out displays make this place feel as much like a museum as a gallery. 10a Av. 5-49, Zona 14. ℂ **502/2366-6883**. www.carloswoodsarte.com.

El Atico   This stylish gallery features paintings, sculptures, and installation art by contemporary Guatemalan artists. Featured artists and exhibits change regularly. 4a Av. 15-45, Zona 14. ℂ **502/2368-0853**.

Galería El Túnel ★   For a long time this was easily the best art gallery in the Old Town. Relocated to the Zona Viva, it continues to be a great place to see contemporary and classic Guatemalan art, with a permanent collection and rotating exhibits of art and sculpture. With a stable of over 100 working artists, there's always an interesting and varied selection on hand. They also occasionally offer painting classes and other workshops. Plaza Obelisco 16a Calle 1-01, Zona 10. ℂ **502/2367-3266**.

BOOKS

Sophos ★★   This hip and contemporary bookstore and cafe would fit right into the landscape in Seattle, New York, or Paris. They carry a wide selection of titles in Spanish and English, and feature rotating art exhibits and regular workshops, performances, readings, and book signings. 4a Av. 12-59, Plaza Fontabella, Zona 10. ℂ **502/2419-7070**. www.sophosenlinea.com.

HANDICRAFTS, SOUVENIRS & TEXTILES

Colección 21 ★   This is an excellent shop and gallery with a wide range of arts, crafts, textiles, and jewelry of generally high quality. They also have a collection of contemporary painting, as well as some antiques. 12a Calle 4-65, Zona 14. ℂ **502/2363-0649**. www.coleccion21.com.

In Nola ★★ 🎁   This place is the Zona Viva outgrowth of the long-standing **Lin Canola** (below). It has a broad and generally high-quality selection of Guatemalan goods. The emphasis is on textiles, and this is a great place to buy fabrics by the yard. They also stock clothing, bedroom linens and coverings, and table settings. In addition, you can find a wide range of woodcarvings, leather goods, and ceramic wares. 18a Calle 21-31, Zona 10. ℂ **502/2367-2424**. www.in-nola.com.

Lin Canola ★★   This popular store features a massive selection of Guatemalan cloth and textile products, as well as other arts and crafts items. This is a great place to buy local fabrics in bulk. Originally operated out of the Mercado Central, they now have this downtown outlet, as well as their sister storefront, **In Nola,** in the upscale Zona 10 neighborhood. 5 Calle 9-60, Zona 1. ℂ **502/2253-0138**. www.lin-canola.com.

Mercado Central (Central Market) ★ 🔪   This massive indoor market takes up several floors, covering a square city block in a building just behind the Catedral Metropolitana. This is your best bet for getting good deals on native wares. Offerings range from clothing and textiles to housewares and handicrafts. This market is actually frequented by Guatemalans more than tourists. Be careful of pickpockets. 9a Av. btw. 6a Calle and 8a Calle, Zona 1. No phone.

Mercado de Artesanías (Artisans' Market) 🔪   This massive market area is geared toward tourists, but is the place to come in Guatemala City for the broadest range of crafts and souvenirs. Because of its convenient location near the airport and the Finca La Aurora, you can combine a visit to this market with several museums and attractions in the same zone. 6a Calle 10-95, Zona 13. ℂ **502/2472-0208**.

JEWELRY

Albuhi ★   This pretty shop specializes in silver and pewter ware. In addition to handmade jewelry, you can also get picture frames and an assortment of religious items, from crosses to ornate saints. Centro Comercial La Plaza 20, 20s Calle 25-96, Zona 10. ℂ **502/2368-3842**.

Aparicio ★   These folks carry high-end, one-of-a-kind jewelry in gold and silver, either plain or set with a wide range of gemstones. They also carry a broad selection of fine watches, as well as Swarovski jewelry and crystals. In addition to the storefront listed here, they have another outlet at the Gran Centro Comercial in Zona 4. 12a Calle 1-25, Centro Comercial Gémenis 10, Zona 10. ℂ **502/2335-3404**. www.aparicio.com.gt.

LIQUOR

The Guatemalan **Zacapa rum** ★★★ is one of the finest rums in the world. The 23-year-old Zacapa Centenario dark rum is as rich and smooth as a fine cognac. It has won widespread acclaim in international tasting competitions, and the company claims that part of their success and secret lies in the fact that the rum is initially distilled at sea level, near where the sugar cane is grown, and brought to a separate facility high in the Guatemalan mountains to age. Zacapa rums also come in 15- and 25-year aged varieties. For decades, the Centenario came in a bottle entirely covered in a woven reed. Today, these bottles are increasingly rare, and while the newer packaging features only a thin band of the weaving, the rum is just as good. You can get Zacapa rum at liquor stores and supermarkets across the city (and country). However, you'll find the best prices, oddly, at the airport. It's convenient to know you can save that last bit of shopping until the last minute.

GUATEMALA CITY AFTER DARK

Guatemala City is a large, metropolitan city. However, its after-dark pleasures are somewhat limited. Part of this is due to the famously dangerous nature of much of the city, especially after dark. Many of the late-night offerings are confined to a couple of very concentrated and centralized "safe" areas, which gives the scene a little bit of an apartheid feel. Still, if you're looking for a concert, theater performance, or night on the town, you should be able to find something here to fit the bill.

The Performing Arts

Guatemala's performing arts scene is relatively thin, which could be due to the high levels of poverty and illiteracy.

The greatest number of high-quality performances take place at the **Centro Cultural Miguel Angel Asturias** ★★, 24a Calle 3-81, Centro Cívico, Zona 1 (ℂ **502/2232-4041;** www.teatronacional.com.gt), which features the country's largest, most modern, and most impressive theater. Offerings range from local and visiting ballet companies and symphonies to theater and modern dance. A couple of satellite theater and gallery spaces often host smaller events, which include conferences, poetry readings, and film cycles.

Another principal venue for the performing arts is the theater at the **Instituto Guatemalteco Americano** ★ (IGA; ℂ **502/2422-5555;** www.iga.edu), which is located at Ruta 1, 4-05, Zona 4, on the outskirts of Cuatro Grados Norte. These folks maintain a steady schedule of events that range from children's and traditional theater to art film cycles and dance performances. Check out their website for current event schedules.

The **Centro Cultural de España,** Vía 5, 1-23, Zona 4 (© **502/2385-9066;** www.cceguatemala.org), is located right on the main drag of Cuatro Grados Norte, close to the IGA. In addition to their small gallery space, they have a regular schedule of artistic, literary, and cultural events.

Your best bet for finding out what might be playing is to ask your hotel concierge, check the websites listed above, or pick up a copy of the free monthly *Revue Magazine* (www.revuemag.com), which is widely available at hotels and other tourist haunts around the country.

Ticket prices can range from Q30 to as high as Q480 depending on the event and the star power of the main act.

The Bar Scene

For visitors and locals alike, there are two main after-dark destinations: the Zona Viva and Cuatro Grados Norte. Both offer a broad range of bars, restaurants, and clubs in a compact area that's safe and pedestrian-friendly. Most bars don't charge a cover unless there's a live act, in which case the cover is anywhere from Q10 to Q80. Discos and dance clubs often have a cover of between Q15 and Q40.

Cheers North American tourists feeling homesick, or those looking for some classic rock, a pool table, or a sporting event on television, should come here. The menu is classic American-style bar food (although the owners are actually Canadian), with spicy chicken wings, nachos, and burgers. In addition to the three pool tables, they've got dartboards and a foosball table. Open Monday through Saturday 9am to 1am, Sunday noon to midnight. 13a Calle 0-40, Zona 10. © **502/2368-2089**.

Del Paseo This is a great spot in Cuatro Grados Norte for a few drinks, some conversation, and a light bite with friends. As much a cafe and bistro as a bar, this place has live music most Thursdays and some weekends. Open daily noon until around 2am. Cuatro Grados Norte, Zona 4. © **502/2385-9046**.

Kahlua ★ This is one of the better dance spots in town, with a loud and lively vibe. The sound system is excellent, the main dance floor is quite large, and there's an interesting light show. There are several side rooms here, as well as a restaurant if you want a break from the pounding rhythms. Open Wednesday through Saturday 8pm to 3am. 1a Av. 15-06, Zona 10. © **502/2333-7468**.

Kloster This German-style pub has its own selection of microbrew beers. Tap beer is served in a variety of sizes, including by the meter, which is a massively tall glass that rests with an air of precarious danger on the tables or long wooden bar. The bar menu features several fondue options. In addition to the bar listed here, these folks have another outlet on the main drag in Cuatro Grados Norte. Open daily noon to 1am. 13a Calle 2-75, Zona 10. © **502/2334-3882**. www.restaurantekloster.com.

La Bodeguita del Centro ★★ 🎁 The spirit of the beatnik culture is alive here. You can't miss the brightly contrasting primary colors that define the exterior of this popular spot. La Bodeguita often has live music, as well as the occasional theater piece or poetry reading. The programming here is nothing if not eclectic. The live music might be jazz, folk, classic rock or hard-core punk. Open Tuesday through Sunday noon to 2am. 12a Calle 3-55, Zona 1. $\mathcal{C}$ **502/2230-2976**. Cover ranges Q5–Q50.

Rattle 'N' Hum ★★ This Australian-owned bar fills up quickly most nights with a broad mix of Guatemalans and expats. In addition to tall cold cans of Fosters and classic Men Down Under cuts on the sound system, you'll find a good menu of bar food and plenty of drink options. There's a lively happy hour scene, and live music several nights a week. Open daily noon to 1am. 4a Av. 16-11, Zona 10. $\mathcal{C}$ **502/2366-6524**.

Trovajazz ★★ This hip bar in Cuatro Grados Norte is one of my favorite haunts for live music. There's a band or act playing here most nights, and as the name implies, the music can range from *trova* (Latin American folk songs) to jazz. Open nightly until 1 or 2am, depending on the crowd. Vía 6 3-55, Zona 4. $\mathcal{C}$ **502/2334-1241**. www.trovajazz.com.

William Shakespeare Pub This simple English-style pub is popular with the local expatriate crowd and visitors. Their motto is "No tragedy, no comedy, just good times." You'll find it just below the ground floor of a high-rise building and commercial center (though it's visible from the street). Open daily noon to 1am. 13a Calle and 1a Av., Torre Santa Clara II, Zona 10. $\mathcal{C}$ **502/2331-2641**.

The Gay & Lesbian Scene

Guatemala is a largely Catholic, socially conservative Central American nation, and in general terms the nation can be rather homophobic. Public displays of same-sex affection are rare, and violence against prominent gay and lesbian activists is not unheard of. For these reasons, the local gay and lesbian communities are pretty discreet. Many gay and lesbian organizations guard their privacy, and the club scene is changeable and not well publicized.

For good, comprehensive information on the current situation for gay men, check out **Gay Guatemala** (www.gayguatemala.com), which appears in both English and Spanish. Information on the lesbian scene, and specifically lesbian clubs and bars, is much harder to come by. In general, the clubs and bars mentioned below tend to be predominantly gay, but all are pretty lesbian-friendly.

The most established gay and lesbian bars are **Black & White,** 11a Calle 2-54, Zona 1 ($\mathcal{C}$ **502/5904-1758;** www.blackandwhitebar.com); **Metropole,** 6a Calle, between 3a Avenida and 4a Avenida, Zona 1; **Ephebus Bar,** 4a Calle 5-30, Zona 1 ($\mathcal{C}$ **502/2253-4119**); **Genetic,** Ruta 3, 3-08, Zona 4 ($\mathcal{C}$ **502/2332-2823**); and **El Encuentro,** 5a Av. 10-52, Zona 1 ($\mathcal{C}$ **502/2232-9235**).

Cinemas

All of the modern malls have multiplex cinemas showing late-run American movies, usually subtitled, but sometimes dubbed. Your best bets are the **Cinépolis,** Centro Comercial Miraflores, Calzada Roosevelt, Zona 11 ($\mathcal{C}$ **502/2470-8367;** www.cinepolis.com.gt); **Cinépolis,** Oakland Mall, Diagonal 6 13-01, Zona 10 ($\mathcal{C}$ **502/2269-6990;** www.cinepolis.com.gt); **Cines Tikal Futura,** Centro Comercial Tikal Futura, Calzada Roosevelt, Zona 11 ($\mathcal{C}$ **502/2440-3297**); and **Cines Próceres,** Centro Comercial Los Próceres, 16a Calle, Zona 10 ($\mathcal{C}$ **502/2332-8508**). Check any of the local, Spanish-language daily papers for current schedules.

SIDE TRIPS FROM GUATEMALA CITY

Several side trips from Guatemala City are possible, ranging from day trips and tours to multiday excursions. I highly recommend you take any of these trips as part of an organized tour. All of the major hotels have tour desks that can arrange these for you. Alternatively, you can contact **Clark Tours,** 7a Av. 14-76, Zona 9, inside Clark Plaza (𝄐 **502/2412-4700;** www.clarktours.com.gt); **Maya Expeditions,** 15a Calle "A" 14-07, Zona 10 (𝄐 **502/2363-4955;** www.mayaexpeditions.com) and **Turansa,** Carretera Roosevelt, Km 15, Zone 11, Super Centro Molino (𝄐 **502/2390-5757;** www.turansa.com).

In addition to the tours listed below, day tours by land are available to the Maya sites of Quiriguá and Copán in Honduras. Multiday trips to any of the other regions in Guatemala mentioned below can also be arranged.

Top Tours & Excursions

Antigua ★★★   The fabulous colonial city of Antigua is just 45 minutes away from Guatemala City by car or bus. All of the local tour companies offer half- and full-day tours to Antigua. I definitely recommend you sign up for a full-day tour if possible. Antigua is *that* beautiful, and there is *that* much to see. Half-day tours cost $30 to $50, including lunch and entrance fees to all attractions. Full-day tours cost $50 to $80, including lunch. For more information on Antigua, see chapter 6.

Chichicastenango on Market Day ★★★   If you're in Guatemala City with a free Thursday or Sunday, you'll want to take a day trip to the fabulous market in Chichicastenango. These tours also hit Panajachel and Lake Atitlán on the way back, so you get to kill two or more birds with one stone. This is a full-day tour, with a fair amount of travel time, but it's worth it. These tours cost between $45 and $90, and include lunch. For more information on Chichicastenango and its market, see chapter 8.

Lake Atitlán ★★   Even if there's no market happening in Chichicastenango, you might consider a day trip to Lake Atitlán, one of the most beautiful spots in all of Guatemala. All of the tour agencies in town can arrange this outing, which takes a full day, and includes visits to Sololá, Panajachel, and one or two of the villages around the shores of the lake. These tours cost between $50 and $100, and include lunch. For more information on Lake Atitlán and its surrounding villages, see chapter 7.

Tikal ★★★   Perhaps the most popular day tour out of Guatemala City is to the amazing Maya ruins of Tikal. These tours generally involve a very early morning flight and even earlier hotel pickup. The tours give you a good, full day in Tikal. However, if you've got the time, I seriously recommend you add at least a 1-night extension to the tour. These tours run around $300 to $350, including round-trip airfare, park entrance fee, and a guide. Budget an additional $50 to $150 per person per day for multiday excursions, depending on the level of accommodations chosen. For more information on Tikal, see chapter 9.

Mixco Viejo This interesting site was an ancient Maya city built during the 12th and 13th centuries. Like many other Maya cities of the era, it was built on a plateau with steep canyon walls to protect it from other Maya groups. It was also one of the last Maya cities to fall against the Spanish conquistadors. The site features several pyramids and a well-preserved ball court. Tours here usually stop at the large and abundant fruit-and-vegetable market just outside the ruins. Full-day tours cost between $38 and $63, including lunch.

ANTIGUA

S imply put, Antigua ★★★ is a gem, an enchanting blend of restored colonial-era architecture and rugged cobblestone streets, peppered with ruins and brimming with all the amenities a traveler could want—beautiful boutique hotels, fine restaurants, and plenty of shopping and activity options. Antigua sits in a small valley surrounded by towering volcanoes, which are clearly visible over the red tile roofs and church bell towers that dominate the small city's skyline. The colonial core of Antigua is extremely compact and well suited to exploring on foot.

Antigua was Guatemala's capital from 1543 until 1776. It was founded after mudslides and flooding destroyed the country's first capital, in what is today Ciudad Vieja, in 1541. Designed by Italian civil architect Juan Francisco Antonielli and originally christened La Muy Noble y Muy Leal Ciudad de Santiago de los Caballeros de Goathemala (the Very Noble and Very Loyal City of Santiago of the Knights of Guatemala), it was for centuries perhaps the New World's finest city. In fact, it was declared the Capitancy General, which in effect granted it status as the government seat for all of Mexico and Central America. Antigua flourished throughout the 17th and on into the 18th centuries, with the massive wealth generated by the Spanish conquest being poured into the construction of churches, government buildings, universities, convents and monasteries, private homes, and military garrisons.

Many of those impressive buildings were knocked down in a steady string of earthquakes, and after a massive earthquake in 1773 destroyed most of the city, the government seat was relocated to present-day Guatemala City. There was great resistance to the move, and in 1777, the government actually instituted a law making it illegal to live in Antigua. Eventually, the city was almost entirely abandoned and stayed that way until the 20th century. It wasn't until the capital was moved to Guatemala City that the former city of Santiago de Guatemala was renamed Antigua, or La Antigua, which was a short way of saying "the old capital." In 1944, Antigua was declared a National Monument by the Government of Guatemala, and in 1979, UNESCO named it a World Heritage Site.

Antigua has the most elaborate and stunning **Holy Week celebrations** ★★★ in all of Guatemala, and perhaps even the Americas. During Holy Week, the streets are decorated with intricate and beautiful *alfombras* (rugs) made of colored sawdust and flower petals. A steady stream of religious processions parade through the streets and over these *alfombras,* which are quickly replaced with new ones. While the Holy Week celebrations here are the city's principal civic celebration, Antigua also goes all out each year on and around July 25, the feast day of the city's patron saint Santiago, or Saint James.

ORIENTATION

40km (25 miles) SW of Guatemala City; 108km (67 miles) SE of Chichicastenango; 80km (50 miles) SE of Panajachel

Arriving

BY PLANE

The nearest airport to Antigua is **La Aurora International Airport** (© **502/2321-0000** or 502/2260-6257; www.dgacguate.com; airport code GUA) in Guatemala City. Since Antigua is so close to Guatemala City, many visitors book their first and last nights—and often a few more—in Antigua. Once you've made it through Customs, you can be settled into your hotel in Antigua in less than an hour, if you don't hit too much traffic.

Getting into Town from the Airport

BY SHUTTLE   The most common way to get to and from Antigua is on a minivan shuttle. Several companies operate regular minivan shuttles between Antigua and most major tourist destinations, including the airport, downtown Guatemala City, Lake Atitlán, and Chichicastenango. If you're coming to Antigua directly from the airport, you'll usually find several shuttles waiting, just after clearing Customs. All charge between Q50 and Q80 per person. Some will leave as soon as they are full, while others leave on fixed schedules.

If you're already in Guatemala City, or arriving from any other destination, ask your hotel or any tour agency about booking a shuttle to Antigua. Alternately, you can book directly with one of the shuttle companies, like **Atitrans** (© **502/7832-3371;** www. atitrans.net).

Rates between Antigua and other popular destinations run around Q160 for Panajachel, Q160 for Chichicastenango, and Q640 for Flores/Tikal.

BY TAXI   A taxi is the fastest, and easiest way to get from the airport or Guatemala City to Antigua. A taxi should cost between Q200 and Q320. Expect to pay the higher rate, maybe even a little more, after dark.

BY BUS   Buses from Guatemala City to Antigua leave from the El Trebol intersection in Zona 8. Buses leave every 15 minutes or so, usually as they fill up, between 5:30am and 7pm. The fare is Q8 for the 1-hour ride. The main bus terminal in Antigua is at the end of 4a Calle Poniente, next to the Municipal Market. Buses leaving Antigua for Guatemala City follow roughly the same schedule. Safety is a serious concern on these buses, and I recommend you take a taxi or shuttle.

BY CAR   The best route to Antigua from Guatemala City is to take the Calzada Roosevelt out of town. The Calzada Roosevelt heads northwest out of Guatemala City, through Zona 11 (passing right in front of the Tikal Futura Hotel), before turning into the Pan-American Highway (CA-1). Take this and exit at San Lucas. From here you'll take the well-paved, windy highway (RN10) into Antigua. The ride takes about 40 to 45 minutes with no traffic.

Visitor Information

The Guatemala Tourism Commission, **INGUAT,** 2a Calle Oriente, #11 (© **502/7832-3782;** www.visitguatemala.com), has a helpful bilingual staff, and offers regional brochures, basic maps, and a score of hotel and tour fliers. The office is open Monday through Friday 8am to 5pm, and Saturday and Sunday 9am to 5pm.

Local travel agencies and hotel tour desks are another good source of information. There are numerous travel agencies all over town. Some of the best include **Lax Travel Antigua ★**, 3a Calle Poniente, #12 (© **502/7832-1621**); **Sin Fronteras ★**, 5a Av. Norte, #15A (© **502/7720-4400;** www.sinfront.com); **Rainbow Travel Center ★**, 7a Av. Sur, #8 (© **502/7931-7878;** www.rainbowtravelcenter.com); and **Via Venture ★★**, 2a Calle Oriente, #22 (© **502/7832-2509;** www.viaventure.com).

If you need assistance, dial **Asistur** (© **1500**) toll-free from any phone in Guatemala. Asistur has bilingual operators who can answer questions or put you in direct contact with the appropriate authorities in the case of an emergency. You can also contact the **tourism police** (© **502/7832-7290**), which has its 24-hour office on 4a Avenida Norte on the side of the Palacio del Ayuntamiento.

GETTING AROUND

ON FOOT Antigua is walkable, and cars and taxis are unnecessary to explore the colonial core of the city. The entire downtown section of Antigua, which is where most tourist attractions are, extends less than 10 blocks in any direction from the Plaza Mayor. However, watch your step: Several hundred years and a few serious earthquakes have made Antigua's streets and sidewalks rather treacherous in spots. It's very easy to twist an ankle, trip, or fall if you're not careful. Bring comfortable, flat walking shoes or sneakers. Also, sidewalks tend to be narrow, forcing you frequently to walk in the street; keep an eye out for cars and motorcycles.

BY TAXI Taxis and tuk tuks are plentiful in Antigua. A ride anywhere in the city should cost between Q20 and Q30. Some of the taxis in Antigua use meters, but if the one you get into doesn't, be sure to negotiate a firm price beforehand. If you need to call a cab, ask your hotel, or try **Taxis Antigua** (© **502/7832-2360**).

BY CAR While you won't need a car to explore Antigua, you may want one for a trip to Chichicastenango, Lake Atitlán, or other nearby towns. In Antigua, try **Tabarini,** 6a Av. Sur, #22 (© **502/7832-8107;** www.tabarini.com).

City Layout

Antigua is laid out in a simple grid, with the **Plaza Mayor,** or Parque Central (Central Park), at its center. *Avenidas* (avenues) run north-south, and *calles* (streets) run east-west. North of Plaza Mayor, the *avenidas* carry the suffix *norte;* south of Plaza Mayor they are followed by the suffix *sur.* Directions on *calles* east of Plaza Mayor are indicated by the suffix *oriente;* while those to the west are *poniente.* Unlike most cities in Guatemala, Antigua doesn't use the Zona system; instead each individual building is numbered.

Three main volcanoes are visible from various points in Antigua and can help you stay oriented. The solitary **Volcán de Agua** is almost due south of the city. A bit more to the southwest are **Volcán Acatenango** and **Volcán Fuego.** The latter is quite active, and you can often see a long plume of smoke rising from its crater. To the north of the city is the **Cerro de la Cruz,** a high hilltop with a large Catholic cross atop it.

ACCOMMODATIONS ■

Black Cat Hostel **19**
Casa Azul **25**
Casa Capuchinas **32**
Casa Concepcion **30**
Casa Encantada **3**
Casa Ovalle **33**
Casa Santo Domingo **31**
Cissus Hotel **5**
Hotel El Convento **34**
Hotel Posada de Don Rodrigo **38**
Hotel Posada La Merced **47**
Hotel San Jorge **7**
Jungle Party Hostel **50**
Kafka **48**
Mesón Panza Verde **1**
Palacio de Doña Leonor **26**
Porta Hotel Antigua **4**
Posada Asjemenou **40**
Posada de los Leones **55**
Posada del Angel **2**
Posada San Pedro **6**
The Cloister **39**

DINING ◆

Bistrot 5 **28**
Café Condesa **16**
Café Flor **12**
Café Mediterraneo **8**
Café Sky **9**
Caffé Opera **49**
Como Como **13**
Doña Luisa
  Xicoteneatl **27**
El Sabor del Tiempo **21**
El Sereno **37**
Fusion **45**
Gaia **42**
Hector's **44**
La Fonda de la
  Calle Real **20, 22, 23**
Mesón Panza Verde **1**
Nokiate **10**
Queso y Vino **43**
Tartines **15**
Welten **30**

ATTRACTIONS ●

Casa del Tejido Antiguo **53**
Catedral San José **18**
Cerro de la Cruz **54**
Convento de las Capuchinas **35**
Iglesia La Merced **46**
Mercado de Artesanias y
  Campañia de Jesús **51**
Mercado Municipal **52**
Museo de Arte Colonial **11**
Museo de Santiago **24**
Museo del Libro Antiguo **24**
Nim Po't **41**
Palacio de los Capitanes
  Generales **14**
Palacio del Noble
  Ayuntamiento **24**
Plaza Mayor **17**

115

Babysitters Hotels offering regular, dependable babysitting service are few and far between. If you'll need a babysitter, make sure that your hotel offers this service, and be sure to ask whether the babysitters are bilingual. In many cases, they are not. This is usually not a problem with infants and toddlers, but it can cause problems with older children. Babysitters charge between Q15 and Q40 per hour.

Banks Several banks have branches right on the Plaza Mayor or within a 2-block radius, including **Banco Industrial,** 5a Av. Sur, #4 (✆ **502/2420-3000**); and **Banco Reformador,** 4a Calle Poniente, #1A (✆ **502/7832-4876**). All of these have ATMs, will change money, and will make cash advances against a credit card.

Bookstores There are several good bookstores in Antigua. The best one for tourists is **La Casa del Conde,** 5a Av. Norte, #4 (✆ **502/7832-3322**), located in a small shopping complex on the west side of the Plaza Mayor. Also try **Librería del Pensativo ★**, Calle del Arco, #29 (✆ **502/7832-0729**) for literature; or **Rainbow Café and Bookstore,** 7a Av. Sur, #8 (✆ **502/7832-1919**).

Currency Exchange All banks (see above) will exchange money for a nominal service charge.

Almost all of the hotels, restaurants, and shops in Antigua will also accept U.S. dollars and euros, though many give less than advantageous exchange rates.

Dentists Try **Clínicas Ovalle,** 2a Av. Norte, #3 (✆ **502/7832-0275**); call your embassy, which should have a list of recommended dentists; or ask at your hotel.

Doctors Contact your embassy for information on doctors in both Antigua and Guatemala City, or ask your hotel for a recommendation. Also, see "Hospitals," below.

Drugstores A drugstore or pharmacy is called a *farmacia* in Spanish. There are scores of *farmacias* around Antigua, and you can probably find one simply by walking around. **Farmacia Fénix,** 6a Calle Poniente, #35 (✆ **502/7832-5337**), offers free delivery and has several outlets.

Embassies & Consulates See "Fast Facts" in chapter 13.

Emergencies Dial ✆ **1500** from anywhere in Guatemala. This will connect you to Asistur, which will have a bilingual operator who can put you in contact with the police, fire department, or ambulance service.

Express Mail Services Many of the shops around Antigua offer courier

shipping of your purchases. If you want to do it yourself, head to **DHL,** 6a Calle Poniente and 6a Avenida Sur (✆ **502/7832-3718;** www.dhl.com).

Eyeglasses There are several *ópticas* (eyeglass stores) around Antigua, including **Optyma,** 7a Calle Poniente, #15 (✆ **502/7832-4281**), and **Centro Visual G&G,** 4a Av. Sur, #1 (✆ **502/7832-6554**), both of which have resident ophthalmologists.

Hospitals The best hospital in Antigua is **Hospital Privado Hermano Pedro,** Av. La Recolección, #4 (✆ **502/7832-1190;** www.hopsitalpedrohermano.net), a modern 24-hour private hospital offering a wide range of services, including emergency and trauma units.

Internet Access There are a host of Internet cafes around Antigua, and a growing number of hotels are offering Wi-Fi. **Conexiones,** 4a Calle Oriente, #14 (✆ **502/7832-3768;** www.conexion.com), or the **Funkey Monkey,** 5a Av. Sur, #6 (✆ **502/7832-7181**), are two good bets. Rates run Q3 to Q8 per hour.

Laundry & Dry Cleaning Most folks use their hotel's laundry service, but if your hotel can't do it or is too expensive, try **Detalles Dry Cleaning & Lavandería,** 6a Av. Norte, #3B

(📞 **502/7832-5973**), which has coin-operated machines as well as wash and fold options.

Maps The city map in this book should be just fine, but you can also ask your hotel or go to the Guatemalan Tourism Commission, **INGUAT,** 2a Calle Oriente, #11 (📞 **502/7832-3782;** www.visitguatemala. com), to pick up a useful city map.

Photographic Needs There are a host of photo shops and 1-hour developing outfits in Antigua. If you have camera troubles, your chances of having any serious repair work are slim. Your best bet is **Foto Angel,** 5a Calle Poniente, #3B (📞 **502/7832-2919**).

Police The main Antigua police station is at the Palacio de los Capitanes Generales (📞 **502/7832-2266**), right on Plaza Mayor. The **tourism police** (📞 **502/7832-7290**) is a division of the larger police force with bilingual officers trained specifically to deal with tourists. Their office is just around the corner on 4a Avenida Norte, and is open 24 hours.

Post Office The main post office (📞 **502/7832-2164**) is located at 4a Calle Poniente and Alameda Santa Lucía.

Restrooms Most hotels and restaurants will let travelers use their facilities, although they are happiest about providing the service to clients.

Safety Antigua is one of the safest cities in Guatemala, and has a strong police presence. Both regular police and specialized tourist police patrol the city, particularly around the central downtown core. The farther away from Plaza Mayor you venture, the greater your chances of encountering trouble. Be especially careful about hiking to the Cerro de la Cruz without a guide, large group, or tourist police escort. Practice common sense. Don't wear flashy jewelry or wave wads of cash around, be aware of your surroundings, and avoid any people and places that make you feel uncomfortable.

Useful Telephone Numbers To get an international outside line, dial 📞 **00** before the country code. To make a local or international collect call, dial 📞 **147-120.** Most of the international phone companies have direct access numbers. If you have a calling plan, you can connect directly to **AT&T** (📞 9999-190); **MCI** (📞 9999-189); **Sprint** (📞 9999-195); **Bell Canada** (📞 9999-198); and **British Telecom** (📞 0800/890-502).

Water Drink only bottled water in Antigua.

WHERE TO STAY

Whether you're looking for a budget room in which to plop down your backpack or a top-notch luxury inn in which to kick up your feet, your choices are endless. The high-end boutique hotels here are unmatched in any other area of Guatemala or anywhere else in Central America, for that matter. I've picked the best I can find in each price range and category, but note that new hotels are opening all the time.

Very Expensive

There's a glut of outstanding options in this price range in Antigua. If the following are all full or don't suit your tastes, you might also try the **El Convento** (📞 **502/7720-7272;** www.elconventoantigua.com) or the boutique **Cissus Hotel** (📞 **502/7832-7938;** www.cissushotel.com).

Casa Santo Domingo ★★   This grandiose hotel lives up to the hype. A tourist attraction in and of itself, it is spread over massive grounds that include the colonial-era ruins of an old convent, a working chapel, several museum-quality display areas, and a large amphitheater. Most rooms have working fireplaces, and the best have balconies and/or Jacuzzis. I highly recommend the rooms found along the row of nos. 237 to 241, which are wonderfully situated with volcano and sunset views from their private balconies.

Even if you're not staying here, be sure to visit the Casa Santo Domingo, particularly around sunset. The grounds and facilities are impressive, and they have a sunset terrace with a perfect view of the nightly setting behind Volcán de Agua. Stick around for a drink or dinner as night falls, and the whole place is transformed into a candlelit fantasy. The restaurant here is excellent.

3a Calle Oriente, #28. (C) **502/7820-1220.** Fax 502/7820-1221. www.casasantodomingo.com.gt. 129 units. $210 double; $445 suite. AE, DC, MC, V. Free parking. **Amenities:** Restaurant; bar; Jacuzzi; large outdoor pool; room service; sauna. *In room:* TV, hair dryer, minibar.

Mesón Panza Verde ★★★   Although not nearly as massive in scale, I find this place every bit as captivating and special as the Casa Santo Domingo. The standard rooms are certainly acceptable, with small semi-private garden terraces, however, it's worth a splurge for one of the amazing, and varied suites. All are quite spacious and beautifully decorated, with an eclectic mix of furnishings, artwork, and design touches from Guatemala and around the world. My favorite rooms here are nos. 9 and 10, which are ground-floor suites with large private garden patios and huge bathrooms. Number 12, the Grand Suite, was originally intended to be the owner's residence, and features a private staircase, entrance, and balcony. The restaurant, also called **Mesón Panza Verde** (see review below) is one of the best in Antigua. There's also a small lap pool, adventurous art gallery, and wonderful rooftop terrace that winds around the building with several different places to sit and admire the view.

5a Av. Sur, #19. (C) **502/7832-2925.** www.panzaverde.com. 12 units. $100 double; $165–$190 suite; $250 master suite. Rates include full breakfast and taxes. Rates lower in the off season and for extended stays; higher during peak periods. AE, DC, MC, V. Free parking. **Amenities:** Restaurant; bar; small lap pool; free Wi-Fi. *In room:* TV.

Palacio de Doña Leonor ★★★ 📖   This beautiful hotel occupies the former home of Pedro de Alvarado's daughter, Leonor. Located just off the Plaza Mayor, this massive old colonial-era mansion features an immense and immaculate interior courtyard, broad interior verandas, and stunning architectural details. The rooms are large and equipped with plenty of modern amenities while maintaining their ancient charms. Some of the suites come with either Jacuzzi tubs or steam showers. The Don Pedro de Alvarado suite is a huge corner unit with a working fireplace, gigantic carved four-poster bed, 42-inch plasma television, and two balconies with great views.

4a Calle Oriente, #8. (C) **502/7832-2281.** Fax 502/7832-0226. www.palaciodeleonor.com. 13 units. $195 double; $235 junior suite; $300 master suite. Rates include full breakfast. AE, DC, MC, V. Free parking. **Amenities:** Restaurant; bar; babysitting; concierge; Jacuzzi; small pool; all rooms smoke-free; room service; small spa; free Wi-Fi. *In room:* TV, hair dryer, minibar.

Portahotel Antigua ★ ☺   This large hotel is designed and decorated in neocolonial style, with architectural details such as cupolas. All of the rooms are spacious and modern; however, it's worthwhile to upgrade to a deluxe unit, which comes with a private balcony or patio. Most of the rooms have two double beds; about 25 have either one king- or queen-size bed. Some of the rooms come with a working fireplace. You can get a better value and more ambience in the many boutique hotels listed in this section, but if you're looking for a business-class hotel with a wide range of services and amenities, this is still a fine option. These folks also offer babysitting and a children's program, making it a good choice for families.

8a Calle Poniente, #1. ☎ **502/7832-2801.** Fax 502/7832-0807. www.portahotels.com. 110 units. $165 double; $275 suite. AE, DC, MC, V. Free parking. **Amenities:** Restaurant; bar; babysitting; midsize out-door pool; room service. *In room:* TV.

Posada del Angel ★★   Yet another wonderful boutique hotel housed in a con-verted old home, this intimate bed-and-breakfast hosted former U.S. President Bill Clinton. Don't be deceived by the decrepit door letting out onto 4a Avenida Sur. Pass-ing through this faded and falling entrance is part of the charm. All the rooms are artistically decorated, and several feature beautiful showers with a high wooden door-way and hanging star-shaped light fixture. The second-floor Rose Suite is very large, with polished wood floors and a vaulted ceiling with exposed worn beams. This suite has a private section of rooftop terrace, but another large section is available for all guests to enjoy. There's a pretty little lap pool in the narrow interior courtyard.

4a Av. Sur, #24A. ☎/fax **502/7832-0260.** www.posadadelangel.com. 7 units. $214 double; $282–$364 suite. Rates include full breakfast. AE, DC, MC, V. Free parking. **Amenities:** Lounge; small lap pool; free Wi-Fi. *In room:* No phone.

Posada de los Leones (the Lion's Inn) ★★ 🏨   This intimate and elegant hotel is located just outside the hustle and bustle of downtown Antigua. The rooms are all large and beautiful, with built-in fireplaces and a refined sense of style. Of the standard rooms, I recommend La Magia, which has its own private garden terrace. The massive Shaha-razad Grand Suite features a four-poster king-size bed, a huge walk-in closet, and an oversize bathroom with a combination Jacuzzi-steam bath. The narrow pool is slightly more decorative than functional, but those decorations include a backing wall of stone, brick, and ivy with a three-headed lion fountain filling the pool. Meals can be taken alfresco on a rooftop terrace or in a beautiful dining room with a vaulted brick ceiling.

Calle de los Duelos, Las Gravileas, #1. ☎ **502/7820-7371.** Fax 502/7832-7378. www.posadadelos leones.com. 6 units. $280 double; $380 suite. Rates include full breakfast and taxes. Rates higher during peak periods. AE, DC, MC, V. Free parking. **Amenities:** Restaurant; bar, small outdoor pool; free Wi-Fi. *In room:* TV (upon request).

Expensive

In addition to the hotels listed here, **Casa Concepcion ★** (☎ **502/7832-5821;** www.hotelcasaconcepcion.com) is a pretty, well-run boutique bed-and-breakfast owned by the folks at Antigua Tours (see later in this chapter).

Casa Encantada ★★   This boutique B&B has a refined air about it, in terms of both the decor and service. Although most rooms are rather compact, they make up in comfort and style what they lack in size. The best room here is the large, rooftop suite, which has plenty of space and a private Jacuzzi. However, my favorite room is no. 7, which is tucked in the back of the hotel and reached by a rock walkway over a small pool. At night this pathway is lit with candles and is quite romantic. The whole hotel is really meant for couples and honeymooners, and only one room here—the second-floor room—has two beds; the rest have either one king-size or one queen-size. Breakfast is served on the delightful open-air rooftop, with great views of the red-tile roofs and the surrounding hills and volcanoes. In the afternoons and eve-nings, the little bar up here is *the* place to be for cocktails and snacks.

9a Calle Poniente Esquina, #1. ☎ **866/837-8900** toll-free in the U.S. and Canada, or 502/7832-7903 in Guatemala. www.casaencantada-antigua.com. 10 units. $95–$155 double; $190–$275 suite. Rates include full breakfast. These are weekend rack rates; rates lower midweek and off season, higher during peak periods. AE, DC, MC, V. Parking nearby. **Amenities:** Bar; small pool; free Wi-Fi. *In room:* TV, hair dryer, minibar.

The Cloister ★ 🛏 Fabulously located beside the Santa Catalina Arch, this converted convent is about as atmospheric a hotel option as you can find in Antigua, and that's saying a lot. The rooms are spread around the interior of this 17th-century building, and all feature antique tile or stone floors, high exposed-beam ceilings, and a tasteful mix of antiques, local crafts, and textiles. One room fronts the street, but I'd avoid it unless it's Holy Week. A couple of interior courtyards and gardens offer fountains, chairs, and several nooks in which to sit with a book or journal. The hotel doesn't have a restaurant, but they do serve a delicious breakfast.

5a Av. Norte, #12. ⓒ **502/7832-0712.** www.thecloister.com. 7 units. $125–$150 double. Rates include full breakfast. AE, DC, MC, V. Parking nearby. **Amenities:** Free Wi-Fi. *In room:* No phone.

Hotel Posada de Don Rodrigo ★ This popular, centrally located hotel is spread around the buildings and courtyards of three old houses that have been knit together. At the center of the largest courtyard stands a large pine tree, while fountains and gardens are sprinkled through the rest. Marimba bands play in the restaurant and common areas throughout much of the day, and local artisans make and sell their crafts in the main courtyard. All of the above can give this place a little bit of a kitschy feel. The rooms are simple, with attractive handmade wood furniture and decor that reflects the colonial era. Most are quite spacious, and some have fireplaces. Room nos. 300 to 303 feature small balconies overlooking the street. These rooms are particularly sought-after for Semana Santa.

5a Av. Norte, #17. ⓒ **502/7832-0387** or 7832-9858. Fax 502/7832-9858. www.hotelposadadedon rodrigo.com. 41 units. $100–$110 double. AE, DC, MC, V. **Amenities:** Restaurant; bar; room service. *In room:* TV.

Moderate

In addition to the places listed below, **Casa Ovalle** (ⓒ **502/7832-3031;** www. hotelcasaovalle.com) is another excellent, intimate bed-and-breakfast housed in a converted home.

Casa Azul ★ Unlike most of the other hotels in Antigua, this place has a modern and eclectic style, with an array of furniture styles from Art Deco to contemporary. The rooms all have very high ceilings, especially those on the second floor. My favorite room in the house is no. 8, a second-floor corner unit with lots of space and great views over the rooftops of Antigua. Casa Azul is very well located, just a half-block from the Plaza Mayor. There's no restaurant here but breakfast is served, and a host of restaurants are located nearby.

4a Av. Norte, #5. ⓒ **502/7832-0961.** Fax 502/7832-0944. www.guate.com/casaazul/english. 14 units. $90 double. Rates include breakfast. Rates lower in the off season, higher during peak periods. AE, DC, MC, V. Parking nearby. **Amenities:** Jacuzzi; small outdoor pool; sauna. *In room:* TV.

Casa Capuchinas ★ This small bed-and-breakfast sits right across the street from the Convento de las Capuchinas. A large lawn and garden area sits just behind the high wall that runs along 2a Avenida Norte. The hotel is built in an L shape, with a couple of rooms set near the street, and the rest farther back. I recommend room no. 2, a very large second-floor room with a king-size bed, a beautiful mosaic tub and shower, and a great view of the hotel's gardens and the convent. All of the rooms have fireplaces and lively decor, with contrasting pastel walls and local textiles and furniture.

2a Av. Norte, #7. ⓒ **502/7832-0121.** Fax 506/7832-7941. www.casacapuchinas.com. 8 units. $79–$99 double. Rates include full breakfast. AE, MC, V. **Amenities:** Room service. *In room:* TV.

Hotel San Jorge   This simple hotel provides clean and comfortable rooms at a reasonable price, but you won't get many frills, and very little in the way of colonial ambience. The rooms, which front a small garden with a fountain and white wrought-iron garden furniture, are all carpeted, feature a working fireplace, have a small desk and chair, and share a common veranda. There's no restaurant here, but a good breakfast is served.

4a Av. Sur, #13. ℂ/fax **502/7832-3132.** www.hotelsanjorgeantigua.com. 12 units. $61 double. Rates include tax and continental breakfast. Rates slightly higher during peak weeks. AE, DC, MC, V. Free parking. **Amenities:** Room service; free Wi-Fi. *In room:* TV.

Inexpensive

Backpackers and budget hounds might want to look into **Kafka** (ℂ **502/5270-6865;** kafkaantigua@gmail.com), the **Black Cat Hostel** (ℂ **502/7832-1229;** www.blackcathostels.net), or **Jungle Party Hostel** (ℂ **502/7832-0463;** www.junglepartyhostal.com).

Hotel Posada La Merced ☺   This economical option is located right near La Merced church. The rooms are spread around a sprawling, converted colonial-style home, and all open on to one of two central courtyard areas. The rooms are simple, clean, and homey. A modest amount of local artwork and neo-colonial wooden furniture livens up the rooms. There are a couple of apartments with kitchenettes for longer stays, and two-bedroom/one-bathroom "suites" that are good for families. There's also a large communal kitchen for all of the guests to use. The owner and staff here are quite personable and helpful.

7a Av. Norte, #43. ℂ **502/7832-3197** or 7832-3301. www.posadalamercedantigua.com. 23 units. $40–$60 double. Rates lower in the off season; higher during peak periods. Rates include taxes. AE, DC, MC, V. Parking nearby. **Amenities:** Free Wi-Fi. *In room:* No phone.

Posada Asjemenou   Located near the Santa Catalina Arch, this budget hotel has a friendly, hostel-like vibe to it. Common areas are quite inviting, and are usually filled with fellow travelers reading books or playing some cards or a board game. The rooms, arranged around an interior courtyard, all feature antique tile floors, minimal furnishings, and double French doors that open onto the central courtyard. (**Note:** The panels on these doors are the only "windows" in the rooms.) Most of the bathrooms are a good size, with hot showers. There's a small Italian restaurant and pizzeria attached to the hotel. Nearby bars and clubs can be noisy at night.

Calle del Arco, #31. ℂ **502/7832-2670.** www.hotelposadaasjemenou.com. 12 units, 9 with private bathroom. $28 double with shared bathroom; $35 double with private bathroom. AE, DC, MC, V. Parking nearby. **Amenities:** Restaurant; bar; free Wi-Fi. *In room:* No phone.

Posada San Pedro 🗡   This simple budget hotel has a calm and almost refined feel when compared to the glut of hostels and hostel-like options in this price range. Most rooms come with one double and one twin bed, and all have private bathrooms. Room nos. 4, 5, and 6 on the second floor are the best rooms here, with good views from their shared veranda. There are two lounge areas with cable television. Posada San Pedro has a second location on the north side of town at 7a Av. Norte, #29 (ℂ **502/7832-0718**).

3a Av. Sur, #15. ℂ/fax **502/7832-3594.** www.posadasanpedro.net. 10 units. $40 double. Rates include tax. AE, DC, MC, V. Parking nearby. *In room:* TV, no phone.

WHERE TO DINE

Matching Antigua's abundance of top-notch hotels, boutique inns, and B&Bs, the city has a wide range of excellent dining options. In addition to the places listed below, **Fusion,** 1a Calle Poniente, #9 ★ (🕾 **502/7882-4516**), is a lively spot serving up its namesake cuisine, while **Como Como ★★**, 6a Calle Poniente, #6 (🕾 **502/7832-0478**), is a new restaurant earning rave reviews for its creative French/Belgian cuisine. Finally, **Café Mediterráneo,** 6a Calle Poniente, #6A (🕾 **502/7832-7180**), and **Queso y Vino,** 1a Calle Poniente, #1 (🕾 **502/7832-7785**), are both very good bets for Italian cuisine.

Expensive

For fancy, high-end fusion cooking in an elegant setting, you can also try the in-house restaurant at the **Palacio de Doña Leonor ★★** (see above).

El Sereno ★ INTERNATIONAL   The dining here is some of the most romantic and atmospheric in Antigua. The restaurant occupies the former home of the Royal Mercedarian Order, a religious order founded in the early 1200s by Saint Peter Nolasco that oversaw the construction of the Iglesia La Merced. The fusion-tinged Continental cuisine is quite good. The regularly changing menu might include a tomato-curry soup for starters, and some imported New Zealand lamb with a rich wine reduction for a main course. Local ingredients and traditional Guatemala dishes are often featured as well.

My favorite spot is the small rooftop terrace with its small bar area and fabulous views over the town. Even if you don't dine here, be sure to come for a drink. In addition to the terrace, there are a number of elegant dining rooms with fireplaces and rich decor.

4a Av. Norte, #16. 🕾 **502/7832-0501.** www.elsereno.com.gt. Reservations recommended. Main courses Q110–Q250. AE, MC, V. Daily noon–10pm.

Mesón Panza Verde ★★★ 🛏 INTERNATIONAL/FUSION   This hotel houses my favorite restaurant in Antigua. The ambience is fabulous, the service professional and attentive, and the food superb. Chef Christophe Pache blends traditional French techniques and training with a wide range of world influences. Try the sea bass with fresh grapes in a white-wine cream sauce, or the *Geschnetzeltes Zurich*—pork tenderloin in a cognac and demi-glace sauce—from the chef's native Switzerland. Tables are spread around several open-air terraces, assorted rooms, and nooks; my favorite seats are poolside under a vaulted stone roof. Enjoy live jazz Wednesday through Friday nights, and Sunday during brunch. This place has an extensive and reasonably priced wine list, as well as some good top-shelf cognacs, tequilas, rums, and single-malt whiskeys.

5a Av. Sur, #19. 🕾 **502/7832-1745.** www.panzaverde.com. Reservations recommended. Main courses Q80–Q160. AE, DC, MC, V. Mon–Sat noon–3pm and 7–10pm; Sun 10am–4pm and 7–10pm.

Nokiate ★ SUSHI/PAN-ASIAN/LATIN FUSION   With an extensive and eclectic menu, this dimly lit restaurant and lounge is a good place to go for a real change of pace, scenery, and cuisine. The small sushi bar puts out some creative rolls, including one featuring shrimp, tempura avocado, mango, and eel sauce. I particularly like the marinated grilled spicy calamari skewers, which are a fusion of Japanese yakitori and Peruvian *anticuchos*. The adjacent bar features chill-out music and regular martini nights.

1a Av. Sur, #7. ℂ **502/7832-9239.** www.nokiate.com. Main courses Q80–Q145. AE, MC, V. Mon–Fri 6:30–10:30pm; Sat–Sun 12:30–10:30pm.

Welten ★★ INTERNATIONAL   This refined restaurant is an Antiguan institution. Tables are spread through several rooms of a converted old mansion, as well as under verdant vines in an interior courtyard. My favorite seats, however, are under a canvas awning around the edge of a small pool, which is filled with rose petals and floating candles at night. The food is wonderfully prepared and the service excellent. The menu features a broad range of Continental fare with heavy French and Italian influences. You can get a tender steak in green peppercorn sauce, or a fresh fish filet with white wine, cream, and mushrooms. There are several pasta selections, of which I recommend the homemade *cannelloni* stuffed with turkey and chicken in a cognac and pepper sauce.

4a Calle Oriente, #21. ℂ **502/7832-4335** or 7832-6967. www.weltenrestaurant.com. Reservations recommended. Main courses Q90–Q165. AE, DC, MC, V. Mon, Wed–Thurs 11am–10pm; Fri–Sat noon–11pm; Sun noon–10pm.

Moderate

Bistrot 5 ★★★ FRENCH/BISTRO   This homey restaurant offers a wide-ranging menu of classic French dishes, as well as a mix of more contemporary bistro concoctions and a chalkboard list of daily specials. Start things off with some traditional escargot or frog legs, or venture further afield and try the shrimp sliders. Whatever you do, don't pass up the *pied du cohon,* a classic French preparation of pigs feet. Main courses are all excellent; check out the daily special, or try the short rib risotto or honey-glazed duck. Despite the large space, the restaurant is cozy and romantic, with an open kitchen, marble-topped tables, a high vaulted wooden plank ceiling with a beautiful wine-bottle chandelier, and plenty of candles spread all around.

4a Calle Oriente, #7. ℂ **502/7832-5510.** www.bistrotcinq.com. Reservations recommended. Main courses Q78–Q145. AE, MC, V. Mon–Fri 6–10:30pm; Sat–Sun noon–11pm.

Caffé Opera ★ ITALIAN   With the casual feel of a neighborhood trattoria, this place serves up excellent pasta dishes, traditional panini, and more hearty entrees, such as tenderloin with arugula or rabbit in red-wine sauce. The wine list is excellent, and be sure to save room for dessert, say some tiramisu, with a cup of expertly prepared espresso or cappuccino.

6a Av. Norte, #17. ℂ **502/7832-0727.** www.cafe-opera.com. Reservations recommended. Main courses Q45–Q120. AE, DC, MC, V. Thurs–Tues 12:30–10:30pm.

El Sabor del Tiempo INTERNATIONAL/ITALIAN   This dimly lit place feels cozy and well-worn (in a good way). There's a range of reasonable pasta dishes, pizza, and panini. For something more substantial, I recommend the rabbit in rosemary sauce. They also have beer on tap and a good wine list.

3a Calle Poniente and Calle del Arco. ℂ **502/7832-0516.** Main courses Q60–Q134; pastas Q60–Q75. AE, MC, V. Daily noon–10pm.

Gaia MIDDLE EASTERN   This Middle Eastern restaurant is a pleasant change of pace in Antigua. I like to come here in the afternoon for a cooling mint iced tea and a light bite, as well as for a meal in the evening, which could include staples such as falafel, hummus, chicken kabobs, and couscous, and bigger entrees such as a full steak or a grilled chicken plate. Throw pillows are strewn on low benches in the front and back rooms, and the courtyard offers several semi-private gazebos and a few low tables with sturdy ottomans.

5a Av., #35A. ℂ **502/7832-3670.** www.gaiarestaurante.com. Main courses Q58–Q110. AE, DC, MC, V. Daily noon–1am.

Hector's ★★★ 🖥 INTERNATIONAL   Almost always bustling, this tiny little restaurant serves up excellent bistro-style fare in a cozy and amiable space. There are only six or so tables and a few chairs at a small bar, which fronts the open kitchen. There are always daily specials, a pasta option, and some regular favorites such as beef bourguignon. I recommend the seared duck breast served over a potato-and-carrot gratin, with some balsamic-roasted grapes along for the ride. There's no sign here, and owner/chef Hector Castro says the place really doesn't have an official name, but you'll be able to find it, right across from La Merced Church.

1a Calle Poniente, #9A. ℂ **502/7832-9867.** Main courses Q55–Q135. AE, MC, V. Daily 12:30–10pm.

La Fonda de la Calle Real ★ GUATEMALAN   This is *the* place to come in Antigua for authentic Guatemalan cuisine, but don't expect a quiet, laid-back joint. This place is so popular, in fact, that they have three branches in town—all within a block of one another. The menu features a range of classic Guatemalan dishes from *pepian,* a spicy chicken dish, to *kac ik,* a filling turkey soup from the Cobán region. All of the branches do a good job of re-creating a sense of colonial ambience with wood furniture and tall-backed chairs. I like the second-floor seating at the original outlet listed below, but the location at 3a Calle Poniente, #7, is much more spacious.

5a Av. Norte, #12. ℂ **502/7832-0507.** www.lafondadelacallereal.com. Main courses Q75–Q125. AE, DC, MC, V. Mon–Thurs 8am–10pm; Fri–Sat 8am–11pm; Sun 8am–9pm.

Tartines ★ 🖥 FRENCH/INTERNATIONAL   Guatemala City's longstanding favorite French chef Jean Francois has moved to Antigua, and downsized somewhat with this casual bistro-style restaurant. The menu features a small selection of main courses, featuring duck with a different sauce daily, and steak served several ways, as well as some pasta dishes, a few crepe options, and a range of salads, soups, and Panini. The highlight here, for me, is the lovely second floor covered patio seating overlooking the ruins of the city's main Cathedral.

4a Calle Oriente, #1C. ℂ **502/7882-4606.** Main courses Q60–Q180. AE, DC, MC, V. Tue–Wed 11am–7pm; Thurs–Sat 11am–10pm; Sun 11am–4pm.

Inexpensive

Café Condesa 🍴 INTERNATIONAL   Located just off the central park, this place is a great choice for breakfast, coffee, or a light lunch. The sandwiches are very creative and made with homemade bread. I like the vegetarian La Tara, with home-made herb garlic cheese and tomato pistou. You can also opt for one of several quiche options or a large salad, and finish with one of the fresh pies or desserts. Sundays feature an all-you-can-eat brunch. Even when this place is packed—which it often is—the service is extremely fast. The restaurant is tucked in the back of a small collection of shops, inside the Casa del Conde.

5a Av. Norte, #4. ℂ **502/7832-0038.** Breakfast Q30–Q50; salads and sandwiches Q32–Q50; dessert Q16–Q22. AE, DC, MC, V. Sun–Thurs 7am–8pm; Fri–Sat 7am–9pm.

Café Flor 🍴 THAI/PAN-ASIAN   This place is consistently packed with backpackers, language students, and assorted tourists, and while I can find no fault with the welcoming and lively ambience or the prices, the food, which is often bland and inauthentic, and service, which is lax, are severe disappointments. Still, if you want a filling and very reasonably priced plate of curried vegetables or chicken in a convivial spot with live piano music, this place is just fine.

4a Av. Sur, #1. ✆ **502/7832-5274.** Main courses Q52–Q80. AE, MC, V. Daily 11am–11pm.

Café Sky 📷 INTERNATIONAL   If you're looking for a relaxed restaurant with a great ambience, hearty food, and fantastic views, you can't beat Café Sky. I love coming here for drinks and appetizers, but their grilled steaks, baby back ribs, and grilled chicken main courses are also good. They also do excellent breakfasts, which are served throughout the day. There's view seating on the second and third floors here, as well as indoor dining rooms, when neither the weather nor view are up to snuff.

1a Av. Sur, #15. ✆ **502/7832-7300.** Main courses Q80–Q130. AE, DC, MC, V. Daily 8am–10pm.

Doña Luisa Xicoteneatl GUATEMALAN/BAKERY   This is Antigua's original backpacker hangout, and it's still going strong. The crowded bulletin board continues to be a major resource for fellow travelers to leave and receive information. Breakfast is wonderful here, with strong Guatemalan coffee and fresh-baked bread and goodies. Later in the day you can get sandwiches, burgers, burritos, or more substantial main dishes. Try to grab a view table on the second floor, though the fauna-filled, open-air courtyard is also delightful.

4a Calle Oriente, #12. ✆ **502/7832-2578.** Main courses Q24–Q80. AE, DC, MC, V. Daily 7am–9:30pm.

WHAT TO SEE & DO

Antigua is a fabulous city for a leisurely stroll, and along the way you can visit a museum or do some shopping. If you want to see things on your own, the following descriptions of the main attractions will help you choose what interests you most. There are also a number of tour agencies in town, and most hotels have a tour desk. All of these offer a standard city tour, as well as visits to volcanoes, Chichicastenango market, Lake Atitlán, and 1-day and multiday trips to Tikal. If you're not happy with the offerings at you hotel's tour desk, try **Lax Travel Antigua** ★, 3a Calle Poniente, #12 (✆ **502/7832-1621**); **Sin Fronteras** ★, 5a Av. Norte, #15A (✆ **502/7720-4400;** www.sinfront.com); and **Rainbow Travel Center** ★, 7a Av. Sur, #8 (✆ **502/7931-7878;** www.rainbowtravelcenter.com).

The best city tours available are the walking tours offered by **Antigua Tours** ★★ (✆ **502/7832-5821;** www.antiguatours.net). They offer a wide range of tour and hotel booking options, but are best known for their walking tours with longtime resident and author Elizabeth Bell, whose books about Antigua include *Antigua Guatemala: The City And Its Heritage*. The 3-hour tour leaves Tuesday through Saturday at 9:30am and Monday and Thursday at 2pm and costs $20. On days when Bell is not available, other well-trained and personable guides lead the tour. These folks have an office on the west side of the main plaza, next to the Café Condesa, and another next to the Casa Santo Domingo.

If you're looking for adventure, contact **Old Town Outfitters** ★★ (✆ **502/5399-0440;** www.adventureguatemala.com) for mountain biking, hiking, and other activities around Antigua and the country.

Attractions

The **Plaza Mayor ★★** is the central axis of all Antigua. In colonial times, this was the city's main market and meeting area. Today, it's a great place to grab a shady seat and watch the parade of life pass before you. The current park was built in the 20th century, and covers a full city block with towering trees, well-tended gardens, various pathways lined with sturdy benches, and a beautiful fountain at its core. Teenage boys get a big kick out of the sculpted sirens lining the inside of the fountain, which is filled by a steady stream of water shooting out of their breasts.

Catedral San José ★   Vowing to learn from the destruction of the cathedral during the earthquakes of 1583, the city (then called Santiago de los Caballeros de Guatemala) began construction of a new, more complex, and supposedly stronger cathedral in 1669. The structure, completed in 1680, contained seven entrances, five naves, 78 arches, 18 chapels, a main sacristy, and a main chamber. Unfortunately, seismology tends to repeat itself, and that cathedral was leveled in the great earthquake of 1773. You can visit the ruins from the south gate on 5a Calle Oeste. The entire structure was rebuilt in the 19th century (the sacrarium is the only piece used from the original). Embedded in the facade are several figures: the Virgen de la Asunción (Virgin of Assumption), Santiago Apóstol (Protector of the City), Padre Eterno (Eternal Father), the Doce Apóstoles (Twelve Apostles), and the four Padres de la Iglesia (Church Fathers), as well as the Protectoral Coat of Arms and a shell crossed by swords (a symbol of the Holy Protector). The interior is less impressive but houses a statue of Christ carved by Quirio Cataño, famous for carving the **Black Christ** of Esquipulas (p. 229).

4a Av. Norte, on the east side of Plaza Mayor. *Ⓒ* **502/7832-0909.** Admission Q10 to visit the ruins; free for the main cathedral. Daily 9am–5pm.

Museo del Libro Antiguo   The site of the first printing press in Guatemala (1660), this museum lies within the Palacio del Noble Ayuntamiento. There are three exhibition rooms. The first is an overview of the history of Gutenberg's invention, including a wooden replica of the original printing equipment and works printed on the original Guatemalan press. The second goes into more technical detail about the processes of xylography (printing on wood) and lithography (printing on stone). The last exhibition is dedicated to books decorated with a range of marbling techniques which give them a special appearance and texture. The museum's prized possession is a copy of *Explicatio Apologetica,* which, when published in 1663, was the first book printed in Guatemala. Because of the fragile state of much of the collection, photography, with or without flash, is prohibited.

4a Calle Poniente, on the north side of the Plaza Mayor, inside the Palacio del Noble Ayuntamiento. *Ⓒ* **502/7832-5511.** Admission Q30. Tues–Fri 9am–4pm; Sat–Sun 9am–noon and 2–4pm.

Museo de Santiago   In 1956, the colonial-era jail in the Palacio del Noble Ayuntamiento was converted into a museum, presenting relics from the glory days of the city to a captive audience. Its five exhibition rooms take visitors back to the city's founding as Santiago de los Caballeros de Guatemala, displaying centuries-old artwork, tools, and other objects. The collection includes sculptures, ceramics, heraldry (official crests of families, cities, or institutions), metalwork, furniture, and weapons. Most of the pieces here date from between the 16th and 18th centuries. Some of the most popular items are the cannons, shields, and muskets in the collection of arms, some of which visitors can hold in order to feel their impressive weight.

4a Calle Poniente, on the north side of the Plaza Mayor, inside the Palacio del Noble Ayuntamiento. ✆ **502/7832-2868.** Admission Q30. Tues–Fri 9am–4pm; Sat–Sun 9am–noon and 2–4pm.

Palacio del Noble Ayuntamiento   This 1743 structure was designed by Luis Diez de Navarro, Juan de Dios Aristondo, and Diego de Porras. Its impressive two-story facade is constructed of a double layer of stone archways supported by columns. The eastern wall has one of the few carved stone exteriors surviving from the 18th century. Originally the seat of the Spanish colonial government and a jail, it now houses the *municipalidad,* or city government, the Museo del Libro Antiguo, and the Museo de Santiago.

4a Calle Poniente, on the north side of Plaza Mayor. No phone. Free admission. Daily 9am–4pm.

Palacio de los Capitanes Generales   For 200 years, this was the home of the Spanish viceroy, making it the seat of power for all of Central America. The original building, modified many times over the centuries, was constructed in the late 1500s and held the court of law, provincial offices, post office, treasury, royal office, servants' quarters, and horse stables within its more than 20,000 sq. m (215,000 sq. ft.).

5a Calle Poniente, on the south side of the Plaza Mayor. No phone.

NORTH OF THE PLAZA MAYOR

The most distinguishing architectural feature north of Plaza Mayor—even more so than the Convento de las Capuchinas and the Iglesia La Merced (see below)—is the **Arco de Santa Catalina (Santa Catalina Arch).** This high arch spans 5a Avenida Norte, about 3 blocks north of the Plaza Mayor. The arch was built in the mid–17th century to allow nuns to pass from one part of the Santa Catalina Convent to the other without being seen. In the 19th century, a clock was added to a large cupola atop the center point of the beautiful yellow arch. Today, 5a Avenida Norte is often called Calle del Arco.

Cerro de la Cruz ★   The Cerro de la Cruz, a hill north of the city with a big cross mounted on it, offers the best view of Antigua. You can climb the hill on foot (20–30 min. from the Plaza Mayor), or get there by car or taxi. The trail leading up to the overlook has a well-earned reputation for petty crime, so never go alone. The tourist police will accompany you during certain hours; check in at their office at 4a Avenida Norte, next to the Palacio del Noble Ayuntamiento.

Out beyond 1a Av. Norte. No phone. Free admission. Daily 9am–5pm.

Convento de las Capuchinas ★★   The Capuchins are a Roman Catholic order who seek sanctification through a life of work, privation, and continual penitence. Unlike other convents of old, the Convento de las Capuchinas did not require women to donate a dowry to join, though in Antigua that egalitarian outlook kept their ranks at less than 28 nuns. Completed in 1736, the impressive convent was abandoned after an earthquake in 1773 scared the nuns to safer ground. Fortunately the damage was relatively minor, and the well-preserved courtyards, gardens, bathing halls, and nuns' private cells are now open to the public. Mannequins now occupy some of those cells, demonstrating cloistered life. The roof is a great place to take in a sweeping view of the city.

2a Av. Norte and 2a Calle Oriente. ✆ **502/7832-0743.** Admission Q40, Q20 students and children 11 and under. Daily 9am–5pm.

Iglesia La Merced ★★★ This church's central plaza is one of the most important launching points for processions during Holy Week. Built in a baroque style and adorned with stucco pilasters, it's also one of the best restored and preserved in the city. Famous architect Juan de Dios began work on the building in 1749, and completed it in 1767. The facade of the yellow temple is adorned with amazing detail, and several impressive paintings can be found inside, including the well-known work *Jesus Nazareno*. The previous incarnation of the church had, like all the others in town, been destroyed by an earthquake some years before. This incarnation was to suffer the same fate, though it has been restored after years of abandonment.

Just to the side of the church are the ruins of the **Convento La Merced,** a 16th-century convent with an enormous star-shaped pond and a beautifully decorated octagonal fountain in the courtyard. There are excellent views from the convent's second floor and rooftop.

1a Calle Poniente and 6a Av. Norte. No phone. Free admission to the church; Q5 to visit the convent ruins. Daily 7am-8pm.

SOUTHEAST OF THE PLAZA MAYOR

Museo de Arte Colonial The Museum of Colonial Art is located on the premises of what was once the University of San Carlos, a building whose cloisters are relatively well preserved given the city's shaky past. The museum's collection consists largely of paintings and statues commissioned by Spanish *hidalgos* (noblemen) in the 17th century, but includes photographs of contemporary Semana Santa (Holy Week) celebrations.

4a Av. Sur and Calle de la Universidad. ✆ **502/7832-0429.** Admission Q50. Tues-Fri 9am-4pm; Sat-Sun 9am-noon and 2-4pm.

WEST OF THE PLAZA MAYOR

Casa del Tejido Antiguo ★ This museum will tell you everything you ever wanted to know about textiles. It has a sizeable collection of typical clothing from various regions of Guatemala. The exhibits of colorful, vintage *cortes* and *huipiles* are complemented by ample information on how they're woven, the history of the process, and the broader cultural significance of Maya cloth. Informative placards explain the exhibits, but guided tours in English and Spanish are available and recommended if you're deeply interested in the subject. A gift shop has various handmade items for sale. The selection is good, and the products are guaranteed to be authentic, but you'll probably find better prices elsewhere.

1a Calle Poniente, #51, btw. Ruinas Recolección and San Jerónimo. ✆ **502/7832-3169.** Admission Q5. Mon-Fri 9am-5:30pm; Sat 9am-4pm.

Centro Cultural La Azotea ★★ This complex of attractions gives a good glimpse into several facets of local life. My favorite museum here is dedicated to Maya music (*K'ojom* is the word for "music" in three Mayan languages), and is based on the field work of ethnomusicologist Samuel Franco. The extensive multimedia archive contains hours of music and sounds, video footage, and color slides recorded during patron-saint festivals and other rituals. A small gift shop sells crafts, recordings of Guatemalan music, and a few instruments. However, you'll also want to leave time for the neighboring coffee museum and small working coffee plantation, which has been roasting and harvesting beans since 1883. Other exhibits here present peeks into the daily life of typical Mayan indigenous communities around the country. La Azotea is located in the neighboring town of Jocotenango, about a mile from

SEMANA santa (HOLY WEEK)

The Christian **Semana Santa** ★★★ celebrations in Antigua are an extravagant mix of religious fervor, civic pride, and artistic achievement. Throughout the week there are a score of masses, vigils (*velaciones*), and public processions. The processions can vary in size, and are often made up of hundreds of worshipers, who include men in regal purple robes, women in white linens and lace, and ubiquitous incense carriers. Other processions feature men in white hooded costumes (whose style was later borrowed by the Ku Klux Klan), women in somber black dresses (as if in mourning), and the occasional horseback-riding members. Most carry large floats (*andas*) with sculptures of Jesus Christ, Mary Magdalene, and other saints.

Some of the *andas* are enormous (as much as 3 tons) and require as many as 100 men to carry each on their shoulders. As these huge floats make their slow way down the rugged streets, they lurch from side to side, often seeming as if they will topple (they *very* rarely do). Individual processions can last for many hours, and you'll notice a complex choreography used to keep the shoulders and legs of those carrying them fresh.

Although the celebrations officially begin on Ash Wednesday, the real spectacle begins on Palm Sunday and peaks on Good Friday. Throughout the week, elements of the Passion, Crucifixion, and Resurrection are reenacted and celebrated. The sheer scope and abundance of the celebrations are hard to describe. The smell of incense and a thick smoke often hang heavy over the whole city.

If you plan on coming during Semana Santa, book your room well in advance, as much as a year or more in some of the more popular hotels here. The real score during Holy Week are rooms overlooking some of the streets on the processional routes. Of the hotels listed earlier, **Hotel Posada de Don Rodrigo** and the **Palacio de Doña Leonor** both have choice second-floor rooms with balconies fronting one or more of the processional routes. *Warning:* Be careful as you enjoy the Semana Santa celebrations. Pickpockets and petty thieves thrive in the crowded streets. Leave your money and valuables in your hotel safe.

Antigua. The center provides hourly transportation to and from Antigua from several convenient pick-up points, otherwise, taxis charge between Q20 and Q40 ($2.50–$5) each way.

At the end of Calle del Cemetario Final, Jocotenango. ℂ **502/7831-1120.** www.centroazotea.com. Admission Q50; Q25 students. Mon–Fri 8:30am–5pm; Sat 8:30am–3pm.

Other Activities

There are a host of Spanish-language schools in Antigua. Most offer small group or individual immersion-style classes between 4 and 5 hours daily, as well as various other activities and guided trips and tours. Most offer the option of a homestay with a local family, or a booking at any one of many hotels around the city. The schools I recommend include **Academia de Español Antigüeña,** 1a Calle Poniente, #10 (ℂ **502/7832-7241;** www.spanishacademyantiguena.com); **Academia de Español Guatemala** ★, 7a. Avenida Norrte # 63 (ℂ **502/7832-5057;** www.acad.conexion.com); **Centro Lingüístico Maya** ★, 5a Calle Poniente, #20 (ℂ **502/7832-0656;**

www.clmaya.com); and **Escuela de Español San José el Viejo** ★★, 5a Av. Sur, #34 (𝄞 **502/7832-3028**; www.sanjoseelviejo.com).

Rates run $125 to $300 per week including classes, excursions, homestay, and airport transfers.

If you want to do volunteer work in the area, check in with **Proyecto Mosaico** ★, 3a Av. Norte, #3 (𝄞/fax **502/5817-6660**; www.promosaico.org), an organization that formed in the wake of Hurricane Mitch and works as a clearinghouse to connect volunteers with worthy projects and organizations around Guatemala.

OUTDOOR ACTIVITIES

Most visitors come to Antigua for the history, culture, dining, and shopping, but outdoor enthusiasts will find there's plenty here for them, too.

BIKING   The rural back roads, volcanoes, and mountains around Antigua are perfect for mountain biking. **Old Town Outfitters** ★★ (𝄞 **502/5399-0440**; www.adventureguatemala.com) has quality equipment and offers a variety of rides and tours, ranging from half-day mellow rides to multiday excursions. "The Spinal Cord" journeys along a narrow ridge through the mountains above Antigua. Multiday tours might include a 2-day pedal (mountain bike) and paddle (kayak) around Lake Atitlán. Rates average around $35 for a half-day tour, and $70 for a full-day outing, to $150 to $250 for the 2-day excursions.

GOLF   Golf is not a major attraction in Guatemala, but avid golfers will want to head to the outskirts of Antigua and check out the Peter Dye–designed "Mayan Fire" course at **La Reunion** ★★ (𝄞 **502/7873-1440**; www.lareunion.com.gt). Greens fees run $80 Sunday through Friday, and $100 on Saturday. Club and cart rentals are also available.

HIKING & CLIMBING   Building on their success in the mountain bike arena, the folks at **Old Town Outfitters** (see above) have also emerged as the best agency for those looking to hike one of the nearby volcanoes such as Acatenango, Pacaya, or Agua (see later in this chapter) or do some rock climbing. These hikes range from $30 to $50 for a day hike to around $75 to $100 for overnight camping trips to any of the volcanoes.

HORSEBACK RIDING   The same back roads and trails that are so well suited to mountain biking are also perfect for horseback rides. If you want to explore the region by horseback, contact Fred and Paula at **Ravenscroft Riding Stables,** on the road to Santa María de Jesús (𝄞 **502/7830-6669**). Rates run around $25 to $30 per hour.

JOGGING   Be careful jogging around Antigua; if the tight streets and unforgiving drivers don't get you, muggers just might. The popular and attractive Cerro de la Cruz makes a great jogging route. However, I know of several incidents over the years when joggers were attacked. Single women in particular should be on guard.

YOGA, SPAS & GYMS   Many of the higher-end hotels have a small gym or spa. If yours doesn't, and you're looking to stretch out, burn some calories or get pampered, there are several options around town. For yoga classes I recommend contacting the folks at **Yoga Antigua** (✆ 502/7832-8202), who offer a range of regularly scheduled and private class options.

For a good workout, head to **Antigua's Gym** (✆ 502/7832-7554) at 6a Calle Poniente, #31, or **La Fábrica Gimnasio** (✆ 502/7832-0486; www.gimnasiola fabrica.com) at Calle del Hermano Pedro, #16. Rates for a specific class or day pass run between Q40 and Q80.

For some pampering, head to the **Healing Hands Therapy Spa** (✆ 502/7832-1648), 3a Av. Norte, #20A, or **Mayan Spa** (✆ 502/7832-8987; www.mayan-spa.com), with two convenient downtown locations. Both offer a wide range of massages and spa treatments.

SWIMMING   If your hotel doesn't have a pool, you can use the one at the **Porta-hotel Antigua,** 8a Calle Poniente, #1 (✆ 502/7832-2801), for Q80. Children 12 and under are Q40. Open daily from 6am to 8pm.

A Coffee Tour . . . and More

Just outside of Antigua, in the tiny village of San Felipe de Jesus, sits **Finca Filadelfia ★★** (✆ 502/7728-0812; www.filadelfiaresort.com), a large coffee farm and plantation. In addition to coffee tours and cupping demonstrations, this place offers mule rides, bird watching expeditions, mountain bike and hiking tours, and a zip-line canopy adventure, with two separate zip-line courses. They also have a few luxury rooms and suites, as well, and an excellent restaurant on site. Free transportation is offered four times daily from points in downtown Antigua. The traditional coffee tour costs $18, while other adventure tour options run from $20 to $75. Various packages are available, and reservations are recommended. The plantation is open daily from 9am to 5pm, though the last coffee tour heads out at 2pm.

Going Nuts: Valhalla Macadamia Nut Farm

The **Valhalla Macadamia Nut Farm** (✆ 502/7831-5799; www.exvalhalla.net) is an interesting project working toward reversing global warming, assisting local indigenous populations in finding alternative and sustainable sources of food and income, reforesting tropical forests, and providing public education in the areas of conservation and sustainable development. The folks at this farm offer a free educational tour of their macadamia farm. They also offer up their very famous macadamia pancakes and other macadamia and homemade chocolate products. If you're willing to commit a full month to the task, ask about volunteer opportunities here. This working farm is located at Km 52.5 on the route to San Miguel Duenas and is open daily, but advance reservations are highly recommended.

SHOPPING ★★★

Antigua is probably the best city for shopping in all of Central America. Options range from high-end jewelry and clothing stores to fine art galleries and open-air street vendors selling locally produced crafts and textiles. There are shops to fit all budgets and tastes.

The streets closest to Plaza Mayor are peppered with souvenir stores hawking T-shirts and key chains, shops selling high-end jewelry, top-notch art galleries, and more. About 3 blocks west of Plaza Mayor is the *mercado municipal,* or public market, as well as an organized handicraft and artisans market.

In general, prices are higher in Antigua than anywhere else in Guatemala. The higher-end stores have set prices, and rarely budge on them. However, the handicraft and souvenir outlets, as well as the larger markets and street vendors, will all bargain.

Shopping A to Z

ART

Galería Panza Verde   This small gallery on the second floor of Mesón Panza Verde features a regularly rotating exhibition of contemporary Guatemalan and international art, as well as a small semi-permanent collection, including excellent works by one of the owners. Open daily 11am to 7pm. 5a Av. Sur, #19, La Antigua. 🕾 **502/7832-7920**.

La Antigua Galería de Arte ★   This gallery features artists from all over Latin America and a few from the U.S. and Europe. The works are all well displayed in the rooms of a beautiful colonial-era home. Open Mon-Sat 10am to 7pm and Sunday noon to 6pm. 4a Calle Oriente, #15. 🕾 **502/7832-2124**. www.artintheamericas.com.

Wer ★★   Owned by local artist Alejandro Wer, this converted 250-year-old home houses a massive collection of contemporary Guatemalan art by more than 100 artists in several of its rooms. Open daily 9am to 5:30pm. 4a Calle Oriente, #27. 🕾 **502/7832-7161**.

CANDIES & CHOCOLATE

Doña María Gordillo ★   This place, which traces its origins to 1874, is an institution, and justifiably so. A glass counter filled with a wide range of homemade sweets—made from marzipan, shredded coconut, dulce de leche, and candied fruit—runs the length of the storefront. You'll have plenty of time to marvel at the extensive collection of children's ceramic savings banks, most in the shape of owls,

---

Before You Buy

If you're planning to head to the large and hectic markets—whether here, in Chichicastenango, or around the country—to bargain and shop, it's good to get an idea of what to look for before you dive in. I recommend visiting **Casa de Artes** or **Nim Po't** before setting out in search of any arts, crafts, or textiles. The folks at Casa de Artes carry high-end pieces, and their staff is very knowledgeable, so you can learn the difference between a quality piece of work and something that's mass produced. Be sure to ask where the different styles are from, and see if any specific town or region strikes your fancy. Their selection of *huipiles* is top-notch.

since this place is almost always packed, and there's little rhyme or reason to their method of dealing with the crowds. Open daily 10:30am to 2pm and 3 to 7pm. 4a Calle Oriente, #11. ✆ **502/7832-0403**.

CLOTHING

K'frans ★   These folks manufacture and sell cotton clothing for men and women featuring their original designs. They have a sister shop in Panajachel. Open daily 9am to 7pm. 4a Calle Poniente #19. ✆ **502/7832-9264**.

HANDICRAFTS & SOUVENIRS

Casa de Artes ★   If you're looking for the best, this is it—but you'll pay for it. This is probably the art-and-handicraft shop with the highest-end selection. Different rooms are dedicated to woodcarvings, traditional textiles, ceramics, jewelry, and paintings. Open Monday to Saturday 9am to 1pm and 2:30 to 6:30pm, and by appointment. 4a Av. Sur, #11. ✆ **502/7832-0792**. www.casadeartes.com.gt.

Colibrí   This is a good shop for a variety of craft and textile products from around Guatemala, particularly baskets and other woven works. Open daily 9am to 6pm. 4a Calle Oriente, #3B. ✆ **502/7832-0280**.

JEWELRY

There's a glut of shops and street vendors selling jewelry around Antigua. Many specialize in jade and are truly superlative, and at the better shops, you can even design a custom piece.

Jades Imperio Maya ★   This shop produces high-quality works in jade, including some interesting and original jewelry designs, which are displayed in a showroom with plenty of light and accessible displays. In addition to the main branch listed here, these folks also have storefronts on 4a Calle Poniente, #16B and 4a Calle Oriente, #5C. Open daily 9am to 6:30pm. 5a Calle Oriente, #2. ✆ **502/7832-0925**. www.jades imperiomaya.com.

Jades S.A.   These folks are pioneers of Guatemala's jade industry, and this location, their main factory, is a museum of their impressive history and dedication to quality production. Wares range from jewelry and replica masks to assorted gift items and sculptures. They have two other storefronts in Antigua, in addition to outlets at the Hotel Casa Santo Domingo and the Marriott and Camino Real hotels in Guatemala City. Open daily 9am to 6:30pm. 4a Calle Oriente, #34. ✆ **502/7832-3841**. www.jade maya.com.

Joyería del Angel ★★ 🎁   Custom-made one-of-a-kind pieces are the forte of this place. Though many of the pieces are quite expensive, there are some more moderately priced works, as well as the occasional sale items. Open daily 9am to 6pm. 4a Calle Oriente, #5A. ✆ **502/7832-3189**. www.delangel.com.

LEATHER

Kuero's & Mucho Más ★   From run-of-the-mill belts to handbags, these are some of the best leather goods I've found around Antigua. Their goods vary in quality, but if you shop carefully, you can find great pieces at very reasonable prices. Their women's handbags and leather and textile luggage pieces are particularly good. They have another location in the Mercado de Artesanías y Compañía de Jesús (see below). Open daily 9am to 5:30pm. 4a Calle Oriente, #5. ✆ **502/7832-5006**.

GREEN WITH ENVY: THE HISTORY OF jade

The ancient Maya, Olmec, and Aztecs all treasured jade, more so than gold, and because of its durability, it was often considered strong currency in the afterlife. The name comes from the Spanish conquistadors who dubbed it *piedra de ijada* (stone of the kidney, or loins) when they saw the Maya use it to cure kidney disease. This was soon shortened to *jada,* or jade.

There are two distinct silicate rocks that are truly considered jade—nephrite and jadeite. Guatemalan jade is jadeite, which is the harder and more brilliant of the two. It's scarce and thus more valuable. Contrary to popular belief, jade is not always green. In fact, it comes in a wide range of colors, from lavender to black.

Be careful when buying jade, as jewelry made from lesser stones is pawned off as true jade. The more reputable shops in Antigua offer guarantees that their stones are authentic, and many can document the actual mine from which the stone was extracted.

MARKETS

While the prices at Nim Po't are fairly solid (they will offer slight discounts for bulk purchases if you ask), the prices at the other two markets listed here are very negotiable. Be pleasant, but persistent, and you should be able to walk away with your goods and a heavier wallet.

Mercado de Artesanías y Compañía de Jesús ★ This clean and modern facility was built to give a semi-permanent home to the many street vendors who had set up shop around Antigua. It features a tightly packed maze of small souvenir stands selling standard, mass-produced fare aimed at the unsuspecting tourist market. However, there are a few vendors selling quality wares, but you'll have to know your stuff and sift through a lot of junk to get to anything good. Open daily 8am to 7pm. 4a Calle Poniente. © **502/7832-5599**. www.munideantigua.com.

Mercado Municipal Local residents on the west end of the city come here to do their shopping among the numerous stalls connected by narrow passageways. Basic household goods, flowers, vegetables, grains, and spices are all sold here, plus some crafts and textiles. It's worth walking through just to soak in the sights and sounds, but be aware that crowded tight walkways are prime haunts for pickpockets. Open daily 7am to 5pm. 4a Calle Poniente. **No phone.**

Nim Po't ★★★ This large indoor market works as a sort of consignment warehouse for local craft and textile cooperatives selling arts, crafts, and textiles from around Guatemala. The prices here are very fair, but the quality of the merchandise varies greatly. You can, however, find excellent *huipiles* and carved masks, as well as artisanal ceramics and glasswares. In addition, they have an excellent selection of tee shirts, and more contemporary souvenirs. Open daily 9am to 9pm. 5a Av. Norte, #29. © **502/7832-2681**. www.nimpot.com.

TEXTILES

In addition to the places listed below, the **Casa del Tejido Antiguo** (see "West of the Plaza Mayor" under "Attractions" earlier in this chapter) also has a well-stocked shop. Moreover, all of the listings in the "Markets" section above have ample offerings of traditional Guatemalan textiles.

El Telar ★   The workmanship on these bedspreads, tablecloths, curtains, and other home decor items is superb, but the colors and designs tend to be rather sober. They also sell fabric in bulk. Open daily 9am to 6pm. 5a Av. Sur, #7; and 5a Av. Norte, #18. ℂ **502/7832-3179**.

Textura ★★   If you're looking for a bedspread, table settings, or a throw pillow, this is another good option. The different rooms in this store are loosely organized by color (a blue room, a red room, and so on). You can also buy fabrics in bulk here. The prices here are on the high side, but the quality is top notch. Open daily 10am to 6pm. Open until 7pm on Thursdays, Fridays, and Saturdays and until 5pm on Sundays. 5a Av. Norte, #33. ℂ **502/7832-5067**. www.cuidatuplaneta.com.

Tienda Típica Santa María 📩   Located inside the Mercado de Artesanías (see above), this stall is run by a wonderful Maya woman from Santa María. Hundreds of *huipiles* from around Guatemala are on display and stored in huge piles. While there's a lot of mediocre stuff, you can find some real gems if you're willing to dig a little. I purchased several fabulous *huipiles* from Nebaj and another from Chichicastenango from this stall. Open daily 8am to 7pm. 4a Calle Poniente. ℂ **502/5929-5083**.

ANTIGUA AFTER DARK

You'll find plenty of bars and clubs in Antigua, but overall, the nightlife scene is pretty mellow. In fact, by city ordinance, all bars and clubs must shut down by 1am. Adaptive as always, what follows are several nightly "private" after-hours parties, which are safe for tourists to attend. The parties change locations, and you'll almost certainly be handed a flier "inviting" you to one if you are still hanging around any of the bars in Antigua as the witching hour approaches.

In addition to the places listed below you can check out **La Sala,** 6a Calle Poniente, #9 (ℂ **502/7882-4237**), for everything from live sports on large screens to dancing; **Kafka,** 6a Av. Norte, #40 (ℂ **502/5270-6865**) for a mellow bar scene; and either **La Peña de Sol Latino,** 5a Calle Poniente, #15C (ℂ **502/7882-4468**; www.lapenadelsollatino.com), or **La Esquina** ★, at 6a Calle Poniente #7 (ℂ **502/ 7882-4761**), for live music.

Café No Sé ★★★   This bar is popular with a mixed crowd of locals and tourists, and just reeks of bohemia. Guitars hang from the walls, and jam sessions and poetry readings are not uncommon. They import high-quality and reasonably priced tequila and mescal from Mexico. In fact, be sure to visit the specialized mescal bar in the back, where you'll find a shrine to original owner Bo, which includes his ashes and a Bo-ximon statue, a play on Maximon statues found elsewhere in Guatemala. Open daily 11am to 1am. 1a Av. Sur, #11C, btw. 5a Calle and 6a Calle. No phone. www.cafenose.com.

Café 2000 ★   Contemporary dance, house, trance, and techno, sometimes spun by a DJ, are always on deck here. They often project free films on a large screen. Open daily 9am to midnight. 6a Av. Norte, #2. ℂ **502/7832-2981**.

Frida's   While this is a popular Mexican restaurant (with another branch in Guatemala City), I prefer to think of it, and use it, as a drinking establishment. The food is certainly acceptable, but there are better restaurants in town. However, if you want to sit around sipping margaritas and noshing on nachos while a mariachi band serenades you, this is the place to be. Open daily noon to midnight. 5a Av. Norte, #29. ℂ **502/7832-1296**. www.lasfridas.com.

JP's Rumbar ★★   This homey bar is a great place to meet, greet and converse. There are several rooms here, including a covered patio area, a good menu of New Orleans inspired dishes, and nightly live music. Open daily 11am to 11pm. 7a Calle Poniente, #12. ℂ **502/7882-4244**. www.rumbarantigua.com.

La Casbah   Located near the Santa Catalina Arch, this is Antigua's principal dance club. The music ranges from salsa and reggaetón to modern house and dance grooves, and is played loud. Casbah is known for being gay- and lesbian-friendly. Open Monday through Saturday 8pm to 1am. 5a Av. Norte, #30. ℂ **502/7832-2640**. www.lacasbah antigua.com.

La Sin Ventura   Nights here may start off mellow with a late-run movie, but things heat up later in the evening, making this a contender with **La Casbah** (above) for the best dance spot. Most nights you'll find a good mix of locals and tourists grooving to salsa, merengue, and cumbia on the crowded dance floor. Open daily noon to 1am. 5a Av. Sur, btw. 5a Calle Poniente and 6a Calle Poniente. ℂ **502/7832-0581**.

Monoloco ★   Occupying two floors of a complex that includes a popular Internet cafe, beauty salon, and gift shop, this U.S.-style sports bar and restaurant is a great place to grab a drink and some hearty bar grub. Two large flatscreen televisions show whatever game is on, and even if there's no game on, you'll still find plenty of action here most nights. Open daily 7am to 1am. 5a Av. Sur, #6. ℂ **502/7832-4235**.

Reilly's ★   The small bar area near the front of this Irish-style pub is often packed, but you'll find more space, as well as some tables and chairs, toward the side and back. This place draws a mixed crowd, but it's popular with expatriates and tourists. Open daily 2pm to 1am. 5a Av. Norte, #31. ℂ **502/5499-2331** or 5640-9860. www.reillysantigua.com.

Riki's Bar   Located inside the Café La Escudilla, this place attracts a lot of expatriates and language students, as well as Guatemala City's visiting hip and well-heeled crowd. Open daily 8am to midnight. 4a Av. Norte, #4. ℂ **502/7832-1327**.

VOLCANOES NEAR ANTIGUA

There are a handful of both dormant and active volcanoes close to Antigua. You can see several of them from almost any vantage point in the city. A couple are popular destinations for day hikes. Your best bet for hiking any of the volcanoes is to sign up for an organized tour. All of the hotel tour desks in town can set you up, or you can contact **Lax Travel Antigua** ★, 3a Calle Poniente, #12 (ℂ **502/7832-1621**); **Sin Fronteras** ★, 5a Av. Norte, #15A (ℂ **502/7720-4400;** www.sinfront.com); **Rainbow Travel Center** ★, 7a Av. Sur, #8 (ℂ **502/7931-7878;** www.rainbowtravel center.com); or **Old Town Outfitters** ★★, 5a Av. Sur, #12 (ℂ **502/5399-0440;** www.adventureguatemala.com).

VOLCÁN PACAYA ★★

About an hour-and-a-half from Antigua is the country's most popular volcano destination, **Volcán Pacaya.** Rising to 2,552m (8,370 ft.), Pacaya is in a near constant state of eruption. Tours tend to leave either very early in the morning or around 1pm. I recommend the later tours, especially in the dry season, as you may get to see some of the lava glowing red against the night sky, and it's more likely you'll be treated to the sight, sound, and smell of volcanic gases and steam.

Most ascents of Volcán Pacaya begin at **San Francisco de Sales,** where you must pay the Q30 national park entrance fee. From here you'll hike for about an hour-and-a-half to reach the base of the crater's rim, where the steep hiking trail gives way to a solid slope of loose debris made of lava rocks and ash. This final stretch is a steep and arduous scramble, with loose footings and many mini–rock slides—don't climb directly behind anyone else in your group. On the way down, more adventurous and athletic hikers can "ski" down. Some tour companies actually offer sled rides or snowboard descents.

Those who make it to the summit will encounter an otherworldly scene of smoke and gas, with the occasional volcanic belch. Some of the rocks will be very hot to the touch. When the skies are clear, the views are amazing. At times, Pacaya will let loose with a spectacular eruption. In 2010, in fact, the eruptions were quite severe, killing several people and closing Guatemala's main airport for several days.

Be sure to come well prepared. Sturdy, closed-toe hiking shoes or boots are necessary. You'll also want to bring water, a warm sweatshirt, and (if it's in the forecast) rain gear. Finally, if you're coming on one of the later tours, be sure to either bring a flashlight or make sure your tour agency provides one.

Before you go, get current safety information, in terms of both volcanic and criminal activity, from your tour agency, INGUAT, or the Antigua tourism police. It's sometimes possible to camp here, which is your best chance of seeing the nighttime lava show. If this interests you, many of the tour agencies listed above also offer camping options.

Tour prices range between Q80 and Q320 depending on the size of your group and whether or not lunch and the national park entrance are included. Some of the cut-rate agencies around Antigua will offer the trip for as little as Q50, but I'd recommend going with a reputable agency like the choices listed above and paying a few extra dollars.

VOLCÁN DE AQUA ★

Although higher than Pacaya, the 3,760m (12,333-ft.) **Volcán de Agua** is actually an easier ascent. It's also decidedly less exciting, in large part because Volcán de Agua has been dormant since the mid–16th century. Called Hunapú in the local Kaqchiquel Mayan language, its Spanish name traces back to 1541, when water and mudslides from the volcano wiped out Guatemala's then–capital city, today known as Ciudad Vieja. The hike to the summit of Volcán de Agua leaves from the town of Santa Maria de Jesus. The hike is relatively gentle and should take about 4 to 5 hours from Santa Maria to the summit. The hike down is somewhat quicker, but be careful and don't push it.

Other Volcanoes

ACATENANGO ★★

The tallest of the volcanoes ringing Antigua and the third tallest in Guatemala, **Volcán Acatenango** has two main peaks, Pico Mayor and Tres Marias. Pico Mayor is the taller of the two and peaks out at some 3,975m (13,040 ft.). Tres Marias, which is also known as Yepocapa or Tres Hermanas, rises to 3,880m (12,730 ft.). Acatenango is dormant, although it does have several small craters spewing sulfur gases. Acatenango is very close to Volcán Fuego, and the two are actually connected by a high ridge. This is the best volcano hike in the area for your money, providing spectacular panoramic views on clear days. However, the ascent is long and arduous, taking most climbers between 5 and 6 hours. Overnight trips are common here, and can sometimes be rewarded with a nighttime show from Volcán Pacaya.

FUEGO

Volcán Fuego is very active, and ascents here never get very close to the crater and are entirely dependent on current volcanic activity. Fuego's last major eruption was as recent as 1974. Fuego stands some 3,760m (12,350 ft.), although its exact altitude often changes due to volcanic activity. The Kaqchiquel called this volcano Chi Gag, or "Place of Fire."

LAKE ATITLÁN

Aldous Huxley famously claimed that Lake Atitlán ★★★ was "the most beautiful lake in the world," and that Italy's Lake Como paled in comparison. Formed thousands of years ago in the crater of a massive volcano, Lake Atitlán is more than 10 miles across at its widest point. It sits at nearly a mile high in altitude, and is surrounded on all sides by steep, verdant hills, picturesque Maya villages, and massive volcanoes with striking pointed cones. The views from the lakeshore, the hillsides above the lake, and the boats plying its waters are all stunning, and seemingly endlessly varied, as the light and cloud cover shift constantly throughout the day.

The shores of Lake Atitlán are sparsely populated with a series of small villages and a few larger towns connected by rugged roads and frequent boat traffic.

The Lake Atitlán region was severely affected by Hurricane Stan in October 2005 and again by heavy rains and storms in subsequent rainy seasons. The damage that Stan and these other storms has caused is still very evident, especially in Panajachel, Santiago Atitlán, and Santa Catarina Palapo, where landslides mark the hillsides, and the physical scars are visible on roadsides, riverbeds, and the lake shore. Landslides, flooding, and overflowing rivers continue to plague various communities around the lake, and their muddy scars are visible on the surrounding mountains and hillsides.

PANAJACHEL ★

115km (71 miles) W of Guatemala City; 37km (23 miles) S of Chichicastenango; 80km (50 miles) NW of Antigua

Panajachel is the gateway to Lake Atitlán. It's the largest city on the lake's shore and the most easily accessible by car and bus from the rest of Guatemala. Boats leave from Panajachel throughout the day bound for the various towns and villages that ring Lake Atitlán. Many, including me, find Panajachel a bit too chaotic and crowded, and prefer the quieter villages and isolated hotels around the lake. Still, Pana, as it's most commonly known, offers a wealth of dining, shopping, and tour options, and you can't beat the views, with the three major volcanoes—San Pedro, Toliman, and Atitlán—clearly visible from anywhere along the lakeshore.

Panajachel, and the rest of the north shore of Atitlán, is a predominantly Kaqchiquel Maya area. During the Spanish Conquest, the Kaqchiquel allied themselves with the Spaniards against their Tz'utujil neighbors. The tension is still present—there is very little mixing between the two groups, though Maya from the different villages around the region all come to Panajachel to sell their wares.

Essentials

GETTING THERE

BY BUS   **Transportes Rebuli** (© **502/2230-2748**) has buses leaving roughly every hour between 5am and 4pm to Panajachel from 21a Calle 1-34, Zona 1, in Guatemala City. The ride takes around 3 hours. Fare is Q20 ($2.50). The return buses run along a similar schedule and depart from the crossroads of Calle Principal and Calle Santander.

BY SHUTTLE   Panajachel is connected to Guatemala City, Antigua, and Chichicastenango by regular tourist shuttle buses. These range from minivans to standard buses. Fares between Panajachel and Guatemala City run around Q80 to Q200; between Panajachel and either Antigua or Chichicastenango is about Q40 to Q160. Any hotel tour desk or local tour agency can book you one of these shuttles, or you can contact **Atitrans** (© **502/7832-3371;** www.atitrans.net) or **Turansa** (© **502/ 5651-2284;** www.turansa.com). *Warning:* Almost all of the shuttles from Guatemala City to Panajachel stop first in Antigua, where there is often a wait and/or switch of vehicle.

BY CAR   To drive to Panajachel and other cities along the lake, take the Pan-American Highway (CA-1) to the junction at Los Encuentros. A few miles north of Los Encuentros is the turnoff to Sololá. In Sololá, follow the signs and flow of traffic to the road to Panajachel. The drive takes around 2½ hours from Guatemala City.

GETTING AROUND

Panajachel is relatively compact, so it's fairly easy to walk anywhere in town. In fact, most people spend their time walking up and down the long strip that is Calle Santander. If you need a taxi or tuk tuk, they are plentiful and can almost always be flagged down anywhere in town. Most rides will run you Q5–Q10. If you need to call one, ask your hotel to ring for you.

BY BOAT   Panajachel is connected to all the towns and villages ringing the lake by regular boat taxi service. There are two separate dock areas. The docks below the end of Calle Santander are used by boats heading east around the lake, as well as those going directly to Santiago de Atitlán. The docks at the end of Calle del Embarcadero are used by the boats heading west around the lake, as well as those going directly to San Pedro La Laguna.

There are several types of boats providing service around the lake. The least expensive boats are large and slow, and follow a regular schedule. However, smaller, faster

---

Gringotenango

Panajachel was one of the earliest and most popular spots on the "hippie trail" of backpacking travelers who made their way up and down Central America in the 1960s, 1970s, and 1980s. Many stayed, and this prevalent expatriate population has earned Panajachel the rather derogatory nickname of Gringotenango. The suffix *tenango* means "village" or "place of," which makes Gringotenango "the Place of Gringos."

boat taxis leave throughout the day—some by regular schedule, others as they fill up—and are definitely worth the few extra dollars. The slower boat taxis take about an hour to go from Panajachel to either San Pedro La Laguna or Santiago de Atitlán. The smaller, faster boats cut that time in half.

The boats operate from around 5am until 6pm. However, if you're coming back to Panajachel from any of the villages across the lake, you should try to grab a boat by around 4pm, as service after that becomes less frequent and less reliable. Schedules change according to demand, but you should never have to wait more than a half-hour to find a boat heading in your direction.

Boat taxis, their captains, and street touts almost always try to gouge tourists. There is a de facto difference between what locals pay and what tourists pay, and it's often hard to get a firm sense of what the official rates are or should be. Always ask your hotel or the INGUAT office about current fares before heading to the docks, and then try to be polite but firm in sticking to those guidelines.

In general, a small, fast boat taxi between Panajachel and San Pedro La Laguna or Santiago de Atitlán should cost around Q25 each way; between San Pedro and Santiago, or between San Pedro and San Marcos, about Q15. The slow water taxi

Look Out for Lookouts

There are a couple of lookouts, or *miradores,* which are places you can pull off the road for a good view, just before you enter Panajachel on your way from Sololá. You'll notice them because local crafts vendors are set up waiting to pounce on tourists trying to take in the view, which encompasses Lake Atitlán and a couple of tall volcanoes behind it. These vendors have a wide range of typical tourist wares for sale—jewelry, stone carvings, ceramic goods—but you'll find a much broader selection and better prices in town.

between Panajachel and either San Pedro or Santiago should cost Q20. **Note:** Only pay for the leg of the ride you are actually taking. There is absolutely no reason to reserve a return trip in advance, and you run the risk of not meeting up with that specific boat or captain at the appointed time and losing your fare.

If you don't want to wait for a taxi and you've got a small group together, or if you'd prefer a private ride, you can always hire an entire boat that will hold up to 10 to 12 people. These boats charge around Q150 to Q300 for a trip to any of the towns around the lakeshore. The higher fares are for those towns farthest away from Panajachel.

ORIENTATION

Panajachel sits on the north shore of Lake Atitlán. As you enter Panajachel from the Pan-American Highway and Sololá, you'll be on Calle Principal (also known as Calle Real), which continues on around the lake toward Santa Catarina Palopó. Soon after you enter Panajachel, you'll come to a major intersection at Calle Santander. The actual center of the town, called the **Old Town,** or *Ciudad Vieja,* is about 3 blocks from this intersection and about 10 or so blocks from the lakeshore. This is where you'll find Pana's main church and large market, as well as a few hotels, restaurants, bars, and language schools. The majority of the action in Panajachel is centered on Calle Santander, which runs from this intersection directly toward the lake, where it dead-ends. The sidewalks are so crowded with street vendors that most people walk in the center of the street, making way, as necessary, for the sporadic traffic.

FAST FACTS There's an **INGUAT** (Guatemala Tourism Commission) office (② 502/7762-1392) on Calle Santander 1-87, in the Centro Comercial San Rafael. It's open Monday through Friday from 9am to 5pm. They can give you a map of Panajachel and the Lake Atitlán area, and help you with hotel reservations and figuring out the current bus and boat taxi schedules. To contact the local **tourist police,** dial ② 502/7762-1120.

There are a host of banks on Calle Principal and around the Old Town, including **Banco de Comercio, Banco Industrial,** and **Banco G&T.** There are also scores of Internet cafes around Panajachel, both in the Old Town and along Calle Santander. Most charge between Q3 and Q6 per hour. The **post office** is located at the corner of Calle Santander and Calle 15 de Febrero. The nearest hospital is the **Hospital Nacional Sololá** (② 502/7762-4121) in Sololá, although in a pinch you can contact the small **Centro de Salud Panajachel** (② 502/7762-1258).

You'll find internet cafes all up and down Calle Santander. If your hotel can't handle your laundry needs, head to **Lavenderia Il Bucato** (② 502/4705-8531),

DINING ◆
Café Bombay **12**
Casablanca **3**
Crossroads Café **2**
Deli Jasmin **15**
El Bistro **16**
Guajimbo's **9**
Las Chinitas **5**
Sunset Café **18**
Tocoyal **20**

ATTRACTIONS ●
Catholic church **1**
Museo Lacustre Atitlán **17**
Reserva Natural Atitlán **7**

ACCOMMODATIONS ■
Hotel Atitlán **8**
Hotel Dos Mundos **13**
Hotel Primavera **4**
Hotel Real Santander **6**
Hotel Regis **11**
Porta Hotel del Lago **19**
Posada de los Volcanes **14**
Posada Don Rodrigo **17**
Rancho Grande Inn **10**

Gone with the Wind

Lake Atitlán has many moods. Mornings are usually calm, and the lake can have a mystical quality with the mirrorlike reflection of clouds and volcanoes in its flat surface. However, most afternoons, sharp winds kick up. These winds are known locally as *Xocomil,* which translates to "the wind that takes away sin." The lake gets choppy and rough, with steep white caps, which makes the taxi boat crossings wet and almost harrowing at times.

which is located in the Comercial El Dorado, right at the intersection of Calle Principal and Calle Santander, and which offers both full- and self-service laundry options.

What to See & Do in Panajachel

The principal activities in Panajachel are strolling along Calle Santander and the lakeshore, shopping, and hanging out in one of the cafes, bars, or restaurants.

The main **Catholic church,** located in the heart of the Old Town, dates back to 1567, and was meticulously restored in 1962. This small church is wonderfully maintained and remains very active. The old stone facade looks almost whitewashed, and the diminutive plaza in front of the church is a major meeting place for locals.

Language schools attract many visitors to Guatemala. While most of the language school action is centered across the lake in San Pedro, there are several Spanish schools in Panajachel. The best of these include **Jardín de América Spanish School ★** (⊘ **502/7762-2637;** www.jardindeamerica.com) and the **Spanish School Jabel Tinamit** (⊘ **502/7762-6056;** www.jabeltinamit.com). Rates are around $125 to $200 per week, and include 4 hours of class per day and a homestay with a local family.

Museo Lacustre Atitlán ★ ☺ A series of excellent and informative displays explains the geology and geography behind the formation of the lake. One of my favorite displays here is the 3-dimensional scale model of the lake and its surrounding mountains and volcanos. The museum also showcases a collection of ceramic pieces discovered in the area, many of which were brought up from the depths of the lake by scuba divers. Plan on spending about a half-hour to 45-minutes here.

At the Posada Don Rodrigo. At the south end of Calle Santander, Zona 2. ⊘ **502/7762-2326.** Admission Q40, free for children 11 and under. Mon–Fri 8am–6pm; Sat–Sun 8am–7pm.

Reserva Natural Atitlán ★★ A zip-line canopy tour, nature trails and suspended bridges, a butterfly garden, and botanical gardens are the main offerings at this reserve. The trails pass through an old coffee farm, as well as areas of dense forest and close to a powerful waterfall. They also feature three high-hanging bridges to take you up into the canopy and across deep ravines. You'll certainly see a range of tropical bird species, and if you're lucky you may see a monkey or two. The zip-line canopy tour here features eight different cables. The longest of these cables is 320m (1,050 ft.). The reserve has a visitor center, restaurant, and small section of private beach. If you want to stay here, you can either camp, or choose one of the six plain, but pretty, rooms set in the forest just behind the main operation. In addition to conservation efforts, these folks are actively involved in working with the local community to increase recycling and the use of renewable energy. They have also planted over

200,000 trees in the past decade, and participate in the *Todos por el lago* (All for the Lake) project to reduce pollution in Lake Atitlan and promote long-term sustainable solutions for the lake and its resources.

In the San Buenaventura valley, just down the road from the Hotel Atitlán (see below). About .4km (¼ mile) before Panajachel, on the road in from Sololá. ✆ **502/7762-2565.** www.atitlanreserva.com. Admission $5.50, $3.35 for students and children 11 and under includes a guided tour through the butterfly garden and breeding exhibit; $24 canopy tour. Daily 8am–5pm.

OUTDOOR ACTIVITIES

In addition to the attractions listed above, Panajachel and Lake Atitlán are good bases for active adventures. Most hotels have a tour desk that can arrange most of the activities listed below. You can also book through **Adrenalina Tours ★★** (✆ 502/ 7762-6236; www.adrenalinatours.com), **Hunab Kú Travel & Adventure ★** (✆ 502/7762-6060; www.hunabkutours.com) or **Atitrans** (✆ 502/7762-0146; www.atitrans.net), all three with offices on Calle Santander.

BOATING Boat tours ★★ on the lake are one of the most popular activities in Panajachel. All the hotel tour desks and tour agencies in town offer organized tours, most of which depart from Panajachel in the morning and make stops in San Pedro La Laguna, Santiago de Atitlán, and San Antonio Palopó. The tours generally last around 5 to 6 hours. Most cost between Q50 and Q120, which gets you the guaranteed boat ride and an hour to 90-minute layover in each town. You can also sign on for a more elaborate tour that includes a bilingual guide and lunch. These generally run between Q240 and Q480 per person.

If you prefer to venture on your own, it's easy; see "Getting Around: By Boat" above. As soon as the boat lands in each town, you'll be met by local touts and tour guides offering to show you around. For example, in Santiago de Atitlán, they offer to take you to see Maximón; in Santa Catarina Palopó, they'll take you to see some weaving. For more detailed information on the different towns and villages, see their individual sections below.

FISHING Fishing for *mojarra* (black bass) is a popular yet somewhat controversial lake activity: The black bass are nonnative to the lake, having been introduced as a game fish in 1958. Moreover, this aggressive fish has decimated many of the native species, and along with them, the local subsistence fishing industry. If you're interested in fishing, ask your hotel or one of the local tour agencies, or simply head down to the waterfront docks.

PARAGLIDING For a bird's-eye view of the lake and volcanoes, try paragliding. **Roger Lapointe** (✆ 502/5595-7732; www.paraglidingguatemala.com), a Canadian paraglide pilot, offers daily rides in a tandem rig from several different takeoff points on the volcanic hillsides surrounding Lake Atitlán. The cost is $80 for a 40-minute flight. There are no requirements, but any child 8 and older with enough courage and parental permission can give it a shot.

SCUBA DIVING Lake Atitlán offers an excellent introduction to the world of high-altitude freshwater diving. This type of diving is slightly more technically challenging than open-water diving at sea level. Because of altitude and decompression, divers must stay in the area for at least 18 hours after diving. Most dives take place in 9 to 11m (30–35 ft.) of water, and because of limited visibility, are a mixed bag. On a good day (usually during the dry season), you may actually see underwater ruins and relics, as well as volcanic steam vents. The main dive operator here is **ATI Divers**

(© 502/5706-4117; www.laiguanaperdida.com), which is based out of La Iguana Perdida hotel in Santa Cruz, but also maintains a business office on Calle Santander in Panajachel. A single-tank dive with all equipment costs $30. Certification courses are also offered.

SWIMMING   The lakeshore along the front of Panajachel is filled with public beaches. You will almost always find local kids and, to a lesser extent, tourists, swimming here. However, I think the boat and foot traffic and pollution make it unappealing. If you want to swim in the lake, I recommend heading to the beach at the **Reserva Natural Atitlán** (see above) or **San Pedro La Laguna** (p. 150). You could even hire a boat to take you to a more tranquil and picturesque spot of your guide's choosing.

TWO-WHEEL TOURING   The rugged back roads and mountain trails around Lake Atitlán are well suited to two-wheel travel, either by mountain bike or off-road motorcycle. Several tour operators and a couple of rental agencies offer guided tours of this type. If you're interested, try **Emanuel's Moto & Bike Rental** (© 502/7762-2790); they rent mountain bikes, scooters, and dirt bikes. Hourly rental of a high-quality mountain bike will run you just Q5, while an hour on a scooter costs around Q70. They also offer guided tours. A full-day tour should run you Q250 to Q400. Emmanuel's asks that you be 21 or older and have a motorcycle license if you plan to go off-roading on a motorized vehicle

Shopping

Calle Santander and the road ringing the lakeshore are crammed with street vendors selling all sorts of Guatemalan handicrafts, ranging from clothing and other textile products to stone and woodcarvings and leather goods. There are also a fair number of stalls selling handmade jewelry and trinkets, but these are relatively run-of-the-mill works that have no real connection to the land or its people and are nothing compared to native arts and crafts.

Just uphill from the Catholic church is the main market area of Panajachel. Here you will find vendors selling fruits, vegetables, household goods, and flowers mixed in with butchers and some stalls selling arts, crafts, and textiles.

If you're looking for higher-quality pieces, check out **K'frans** ★, Calle Santander 1-83, Zona 2 (© 502/7762-0332), which has high-end cotton clothing for both men and women with interesting designs and excellent workmanship. For leather goods—belts, handbags, and shoes—try **Pajayub,** Calle Santander, across from Tel-gua (© 502/7762-0040).

The nearby towns of **Santiago de Atitlán, Santa Catarina Palopó,** and **Sololá** have deep and highly developed arts, crafts, and textile traditions. It's worth taking a trip to one or all of these towns to shop for the local wares. See below for more information on these towns and how to visit them. In addition, Panajachel makes a perfect base for visiting nearby **Chichicastenango** (p. 166) on market day. All of the tour operators in town offer day trips to Chichi on Thursdays and Sundays.

Where to Stay
VERY EXPENSIVE
Hotel Atitlán ★★★   Beautiful and luxurious rooms, fabulous grounds, impeccable service, and an excellent restaurant make this the top choice in Panajachel. The hotel is jampacked with colonial-era and local art, sculpture, and religious iconography.

The rooms are all distinct and come with a private balcony or garden-front patio. Ask for a third-floor room to get the best lake and volcano views. Room no. 315 is the best standard room in the house, while master suite no. 314 and junior suite no. 308 have slightly better views. The extensive botanical gardens and aviary are true treasures, and the lake-view pool and infinity-edge Jacuzzi may make it hard for you to get up the impetus to tour the lake, towns, and markets just off the hotel's grounds.

Finca San Buenaventura. ☏ **502/7762-1441** or 7762-2060 reservations office. Fax 502/7762-0048. www.hotelatitlan.com. 62 units $120 double; $200 junior suite; $250 master suite. AE, DC, MC, V. **Amenities:** Restaurant; bar; lounge; babysitting; concierge; Jacuzzi; outdoor pool; room service; small spa with sauna; all rooms smoke free; unlit outdoor tennis court; free Wi-Fi. *In room:* TV, hair dryer.

EXPENSIVE

Porta Hotel del Lago ★ ☺ This towering, six-story, crescent-shaped, lakefront building feels a bit out of place in Panajachel, since almost no other buildings are more than two stories tall. Rooms are on floors two through five, with the best views in rooms on the higher levels. Standard rooms in the center have better views, as they directly face the lake and volcanoes, while those at the ends (the suites) of the floor have angled views. Most rooms have two double beds, modern decor, and 27-inch televisions, while the suites boast large, wraparound balconies. Suites and executive-level rooms come with extra amenities such as coffeemakers, minibars, and in-room safes. There's also a large pool, midsize gym, and two outdoor Jacuzzis. This place is popular with Guatemalan families, especially on weekends, and even has a kids' club.

2a Av. 06-17, Zona 2. ☏ **502/7762-1555** or 7762-1556. Fax 502/7762-1562. www.portahotels.com. 100 units. $99 double; $109 executive level; $139 suite. AE, DC, MC, V. **Amenities:** 2 restaurants; 2 bars; lounge; babysitting; children's program; gym; 2 Jacuzzis; large outdoor pool; room service; sauna. *In room:* TV, hair dryer.

Posada Don Rodrigo ★ ☺ This lakefront property at the end of Calle Santander is my top choice in the heart of Panajachel. The sprawling grounds, tasteful rooms, fabulous terrace views, and in-house attractions set it apart from the competition. The standard rooms feature dark, colonial decor with heavy wood furniture, stucco walls, and a fireplace. The lakefront rooms are a bit more spacious and worth the modest splurge, which gets you a small private balcony and shared lawn. Tall guests will catch views of the lake and volcanoes over the trees and shrubs. The pool, with a big spiral slide, and a very well done museum (**Museo Lacustre Atitlán,** see above) make this an excellent choice for families.

At the south end of Calle Santander, Zona 2. ☏ **502/7762-2326** or 7832-9858. www.hotelposadade donrodrigo.com. 39 units. $100–$110 double. Rates include full breakfast. AE, DC, MC, V. **Amenities:** Restaurant; bar; lounge; babysitting; outdoor pool; room service; free Wi-Fi. *In room:* TV, no phone.

MODERATE

Hotel Dos Mundos ★ ✦ Not as stylish or fancy as the Don Rodrigo (above), this is still an excellent option right on Calle Santander. The rooms, as well as the pool and gardens, are set back off the main drag. All the rooms are spacious and well kept. I prefer room nos. 11 through 23, which front the pool and garden area and share a veranda. The other rooms are a bit closer to the street, though not so close that noise is a problem. The hotel has a popular Italian restaurant, La Linterna, as well as a separate cafe and bar.

Calle Santander 4-72, Zona 2. ☏ **502/7762-2078** or 7762-2140. Fax 502/7762-0127. www.hoteldos mundos.com. 22 units. $70 double. AE, DC, MC, V. **Amenities:** Restaurant; bar; cafe; outdoor pool; room service. *In room:* TV.

Hotel Real Santander   This four-story hotel right on the main drag features clean and comfortable, if somewhat nondescript, rooms. The rooms, all on the second and third floors, feature a large, varnished-wood bay window that lets out on to a shared veranda, a 21-inch flatscreen TV, and faux stucco walls and ceilings. The windows don't offer any real views, but there's an unfinished rooftop terrace for those who want to gaze around. This place is located right smack on the center of Calle Santander, and street noise can be a problem in some rooms, so try to grab a room as far in from the street as possible.

3a Av. 3-45, Calle Santander, Zona 2. ✆ **502/7762-2915.** Fax 502/7762-1117. necos@itelgua.com. 12 units. $55 double. AE, DC, MC, V. **Amenities:** Free Wi-Fi. *In room:* TV, no phone.

Hotel Regis   This 1934 hotel is run by the granddaughter of the original owner, and the rooms show the bridge between old and new, with some showing their age and others somewhat more recently updated. (It's worth asking to see a few rooms before settling in.) The spacious rooms have tile floors and brightly painted walls, and some even come with a brick fireplace or kitchenette. The most appealing features here are the expansive gardens and two large natural hot spring-fed Jacuzzis.

3a Av. 3-47, Calle Santander, Zona 2. ✆ **502/7762-1149.** Fax 502/7762-1152. www.hotelregisatitlan. com. 25 units. $61–$75 double. AE, DC, MC, V. **Amenities:** 2 Jacuzzis. *In room:* TV.

Posada de los Volcanes   This is a good choice among the hoard of budget lodgings in Pana. There are three rooms on each of the four floors, and each floor has a shared veranda with some tables and chairs. The fourth floor offers a glimpse of the lake and a better view all around. The rooms are compact, but clean and well-kept. The best room in the house is no. 402, which has a picture window with a view of the nearby mountains. The owner and staff are very friendly and helpful.

Calle Santander 5-51, Zona 2. ✆ **502/7762-0244.** Fax 502/7762-2367. www.posadadelosvolcanes. com. 12 units. $50–$60 double. AE, DC, MC, V. *In room:* TV, no phone.

Rancho Grande Inn   If you're looking for a clean and comfortable room that's close to the action without feeling like it is, this longtime favorite is a good option. All of the rooms are fairly similar, with plenty of space, a working fireplace, and simple decor. The individual bungalows are the best and biggest options, spread among the grounds, gardens, and pool. If you can, get a room that's away from the street. Despite being more than 65 years old, the hotel has aged remarkably well. There's no restaurant here, but the daily breakfast, in particular their fresh pancakes, is considered by many a large part of the attraction.

Calle Rancho Grande. ✆ **502/7762-2255.** Fax 502/7762-2247. www.ranchograndeinn.com. 12 units. $66 double; $77 suite. Rate includes full breakfast. AE, DC, MC, V. **Amenities:** Small outdoor pool; free Wi-Fi. *In room:* TV.

INEXPENSIVE

Hotel Primavera ⚑   This small hotel is a step above the score of budget options on Calle Santander. Most of the rooms are on the second floor and feature bay windows that overlook the street. However, street noise can be a problem at night, with several popular bars and discos nearby. The rooms, though relatively small and basic, are immaculate. I like no. 9, which has a private staircase and balcony, and is set back from the busy street.

Calle Santander. ✆ **502/7762-2052.** Fax 502/7762-0171. www.primaveratitlan.com. 10 units. $40–$50 double. AE, DC, MC, V. **Amenities:** Restaurant. *In room:* TV, no phone.

Where to Dine

In addition to the places listed below, **Guajimbo's,** Calle Santander (𝕮 **502/7762-0063**), is a popular Uruguayan-style steakhouse that often has live music and is a great spot for people watching, while **Las Chinitas,** Calle Santander (𝕮 **502/7762-2612**), is the town's most popular Asian restaurant, with a mix of Chinese, Thai, and Indian options. For a casual meal, try **Deli Jasmín,** Calle Santander (𝕮 **502/7762-2586**).

For a coffee break and something sweet, try the **Crossroads Café,** Calle del Campanario 0-27 (𝕮 **502/5292-8439**).

EXPENSIVE

Hotel Atitlán ★★ 🏠 INTERNATIONAL   This hotel restaurant is by far the most elegant dining option in Panajachel. Wood tables and chairs, beautiful place settings and glassware, and candles and a fireplace contribute to the ornate setting, while patio tables add lake and volcano views to the menu. Standout entrees include grilled salmon braised with pesto and filet mignon with Roquefort sauce. They also offer a selection of pastas and a few refined takes on Guatemalan classics, including *pupusas* (cornmeal patties usually stuffed with beans, cheese, or meat) and the typical Chapin plate of grilled meat, fried plantain, refried beans, and local cheese. For lunch, you can get hearty sandwiches and burgers in addition to the regular menu, and the Sunday brunch buffet is justifiably popular.

Finca San Buenaventura. 𝕮 **502/7762-1441.** Reservations required. Main courses Q65–Q180. AE, DC, MC, V. Daily 6:30am–10pm.

MODERATE

Casablanca ★ INTERNATIONAL   The Bogart and Bergman photos and namesake movie posters, combined with antique lamps, crisp white table linens, professional service, and cozy vibe give this place the most atmospheric and romantic ambience in Pana. The long menu ranges far and wide, featuring everything from a variety of pastas to rabbit in a cream-and-bacon sauce to a couple of types of schnitzels. Grab a seat along the wall of picture windows fronting Calle Principal and watch the town pass by while enjoying this elegant and intimate restaurant.

Calle Principal. 𝕮 **502/7762-1015.** Reservations recommended. Main courses Q50–Q160. AE, DC, MC, V. Daily 11am–11pm.

El Bistro ★ ITALIAN   This long-standing local favorite serves up excellent pastas and entrees in a convivial open-air setting. While there's some indoor seating, the best tables are found in a large covered courtyard just off Calle Santander that's lined with plants, palms, and bamboo. The proper tablecloths and candlelight are offset by the plastic lawn chairs. The homemade fettuccine is available with more than 15 different sauces, and other pasta options include lasagna and cannelloni. For something heartier, opt for grilled fish, chicken parmigiana, or steak pizzaola. When you order, the waiter will ask if you want your pasta "al dente" or "normal." "Normal" would be overcooked for most people accustomed to good Italian cooking. This place also serves up good, standard breakfast fare, including the traditional Guatemalan refried beans, tortillas, and eggs, on most days.

Southern end of Calle Santander. 𝕮 **502/7762-0508.** Reservations recommended. Pasta Q50–Q60; main courses Q50–Q80. AE, DC, MC, V. Tues–Sun 7:30am–10pm; Mon noon–10pm.

Sunset Café GUATEMALAN/MEXICAN   As the name suggests, sunset is a good time to come here, when you can marvel at the reflection of the moon in Lake Atitlán and the flickering of the lights in San Pedro. The spectacular setting here makes the standard Mexican fare acceptable, but I still like the *fajitas de pescado* (fish fajitas) and *enchiladas verdes* (chicken enchiladas in a green tomatillo sauce). There's live music here most nights, so grab a drink, a plate of nachos, and a seat under the tree (heavily hung with orchids and bromeliads) that grows through the thatch roof.

Calle Santander and Calle del Lago. ⓒ **502/7762-0003.** Reservations recommended for large groups. Main courses Q40–Q100. AE, DC, MC, V. Daily 11am–midnight.

Tocoyal GUATEMALAN   The front wall of picture windows allows great views of the lake, but passing traffic and souvenir stands sometimes get in the way. The food here is well prepared and attentively served by waiters in starched white shirts, black bow ties, and red Guatemalan vests. You can order up a grilled steak, or some fresh lake fish, or opt for a traditional chicken *pepian,* served in a mildly spicy broth.

The restaurant is named after a traditional headdress made from a very long ribbon tightly wound around itself and worn almost like a halo by Maya women.

Calle del Lago, Playa Publica, Zona 2. ⓒ **502/7762-1555.** Main courses Q50–Q150. AE, DC, MC, V. Daily 8am–9pm.

INEXPENSIVE

Café Bombay ★ 🍴 INDIAN/VEGETARIAN   The name of this place would indicate Indian cuisine, which you'll find here, but you'll also get everything vegetarian from pad Thai and tacos to lasagna and falafel. Excellent sandwiches, soups, and smoothies are also served, as well as vegan fare. The atmosphere is casual, and on a nice day you can grab a seat on one of the umbrella-covered tables just off Calle Santander.

Calle Santander. ⓒ **502/7762-0611.** Reservations not accepted. Main courses Q50–Q75; sandwiches Q20–Q40. No credit cards. Wed–Mon 11am–10pm.

Panajachel After Dark

Panajachel has a fairly active nightlife. For nearly 20 years, my favorite place has been the **Circus Bar** ★★ (ⓒ **502/7762-2056**), Avenida Los Arboles, which has a relaxed vibe, simple menu, and decor to match the joint's name. They also frequently have live music. This is also the first place I ever tried **Ron Zacapa** ★★★, Guatemala's world-class 23-year-old aged rum. Circus Bar, just north of Calle Principal, is located in what's considered Panajachel's mini–Zona Viva.

Of the bars on Calle Santander, I like the **Pana Rock Café** (ⓒ **502/7762-2194;** www.panarockcafe.com), which is a takeoff on the Hard Rock chain.

For loud and late-night dancing, try **Rumba Disco,** Calle Principal (ⓒ **502/7762-1015**); **El Aleph,** Avenida Los Arboles (ⓒ **502/7762-0192**); or **El Chapiteau Discoteque,** Avenida Los Arboles (ⓒ **502/7762-0374**).

SAN PEDRO LA LAGUNA ★

8km (5 miles) SW of Panajachel across the lake

Panajachel has become more commercial and upscale over the years, so the hippie and backpack crowd moved across the lake to San Pedro La Laguna. Today, with a growing number of budget lodgings, Spanish schools, international restaurants, and late-night bars, San Pedro is starting to give Pana a run for its money. San Pedro has a reputation

To San Pablo, San Marcos & Santa Cruz

To Panajachel

To San Juan

Evangelical School

Gringo

Lake Atitlán

Alley

To Santiago de Atitlán

Bus Stop

Market

Bank

Post Office

Cemetery

--- Ferry
--- Trail

0   500 m
0   500 yds

ATTRACTIONS ●
Boats to Panajachel **3**
Boats to Santiago
  de Atitlán **17**
Catholic Church **18**
Centro Cultural Comunitario
  Tz'unun Ya' **9**
Los Thermales **12**
Volcan San Pedro **19**

NIGHTLIFE ★
Alegre Pub **4**
Buddha **11**
El Barrio **14**

ACCOMMODATIONS ■
Casa Elena **8**
Hotel Gran Sueño **7**
Hotel Mansion
  del Lago **5**
Hotelito Sak'cari **13**
Mikaso Hotel **16**

DINING ◆
Chile's **2**
Fata Morgana **6**
Jarachick **15**
Shanti Shanti **1**
Zoola **10**

as a party town. It also has a less developed and less commercial vibe to it than Pana-jachel. On the other hand, San Pedro exhibits much more of a foreign influence than either Santiago de Atitlán or Santa Catarina Palopó (see later in this chapter).

Essentials
GETTING THERE
BY BOAT   From Panajachel, the docks for boats to San Pedro are found at the end of Calle del Embarcadero. The boats operate roughly every half-hour from around 5am until 7pm. However, if you're coming back to Panajachel, try to grab a boat by around 4pm, as service after that becomes less frequent and less reliable. Schedules

change according to demand, but you should never have to wait more than a half-hour to find a boat heading in your direction. These boats ply a route that stops at Santa Cruz La Laguna, Jaibalito, and San Marcos La Laguna en route to San Pedro La Laguna. In addition, they will stop at any number of other smaller docks, whether they are for tiny communities, individual homes, or hotels.

Boat taxis, their captains, and street touts almost always try to gouge tourists. There is a difference between what locals pay and what tourists pay, and it's often hard to get a firm sense of what the official rates are or should be. Always ask your hotel or the INGUAT office about current fares before heading to the docks, and then try to be polite but firm in sticking to those guidelines.

A boat taxi between Panajachel and San Pedro La Laguna should cost around Q25 each way. Between San Pedro and Santiago or San Pedro and San Marcos should run Q15. *Note:* Only pay for the leg of the ride you are actually taking. There is absolutely no reason to reserve a return trip in advance, and you run the risk of not meeting up with that specific boat or captain at the appointed time and losing your fare.

The slow (about an hour-long ride) water taxi between Panajachel and San Pedro leaves about twice a day from the docks below the end of Calle Santander and should cost Q20. However, I recommend you take the much faster and more frequent boats from the end of Calle del Embarcadero, which charge just a few *quetzales* more.

You can always hire an entire boat to make the trip for around Q150 to Q300. These boats hold between 10 and 12 people, so if you can round up a group, it's not too expensive.

BY CAR   To reach San Pedro La Laguna by car, take the exit for Santa Clara La Laguna and San Pedro La Laguna off the Pan-American Highway (CA-1) about 20km (13 miles) west of Los Encuentros. Don't take the exit for Sololá and Panajachel. San Pedro La Laguna is also connected to Santiago de Atitlán by a paved road.

BY BUS   There are no express or luxury buses to San Pedro. If you're coming by bus, your best bet is to head to Panajachel first (see "Panajachel: Getting There: By Bus," earlier in this chapter), and then catch a boat taxi to San Pedro (above). However, San Pedro does have regular "chicken bus" service (cheap, local, commuter buses) to and from both Guatemala City and Quetzaltenango. Ask your hotel, or contact **Asistur** (② **1500**) for current schedules.

GETTING AROUND

Although distances are short, the hill between the docks and the center of town is formidable. You can usually find a taxi or tuk tuk near either dock to take you to the center of town for around Q8. Alternately, you can pile into one of the pickup trucks that waits at the pier, then heads to the center of town for just Q6.

For information about getting around the lake by boat, see "San Pedro La Laguna: Getting There: By Boat" and "Panajachel: "Getting Around: By Boat," above.

ORIENTATION

San Pedro La Laguna is located on the southwestern shore of Lake Atitlán. The center of the town sits on a small plateau a steep climb up from the shores. This is where you'll find San Pedro's Catholic church and central plaza, as well as most of the town's shops and services. From this plateau, streets run down on either side of a steep ridge. The roads heading down the west side of this ridge lead toward the *muelle municipal,* which is the main dock for boats arriving from and departing to Panajachel. The roads heading down the east side of this ridge lead toward an area known as *la playa,* or "the beach," and the *muelle santiago,* the main dock for boats arriving from and departing for Santiago de Atitlán. These two main docks are connected by a winding, narrow road, known locally as "Gringo Alley," where you will find most of the hotels, restaurants, and bars listed in this section.

FAST FACTS There is a **Banrural** office (3a Av. 1-51, Zona 3) in the center of town just up from the church. You'll also find the **post office** and a **Telgua** telephone office on the street behind the church. To contact the local **police,** dial ✆ **502/7762-4000.** There's no hospital or major medical clinic in San Pedro. In the event you need medical care, ask your hotel. There are several Internet cafes around San Pedro. I like **Dnoz.com** (✆ **502/7721-8078**), which is also an inviting little coffee shop and simple restaurant, with a good book exchange. Most hotels and several private operations will launder your clothes.

Fun On & Off the Lake

San Pedro is a laid-back lakeside town, with most visitors opting to spend the day at a cafe or restaurant. However, if you want to get active, there are plenty of options. To set up any sort of organized tour, head to **Atitlan Adventures** (✆ **502/4130-5205;** www.lakeatitlanadventure.com), **Big Foot Tourist Info Center** (✆ **502/7721-8203**), or **Casa Verde Tours ★** (✆ **502/5837-9092;** www.casaverdetours.com). If you happen to be here on June 29, take part in the feast day of San Pedro, when the town pulls out all the stops with a major street fair, bullfights, carnival rides, and live music and dancing.

CANOEING & KAYAKING You can rent canoes and kayaks from several operators in town. Just head down to either one of the main docks. Rates run around Q10 per hour and Q30 to Q40 per day. If you're in good shape, you can paddle to one of the nearby towns or villages. Be careful of the regular boat taxis, and try to avoid spending too much time near the busy dock areas. Also, remember that the winds and chop tend to kick up in the afternoons.

HIKING At 3,020m (9,905 ft.), **Volcán San Pedro** towers over and behind the town. The trail is generally wide and well maintained, and the round-trip hike should take between 5 and 6 hours. Tour desks all over town offer guided hikes to the summit for around Q40 to Q120 per person. Other hikes around San Pedro head to **Cerro de la Cruz,** a beautiful hilltop with great views, and to **La Nariz del Indio (Indian's Nose),** another lookout spot that allegedly looks like a Maya profile from afar.

HORSEBACK RIDING & MOUNTAIN BIKING This is hilly, rustic, and rural country and an excellent area to explore by horseback or on a mountain bike. Horseback and mountain bike tours can be set up by any hotel tour desk or in-town tour agency (see above).

 Be Careful

The beautiful countryside and volcanic peaks around Lake Atitlán are quite enticing to climbers and hikers. However, due to the current security situation, poverty, and a history of violence, it's often not safe for tourists to be on isolated trails or back roads. It's best to sign up for a guided tour if you want to scale a volcano or hike to one of the nearby villages or lookout points.

LANGUAGE LESSONS   San Pedro has become a hot spot for foreign students looking to learn or brush up on some Spanish. There are a half-dozen or more language schools in San Pedro. Most offer either individual or small-class, intensive instruction combined with a homestay with a local family and various organized activities and tours. Try **Corazón Maya Spanish School** (*©* **502/7721-8160;** www.corazonmaya.com) or **San Pedro Spanish School** (*©* **502/5715-4604;** www.sanpedrospanishschool.com). Rates range from $100 to $150 per week and include 4 hours of class per day and a homestay with a local family. More adventurous students might want to learn some of the Tz'utujil Mayan dialect. Ask at any of the language schools, and they'll be able to set you up with a local instructor.

A SOAK AND A SAUNA   If you have sore muscles from hiking to the summit of Volcán San Pedro or horseback riding around the shores, book yourself a tub and sauna at **Los Thermales** (*©* **502/5897-5319**). Solar-heated water is used to fill several large hot tubs. They also have a wood-fired sauna. Open daily 8:30am to midnight. Rates run around Q30 per person.

A SMALL LOCAL MUSEUM   For a fascinating glimpse into the geological, anthropological and contemporary social life of the lake, check out the **Centro Cultural Comunitario Tz'unun Ya'** ★ (*©* **502/5846-1923**). Open Tuesday to Friday 8am to noon and 2 to 6pm, and Saturday to Sunday 8am to noon. Admission is Q35 per person and includes a guided tour.

Where to Stay
INEXPENSIVE

Casa Elena   Most of the rooms at this popular budget option are bare-bones concrete-block affairs, with minimal furnishings, shared bathrooms, and little ambience. Service and upkeep here are pretty lax. However, room nos. 9 and 10, at the end of the third and fourth floors, are real steals, with private bathrooms and large picture windows with fabulous views overlooking the lake.

7a Av. 8-61, Zona 2. *©* **502/5980-4400.** 20 units, 7 with private bathroom. Q50 double with shared bathroom; Q100 double with private bathroom. AE, DC, MC, V. *In room:* No phone.

Hotel Gran Sueño   This hotel is clean and well run. The rooms are on the small side, but all come with cable TV, rough stucco walls, and a private bathroom with heated shower head. Most of the rooms have just one double bed and feature a large round picture window with intricate wood and brick framing.

8a Calle 4-40, Zona 2. *©* **502/7721-8110.** 7 units. Q100 double. AE, DC, MC, V. *In room:* TV.

Hotelito Sak'cari ★ 🍃   This small hotel is probably my favorite option in San Pedro. The second-floor rooms are the best, with a shared veranda overlooking the lake, though the few individual bungalows are also good options. Only three of the rooms have queen-size beds, so be sure to request one of these if you're traveling as a couple. The hotel also has a large, clean steam bath. The name *sak'cari* mean "sunrise" in Tz'utujil, and the sunrise over the lake is gorgeous here.

7a Av. 2-10, Zona 2. *©* **502/7721-8096** or 2475-1802. www.hotelsakcari.com. 16 units. Q256 double. AE, DC, MC, V. **Amenities:** Free kayaks; steam bath; free Wi-Fi. *In room:* No phone.

Hotel Mansión del Lago   This hotel is set on the hillside above the *muelle municipal,* and the rooms on the top floor have the best views, especially from their shared veranda. Most rooms, which are named after different cities and archaeological sites around Guatemala, are rather small, and lack anything in the way of style, but all come with a small television and private bathroom. There are two concrete rooftop terraces, and one of these has an unheated Jacuzzi. These folks have a good Internet cafe on-site.

4a Av. and 8a Calle, Zona 2. ✆ 502/7721-8041 or 7721-8124. www.hotelmansiondellago.com. 17 units. Q150 double. AE, DC, MC, V. **Amenities:** Jacuzzi. *In room:* TV, no phone.

Mikaso Hotel ★   Located just off the water's edge near the Santiago dock, this three-story hotel offers large, clean rooms. The rooms themselves are rather plain, but are kept immaculate. The best feature here is the rooftop patio and restaurant, which offers excellent views of the lake and surrounding mountains. In addition, the service is friendly and accommodating. This place is a tad more expensive than other options in town, but I think it's worth the splurge

On the waterfront, just off the Santiago dock. ✆ 502/5973-3129 or 7721-8356. www.mikasohotel.com. 11 units. Q280–Q360 double. AE, DC, MC, V. **Amenities:** Restaurant. *In room:* No phone.

Where to Dine

In addition to the places listed below, **Shanti Shanti,** 8a Calle 3-93, Zona 2 (✆ **502/5561-8423**), is a popular and laid-back breakfast-and-sandwich joint, with a good lake view, while **Fata Morgana** (no phone) is the place to go for pizzas, fresh pasta and Italian fare, and **Jarachik** ★ (✆ **502/5958-9417**) is a popular hostel, restaurant, and bar with a varied menu and equally varied clientele.

INEXPENSIVE

Chile's 🍴 INTERNATIONAL   Good food and a great view of the lake make this one of the best and most popular options in San Pedro. The menu ranges from pizzas and pastas to beef in orange sauce and red curry chicken with rice. There are several different vegetarian dishes, as well as a selection of salads and hearty sandwiches. Everything is very well prepared, and the service is attentive and jovial. The best seats are on the open-air deck and covered patio closest to the water. After you're stuffed, stick around for dance class. (Tues and Fri introductory lessons are free.) This place actually has two locations; I prefer the one closes to the main Panajachel ferry dock, although for more privacy, you might head to the second location a few doors down.

4a Av. 8-12, Zona 2 (just above the *muelle municipal*). ✆ 502/4188-3229. Reservations not accepted. Main courses Q30–Q50. AE, DC, MC, V. Daily 7am-1am.

Zoola ★★ 🏠 MIDDLE EASTERN/INTERNATIONAL   This popular place serves up hearty, healthy, and tasty fare in a relaxed, convivial atmosphere. Housed under a large, open-air *palapa* roof structure, guests get cozy in a series of spacious nooks on the floor, bedecked with woven rugs, ample pillows, and a long, low table. The menu leans heavily towards Middle Eastern fare, which includes falafel, baba ghanouj, and tabbouleh, but you can also get a range of salads, sandwiches, wraps, and more substantial main dishes like lasagna and homemade quiche. They also serve breakfast, and have a few simple rooms out back. The only downside here is that service can be interminably slow at times—which might be a good thing as it lets your appetite gear up for the immense portions.

On the "Gringo Trail," about midway btw. the Santiago and Panajachel docks. ✆ **502/5847-4857.** Reservations not accepted. Main courses Q30–Q50. No credit cards. Daily 7am-10pm.

San Pedro After Dark

San Pedro is a great town to bar-crawl, since everything is within walking distance. Most of the nightlife is strung along the main road, or "Gringo Trail." On any night you might find things happening at **El Barrio** ★ (*© 502/5577-2601*), the **Alegre Pub** ★ (*© 502/7721-8100;* www.thealegrepub.com), or the **Buddha** ★★ (www. thebuddhaguatemala.com). Most tourists and language students tend to do a simple pub-crawl and congregate at whichever spot is most happening on that night. El Barrio and the Alegre Pub shoot for an Anglo-American pub vibe, and the Alegre Pub shows nightly movies and most sporting events, including Sunday afternoon American football. The Buddha has a more European feel, and often has live music, which might be anything from an open mic jam to rock to Latin Folk to jazz or reggae.

SANTIAGO DE ATITLAN ★★

8km (5 miles) S of Panajachel across the lake

Set on the southern shores of Lake Atitlán, near the start of a long narrow bay, Santiago de Atitlán is a picturesque Tz'utujil town with a distinct character and fiercely independent streak. Santiago de Atitlán was the site of a horrible massacre during the civil war and one of the first villages to organize against the paramilitary and military forces.

The town was severely ravaged by Hurricane Stan in October 2005, and mudslides from the Toliman volcano killed more than 70 people in and around Santiago.

The Santiago de Atitlán *huipil* and men's pants are unique and highly prized by foreigners buying indigenous textiles. The cult of Maximón (see the box on p. 157) is very strong in Santiago, and as soon as you step off of any boat here, you'll be met with offers from local kids and touts to take you to see him. You'll definitely want to visit Maximón, but don't feel obligated to go along with the first person who approaches you.

Essentials

GETTING THERE

BY BUS   There are no express or luxury buses to Santiago de Atitlán. If you're coming by bus, your best bet is to head to Panajachel first (see "Panajachel: Getting There: By Bus," earlier in this chapter), and then catch a boat taxi to Santiago de Atitlán (below). Santiago does have regular "chicken bus" service to and from Guatemala City. From Santiago, they leave from in front of the main plaza, roughly every hour between 4am and 3pm. Ask your hotel, or contact **Asistur** (*© 1500*) for current schedules.

BY BOAT   From Panajachel, the docks for boats to Santiago de Atitlán are found at the public docks and beach area below the end of Calle Santander. The boats operate roughly every hour from around 6am until 5pm; however, if you're coming back to Panajachel, try to grab a boat by 4pm, as service after that becomes less frequent and less reliable. Schedules change according to demand, but you should never have to wait more than an hour to find a boat heading in your direction. Alternatively, you can hire an entire boat (which holds 10–12 people) to make the trip for around Q300.

Boat taxis, their captains, and street touts almost always try to gouge tourists. There is a price difference between what locals pay and what tourists pay, and it's often hard

maximón THE SAINT

The Mayas' introduction to Catholicism often came with the threat of immolation, hanging, or beheading, and they soon rationalized that this new religion could easily be superimposed with their own. When they saw the statue of Mary crushing a snake under her foot, they prayed to Gukumatz, the creator snake god.

The Maya also brought their own saint to their brand of Catholicism. Maximón (pronounced "Ma-shi-*mon*") was a pre-Columbian Maya god of the underworld known as Maam, or Grandfather. The modern name is a blend of Maam and his other name, San Simon. Maximón symbolizes male sexual virility and brings rain to fertilize the earth. He's known as the saint of gamblers and drunkards, and is thought to give wealth and worldly success to his followers.

Despite the Catholic church's attempt to demonize the dark-skinned Maximón by equating him with Judas, he is still found in churches, shops, and homes across Guatemala. He is now depicted as a 20th-century mustached man wearing a black suit, red tie, and wide-brimmed hat, and is represented in life-size wood statues, small dolls, or pictures on votive candles. He's given offerings of tobacco, alcohol, Coca-Cola, and a tropical plant with orange-red berries.

Maximón's feast day is October 28. On this day, and on the Wednesday of Holy Week, he's carried through the streets on the shoulders of his followers. In some villages he's hung from the main church's cross at the end of the ceremony. Maximón's more scandalous side forces most followers to keep him out of public view for the rest of the year, for fear that his famed sexual desires may run amok. He is kept in the house—and sometimes the outhouse—with his whereabouts changing regularly. In most towns with strong Maximón traditions (including Santiago de Atitlán and Zunil), locals will bring you to see him for a small tip. If you go, be sure to bring a cigar or some rum to leave in offering. In most cases, you'll also have to pay a small fee for each photo you take. Most touts want Q10 to Q15 to take you to see Maximón. You may be charged an extra couple of *quetzales* per photo, depending upon who's minding the saint and how much he thinks he can get from you.

to get a firm sense of what the official rates are or should be. Always ask your hotel or the INGUAT office about current fares before heading to the docks, and then try to be polite but firm in sticking to those guidelines.

A boat taxi between Panajachel and Santiago de Atitlán should cost around Q25 each way. Between Santiago and San Pedro the ride should run Q15. **Note:** Only pay for the leg of the ride you are actually taking. There is absolutely no reason to reserve a return trip in advance, and you run the risk of not meeting up with that specific boat or captain at the appointed time and losing your fare.

BY CAR The best route to drive here from Guatemala City is via the Pacific Highway (CA-2). From the Coastal Highway, turn right at Cocales, through the towns of Patutul and San Lucas Tolimán.

Driving from Antigua, the best route is via the Pan-American Highway (CA-1). Take this road to Las Trampas, where you'll turn left toward Godinez. Drive through Aguas Escondidas and on to San Lucas Tolimán.

GETTING AROUND

Santiago is quite compact, and aside from the challenge presented by its steep hill, you should be able to walk anywhere in town. Still, you can always find a taxi or tuk tuk near the dock to take you to the center of town for around Q5. A taxi to Posada Santiago or El Bambu should run you Q15.

ORIENTATION

The boat taxis all land at a busy dock area at the foot of town. Just off the dock area and all along the steep cobblestone road leading up to the center of town, you'll find scores of makeshift stands and stores selling local arts and crafts. The main church and central plaza are at the top of this steep road. There are **Banrural** and **Banco G&T Continental** branches near the main plaza in Santiago; both have ATMs.

What to See & Do

The principal attraction in town, **La Iglesia Parroquial Santiago Apóstol ★★** was built in the late 16th century, and features a plaque and statue dedicated to **Father Stanley Rother,** an American priest who was murdered by a right-wing group in 1981. The main structure consists of large intricately carved altars with numerous niches, each filled with a carved figure of a saint or holy person, many of whom are adorned in traditional Maya clothing.

Visitors will also want to stop in at the small **Museo Cojoyla** (no phone, free admission), which delves into the town's distinctive textiles, explaining both its history and production techniques. You'll find this museum about one block uphill from the main dock in town.

Outdoor enthusiasts will be happy to know that one of the best ways to tour the countryside around Santiago de Atitlán is on horseback. Longtime residents **Jim and Nancy Matison** (© **502/5811-5516** or 5742-8975; wildwestgua@yahoo.com) offer a range of rides in the area, including a full-day tour with lunch for $60 per person; shorter rides for $20 per person per hour, plus $7.50 per hour for the guide; as well as various treks and hikes.

Dolores Ratzan is a Tz'utujil woman who has dedicated herself to the study of traditional Maya healing and religion. She also conducts wonderful tours to the studios and workshops of local artists and weavers. Dolores can be contacted through the Posada de Santiago (© **502/7721-7366;** www.posadadesantiago.com).

If you don't want to swim in the lake, you can use the pool and facilities at **Turicentro Tiosh Abaj** (see below) for Q30 per day.

Shopping

The local **Santiago de Atitlán** *huipil* **★★** is distinctive and beautiful, featuring large embroidered birds and flowers, usually densely displayed around the neck and chest area, on a plain white cloth with thin, blue vertical stripes or a checkerboard pattern. You'll find these at the numerous stands that line the main road between the dock and center of town. Santiago is also a good place to shop for carved-wood masks, as well as local paintings done in a "primitive" style. Friday and Saturday are the principal market days, and you'll find a greater selection on those days, with sellers coming into town from surrounding villages. However, the shopping scene is good here just about any day.

Note: It's become common practice to take old *huipiles,* particularly those from Santiago, and dip them into a large dye vat of either blue or ocher. This gives the

FATHER ROTHER & THE SANTIAGO massacre

For 13 years, Father Stanley Rother of Oklahoma worked in Santiago de Atitlán, translating the Bible and reciting Mass in the local Tz'utujil language, and establishing a small hospital to serve the community. He was first assigned to Santiago de Atitlán in 1968 after he became an ordained Catholic priest of the Oklahoma Archdiocese. Despite, or perhaps because of, his work, he received death threats, and Rother was summoned back to Oklahoma in January 1981. However, missing the work and community he left behind, he returned in April of 1981, in time for Holy Week. On July 28, 1981, four men entered the church rectory and shot him. Rother was one of 10 priests murdered in Guatemala that year, and parish members built a memorial in his living quarters.

Throughout the 1980s, Santiago suffered heavily under the military campaign to combat alleged subversives, guerrillas, and communists. More than 1,000 people from Santiago were killed or disappeared during this time.

On December 1, 1990, a group of drunk soldiers in civilian dress went to the home of a shopkeeper and threatened to break the door down. The family's screams were overheard by

neighbors who, perhaps emboldened by the memory of Father Rother, chased the soldiers away. Someone rang the town bell, and nearly the entire village gathered in the plaza, where they met for several hours.

At 4am, 3,000 shouting people woke the soldiers sleeping at the nearby military base. When a couple of villagers threw rocks over the barbed-wire fence, the army opened fire, killing 11 villagers (of whom three were children) and wounding 17.

Government officials who arrived the next day were presented with a petition signed by more than 20,000 people. The petition demanded that the army withdraw from the area. The killings and the villagers' response had drawn international attention, and the government chose to remove the troops rather than risk an international scandal and the loss of considerable amounts of tourist and foreign aid dollars. To this day, the Guatemalan military is banned from establishing any sort of presence in Santiago.

The site of the massacre is now a small park called Parque del La Paz, or Peace Park. A memorial celebration is held here each year on December 2.

huipil an interesting look, but it's very far from traditional, and often serves to mask an inferior piece of work.

Where to Stay & Dine in Santiago de Atitlan

Santiago de Atitlán is not a dining destination, but **Posada de Santiago** and **Bambú Hotel & Restaurant** (see below) have the best offerings in town. You can also get good, simple Guatemalan fare at **El Pescador,** located on the main road between the docks and center of town.

MODERATE

Bambú Hotel & Restaurant ★ 📷 This is my favorite hotel in Santiago de Atitlán. Rooms include two bungalows with private patios overlooking the lake and those in the two-story building set a bit farther back from the lake. Both options are spacious and cozy with warm earth tones and pretty artwork. The hotel has a pool and an excellent Nuevo Spanish–influenced restaurant with lake and volcano views. The town is just a 15-minute walk or short cab ride away, and any of the boat taxis from Panajachel or San Pedro will drop you off at the hotel's private dock.

Carretera San Lucas Tolimán, Km 16. © **502/7721-7332.** Fax 502/7721-7333. www.ecobambu.com. 11 units. $65–$75 double. Rates include continental breakfast and taxes. AE, DC, MC, V. **Amenities:** Restaurant; bar; midsize outdoor pool; sauna. *In room:* No phone.

Turicentro Tiosh Abaj ★   This hotel makes an effort to introduce some swank to Santiago, but it lacks the personality and charm of the hotel listed above. Still, if you want a large, comfortable room with modern amenities that's in the heart of town, this is your best bet. Most of the rooms come with a king-size bed, and all have a 27-inch flatscreen TV and a private balcony or patio (only a few on the fourth floor have a view of the lake). Walls are painted in soft tones and decorated with local handicrafts and textiles. The suites are massive, and come with a fireplace and even larger flatscreen TV. The pool here is shaped like a fish and features a children's end and two water slides.

Downtown. © **502/7721-7656.** ©/fax 502/7721-7165. www.tioshabaj.com. 30 units. $79 double; $135 suite. Rates include taxes. AE, DC, MC, V. **Amenities:** Restaurant; bar; large outdoor pool; sauna; free Wi-Fi. *In room:* TV.

INEXPENSIVE

Posada de Santiago ★   While the rooms feel a bit rustic, the setting on a lush hillside above the lake makes this a great choice. My favorite rooms are the six individual stone cottages, which each come with a queen- and twin-size bed and a private patio or terrace with a hammock. Casa Maya has a private gazebo and bit of lawn. There are three suites, of which I like Casa Rosa, which has a stone headboard with a Maya-styled face over the queen-size bed. There are also a couple of budget cottages with very basic rooms that share a common kitchen, living area, and bathroom. All but the budget rooms have a fireplace, and the two suites come with TVs. The best feature here is the pool and barbecue area, which has a fabulous perch overlooking the lake, as well as a separate hot tub and sauna. The restaurant is also very good, and serves a mix of traditional Guatemalan food and American/international dishes. A taxi or tuk tuk ride here should cost around Q15.

1.5km (2 miles) south of the dock. © **502/7721-7366** or 5784-9111. Fax 502/7721-7365. www.posadade santiago.com. 19 units, 14 with private bathroom. $30 double with shared bathroom; $45 double with private bathroom; $60–$125 cottage or suite. AE, DC, MC, V. **Amenities:** Restaurant; bar; Jacuzzi; midsize outdoor pool; sauna; free Wi-Fi. *In room:* No phone.

OTHER VILLAGES AROUND LAKE ATITLAN

A dozen or more small towns and villages ring the shores of Lake Atitlán. All are easily accessible by car, taxi, tuk tuk, or boat. Some, in fact, are only accessible by boat. While all of these towns and villages are good destinations for day trips, they also make great places to stay, especially if you want to get away from the heavily beaten tourist path.

Santa Catarina Palopo & San Antonio Palopo

These two Kaquichel Maya towns on the northeastern shore of the lake are connected to Panajachel by a well-paved road, and are also accessible by regular water taxi service. **Santa Catarina Palopó ★** is particularly well known for its distinctive *huipil* ★★★ of dark blues and greens with intricate embroidery. **San Antonio Palopó ★** is where the paved road ends and a dirt road continues around the lake. Both towns have tight streets packed with homes and businesses that rise from the lake shore, as well as churches in their town centers. The brilliantly whitewashed church in San Antonio Palopó is especially pretty, with an enviable perch and fantastic view over Lake Atitlán. San Antonio Palopó is often a featured stop in the organized lake tours sold out of Panajachel.

Although the walk isn't particularly picturesque, and you have to be careful of passing traffic, you can walk from Panajachel to San Antonio. There are some great views from the side of the road as you arrive in San Antonio Palopó. Whether you're walking or driving, be sure to stop here. It takes between 2 and 2½ hours to walk one-way. You could walk there and back, or simply walk one-way and grab a taxi or hitchhike back. Hitchhiking between San Antonio Palopó and Panajachel during the day is relatively safe, but avoid doing so at night or at any other places around the lake.

Where to Stay & Dine

In addition to the places listed below, **Terraza Choi ★** (© **502/5847-4852;** www.terrazachoi.com) is a pretty bed-and-breakfast, with three cozy rooms located on the lakeshore in a converted home.

VERY EXPENSIVE

Casa Palopó ★★★   This small hotel exudes elegance, from the stone tiles on the pool deck to the original art adorning the walls. Most of the rooms have king-size beds, large bathrooms with beautiful Mexican majolica sinks, and large terraces with gorgeous views. My favorite is suite no. 1, whose large terrace is reached through French doors. There's a private villa above the main building with two gorgeous master suites, a Jacuzzi, a full kitchen, dining and living rooms, and a private infinity-edge pool. The villa also comes with a personal butler and cook. Back down at the hotel, the restaurant is worth a visit even if you're not a guest here, and the pool with wood gazebo is a great place to unwind.

Carretera a San Antonio Palopó, Km 6.8, Santa Catarina Palopó. © **502/7762-2270.** Fax 502/7762-2721. www.casapalopo.com. 9 units. $168–$206 double; $220–$263 suite; $930 villa. Rates higher during peak periods, lower during the off season. AE, DC, MC, V. No children under 15 allowed. **Amenities:** Restaurant; bar; concierge; small gym and spa services; small outdoor pool; room service; free Wi-Fi. *In room:* Minibar.

Villas B'alam Ya ★★★ 🏠   The four independent villas here are all unique, yet all overflow with artistic touches and eclectic design elements. The whole complex is set on the lakeside on a quiet stretch between Panajachel and Santa Catarina Palopó. The villas vary in size, from the compact **Casa Jade,** to the two-bedroom, three-level **Villa Bambu.** All come with a working kitchen and a host of modern amenities. I recommend the namesake **Villa B'alam Ya,** which has a large garden and veranda off the main living area, as well as an expansive lakeview deck off the upstairs master bedroom. There's no formal restaurant here, but breakfasts are cooked and served in your villa, and for other meals, you can either cook for yourself, arrange for delivery from a range of Panajachel restaurants, or have an in-house chef come and cook for you.

Carretera a San Antonio Palopó, Km 4, Santa Catarina Palopó. ©/fax **502/7762-2522.** www.balamya.com. 4 units. $150–$350 double. Rates higher during peak periods, lower during the off season. AE, DC, MC, V. **Amenities:** Concierge; Jacuzzi; complimentary kayaks; small outdoor pool; room service; spa services; free Wi-Fi. *In room:* TV w/DVD, hair dryer, full kitchen, minibar, MP3 docking station.

MODERATE

Villa Santa Catarina ★   This pretty hotel is located in the heart of Santa Catarina Palopó, just up from the lake. All of the rooms are spacious, with tile floors and tasteful local decor, and though the lake is nearby, the shape of the building compromises the views from most of the rooms. The best bed in the house is room no. 51, a junior suite with a mosaic-tile bathroom, a balcony with both lake and mountain views, and a large picture window with a full-on view of the water. Of the standard rooms, no. 3 has the best view.

Santa Catarina Palopó. ✆ **502/7762-1291** at the hotel or 2223-5000 reservations in Guatemala City. Fax 502/2334-8134. www.villasdeguatemala.com. 36 units. $75 double; $130 junior suite. AE, DC, MC, V. **Amenities:** Restaurant; bar; outdoor pool; room service. *In room:* TV, no phone.

INEXPENSIVE

Hotel Terrazas del Lago   Simple and relaxed is the best way to describe this place on the eastern edge of San Antonio Palopó. Most of the rooms are on the top floor of this two-story building, and all have terra-cotta tile floors, river stone walls, simple furnishings, private bathrooms, and heavy wool blankets on the beds. Room no. 12 is the pick of the litter: a second-floor end unit with a great view of the lake. This hotel feels very isolated, though it has its own boat dock and is just a short walk to town.

San Antonio Palopó. ✆ **502/7762-0157** or 5820-2020. Fax 502/7762-0037. www.hotelterrazasdel lago.com. 10 units. $25 double. AE, DC, MC, V. **Amenities:** Restaurant; bar. *In room:* No phone.

The Northwest Shore of Lake Atitlan

Many of the boats leaving Panajachel for San Pedro La Laguna make a series of stops at a handful of small villages and isolated hotels that line the northwestern shore of Lake Atitlán.

San Marcos La Laguna ★ and **Santa Cruz La Laguna** ★ are two small communities on the northwestern shores of Lake Atitlán. Both are set on high hillsides above the lakeshore. However, each has a selection of small hotels spread along the water's edge. I particularly like San Marcos, which features a delightful warren of narrow stone and dirt paths winding through thick gardens and forest.

For some reason, these two towns have developed as hot spots for yoga retreats and holistic getaways, with several hotels in each town catering to this niche. The most serious and long-standing yoga retreat and meditation centers in the area are **Las Pirámides del Ka** (✆ **502/5205-7151**; www.laspiramidesdelka.com), which was inaugurated on the summer solstice more than 15 years ago and continues to offer a full range of retreats, classes, and treatments, and **Villa Sumaya** (see below), a somewhat newer option giving them a run for their money.

   Safety First

Dirt paths and roads running close to the lakeshore connect all of the towns and villages along the northwestern shore of Lake Atitlán. Walking between the towns can be an excellent way to spend a day. However, be careful and always ask your hotel or the INGUAT office about the current security situation along these paths. The town of San Pablo La Laguna, in particular, has been known in the past for attacks on tourist hikers.

One of the smallest towns along the lakeshore, **Jaibalito** is home to the hotel **La Casa del Mundo** (see below) and the restaurant **Ven Acá** (see below).

WHERE TO STAY

In addition to the places listed below, I like the eclectic, artistic touches at the **Hotel Aaculaax** (✆ **502/5287-0521**; www.aaculaax.com) in San Marcos. In Santa Cruz, backpackers and adventure travelers tend to congregate and stay at **La Iguana Perdida** ★ (✆ **502/5706-4117**; www.laiguanaperdida.com), located just above the town's main dock.

VERY EXPENSIVE

Laguna Lodge ★★ 📷 This new collection of rustically luxurious rooms and suites is built up a steep hillside, starting right from the water on a quiet cove just outside of Santa Cruz La Laguna. Rooms here feature wood floors and carved wooden doors, marble bath countertops, tasteful decor, private balconies, and lake views. The owners are serious about environmental conservation and sustainable tourism practices. The restaurant serves gourmet, yet entirely vegetarian, cuisine, most of which is locally grown and organic. They are also backed by an extensive private nature reserve, with several trails, and excellent lookout points. There are several lounge areas, with hammocks or cozy couches. I like the thatch-covered area overlooking the lake.

Santa Cruz La Laguna. ✆ **502/7823-2529.** www.fiveleafresort.com. 7 units. $225–$290 double. Rates include full breakfast, and round trip boat transportation from Panajachel. AE, DC, MC, V. **Amenities:** Restaurant; bar; concierge; small gym; Jacuzzi; complimentary kayaks; room service; sauna; spa services; free Wi-Fi. *In room:* No phone.

Moderate

La Casa del Mundo ★ 📷 This hotel sits at the top of several steep flights of steps on a rocky outcropping that juts into the lake. The rooms' distinctive decor mixes local arts and crafts with a European sense of style. Every room has a view of the lake, and a few have private balconies with lake and volcano views. There are also several open-air tiled terraces spread around the grounds, all with great views. On one of these terraces, down near the water, is the hotel's wood-fired hot tub, wonderfully located to allow you to alternate between the hot tub and the cool lake.

Jaibalito. ✆ **502/5218-5332** or 5204-5558. www.lacasadelmundo.com. 16 units, 10 with private bathroom. $36 double shared bathroom; $64–$79 double with private bathroom. Rates slightly higher during peak periods. Rates include taxes. No credit cards. **Amenities:** Restaurant; bar; Jacuzzi; kayak rentals; Wi-Fi ($3.15 per hour). *In room:* No phone.

Villa Sumaya ★★ 📷 If you're looking for spiritual and physical rejuvenation, this is the place for you. The individual cabins are beautifully done with tile floors, soft cotton comforters, local crafts, and a large veranda with several chairs and a hammock. All rooms face the lake, with the towering silhouettes of volcanoes in the background. The hotel's Blue Tiger Temple is a wonderful wood-floored yoga and meditation room that often attracts visiting instructors and retreat guests, and there's always a massage therapist on call. There's both a solar heated pool and a good beach for swimming, and the grounds are lush with tropical flowers.

Santa Cruz La Laguna. ✆ **502/4026-1390** or 4026-1455. www.villasumaya.com. 15 units. $65–$110 double. AE, DC, MC, V. **Amenities:** Restaurant; bar; babysitting; Jacuzzi; pool; sauna. *In room:* No phone.

Inexpensive

Posada Schumann ★ This lodge has a series of private and duplex bungalows spread over lush grounds that slope down to the lake. There's a cozy feel to the whole operation. You'll pay a little more for the best bungalows, which are closest to the water. Some come equipped with kitchenettes and/or minifridges. Kayaks can be rented for tooling around on the lake.

Barrio Tres, San Marcos La Laguna. ✆ **502/5202-2216.** Fax 502/2473-1181. www.posada-schumann. com. 14 units $25–$50 double. Rates include continental breakfast. AE, DC, MC, V. **Amenities:** Restaurant; bar; kayak rentals; sauna. *In room:* No phone.

WHERE TO DINE

Most folks eat all their meals at their hotels, but if you do venture out, there are a couple of good options in each of the towns. In San Marcos, I recommend the pizzas, curries, and creative vegetarian fare at **Restaurante Fe,** or the mixed menu, pool tables, and twice-weekly movies offered up at **Blind Lemon's** (www.blindlemons. com). Over in Santa Cruz, try the vegetarian fare at the lakefront restaurant at **Isla Verde** (www.islaverdeatitlan.com).

Club Ven Acá ★★ 📖 INTERNATIONAL This unique joint serves up some of the best and most creative food around, in a relaxed lakefront setting. Tables are set spread around a large patio surrounding a pool, either under large canvas umbrellas or an open-air red clay tile roof. Definitely start things off with the pumpkin seed, cranberry, and cheese quesadilla. For a light meal, I recommend the seared tuna salad with an Asian citrus dressing. Main dishes are varied and creative. There's a daily Q150 prix fixe meal that includes an appetizer, salad, main course and dessert. Diners here have access to the pool and Jacuzzi, and on weekends, there's sometimes a hip bar and lounge scene here.

In Jaibalito. ✆ **502/5051-4520.** www.clubvenaca.com. Reservations recommended. Main courses Q55–Q95. No credit cards. Wed–Sat 11am–5pm; Sun 10am–4pm.

Solola

Sololá sits at a strategic point between Lake Atitlán and the Pan-American Highway. Even before the highways were built and the Spanish arrived, Sololá was a major trading post connecting various coastal, lake, and highland communities. To this day, **Sololá's Tuesday and Friday markets ★** are some of the largest in the highlands. The markets are anything but the typical tourist haunts, and are primarily for buying and selling among the various highland communities. However, you can find excellent textile products and some arts and crafts here. Sololá is one of the few towns where the men still wear the elaborate traditional garb, with shirts featuring intricate embroidery over multicolored cloth; the cut of the shirt looks like something out of the American Old West.

Sololá is located on a well-paved road 8km (5 miles) from Panajachel. A taxi from Panajachel should cost around Q30 to Q50. You can also hitch a ride here on any number of buses plying the route between Panajachel and Los Encuentros.

Iximche & Tecpan

When Iximché was founded in 1465, the Kaqchiquel were at war with the Ki'ché, and the town's location, atop a long narrow plateau with steep ravines on either side, was chosen for its natural defenses. Today, the ruins at Iximché are made up of four large plazas that demark distinct religious and residential areas. There's one particularly well-maintained ball court and several large temple structures. At one end of the site there's a mound that remains an active site of Maya worship, and it's quite common to see locals lighting candles and incense and making offerings.

When the conquistador Pedro de Alvarado founded the first capital of Guatemala in 1524, he placed it next to Iximché, a Kaqchiquel capital city, near the present-day town of Tecpán. However, Kaqchiquel unrest and uprisings soon forced Alvarado to move the Spanish capital to the site of present-day Ciudad Vieja.

While nowhere near as spectacular as Tikal or Copán, Iximché is very well preserved, and a visit here is definitely worthwhile for anyone interested in ancient Maya culture and architecture.

The archaeological site is open daily from 8am until 5pm. Admission is Q30 ($3.75). Tecpán is located just off the Pan-American Highway about halfway between Los Encuentros and Chimaltenango. From Tecpán it's just 5km (3 miles) along a well-paved road to the ruins. The best way to visit the site is as part of a guided tour. All of the agencies in Panajachel offer guided tours to Iximché and Tecpán. Rates run around Q150 to Q300 for a half-day tour including transportation and a light lunch.

WESTERN HIGHLANDS

The rugged geography of Guatemala's Western Highlands is a dense patchwork of volcanic mountains and lakes populated mostly by small, and often isolated, villages of the country's many Maya people. Some of the primary tribes who call this area home include the Ki'che, Mam, Kekchi, Tz'utujil, Ixil, Kaqchiquel, and Jacaltec. Most still practice small-scale plot farming on milpas, which are fields, usually recently cleared, that are planted with a mix of crops, but most prominently with corn, beans, tomatoes, and other traditional staples. These milpas are family and community-based endeavors.

Locals live on a mix of subsistence farming and bartering. Aside from the food they grow, they also produce intricately designed and brightly colored woven textiles.

In Spanish, the Western Highlands are called the *Altiplano,* comprised of seven distinct provinces: Quetzaltenango, Sololá, Huehuetenango, Quiché, San Marcos, Totonicapán, and Chimaltenanago.

Aside from the area around Lake Atitlán, which is covered in-depth in chapter 7, other highlights of the Western Highlands include the small city of **Chichicastenango** and its remarkable market; the university and language-school hub of **Quetzaltenango;** and the northern outpost of the almost border-town **Huehuetenango.** Surrounding these larger cities are many small, beautiful villages worth exploring. In addition, the area presents opportunities for hiking volcanoes, soaking in hot springs, or trekking through the isolated region known as the **Ixil Triangle.**

CHICHICASTENANGO ★★

144km (89 miles) NW of Guatemala City; 37km (23 miles) N of Panajachel

Santo Tomás de Chichicastenango is a small, highland city with perhaps the most impressive—and certainly the most famous—open-air market in all of Guatemala. Although the twice-weekly market and the city have adapted to the flood of tourists, they both maintain a sense of ancient tradition and the indelible mark of Maya culture that stretches back for millennia. The city center is made of narrow cobblestone streets, and just outside the center, the landscape is one of deep ravines and sparsely populated hillsides. In fact, one local name for Chichicastenango is Tziguan Tinamit, which translates roughly as "surrounded by ravines." However, most people simply refer to it as Chichi.

The town's name derives from a local purple flower, the *chichicaste*. The locals often refer to themselves as Maxeños, with the "x" pronounced as a soft "sh" sound. The Ki'che Maya are the principal linguistic group found in Chichicastenango, although on market days, the town is filled with a cacophony of Mayan dialects, mixed with Spanish and the bargaining banter of Americans, Europeans, and other Central and South Americans.

North of Chichicastenango are several small towns and villages worth visiting, including Santa Cruz del Quiché, Nebaj, and the Ixil Triangle.

Essentials

GETTING THERE

BY BUS   La Masheñita (© 502/2473-4472) buses leave Guatemala City from 10a Calle 10-03, Zona 1, roughly every 20 minutes between 5am and 4pm, with less frequent service during other hours. **Veloz Quichelense** (no phone) buses leave from 41a Calle between 6a and 7a avenidas, Zona 8, on roughly the same schedule. The ride takes 3 hours and the fare is Q30. You can also take any bus to Santa Cruz de Quiché from the Terminal de Autobuses and get off in Chichicastenango.

If you're coming from anywhere else on a bus along the Pan-American Highway, get off in Los Encuentros, and hop on the next bus heading north to Chichicastenango.

On market days, tourist shuttles flock to Chichi from Guatemala City, Panajachel, Antigua, and Quetzaltenango. If you're staying at any of these other towns or cities, ask your hotel or any tour agency to find out current schedules and fares.

Warning: For some reason, the buses plying this route are driven by some of the most reckless and dangerous drivers in Guatemala, frequently passing on blind curves both uphill and down. They pose a threat and danger to themselves, their passengers, and other drivers.

BY CAR   To drive to Chichicastenango, take the Pan-American Highway (CA-1) north out of Guatemala City and the turnoff at Los Encuentros. Follow the exit sign for Chichicastenango and Santa Cruz del Quiché. The drive takes about 2 to 3 hours from Guatemala City; from Panajachel the trip is under an hour.

GETTING AROUND

Chichicastenango is extremely compact, so it's easy to walk just about anywhere in the downtown area. Taxis and tuk tuks can be flagged down all around the central plaza. If you can't readily find one, have your hotel call one for you.

ORIENTATION

The large main plaza is Chichi's central hub. This is ground zero of the market, and where you'll find the city's two main churches, museum, and municipal office buildings. Almost all of the hotels, restaurants, banks, shops, and other services can be found within a 4- or 5-block radius of the central plaza.

FAST FACTS   There's an **INGUAT** tourist office just off the main plaza on 7a Calle (© **502/7756-2022**). The **post office** is located on 7a Av. 8-47, Zona 1. **Banco Industrial, Banrural,** and **Banco G & T** all have branches with ATMs just off the central plaza. There are several Internet cafes around the downtown section of Chichi. The local **Hospital El Buen Samaritano** (© **502/7756-1163**; 6a Calle 3-60, Zona 1) is just off the main plaza. If you need to contact the local **police,** dial © **502/7756-1365.**

What to See & Do

By far the main attraction in Chichicastenango is its twice-weekly market. In fact, Chichi is almost a ghost town on non-market days, with a few vendors set up in permanent stalls on the town's main plaza.

One of the city's only other official attractions is the **Museo Regional,** 5a Av. 4-47, Zona 1 (© **502/4176-2087**), located cater-cornered to the **Iglesia de Santo Tomás** (see below). This small museum has some decent ancient Maya artifacts in jade, stone, and ceramic. The rooms are dimly lit, and the explanatory material is all in Spanish. This place is also sometimes called the Museo Arqueológico Rossbach because much of the collection was donated by the German priest Idelfonso Rossbach. The museum is open Tuesday through Saturday from 8am to 4pm, and Sunday from 8am to 2pm. Admission is Q5.

Chichicastenango's **cemetery** ★ is filled with brightly painted mausoleums and aboveground crypts. While it is very photogenic and atmospheric, there have been reports of attacks on tourists here, so be careful and only visit the cemetery as part of a group or with a tour guide. The cemetery is located along the western end of 8a Calle.

Chichicastenango

ACCOMMODATIONS ■
Hotel Casa del Rey **3**
Hotel Chalet **15**
Hotel Santo Tomás **14**
Mayan Inn **8**

DINING ◆
Las Brasas **13**
Restaurante Los
 Cofradías **12**
Restaurante Casa
 San Juan **10**
Tu Café **11**

ATTRACTIONS ●
Capilla del Calvario **9**
Cemetery **16**
Iglesia de Santo Tomás **5**
INGUAT Office **6**
Moreria Santo Tomás **4**
Museo de las Mascaras
 Ceremoniales **2**
Museo Regional **7**
Pascual Abaj **1**

THE MARKET ★★★

Thursday and Sunday are market days in Chichi, and on these days, the city is a mad orgy of sights, sounds, and smells. Maya craft sellers from across the highlands set up makeshift booths around the central plaza, spilling over on to sidewalks, the church steps, and up various side streets. A broad selection of Guatemalan handicrafts is available, including carved-wood masks and religious figures, ceramic wares, and an immense selection of the country's amazing native textiles. In addition to the craft-works, vendors sell fruits, vegetables, flowers, medicinal herbs, and more. Despite the seeming chaos, there's actually a historical order to the setup, with vendors selling certain products in specific areas that have been designated for as long as anyone can remember. In fact, while tourists might think the entire market is geared toward them, the market is actually the central meeting place for inter-village trade and com-merce among the various highland Maya. **Note:** While a discerning shopper can find quality goods in Chichicastenango's market, much of what is offered is now machine-made and geared toward the mass tourist market.

> ### Seeing Fireworks
>
> Don't be surprised or scared, it's not gunfire, and it's not a bomb—although they are called *bombas*. Guatemalans have an ongoing fascination with fire-works. In many of the major cities (particularly Chichicastenango on market day), you're likely to hear fireworks going off almost any day or night.

Vendors begin arriving in Chichi the afternoon before market day, and set up throughout the evening and into the early morning. The best time to shop is either very early, before the tour buses from Guatemala City and Lake Atitlán begin arriving, or in the afternoon, after everyone's cleared out.

CHURCHES & SHRINES

The **Iglesia de Santo Tomás** ★★★ was built by Dominican priests more than 450 years ago on top of an ancient Maya worship site. It remains the heart and soul of Chichicastenango and—to this day—is used as much for traditional Maya ceremonial purposes as it is for Catholic Mass. Local Maya can almost always be found on the steps leading up to the church, burning copal incense and candles, and offering prayer. Each of the 18 steps represents one of the months in the Maya calendar. Rather than the expected pews, you'll find makeshift shrines and altars spread out on the floor with pine needles and candles. It was in the church's convent that the oldest known copy of the ancient **Popol Vuh** text was discovered.

The church is located on the southeast corner of the main plaza. **Note:** Out of respect, the front door of the church is informally reserved for locals and high church officials. Visitors are encouraged to use the side door.

Capilla del Calvario ★ is the smaller and less active of the two churches on Chichi's main plaza. Inside you'll find hand-painted murals and an intricate wood altar with a carved Christ in a glass coffin in front. You'll notice a dark room off the main body of the church; this holds a second Christ in a glass coffin, and is where many locals prefer to pray.

The Maya shrine, **Pascual Abaj,** is located on a hilltop south of Chichi. A carved stone idol, said to be hundreds of years old, is the centerpiece of the shrine. This is an active site of worship for many locals, who come here to make offerings and pray. Candles, incense, flowers, food, and even booze offerings are brought here to please the gods. Be respectful of the spiritual significance of this site, and don't take pictures or interfere with the worship.

On the way to Pascual Abaj, it's worth stopping at the **Museo de las Máscaras Ceremoniales** ★ (© 502/7756-1915). The museum has been run by the same family since it opened in 1880, and is located near the end of 9a Calle, just up the path to Pascual Abaj. Closer to downtown, you'll find **Morería Santo Tomás,** 5a Avenida and 9a Calle (© 502/7756-1882). Both of these places are actually known as *morerías,* the name for shops where ceremonial masks and costumes are made and stored.

While many tourists visit Pascual Abaj on their own, I recommend you go with a guide, which can be arranged through your hotel or INGUAT. It can be unsafe for solo tourists or small groups, and a local guide insures that visitors won't be robbed, and informs them of cultural sensitivities including local customs and sacred ground.

Where to Stay

Hotels in Chichicastenango fill up Wednesday through Thursday and Saturday through Sunday. On these days it's essential to have a reservation, and the hotels will charge top dollar. Moreover, if you're coming for market, make sure your reservation is totally confirmed and secure. Some hotels will give away rooms on these busy days, unless they are prepaid. On other days, the hotels are empty and usually very willing to negotiate a lower rate.

EXPENSIVE

Mayan Inn This hotel, just off the central plaza behind El Calvario, is a local institution. It's perfectly located, very friendly, and oozes Colonial-era charm. However, you're paying a pretty penny for some very basic accommodations here. Every room comes with a fireplace, which is lit for you during dinner time. Rooms are divided among two facing buildings, and come with two twin beds. I'd definitely ask to see a few before making my choice. The best standard rooms are nos. 12, 14, and 15, while no. 11, a second-floor suite, has great views, tons of space, and two double beds. Each building has a garden courtyard, and Maya glyphs are painted on the walls, mixing somewhat clumsily at times with the colonial-era decor.

8a Calle and 3a Av., Zona 1. © **502/7756-1176.** Fax 502/7756-1212. www.mayaninn.com.gt. 30 units. $134 double. Ten percent discount available for Mon, Tues, and Fri. AE, DC, MC, V. **Amenities:** Restaurant; bar. *In room:* No phone.

MODERATE

Hotel Casa del Rey Though this is the most modern hotel in Chichicastenango, the basic rooms show their age. Some have good views of the town below; the best are in the 300 and 400 blocks of rooms. It's worth the extra money to upgrade to a suite, which is much larger and comes with a spacious sitting room, fireplace, and private porch. The hotel has a pool with a large waterfall, and a separate children's pool and Jacuzzi.

THE popol VUH

The Popol Vuh, often referred to as the Maya Bible, is one of the most important Maya texts. It was first discovered around 1702 by Dominican Father Francisco Ximénez, who found it in the Santo Tomás convent and translated it into Spanish. Not only did he translate the text, but he made a copy of the original, ensuring that a direct connection to the ancient hieroglyphic and oral texts would exist to this day. It was also transliterated into the Ki'che language using Latin letters sometime in the 16th century.

The Popol Vuh contains a treasure-trove of ancient Maya myth, including tales of the twin heroes Hunahpu and Xbalanque and their battles with the lords of Xibalba, or the underworld. Like the Judeo-Christian Bible, the Popol Vuh begins with the creation myth of the Ki'che people.

In 1972, the Popol Vuh was declared Guatemala's national book. Several good English translations exist, including Dennis Tedlock's *Popol Vuh: The Definitive Edition of the Mayan Book of the Dawn of Life and the Glories of Gods and Kings* (Touchstone Press, 1996), and Allen J. Christenson's *Popol Vuh: The Sacred Book of the Mayas* (O Books, 2004).

While the Catholic church and its appointed priests are prominent in Chichicastenango, the city's real seat of religious power rests with the *cofradías* (brotherhoods). There are 14 *cofradías* in Chichi. Each *cofradía* has between six and eight members with specific ranks and responsibilities, which are clearly denoted by their ceremonial dress. The *cofradías* attend church together in their ornate regalia every Sunday, and each *cofradía* is responsible for the care and celebration of their namesake saint. On the celebration day of their saint, the *cofradía* marches in a loud procession through the town. Being the city of Santo Tomás de Chichicastenango, the Santo Tomás *cofradía* is the most important in town. Throughout the week leading up to Saint Thomas's feast day of December 21, Chichicastenango is abuzz in religious fervor, with numerous processions and traditional dances, including the **Palo Volador,** in which dancers descend in flying arcs suspended by their ankles from a high pole or tower.

Km 144, on the road into Chichicastenango. ② **502/7756-1053.** Fax 502/7756-1140. www.hotelcasa delrey.com. 68 units. $80–$100 double Wed–Thurs and Sat–Sun. Rates lower on other days. AE, DC, MC, V. **Amenities:** Restaurant; bar; laundry service; midsize outdoor pool. *In room:* TV, no phone.

Hotel Santo Tomás ★ 👔 This hotel has the best location—just 2 blocks from the central plaza and market—and is easily my top choice in Chichicastenango. Housed inside a former colonial-era mansion, this place has morphed into a sprawling operation, but still maintains its style and ambience. Several large interior courtyards, common verandas, garden fountains, and assorted nooks tie the whole thing together. The rooms are all fairly large and are outfitted with two queen-size beds, wood furnishings, and a fireplace. There's a large terrace with a pool and separate Jacuzzi, and a gym with steam bath and sauna. The restaurant and bar are both stately and popular. There's a fabulous panoramic view of all of Chichi from the hotel's rooftop terrace.

7a Av. 5-32, Zona 1. ② **502/7756-1061** or 7756-1269. Fax 502/7756-1306. hst@itelgua.com. 75 units. $95–$110 double AE, DC, MC, V. **Amenities:** Restaurant; bar; small exercise room; Jacuzzi; outdoor pool; sauna. *In room:* Hair dryer.

INEXPENSIVE

Hotel Chalet 🎣 This bed-and-breakfast is located a few blocks away from the center of the action. The rooms are basic and small, as are the bathrooms, but they have good firm beds, either one queen-size or two twins, and the management is very amiable and helpful. If possible, try for room no. 18, which is on the third floor and features a queen-size bed and a bit of a view. There's a pleasant rooftop terrace where breakfast is often served.

3a Calle C, 7-44, Zona 1. ② **502/7756-1360.** www.chalethotelguatemala.com. 10 units. $28 double. AE, DC, MC, V. **Amenities:** Free Wi-Fi. *In room:* No phone.

Where to Dine

In addition to the places listed below, **Restaurante Los Cofradías,** at the corner of 5a Avenida and 6a Calle (② **502/7756-1643**), is a good option for local food in a pleasant setting; their second-floor corner location offers a view of the activity below, while the **Restaurante Casa San Juan** (🕾 **502/7756-2086;** 4a Av. 6-58, Zona 1) is an artsy oasis with good grub, located just off the **Capilla del Calvario.**

There are a host of stalls set up on the main plaza serving grilled meats with fresh tortillas and other Guatemalan fast food. The food here is hearty and very inexpensive, but only those with well-adapted digestive tracts should partake.

INEXPENSIVE

Las Brasas ★ GUATEMALAN/STEAKHOUSE Get hearty steaks and Chapin fare at very reasonable prices, in addition to thick cuts of beef, shish kabobs, fire-roasted chicken, and a very tasty pork *adobado,* a tangy local tomato-based sauce. The large dining room is sparsely, yet eclectically, decorated, with locally carved masks, drums, and deer skin. Try to grab a table overlooking the street.

6a Calle 4-52, Zona 1, at the entrance to Hotel Giron. 🕾 **502/7756-2226.** Main courses Q45–Q80. MC, V. Daily 7am–9pm.

Tu Café ★ 🍴 GUATEMALAN Tucked into a little space fronting the main plaza and market, this pleasant restaurant and cafe serves well-prepared Guatemalan fare at reasonable prices. Try the grilled chicken smothered in sautéed onions with delicious vegetables and rice on the side. There's always a daily special, which is a full three-course meal, for around Q30.

5a Av. 6-44, Zona 1, fronting the main plaza. 🕾 **502/7756-1448.** Main courses Q25–Q50. No credit cards. Daily 7am–8pm.

Chichi After Dark

Chichicastenango is a sleepy town, with almost no nightlife apart from what you'll find at the bars in the various hotels. On the nights before market days, the central market is abuzz with activity, and you may actually find a marimba band set up entertaining the crowds.

Going Beyond Chichicastenango

SANTA CRUZ DEL QUICHÉ & K'UMARCAAJ

Located some 19km (12 miles) north of Chichicastenango is the small mountain city of Santa Cruz del Quiché, or simply Quiché. Slightly off the main circuit, Santa Cruz del Quiché (the capital of the Quiché province) is much more representative of a modern highland Maya city than its more touristy neighbor. The pace of life here is quite slow, except on Saturday market days.

Quiché is also the gateway to the post-Classic Maya city of **K'umarcaaj,** also known as **Utatlán,** and sometimes spelled Q'uma'rka'aaj. **K'umarcaaj** was the ancient capital of the Quiché region, and is even mentioned in the Popol Vuh. The Maya K'iche offered some of the fiercest resistance ever encountered by the Spaniards. However, they were technologically outmatched and eventually defeated. K'umarcaaj was captured and mostly destroyed in 1524 under the orders of Pedro Alvarado, who had recently defeated the Maya Ki'che King Tucún Umán outside of Quetzaltenango. In fact, the story goes that the surviving Maya Ki'che had put forth a cordial invite for Pedro Alvarado to visit K'umarcaaj, where they planned to ambush him, but he wised up to the plan and sacked the city instead.

The ruins sit on a hilltop surrounded by steep ravines, a testament to the city's strategic wartime position. Little has been done here in the way of excavation, but the ruins of several temples, a ball court, and some well-maintained plazas can be visited.

RIGOBERTA menchú

Rigoberta Menchú is one of Guatemala's best-known and most powerful public figures. Born in 1959 in Chimal, a Quiché village, Menchú is a diminutive woman who almost always dresses in the traditional garb of the Highland Maya. With just a sixth-grade education, she is a Nobel Prize winner and best-selling author.

As an adolescent, Menchú worked with Catholic social reform groups, and in 1979, she became an activist with the Peasant Unity Committee. The following year, Menchú's brother was murdered by the military, and in 1980, her father died, along with 36 others, when the military set fire to the Spanish embassy. The group had sought refuge in the embassy after publicly denouncing the ongoing atrocities. Later that same year, Menchú's mother was taken by paramilitary forces, never to be seen again.

In 1981, Menchú went into hiding after receiving death threats for her work to organize the Maya people against the rampant violence and oppression in Guatemala. She fled the country, remaining in exile for 12 years. During her exile, Menchú returned clandestinely to Guatemala several times in an attempt to continue her work, but was always forced to leave because of death threats and personal danger.

I, Rigoberta Menchú, based on a series of recorded interviews with the Maya activist, was published in 1983. The book had an immense impact in bringing the atrocities being committed by the military against the Maya in Guatemala to the attention of the international community. In 1992, Menchú was awarded the Nobel Peace Prize for her work.

Menchú's selection was criticized by some because she had been a member of organizations that advocated violence. In 1999, further controversy arose when an academic researcher disputed the accuracy of some of the details in her book. Menchú eventually admitted that some of the events and atrocities described in the book were generalized and composite accounts of what was occurring in Guatemala throughout the period, although they may not have occurred on the dates or in the places originally claimed. A member of the Nobel committee stated that Menchú's award was not based exclusively on her autobiography, and he dismissed any suggestion that the Committee should consider revoking her prize.

With the funds from the Nobel prize, Menchú formed a foundation to work for indigenous rights internationally (the rights of women in particular), attempted to have Guatemalan military leaders extradited and tried for crimes against humanity, and became president of a company that distributes low-cost generic medications to the poor. Menchú was named a Goodwill Representative for the 1996 Guatemalan Peace Accords by then President Alvaro Arzu. She is also a representative of the United Nation's Educational, Scientific and Cultural Organization (UNESCO).

K'umarcaaj is still considered a sacred site by modern Maya, and it's not uncommon to find them performing rituals here. This is particularly true of a long tunnel or cave, known locally as *la cueva*. It's wise to plan ahead, bring a flashlight, be respectful, and definitely ask permission of the park guards and anyone you encounter there in prayer before entering the cave.

K'umarcaaj is located just 3km (2 miles) outside of Quiché. The ruins are open daily from 8am to 5pm. Admission is Q30. There's a small museum (no phone) near the entrance with a detailed scale model of the city. A taxi from Santa Cruz del Quiché should cost around Q80 round-trip, with an hour or more set aside to explore the ruins.

Quiché is serviced by frequent buses from Chichicastenango and Guatemala City. If you need or want to spend the night here, check into the **Hotel Rey Ki'che,** 8a Calle 0-39, Zona 5 (© 502/7755-0827).

NEGAJ & THE IXIL TRIANGLE ★★

The Ixil Triangle is a remote region of northern Quiché populated by the Maya Ixil people. The people of this region are deeply tied to their Maya roots, and many speak only their local dialect and little or no Spanish. The small village of Nebaj is the heart of the Ixil Triangle. The town has cobblestone streets and a lovely colonial-era church. The two other principal towns forming the triangle are Chajul and Cotzal. This mountainous region is surrounded by tiny villages and communities, which are tied together by heritage and an active barter economy.

The Ixil Triangle suffered brutal repression during the civil war, particularly under the reign of General Ríos Montt (1982–83). Despite this past, the area is actually one of the safer regions for independent travelers. The local populations tend to be relatively open and friendly to foreigners, although you should still be very respectful and always ask permission before taking anyone's photograph.

The distinctive Nebaj *huipiles* are some of the most beautiful in Guatemala. Predominantly fashioned of purples, greens, and yellows, they feature incredibly tight embroidery of human and animal figures as well as complex geometric designs. The women wear a headdress of colorful ribbons with fluffy pompoms. As in Chichicastenango, market days here are Thursday and Sunday.

Most of your travel needs in and around Nebaj can be arranged with the folks at **El Descanso** restaurant and their sister operation **Guías Ixiles** (© 502/5847-4747; www.nebaj.com). Founded by a couple of former Peace Corps volunteers and a local social activist, this place is the central hub for many travelers into and around the Ixil Triangle. Multiday and overnight hikes and mountain-biking tours are offered around the Ixil Triangle, the most popular to the nearby villages of **Acul** and **Cocop.** They can also hook you up with language classes and homestays with local families, as well as volunteer opportunities in the region.

If you need to spend the night here, check out the **Hotel Villa Nebaj,** Calzada 15 de Septiembre 2-37 (© 502/7756-0005), a somewhat modern hotel in the heart of Nebaj. A room with private bathroom and cable TV is just Q225 double occupancy. Backpackers and budget hounds should head to **Hotel Ixil** (© 502/7756-0036) or **MediaLuna MedioSol Hostal,** at the corner of 3a Calle and 4a Avenida (© 502/5749-7450; www.nebaj.com/hostel). For meals, I recommend **El Descanso** (see above) or **Popi's** (© 502/7756-0092).

Nebaj is located 95km (59 miles) north of Santa Cruz del Quiché. Buses between Santa Cruz del Quiché and Nebaj leave roughly every hour or two. The ride takes around 3 hours and costs Q15.

QUETZALTENANGO (XELA) ★

201km (125 miles) NW of Guatemala City; 90km (56 miles) S of Huehuetenango

The highland city of **Quetzaltenango** is the second largest in Guatemala, with a population of more than 300,000. Like Chichicastenango, this was and still is a principal center of the Maya Ki'che of Guatemala—and many locals still refer to the city by its Ki'che name **Xelajú.** In fact, most people simply call the place **Xela** (pronounced "*Sheh*-la"). Xelajú is close to the sight where Ki'che King Tecún Umán was killed in battle against the Spanish conquistador Pedro de Alvarado. Following Tecún Umán's defeat in 1524, the city was renamed Quetzaltenango, or "place of the Quetzal," which is what Alvarado's Nahuatl mercenaries called it. In 1848, Quetzaltenango declared itself "El Sexto Estado del los Altos," independent from Guatemala. However, while the city retains an independent streak, its political independence lasted only 2 years, and the Guatemalan military quickly brought the rogue state back into the fold.

Thanks to the presence of a large national university and scores of language schools and foreign volunteer programs, there are several good coffee shops and used bookstores in Xela, and even a couple of art-movie houses. You'll also find more nightlife here than anywhere else in the country outside of Guatemala City.

Quetzaltenango makes an excellent base for visiting a host of nearby towns and attractions, including **hot springs,** small villages with impressive **markets and churches,** and towering **volcanoes** waiting to be hiked. The city also serves as a convenient gateway to both Mexico and the Pacific coast of Guatemala.

Essentials

GETTING THERE

BY BUS Several bus lines provide regular service in comfortable modern buses throughout the day between Xela and Guatemala City. **Líneas Dorada** (© 502/2415-8900 in Guatemala City, or 7767-5198 in Xela) has express buses leaving from 16a Calle and 10 Avenida, Zona 1, in Guatemala City, at 7am and 3pm. The return buses leave Xela from 12 Avenida and 5a Calle, Zona 3, at 4:30am and 3:30pm.

Transportes Galgos (© 502/2253-4868 in Guatemala City, or 7761-2248 in Xela) has buses leaving Guatemala City for Xela at 8:30am and 2:30 and 5pm. The return buses leave Xela from Calle Rodolfo Robles 17-43, Zona 1, at 4am and 8:30am, and at 12:30pm.

The trip on either bus line takes about 4 to 5 hours. The fare is around Q55 to Q75 each way.

BY CAR To drive to Quetzaltenango, take the Pan-American Highway (CA-1) north out of Guatemala City. At Cuatro Caminos, take the turnoff for Quetzaltenango, which lies 13km (8 miles) to the southwest, after the small city of Salcajá. The trip takes about 4 hours from Guatemala City. Quetzaltenango is also connected

---

What's in a Name?

The complete Ki'che Mayan name of the city is Xelajú Noj, which translates roughly as "under the 10 mountains," in reference to the surrounding mountains and volcanoes.

Quetzaltenango

Calle Rodolfo Robles
Calle Rodolfo Robles

0   100 m
0   100 yds

To San Marcos

16a Avenida
15a Avenida
14a Avenida
14a Avenida A
13a Avenida
12a Avenida
1a Calle
11a Avenida
10a Avenida
9a Avenida
8a Avenida

Calle Cajolá

Teatro Roma ①

Teatro Municipal ②

2a Calle

③

3a Calle

④

⑤

⑥   ⑦

4a Calle

⑧

⑨

⑲

2a Calle

3a Calle

4a Calle

5a Calle

⑬ ⑩
⑫ ⑪

15a Avenida
14a Avenida

5a Calle

⑮ ⑭

Parque Centro America

21 ㉑

㉒

6a Calle

7a Calle

13a Avenida

⑯

⑰

7a Calle

Museo del Ferrocarril

12a Avenida

⑱

11a Avenida
10a Avenida

✝ ⑳
Catedral Metropolitano de los Altos

To Guatemala City, Chichicastenango

8a Calle

9a Calle

10a Calle

11a Calle

13a Avenida
12a Avenida

9a Avenida
8a Avenida

7a Avenida

8a Calle

9a Calle

10a Calle

11a Calle

■ Bus Station (To Almolonga & Zunil)

To Retalhuleu

Tikal
BELIZE
MEXICO
Livingston
Quetzaltenango
HOND.
Lake Atitlán
Guatemala City
EL SAL.

ACCOMMODATIONS ■
The Black Cat **7**
Casa Doña Mercedes **15**
Casa Mañen **21**
Hotel Bonifaz **19**
Hotel Modelo **4**
Hotel Villa Real Plaza **9**
Villa de don Andrés **14**

DINING ◆
Café Bavaria **13**
Café La Luna **22**
Casa Babylon **12**
El Balcón de Enriquez **11**
El Pasaje Mediterraneo **11**
Restaurante Cardinali **6**
Restaurante y Cantina
   Dos Tejanos **10**
Royal Paris **5**
Sabor de la India **3**
Trattoria La Genovese
   da Alfredo **8**

ATTRACTIONS ●
Casa de la Cultura **18**
Catedral **20**
INGUAT **18**
Museo del Ferrocarril **16**
Parque Centro America **17**
Teatro Municipal **2**
Teatro Roma **1**

to the southern Pacific Coast Highway, which visitors would use to go down to Retalhuleu and the Pacific beaches.

GETTING AROUND

Taxis and tuk tuks are plentiful in Xela. You can always find one around Parque Centro America. Fares around town should run between Q15 and Q30. If you can't flag one down, have your hotel call one for you, or call **Taxi Blanco y Azul** (© 502/7763-2285) or **Mario López** (© 502/4884-7950).

If you want to rent a car for the day, or longer, contact **Tabarini** (© 502/7763-0418; www.tabarini.com). Rates run around Q360 to Q720 per day, depending upon the size and style of the vehicle.

If you want to rent a bicycle for getting around town, check out **Vrisa Bookshop** (© 502/7761-3237). These folks charge Q40 per day, or Q100 per week. However, I find the congested streets and hilly terrain to be very inhospitable to bicycles.

ORIENTATION

The long, narrow **Parque Centro América** is the central hub of Xela. You'll find most of the hotels, restaurants, language schools, and offices, and the main Catholic church either right on this central plaza or within a few blocks. You can see the massive cone of the Santa Maria Volcano 3,677m (12,256 ft.) towering over the southern horizon from almost anywhere in town.

Xela sits at 2,334m (7,656 ft.) above sea level. The climate here is relatively cool, and sometimes damp, particularly from May to mid-November. Be sure to have a light jacket or sweater for the evenings.

FAST FACTS There's an **INGUAT** office (© 502/7761-4931) fronting the Parque Centro America in the Edificio Casa de la Cultura. They can provide you with a city map and basic information on tours and attractions in and around Xela. The main **post office** (© 502/7761-7608) is located about 4 blocks west of the central park at 4a Calle 15-07, Zona 1.

Banco de Occidente, Banrural, and **Banco Industrial** all have branches right on Parque Centro America, and there are dozens of other bank branches around town. Since this is a university and language school city, you'll also find an abundance of Internet cafes in Xela. If your hotel doesn't provide the service, there are several coin-operated and self-service laundromats, and most of these will also wash and fold for you.

In the event of a medical emergency, the **Hospital La Democracia,** 13a Av. 6-51, Zona 3 (© 502/7763-6671), is a well-equipped, modern hospital. You might also try **Hospital Privado Quetzaltenango,** Calle Rodolfo Robles 23-51, Zona 1 (© 502/7761-4381), a well-equipped private hospital. To reach the **National Police** dial © 502/7765-4987. However, for most tourist needs, whether it be for information or an emergency, you should call **Asistur** (© 1500), which is a toll-free call.

What to See & Do

It won't take you long to visit Quetzaltenango's principal attractions. The **Parque Centro América** ★, with its open-air gazebo, is the town's focal point. On the southeastern side of the park you'll find the **Catedral Metropolitano de los Altos,** which is actually two churches. Fronting the park is the ornate facade of the **Catedral del Espíritu Santo** ★, which is all that remains of the city's original 16th-century baroque church. Behind this facade is the more modern, and much larger, **Catedral de la Diócesis de los Altos,** which was inaugurated in 1899.

Also fronting the Parque Centro America is the **Museo del Ferrocarril (Train Museum),** which documents, mostly in photographs, the construction and functioning of the electric train built in the late 19th and early 20th centuries to connect Quetzaltenango with Retalhuleu and the Pacific coast.

Just north of the park center is the **Teatro Municipal (Municipal Theater) ★**, 14a Avenida and 1a Calle (*©* **502/7761-2218**), a wonderfully restored theater built between 1884 and 1908. The theater hosted its first concert in 1903 and is still functioning today. It's worthwhile to catch a show if there's one while you're in town. Just across from the Teatro Municipal is the equally well restored **Teatro Roma,** 14a Avenida A (*©* **502/7761-4950**), the city's first cinema. While they no longer show movies here, they do have occasional performances, which are worth a visit.

On the south side of the park sits the **Casa de la Cultura,** 7th Calle 11-09, Zona 1 (*©* **502/7761-6031**), a large building that houses the INGUAT offices and the Museo de Historia Natural (Natural History Museum; *©* **502/7761-6031 ext.123**), which, in my opinion, can be missed. Should you decide to visit the exhibits, which include dinosaur bones, Maya artifacts, and a room dedicated to the marimba (a large wooden xylophone and the bands that play them), the museum is open Monday through Saturday from 8am to noon and 2 to 6pm. Admission is Q6.

Tours, Treks & Attractions Around Quetzaltenango

While there is little to see in Xela itself, there are a host of tour and activity options within easy reach of the town. All of the hotels and tour agencies listed in this section can arrange any of the tours or excursions listed below.

In addition to the attractions listed here, many visitors use Xela as a jumping-off point to visit the **IRTRA** amusement and theme park complex, the Maya ruins of **Takalik Abaj,** and the lowland city of **Retalhuleu,** continuing on to the beaches of the Pacific coast. For information on all of these places, see chapter 12. All of the tour companies listed here also use Xela as a base for trips to **Nebaj,** mentioned earlier, and **Todos Santos Chuchumatán,** which is covered later in this chapter.

The best and longest-running agencies in Xela include **Adrenalina Tours ★** (*©* **502/7761-4509**; www.adrenalinatours.com), which has its offices in the Pasaje Enriquez building just off Parque Centro America; **Altiplano's Tours** (*©* **502/7766-9614;** www.altiplanos.com.gt); and **Quetzal Trekkers ★★**, Casa Argentina at 12a Diagonal, 8-37, Zona 1 (*©* **502/7765-5895;** www.quetzaltrekkers.com). Quetzal Trekkers is very active in local social work and causes, especially in educating and helping street children, and they can help hook you up with a volunteer gig if you're interested. In addition to the hikes and treks mentioned below, you can also sign up for a 6-day trip through **Nebaj** and **Todos Santos Chuchumatán;** a 3-day hike from **Xela** to **Lake Atitlán;** and a 2-day trek to the summit of **Tajumulco** volcano, at 4,220m (13,842 ft.), the highest point in all of Central America.

ZUNIL & FUENTES GEORGINAS

Zunil ★ is a picturesque little town on the shores of the Salamá River and is surrounded by verdant agricultural fields. It has a beautiful whitewashed church and narrow, cobblestone streets that wind up the hills from the river. Zunil is famous for its worship of **Maximón** (p. 157), who is known as **San Simon** here in Zunil. San Simon is housed in different local homes at different times, and you can ask anyone it town where to find him. A small tip is expected for taking you to see the saint's statue. Monday is market day in Zunil, and while small, it's still a colorful and vibrant market.

Hot springs can be found in several places on the way to Zunil, including Los Vahos, El Recreo, and Los Cirilos, but they all pale in comparison to **Las Fuentes Georginas** ★ (② **502/5704-2959** or 502/7763-0596; www.lasfuentesgeorginas. com), a hot springs resort just beyond Zunil. The large pool here is set in rock and surrounded by steep hills. The hottest water is found closest to the hillside, and gets cooler as you move farther away. There's a restaurant, some changing rooms, and a few basic cabins for overnight stays, but I don't recommend them, as they're very musty and in desperate need of upkeep. As of this writing, Las Fuentes Georginas was closed for reconstruction, following a massive mudslide that filled the main pool. However, the hot springs are expected to reopen by the time this book hits the stands. Traditionally, Las Fuentes Georginas is open daily from 8am to 6:30pm. Admission is Q50 for foreigners with a reduced rate for nationals. A package price, including round-trip transportation runs Q75. Parking is an extra Q10 if you come in your own car.

Zunil is located 9km (5½ miles) south of Xela on the road to Retalhuleu and the Pacific coast. Las Fuentes Georginas is another 8km (5 miles) beyond Zunil up a beautiful, winding road that heads into the mountains. A taxi from Xela to the hot springs should charge around Q100 each way. The fare is a bit less if you're only going to Zunil. Alternately, **Adrenalina Tours** (see above) runs a twice-daily shuttle to Las Fuentes Georginas, leaving Xela at 8am and 2pm, and returning at noon and 6pm. Cost is Q40.

VOLCÁN SANTA MARÍA ★★

The skyline south of Quetzaltenango is dominated by the 3,677m (12,256-ft.) **Volcán Santa María.** All of the tour agencies listed above lead hikes to the summit, and most leave Xela before dawn by car or minivan to the town of Llanos del Pinal. From here it takes between 3 and 4 hours of strenuous hiking to reach the summit. On a clear day, you can see as far as Mexico. You can also see a host of other Guatemalan volcanoes, including Tajumulco, Siete Orejas, and Acatenango, as well as the volcanoes surrounding Lake Atitlán and the volcanoes Fuego and Agua just outside of Antigua. The best view here, however, is of the crater of Santa María's very active sister volcano, **Santiaguito.** Santa María had a major eruption in 1902, which covered much of Quetzaltenango in thick ash and killed more than 1,500 people in the region. It was during this eruption that Santiaguito was born. Santiaguito is in an almost constant state of eruption, belching out gases, volcanic ash, and molten lava. Guided tours run between Q80 and Q240 per person, depending upon group size. During the dry season, it's possible to camp near the summit, which is worth it for the amazing sunrise and sunset views.

SALCAJA

While this small town boasts the oldest Spanish church in Guatemala, it's better known for the private and established vendors lining the streets, particularly the highway leading to Quetzaltenango, with used cars for sale. Of these, the majority seem to be Toyota pickup trucks.

The **Iglesia de San Jacinto** may be small, but it's well maintained and worth a visit. Established in 1524 during Pedro de Alvarado's conquest of the region, the church boasts an ornate altar and some antique paintings.

Salcajá is also famous for its *jaspé* or *ikat* textile weaving. This complex dyeing and weaving process produces intricate abstract designs, although they've been weaving these cloths here since the 1860s. Salcajá is also known for two locally produced liquors—*caldo de frutas* and *rompopo*. *Caldo de frutas* (literally, fruit soup) is a strong brew of fermented fruits and rum or cane alcohol. Rompopo is a somewhat milder concoction of rum, milk, and egg yolks.

Salcajá is located 7km (4⅓ miles) from Xela on the road to Cuatro Caminos.

SAN ANDRÉS XECUL

The ornate church here is definitely worth a visit. Try to come in the afternoon, when the sun hits the church's facade, as it's much harder to get a good photo in the morning, when the sun is behind the church. Up the hill from the main church is a much smaller church worth a visit for two reasons. First, the high perch here offers a wonderful view of the main church and town. Second, this church, and the plot of land beside it, are still actively used for Maya ritual prayers and ceremonies, and you can almost always find local Maya worshiping here.

San Andrés Xecul is located 9km (5½ miles) from Xela, just beyond Slacajá, and off the road to Cuatro Caminos.

SAN FRANCISCO EL ALTO

While Chichicastenango's market gets most of the press and acclaim, insiders know that **San Francisco El Alto's Friday market ★★** is the place to shop the best and largest selection of textiles and garments in Guatemala, plus take in some good views from the hillside location. As in Chichi, San Francisco's central plaza is taken over on market day and packed with merchants from all over the highlands. However, far fewer tourists come here. Instead, large wholesalers and local barterers are the principal buyers. Animal activists should be aware that part of the market here is reserved for live animals, everything from dogs and cats to pigs and chickens. You'll also see caged birds and the occasional captured monkey. San Francisco El Alto is located 17km (11 miles) from Xela beyond Cuatro Caminos on the way to Huehuetenango.

LAGUNA DE CHICABAL

The **Laguna de Chicabal ★** is a gorgeous lake formed in the crater of an extinct volcano. The cone of the lake rises to 2,900m (9,514 ft.), and the emerald-green lake, considered sacred to the Maya, lies a few hundred feet below the rim, surrounded by lush cloud forests. Even if there are no active ceremonies taking place when you visit, you'll notice the many altars around the lakeshore and the ashes, burned candles, and past offerings from recent devotees.

Getting Schooled

Quetzaltenango offers a number of Spanish schools, most with immersion-style lessons, small classes, excursions, and homestay accommodations with a local family. The best among the choices are **Casa Xelaju,** Callejón 15 D, 13-02, Zona 1 (© 502/7761-5954; www.casaxelaju.com); **Celas Maya Spanish School,** 6a Calle 14-55, Zona 1 (© 502/7761-4342; www.celasmaya.edu.gt); **Proyecto Lingüístico**

Quezalteco ★, 5a Calle 2-40, Zona 1 (© 502/7765-2140; www.plqe.org); **Ulew Tinimit Spanish School ★**, 4a Calle 15-23, Zona 1 (© 502/7763-0516; www.spanishguatemala.org); and **Utatlán Spanish School,** 12a Av. 4-32, Zona 1 (© 502/7763-0446; www.utatlan.com). Rates run between $150 and $200 per week, including homestay, most meals, and some organized excursions.

Those interested in volunteering have several excellent options in and around Quetzaltenango. Your best bet is to contact **Entre Mundos** (📞 502/7761-2179; www.entremundos.org), which functions as a bridge between a host of non-governmental organizations and community projects. They specifically work to connect foreign volunteers with appropriate community, social, health, and educational projects.

Laguna de Chicabal is accessed from the village of San Martin Sacatepequez, which is also called San Martin Chile Verde. The hike from San Martin takes about 2 hours. Alternatively, you can drive to a parking lot that is just a 40-minute hike from the lake. The best way to visit the lake is on a guided tour out of Xela. The lake is open daily from 8am to 5pm. Admission is Q10, and parking is an additional Q10. Camping is allowed for Q30 per person.

Shopping

The shopping scene is rather uninspired in Xela, but because of the large university and language school presence here, there are several good used bookstores in town, with selections of both English- and Spanish-language books. **Vrisa Bookshop,** 15a Av. 3-64, Zona 1 (📞 **502/7761-3237**), and **North & South Bookstore,** 8a Calle and 15 Av. 13-77, Zona 1 (📞 **502/7761-0589**), are both good choices. For Guatemalan textiles or craftwork, your best bet is to head to the Friday market at San Francisco El Alto (see above).

Where to Stay

MODERATE

Casa Mañen ★★ The immaculately restored building that houses this B&B might be pushing 200 years, but it's still my top choice in Xela. The rooms all feature thick, antique terra-cotta floors; heavy hand-woven wool blankets and rugs; firm and comfy beds; and a wealth of local art and craft works for decoration, most also have working fireplaces. I prefer the second- and third-floor rooms, which are above the street and away from the action. The hotel's terrace offers great views of the city. The hotel doesn't have a restaurant, but does serve a full and delicious breakfast daily.

9a Av. 4-11, Zona 1. 📞 **502/7765-0786.** Fax 502/7765-0678. www.comeseeit.com. 8 units. $50–$65 double; $70–$100 suite. Rates include full breakfast. AE, DC, MC, V. *In room:* TV.

Hotel Bonifaz This hotel is also called Pension Bonifaz, which is written in large letters above the entrance. It is a rambling, mazelike structure with rooms spread across five floors, accessed via various staircases, and an assortment of lounges and common areas tying the whole thing together. Most of the rooms are spacious and many have good-size private balconies. Those on the fifth floor feature exposed wood-beam ceilings. My favorite room is no. 508, a suite with a large sitting area, fireplace, and good views. Still, most rooms are fairly worn, and you're not getting much value for what you pay here. The somewhat misnamed Presidential Suite is also a good choice, and features a large bathroom with a Jacuzzi tub and a small private outdoor patio. A large atrium on the fourth floor houses a pool and separate Jacuzzi.

4a Calle 10-50, Zona 1. **☏502/7761-2959.** Fax 502/7761-2850. www.quetzalnet.com/bonifaz. 72 units. $83 double; $104 suite. AE, DC, MC, V. **Amenities:** Restaurant; bar; Jacuzzi; small enclosed rooftop pool; room service; free Wi-Fi in the lobby area. *In room:* TV, hair dryer.

Las Cumbres ★★ 🏮 This hotel centers around the hot sulfur springs and steam vents it sits upon, and is located just out of Zunil on the road to Retalhuleu. Each spacious room comes with its own Jacuzzi fed by a hot spring. Some rooms have beautiful stone floors and four-poster beds, some have private Jacuzzi tubs, and four even have their own sauna. However, I prefer the rooms with a view (which don't have their own saunas). My favorites are "Quetzaltenango" and "Cantel," which have beautiful views over the Salamá river valley. The restaurant here is excellent, and there are seven individual steam baths and saunas open to guests and the paying public.

Km 210, Zunil. **☏502/5399-0029;** www.lascumbres.com.gt. 11 units. $50–$60 double. AE, DC, MC, V. **Amenities:** Restaurant; bar; small gym; saunas; squash court; steam baths. *In room:* TV.

INEXPENSIVE

In addition to the places listed below, the **Villa de Don Andrés,** 13a Av. 6-16, Zona 1, near the Parque Centro America (**☏ 502/7761-2014;** www.villadedonandres. com), is another good choice. Backpackers and real budget hounds should head to the **Black Cat,** 13 Av. 3-33, Zona 1 (**☏ 502/7761-2091;** www.blackcathostels. net).

Casa Doña Mercedes 🍴 There are tons of budget options in Xela, but I prefer this joint. The converted old home is located just 2 blocks from the Parque Centro America. The rooms are cheerful and immaculate, there's a shared kitchen, and the service is friendly and efficient.

6a Calle and 14a Av. 13-42, Zona 1. **☏ 502/7765-4687** or 502/5687-3305. www.hostalcasadona mercedes.com. 9 units. $23 double with shared bathroom; $37 double with private bathroom. Rates include taxes. V (with 10% surcharge). **Amenities:** Free Wi-Fi. *In room:* No phone.

Hotel Modelo ★ The rooms here are all clean and spacious, have tile or wood floors, are flooded with natural light, and come with 21-inch flatscreen televisions. The bathrooms tend to be on the small side, and the hotel is very close to Quetzaltenango's lively Zona Rosa, which is convenient if you want to take advantage of the nightlife, but makes those rooms that front the street a bit too noisy. Most of the rooms are housed in the main hotel building, with the least expensive one in a newer annex across the street. Both buildings have small open-air interior courtyards.

14a Av. A 2-31, Zona 1. **☏502/7761-2529** or 7763-0216. Fax 502/7763-1376. www.hotelmodelo1892. com. 19 units. $48 double. AE, DC, MC, V. **Amenities:** Restaurant; bar; free Wi-Fi. *In room:* TV.

Hotel Villa Real Plaza While they are excellently located on a busy corner fronting the Parque Centro America, don't expect much from the basic rooms. All are carpeted and fairly large, and the fireplaces found in many are purely decorative. Several rooms have small balconies overlooking the park, but if you choose one of these, be prepared for the trade-off—you get a great view of the action, but also plenty of street noise. If you want a quiet night's sleep, be sure to ask for an interior room. The ground-floor restaurant features some seating in a pleasant atrium.

4a Calle 12-22, Zona 1. **☏502/7761-4045** or 7761-6033. Fax 502/7761-6780. 54 units. $45 double; $50 suite. AE, DC, MC, V. **Amenities:** Restaurant. *In room:* TV.

Where to Dine

In addition to the restaurants listed below, the **Trattoria La Genovese da Alfredo,** 14a Av. "A" 3-38, Zona 1 (⟨ℂ⟩ **502/5915-3231**), is excellent and a local favorite for pizzas and pastas. For delicious barbecue ribs, pulled pork, and a host of Tex-Mex specialties, head to **Restaurante y Cantina Dos Tejanos ★**, 4a Calle 12-33, Zona 1 (⟨ℂ⟩ **502/7765-4360;** www.dostejanos.com), on the ground floor of the Pasaje Enriquez building. And for a massive menu that ranges from sushi to tacos to Thai spring rolls, you can try **Casa Babylon,** on the corner of 5a Calle and 13 Avenida 1 (⟨ℂ⟩ **502/7761-2320;** www.restaurantecasababylon.blogspot.com).

It's hard to beat the views from **El Balcón de Enríquez,** 4a Calle 12-33, Zona 1 (⟨ℂ⟩ **502/7765-2296**), which I like for breakfast or a light meal. If you're looking for a light meal or simple coffeehouse, try **Café La Luna ★**, 8a Av. 4-11 (⟨ℂ⟩ **502/7761-2242**), with its hodgepodge of antiques; or **Café Bavaria,** 5a Calle 13-14, Zona 1 (⟨ℂ⟩ **502/7763-1855**), which has a wonderful Sunday brunch featuring live jazz.

El Pasaje Mediterraneo ★★ TAPAS/INTERNATIONAL   Tables are spread over several floors, in various nooks and crannies, in this hip restaurant inside the Pasaje Enriquez, a local landmark filled with shops and restaurants. Most of the menu is made up of a range of tapas, although they aren't strictly traditional Spanish-style tapas. You will find dishes with Greek and French, as well as Spanish influences. Don't miss the eggplant rolls with goat cheese and a sun-dried tomato tapenade. Larger combo plates are also available.

4a Calle 12-33, Zona 1, inside El Pasaje Enriquez. ⟨ℂ⟩ **502/5515-6724.** Reservations recommended. Tapas Q35–Q80. AE, DC, MC, V. Daily 11am–3pm and 5:30–11pm.

Restaurante Cardinali ★ ITALIAN/PIZZA   The menu at this long-standing downtown restaurant is massive, featuring over 30 different pasta dishes, and 40 pizza varieties. You can also get veal, chicken, and seafood dishes in an almost equally dizzying array of sauces and presentations. The veal Cardinali is lightly breaded and served in a butter, wine, and lemon sauce. These folks also have an extensive selection of wines, mostly Italian, many of which are pressed into double duty as decorations on tabletops and otherwise spread around the restaurant.

14a Avenida 3-25, Zona 1. ⟨ℂ⟩ **502/7761-0922.** www.restaurantecardinali.com. Reservations recommended. Main courses Q36–Q120. AE, MC, V. Daily noon–10pm.

Royal Paris ★ FRENCH/INTERNATIONAL   This restaurant has the reputation of being the fanciest dining option in town, but the lack of pretense and reasonable prices means it still attracts a good share of the local student crowd. Channel the fancy French experience by ordering a pork chop in an apple-and-cream sauce, or go the bistro route for lunch with one of the excellent sandwiches, made on homemade baguette or whole-wheat bread. Find live music here several nights a week.

14a Av. A 3-06, Zona 1, 2nd floor. ⟨ℂ⟩ **502/7761-1942.** www.royalparis-quetzaltenango.blogspot.com. Reservations recommended. Main courses Q50–Q100. AE, DC, MC, V. Tues–Sun noon–11pm; Mon 6–10pm.

Sabor de la India 🍴 INDIAN   Finding this place is half the battle—it's hard to see from the street and sometimes it's necessary to let yourself in through the gate—but once you do, you'll be treated to delicious, hearty fare that's a welcome change from the other food options in Guatemala. Fish and shrimp curries are on the menu, as are chicken *tikka masala* and *aloo gobi* (potato and cauliflower). Meals are accompanied by lentils, Indian bread, and a thick and tasty yogurt. At Q35, the massive combo plates are a great bargain. While the food is good, the ambience is somewhat lacking, with three bare dining rooms, vinyl tablecloths, and plastic lawn chairs.

2a Calle and 15a Av. A 19, Zona 1. ✆**502/7765-2555.** Reservations recommended. Main courses Q26–Q70. MC, V. Tues–Sat 11am–9pm; Sun 5–9pm.

Xela After Dark

Xela has a very active nightlife. Many start things off at the very popular **Salón Tecún ★** (✆ **502/7761-2350**), in the interior passageway of the Enríquez building, fronting the Parque Centro América. The long wooden tables with bench seating fill up most nights with a mix of locals and language students. A better option is **El Balcón de Enríquez ★★** (✆ **502/7765-2296**), which is in the same building but has second-floor outdoor seating that overlooks the park below.

Several bars and discos are concentrated within 2 blocks around 14a Avenida A, which is known as Xela's Zona Viva (Live Zone). This is the place to come if you want to barhop. Popular dance clubs include **La Parranda;** (www.laparrandadisco.com), 6a Calle and 14a Avenida, Zona 1, **Zona Kokoloko's** (✆ **502/5904-9028**), 15a Avenida and 4a Calle, and **La Rumba Xela** (✆ 502/**4034-7431**), 13a Avenida and 7a Calle, Zona 1.

For a mellower vibe, try **Pool and Beer,** 12a Av. 10-21, Zona 1; **La Fonda del Che** 15a Av. 7-43, Zona 1; or **El Cuartito,** 13a Av. 7-09, Zona 1. A couple of informal cinemas cater to Xela's student population, showing DVDs on a large flatscreen TV or projected onto a screen. **Blue Angel Video Cafe,** 7a Calle 15-79, Zona 1, is the longest running, and features two screening rooms. Films are shown at 8pm and cost Q10. Ask around town, or pick up a copy of the free weekly *Xela Who* (www.xelawho.com) to find the current schedule.

HUEHUETENANGO

266km (165 miles) NW of Guatemala City; 90km (56 miles) N of Quetzaltenango; 84km (52 miles) S of La Mesilla (border with Mexico)

Huehuetenango has a reputation as an unattractive and neglected border outpost, but it's actually a pretty little hamlet, set at the foot of the impressive Sierra de los Cuchumatanes. Commonly known as Huehue (pronounced "*Weh*-weh"), the city functions for tourists primarily as an entry-and-departure point for those coming from or continuing on to Mexico—even though it's a good hour away from the border by car or bus. Aside from the Maya ruins of **Zaculeu,** the city has few attractions, but it serves as an excellent jumping-off point for the isolated mountain hamlet of **Todos Santos Chuchumatán.**

Essentials
GETTING THERE
BY BUS **Los Halcones** buses (✆ **502/2433-9180** in Guatemala City, 7764-2764 in Huehuetenango) leave Guatemala City from Calzada Roosevelt 37-47, Zona 11, at 4, 7, 10am, 2, and 5pm. Return buses leave Huehue from 10a Av. 9-12, Zona 1, at 2, 4, 7, 10am, and at 2pm. The trip takes 5 to 6 hours. The fare is around Q65 each way. There are also several first-class buses throughout the day from Mexico to Guatemala City that stop in Huehue. If there's room, you can always hop on one of these. Ask your hotel for current schedules.

Huehuetenango's **main bus terminal** is located about a mile outside of downtown on the way to the Pan-American Highway, although **Los Halcones** has its own terminal (see above). There are frequent local buses between the bus terminal and downtown. Ask for any bus to El Centro. Fare is Q2. A taxi to the center should cost around Q25. From the main terminal, you can make connections to most other major cities and destinations in the region, including Quetzaltenango.

BY CAR To drive to Huehuetenango, take the Pan-American Highway (CA-1) north out of Guatemala City. At Cuatro Caminos, keep going straight for about 80 km (49.6 miles) where you'll see the prominent exit for Huehuetenango.

GETTING AROUND

The downtown center of Huehuetenango is very compact, and you should have no trouble walking most places. However, taxis and tuk tuks are plentiful. If you can't easily flag one down, call **Taxis Palacios** (© 502/7764-9520).

ORIENTATION

Like most cities across Guatemala and throughout Central America, Huehuetenango features a popular central plaza or park, fronted by the city's Catholic church. To the north, Sierra de los Cuchumatanes are clearly visible from almost any vantage point.

FAST FACTS Huehue's main hospital, the **Hospital Nacional de Huehuetenango** (© 502/7934-3119; www.hospitalnacionalhuehue.gob.gt), is located on the outskirts of downtown, in Zona 10.

The **post office** (© 502/7764-1123) is located about a half-block east of the central plaza at 2 Calle 3-54, Zona 1. You'll also find a cluster of banks within a block or two of the central plaza, including **Banco G&T Continental** (© 502/7764-1290); **Banco Industrial** (© 502/7764-3128). You'll find several Internet cafes around downtown Huehue.

What to Do in & Around Huehue

Huehuetenango doesn't have much to offer tourists, with the exception of a pretty fountain and a Catholic church, which, after suffering great hardships (it suffered massive destruction in the 1902 and 1976 earthquakes, and the church's patron saint, **La Virgen de la Concepción Inmaculada,** was destroyed by fire in 1956), was rebuilt, and once again anchors the plaza with two prominent bell towers and eight white columns dominating its facade.

Most visitors stop in Huehue on their way to **Zaculeu,** the post-Classic city that was once the center of power for the Mam Maya group. It's no coincidence that this ancient Maya city sits on a hilltop with steep ravines on three sides, as the geography works well for defending the site from potential attackers. Zaculeu was occupied for more than 10,000 years until its defeat by Spanish conquistadors in 1525. Not even the Spaniards were able to breech the city's defenses, so they simply laid siege, and in a couple of months starved the Mam into submission.

 Pre-Columbian Palm Springs

Huehuetenango has been inhabited since at least 1500 B.C., and its name is a Haxcalteca word meaning "Place of Old People."

The ruins were restored by the **United Fruit Company** (p. 20) in the 1940s, and are in good shape, although the rather heavy-handed use of concrete and plaster in the restoration has garnered scorn over the years. There's also a ball court and a small museum. Local Mam still use the site for ritual purposes, and you can often see smoldering fires on their altars.

Zaculeu is located 5km (3 miles) west of Huehuetenango. The site is open daily from 8am to 5pm. Admission is Q30. A taxi from town should cost around another Q30.

Where to Stay

In addition to the places listed below, **Hotel Premier** (© 502/7764-9200; www. huehuetenango.com) is a contemporary, business-class hotel located on the outskirts of town, while **Unicornio Azul** ★ (© 502/5205-9328; www.unicornioazul.com) is an isolated lodge, with a specialized horseback riding operation, located about an hour outside of the city.

There are a host of hotels right near the main bus station, but I recommend heading the short distance into downtown to one of the hotels mentioned below.

Hotel Casa Blanca The rooms at this centrally located downtown hotel vary considerably. I'd opt for a third-floor room with a view, in the newer annex, set back from the street. I find a few of the older rooms a bit dark and dour, although the exposed stone work is charming. The hotel's restaurant has some delightful open-air courtyard seating, as well as another more formal indoor dining room, and it's worth trying even if you're not staying here.

7a Av. 3-41, Zona 1. ℗ **502/7769-1086.** Fax 502/7769-0780. www.ecommhuehue.com/casablanca. 15 units. $35–$50 double. AE, DC, MC, V. **Amenities:** Restaurant; bar. *In room:* TV, free Wi-Fi.

Hotel Zaculeu Located just a half-block off the central plaza, this place has been welcoming guests for more than 100 years, which is apparent in some of the front rooms. I find the newer, bigger rooms located in a back annex to be a bit more comfortable. All the rooms are simple, but decorated nicely with local fabrics, furniture, and craftworks. Some have exposed brick patches in the walls. The central courtyard is a lush oasis of tropical flora, and the restaurant serves good local cuisine at excellent prices.

5a Av. 1-14, Zona 1. ℗ **502/7764-1086.** Fax 502/7764-1575. 34 units. $30 double. 5% surcharge for credit cards. AE, MC, V. **Amenities:** Restaurant; bar. *In room:* TV.

Royal Park Hotel ★ 🎈 This five-story contemporary hotel has the plushest rooms and best amenities to be had in downtown Huehue. Rooms have plenty of space, clean tile floors, and large flatscreen televisions. I like the end rooms that face the street (those ending in the numbers "07" and "08"), especially those higher up, since they have large picture windows and good views. Be forewarned, there's no elevator here, so if you do opt for a room on a higher floor, you'll be walking up and down the stairs.

6a Av. 2-34, Zona 1. ℗ **502/7762-7775.** hotelroyalpark1@gmail.com. 33 units. $30–$40 double. AE, MC, V. **Amenities:** Restaurant; free Wi-Fi. *In room:* TV.

Where to Dine

In addition to the places listed below, **Cafeteria Las Palmeras,** 4a Calle 5-10, Zona 1 (℗ **502/5783-2967**), is a bustling and pleasant two-story local joint serving breakfast through dinner in a well-located spot on a corner across from the town's main church.

Café Mi Tierra ★★ 🍴 INTERNATIONAL This place has the most eclectic and bohemian vibe to be found in Huehue, both in terms of cuisine and ambience. There are several rooms and nooks here. All feature bold colors and interesting artworks, and there's a fountain and skylight in the main dining room. The menu ranges from burgers, sandwiches, and pizzas to more filling main dishes like steak, grilled chicken, and tilapia. Their fresh, strong organic coffee and filling breakfasts make this my favorite spot in town to start the day.

4a Calle 6-46, Zona 1. ℗ **502/7764-1473.** Main courses Q15–Q50. V. Mon–Sat. 7am–8:30pm; Sun 8am–3pm.

Las Brasas STEAKHOUSE/INTERNATIONAL This popular local joint is ostensibly a steakhouse, but once you look at the menu, you'll realize how far short that description falls, since most of the offerings are classic Chinese dishes I recommend sticking with the house specialty of grilled steaks, which are prepared over an open-flame grill. However, you can also order from a variety of Chinese dishes, ranging from chow mein to *kung pao* chicken. Portions are large, so you might want to share.

4a Av. 1-55. ℗ **502/7764-2339** or 502/5707-9929. Main courses Q30–Q120. AE, DC, MC, V. Daily 9am–10pm.

Huehue After Dark

Huehuetenango is pretty mellow. **Café Bar Los Estribos** ★ and **Café Bar El Bambu** are probably the two most popular clubs in town. Both are second-floor affairs, conveniently located directly across the street from each other. For dancing, head to **Classic Dance** on the corner of 4a Calle and 8a Avenida.

A Side Trip Out of Huehue

TODOS SANTOS CHUCHUMATÁN ★

Todos Santos Chuchumatán is a beautiful and remote mountain town that remains a major Mam Maya center. Todos Santos suffered some serious atrocities during the civil war, and an army massacre in 1981 is still fresh in the minds of many here.

Both men and women in the area still wear traditional dress. In fact, the *huipiles* and other textile products from Todos Santos are famous throughout Guatemala, and even the men are known for their crocheted handbags. The market, open Saturday and Wednesday, is a great place to purchase the local wares. Todos Santos Chuchumatán is very small, but still attracts a fair number of backpackers and adventurous tourists. There are a few schools catering to foreign tourists looking to learn Mam, Spanish, or traditional weaving technique.

The town's greatest fame comes from its **drunken horse race,** held each year on All Saints' Day, November 1. The *corrida,* or "horse race," dates back to the days of the conquistadors, and is a combination of a drinking game, horse race, and endurance event. Local riders, usually already drunk before the early morning start, race back and forth along a course, drinking after each leg. Racers keep going until they literally fall off their horses, at which point they are dragged to the perimeter to wallow and retch. Over the years there have been deaths and serious injuries. The spectacle is a bit tough to watch for some, as the humor of it all gives way to drunken danger and debauchery. If you plan to come for the *corrida,* be sure to arrive several days early in order to nail down a room, as the limited accommodations in town go fast for these festivities, and it's nearly impossible to reserve anything in advance.

At other times of the year, Todos Santos Chuchumatán serves as a good base for some beautiful hiking. The town sits at 2,500m (8,200 ft.), and the surrounding mountains are much higher. It's often cold here, especially at night, so be sure to bring appropriate clothing. Some popular hiking destinations include the 3,837m (12,585-ft.) summit of **La Torre,** which offers amazing views on clear days. The small village of **San Juan Atitlán** is another popular destination.

Todos Santos is also known for its hot steam baths, or *chuj.* Found in most homes, and often available to tourists for a few *quetzales,* the *chuj* are mud-brick structures with a fire pit at the center. Rocks are heated, and then the bather pours cold water over the rocks and themselves, enjoying the mix of hot steam and refreshing water.

All of the hotels in town are very simple, and none have a phone for reservations. Among those I recommend are **Casa Familiar** (© **502/5580-9579**) and **Hotelito Todos Santos** (© **502/7783-0603**).

Todos Santos Chuchumatán is located 45km (28 miles) northwest of Huehu, and periodic buses connect the two. Buses leave every couple of hours between 6am and 6pm from the main Huehuetenango bus terminal. Ask your hotel in Huehue for the current schedule, which changes according to demand. Fare is around Q12. The ride takes about 3 hours due to the rough road. It's also possible to hike from Huehuetenango or Xela to Todos Santos; all the hotel tour desks and tour companies mentioned above can help arrange this.

TIKAL &
THE PETÉN

Bordering Belize, Mexico, and Honduras, and occupying the entire northeastern section of Guatemala, the Petén is the country's largest and least populated province. Most of the Petén is forest—thick tropical rainforest—and its lush and wild landscape contains some of Mesoamerica's richest archaeological treasures. In 1990, the government of Guatemala officially established the Maya Biosphere Reserve, a tract of 1 million hectares (2.5 million acres) that includes most of Petén province. The Maya Biosphere Reserve adjoins the neighboring Calakmul Biosphere Reserve in Mexico and the Río Bravo Conservation Area in Belize, comprising a joint protected area of more than 2 million hectares (5 million acres).

The Petén Province is home to perhaps the most impressive and best preserved of all ancient Maya ceremonial cities, **Tikal,** as well as other less-excavated sites, including **Yaxhá, El Ceibal, El Mirador,** and **Uaxactún.** The area is also a rich and rewarding destination for bird-watchers and ecotourists.

TIKAL ★★★

548km (340 miles) NE of Guatemala City; 65km (40 miles) N of Flores; 100km (62 miles) NW of the Belize border

Often shrouded in mist and mystery, Tikal is one of the greatest of the surviving Classic Maya cities, and is estimated to have once supported a population of about 100,000 people. Archaeologists have identified more than 3,000 structures, and in its heyday, the city probably covered as much as 65 sq. km (25 sq. miles). The pyramids here are some of the most perfect examples of ceremonial architecture in the Maya world. Standing atop Temple IV, you are high above the rainforest canopy. The peaks of several temples poke through the dense vegetation, toucans and parrots fly about, and the loudest noise you'll hear is the guttural call of howler monkeys.

Essentials
GETTING THERE
BY PLANE TACA Regional Airline (© 502/2470-8222; www. taca.com) has two daily flights to Flores Airport (FRS) from La Aurora International Airport in Guatemala City. Flights depart at 6:30am and

Map: El Petén, showing Ancient Ruins and Park, Reserve.

6pm, with return flights at 8:05am and 7:35pm. **TAG Airlines** (☎ **502/2380-9401**; www.tag.com.gt) has one daily flight departing at 6:30am and returning from Flores at 4:30pm. The flight takes around 50 minutes, and fares range from $150 to $240 each way.

The Flores airport is on the road to Tikal, about 2.4km (1½ miles) east of Santa Elena. A taxi from the airport into Santa Elena or Flores should cost you around Q25. Collective taxis and minivans to Tikal are usually waiting at the airport (if not you'll have to head into Santa Elena or Flores first). These charge around Q50 per person each way. A private taxi can be hired for the drive for around Q400.

BY BUS   There are several companies operating first-class buses to and from Guatemala City. **ADN** (☎ **502/2251-0610** in Guatemala City, or 7924-8131 in Santa Elena; www.adnautobusesdelnorte.com) and **Línea Dorada** (☎ **502/2232-5506** in Guatemala City, or 7926-0070 in Santa Elena; www.tikalmayanworld.com) both operate out of the main bus terminal in Santa Elena, located about 8 blocks south of downtown along 6a Avenida. The trip to Guatemala City takes about 8 to 10 hours, and first-class fares run around Q190 to Q280. If you arrive by bus, you'll have to

Shameless Plug

If you're traveling on to Belize, you'll want to pick up a copy of *Frommer's Belize.*

arrange a taxi, collective taxi, or mini-van ride out to Tikal. Línea Dorado also has service to and from Belize City.

BY CAR To drive to Tikal from Guatemala City, you must first drive to Santa Elena. The best and fastest route is via Río Dulce. Take the Carretera al Atlántico (CA-9) out of Guatemala City to La Ruidosa crossroads at Km 245. From here it's 34km (21 miles) north on highway CA-13 to Río Dulce and another 180km (112 miles) from Río Dulce to Santa Elena. From Santa Elena, you'll need to drive 32km (20 miles) to the crossroads at Ixlú (El Cruce), and turn north toward Tikal, which is 65km (40 miles) away. The route and turnoffs are all well marked, and the drive should take about 8 hours.

Warning: It's strongly advised that you do not drive at night. It's a sad fact that armed groups occasionally set up roadblocks along these isolated, yet frequently trafficked, roads. While this is a rare occurrence, it's better to be safe than sorry.

BY ORGANIZED TOUR Organized day trips leave daily for Tikal from Guatemala City and Antigua. Costs for these all-inclusive trips are approximately $250 to $350 per person including round-trip airfare, ground transportation, park entrance fees, a guide, and lunch. These tours generally leave at around 5am and get back to Guatemala City or Antigua at around 6pm. Budget an additional $50 to $150 per person per day for multiday excursions, depending on the level of accommodations chosen. In Guatemala City, call **Clark Tours** (© **502/2412-4700;** www.clarktours. com.gt), or **Via Venture ★★** (© **502/7832-2509;** www.viaventure.com).

GETTING AROUND

BY TAXI OR MINIVAN If you don't have a car, the best way to get around this area is by minivan. Most are unmarked—the only prominent company, is **San Juan Travel** (© **502/5847-4738**). Minivans from Flores and Santa Elena to Tikal leave roughly every hour between 5am and 10am, and less frequently thereafter. These minivans leave from Tikal for the return trip roughly every hour from noon to 6pm. Every hotel in Flores and Santa Elena can arrange a minivan pickup for you. The trip usually takes an hour and costs around Q50 and Q60 per person each way. You can buy a round-trip fare at a slight savings; however, this commits you to a specific mini-van company, and I've found I prefer paying a little extra to have more flexibility in grabbing my return ride when I'm ready to leave. You'll find vans waiting to collect passengers in the main parking lot at the ruins.

A private cab (which is usually a minivan) from Tikal to Santa Elena/Flores will run around Q350 to Q450 each way. Between Tikal and El Remate, the fare is about Q150 to Q200. Be sure to bargain, as the first price you are quoted is almost certainly above the going rate and subject to some negotiation.

BY CAR There are several local car-rental agencies at the airport. Of these, a good choice is **Tabarini Rent A Car** (© **502/7926-0253;** www.tabarini.com). All rent small jeeps and SUVs. Do get a four-wheel-drive vehicle; even though you may never need the traction or off-road ability, the extra clearance will come in handy. Rates run from Q350 to Q450 per day.

Camera-Ready

Tikal's landscape is so stunning that it was chosen for an exterior shot in George Lucas's *Star Wars* and as the site for a series of famous Nike commercials.

ORIENTATION

Tikal National Park is located 65km (40 miles) north of the sister towns of Flores and Santa Elena. There is no village or town inside Tikal National Park. There is an entrance booth 18km (11 miles) south of the ruins. After paying your Q150 entrance fee and driving in, you will come to the large central parking area and visitor center. This is where you'll find the three hotels and campsite reviewed in "Where to Stay" (later in this section), as well as the two museums, a collection of simple restaurants, and the trail entrance, from which the ruins are about a 15- to 20-minute walk through the forest.

There's a **post office** and **telegraph** office on the left as you arrive at the parking area. You'll find a **public phone** in the Stelae Museum. There's no bank or ATM in Tikal, and most of the little restaurants and gift stands only accept *quetzales*. While some of the hotels here do accept credit cards, the phone connections are spotty, and they sometimes have problems getting the authorizations, so it's best to bring *quetzales* to pay for your entire stay. Also, be sure to bring plenty of insect repellent with you—the bugs here are rapacious.

FAST FACTS There are no banks, medical facilities, laundromats, or other major services available at Tikal. All of these can be found in Flores and Santa Elena, some 65km (40 miles) away (see "Flores & Santa Elena," later in this chapter).

If you arrive by air, you can exchange money at **Banquetzal** (© **502/7926-0711**) in the departure area of the small airport. It's open daily from 7am to noon and 2 to 5pm. You'll also find individuals offering to exchange money (which is safe), but you're better off heading into Santa Elena or Flores if the Banquetzal branch isn't open. Most of the hotels and restaurants in Tikal, in fact, will exchange dollars for *quetzales*, though they may give you a slightly less favorable rate than you would get at a bank.

Exploring Tikal

Tikal is one of the largest Maya cities ever uncovered, and houses the most spectacular ruins in Guatemala, which are comparable to Mexico's Chichén Itzá in pre-Columbian splendor. However, unlike at Chichén Itzá, the ruins of Tikal are set in the middle of a vast jungle through which you must hike from temple to temple. The many miles of trails provide numerous opportunities to spot interesting birds such as toucans and parrots, and wild animals including coatimundis, spider monkeys, howler monkeys, and deer.

No one's entirely sure what role Tikal played in the history of the Maya, whether it was a ceremonial center for priests, artisans, and the elite, or a city of industry and commerce. In the 16 sq. km (6 sq. miles) of Tikal that have been mapped and excavated, only a few of the buildings were domestic structures; most were temples, palaces, ceremonial platforms, and shrines. So far, archaeologists have mapped about 3,000 constructions, 10,000 earlier foundations beneath surviving structures, 250 stone monuments (stelae and altars), and thousands of art objects found in tombs and

Tikal

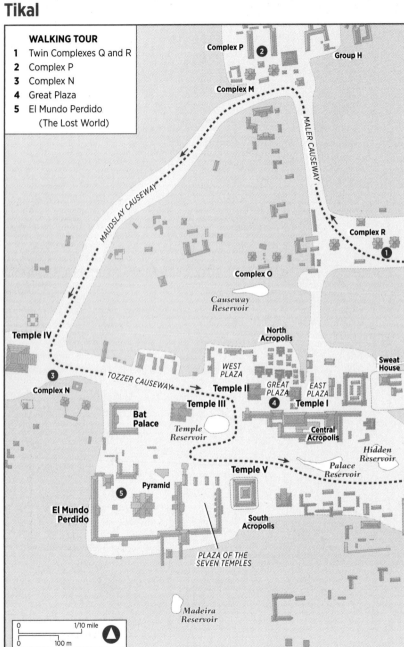

WALKING TOUR

1 Twin Complexes Q and R
2 Complex P
3 Complex N
4 Great Plaza
5 El Mundo Perdido
 (The Lost World)

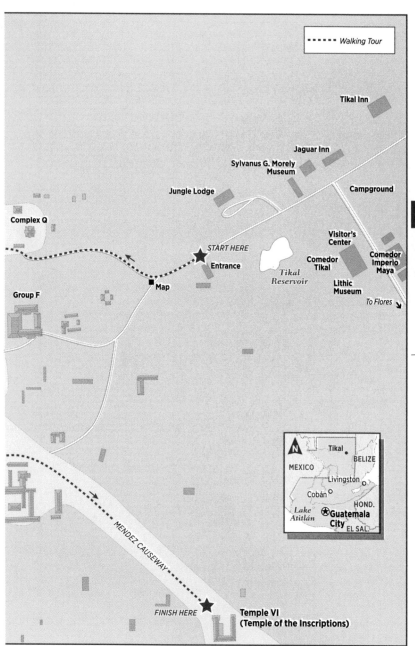

- - - - - - Walking Tour

Tikal Inn

Jaguar Inn

Sylvanus G. Morely
Museum

Jungle Lodge

Campground

Complex Q

Visitor's
Center

START HERE

Entrance

Comedor
Imperio
Maya

Comedor
Tikal

Tikal
Reservoir

Map

Lithic
Museum

To Flores

Group F

MENDEZ CAUSEWAY

FINISH HERE

Temple VI
(Temple of the Inscriptions)

N

Tikal

BELIZE

MEXICO

Livingston

Cobán

HOND.

Lake
Atitlán

⊗Guatemala
City

EL SAL.

cached offerings. There is evidence of continuous construction at Tikal from 200 B.C. through the 9th century A.D., with some suggestion of occupation as early as 600 B.C. The Maya reached their zenith in art and architecture during the Classic Period, which began about A.D. 250 and ended abruptly in about A.D. 900, when for some reason Tikal and all other major Maya centers were abandoned. Most of the visible structures at Tikal date from the Late Classic Period, from A.D. 600 to A.D. 900.

Workers are presently excavating the countless mounds on the periphery of the mapped area, and have been finding modest houses of stone and plaster with thatch roofs. Just how far these settlements extended beyond the ceremonial center and how many people lived within the domain of Tikal are yet to be determined.

MAKING THE MOST OF YOUR VISIT

Tikal is such an immense site that you really need several days to see it thoroughly. However, you can visit many of the greatest temples and plazas in 1 day. First-time visitors should hire a guide, which are available at the visitor center and charge around Q80 to Q160 for a half-day tour of the ruins. In addition, most hotels and all tour agencies in the region offer guided tours for a similar price.

Tikal National Park is open daily from 6am to 6pm. If you'd like to stay in the park until 8pm (for sunset and nocturnal wildlife viewing), get your admission ticket stamped at the office behind the Stelae Museum. If you arrive after 3pm, your admission is good for the following day as well, and if you're staying multiple days, you must pay the admission fee each day. The best times to visit the ruins are in early morning and late afternoon, which are the least crowded and coolest times of day.

There are a host of excellent books on the Maya, some specifically about Tikal. *Tikal: An Illustrated History of the Ancient Maya Capital,* by John Montgomery (Hippocrene Books, 2001), is a good place to start. *The Lords of Tikal: Rulers of an Ancient Maya City,* by Peter D. Harrison and others (Thames & Hudson, 2000), is a similar option. For a more comprehensive view of the ancient Maya, try *A Forest of Kings: The Untold Story of the Ancient Maya,* by David Friedel (William Morrow & Co., 1992). Birders will want to have a copy of *The Birds of Tikal: An Annotated Checklist,* by Randall A. Beavers (Texas A&M University Press, 1992), or *The Birds of Tikal,* by Frank B. Smithe (Natural History Press, 1966). The latter three books are hard to find, but you should be able to order used copies in the U.S., or you can often find copies of all of these in Flores or at Tikal.

WALKING TOUR: TIKAL RUINS

START:	**Visitor Center and Stelae Museum.**
FINISH:	**Temple VI.**
TIME:	**3 to 4 hours.**
BEST TIME:	**Before or after the crowds gather at the Great Plaza. Feel free to reverse the order of this walking tour if it will help you avoid the masses.**
WORST TIME:	**Between 10am and 2pm, when crowds and tour buses stop at the Great Plaza.**

A full tour of Tikal will require an extensive amount of walking—as much as 10km (6 miles). The itinerary described here will take you to most of the major temples and plazas, and can be accomplished in about 3 to 4 hours. If your time is really limited, you should follow the signs and head straight to the Great Plaza. To orient yourself, begin your tour at the visitor center and neighboring Stelae Museum. Here you'll find some informative exhibits and relics, as well as an impressive relief map of the site. See "the Museums," below, for more information on the museum.

From the entrance, walk along the path that goes west toward the ruins, and turn right at the first intersection to get to:

1 Twin Complexes Q & R

Seven of the twin complexes at Tikal have been discovered and mapped (only a few have been excavated), but their exact purpose is still a mystery. Each complex has two pyramids facing east and west; at the north is an unroofed enclosure entered by a vaulted doorway and containing a single stela and altar; at the south is a small palacelike structure. Of the two pyramids here, one has been restored and one has been left as it was found (the latter will give you an idea of just how overgrown and ensconced in the jungle these structures had become).

At the end of the Twin Complexes is a wide road called the Maler Causeway. Turn right (north) onto this causeway, and walk 15 minutes to get to:

2 Complex P

Some restoration has been done at this twin complex, but the most interesting points are the replicas of a stela (no. 20) and altar (no. 8) in the north enclosure. Look for the beautiful glyphs next to the carving of a warrior on the stela, which are all in very good condition. The altar shows a captive bound to a carved-stone altar, his hands tied behind his back—a common scene in carvings at Tikal. Both these monuments date from about A.D. 751.

From Complex P, head south on the Maudslay Causeway to:

3 Complex N

This complex is the site of **Temple IV (Temple of the Two-Headed Serpent).** Finished around A.D. 740, Temple IV is the tallest structure in Tikal at 64m (212 ft.) from the base of its platform to the top. The first glimpse you get of the temple from the Maudslay Causeway is awesome, for the temple has not been fully restored, and all but the temple proper (the enclosure) and its roof comb are covered in foliage. The stairway is covered in earth and roots, but you can get to the top of the temple using a system of roughly made wood ladders set against the steep sides of the pyramid. The view of the setting and layout of Tikal—and all of the Great Plaza—is magnificent. From the platform of the temple, you can see in all directions and get an idea of the extent of the Petén jungle. **Temple III (Temple of the Great Priest)** is in the foreground to the east; **Temples I** and **II** are farther on at the Great Plaza. To the right of these are the **South Acropolis** and **Temple V.**

Temple IV, and all the other temples at Tikal, are built on this plan: A pyramid is built, upon which a platform is constructed. The temple proper rests on this platform and is composed of one to three rooms, which are usually long and narrow and used for priestly rites rather than for habitation. Most temples had beautifully carved wooden lintels above the doorways. The one from Temple IV is now in the Völkerkunde Museum in Basel, Switzerland.

4 Great Plaza

Along the way you'll pass the twin-pyramid Complex N, the **Bat Palace,** and **Temple III.** Take a look at the altar and stela in the complex's northern enclosure—two of the finest monuments at Tikal—and also the altar in front of Temple III, showing the head of a deity resting on a plate. The crisscross pattern shown here represents a woven mat, a symbol of authority to the Mayas.

Entering the Great Plaza from the Tozzer Causeway, you'll be struck by the towering stone structure that is **Temple II,** seen from the back. It measures 38m (125 ft.) tall now, but is thought to have been 42m (140 ft.) high when the roof comb was intact. Also called the Temple of the Masks, because of a large face carved in the roof comb, the temple dates from about A.D. 700. Walk around this temple to enter the plaza proper.

Directly across from Temple II you'll see **Temple I (Temple of the Great Jaguar),** the most striking structure in Tikal. Standing 44m (145 ft.) tall, the temple proper has three narrow rooms with high corbeled vaults (the Maya "arch") and carved wooden lintels made of zapote wood, which is rot-resistant. One of the lintels has been removed for preservation in the Guatemala National Museum of Archaeology and Ethnology in Guatemala City. The whole structure is made of limestone, as are most others at Tikal. It was within this pyramid that one of the richest tombs in Tikal, believed to be the tomb of Tikal ruler Hasaw Chan K'awil, was discovered. When archaeologists uncovered it in 1962, they found the former ruler's skeleton surrounded by some 180 pieces of jade, 90 bone artifacts carved with hieroglyphic inscriptions, numerous pearls, and objects in alabaster and shell. **Note:** Tourists can no longer scale temples I or III. However, those in need of serious cardio workouts will get their fill by climbing some of the other temples.

The **North Acropolis** (north side of the Great Plaza) is a maze of structures from various periods covering an area of 8 hectares (21 acres). Today it stands 9m (30 ft.) above the limestone bedrock and contains vestiges of more than a hundred different constructions dating from 200 B.C. to A.D. 800. At the front-center of the acropolis (at the top of the stairs up from the Great Plaza) is a temple numbered **5D-33.** Although much of the 8th-century temple was destroyed during the excavations to get to the Early Classic period temple (A.D. 300) underneath, it's still a fascinating building. Toward the rear of it is a tunnel leading to the stairway of the Early Classic temple, embellished with two 3m-high (10-ft.) plaster polychrome masks of a god—don't miss these.

Directly across the plaza from the North Acropolis is the **Central Acropolis,** which covers about 1.6 hectares (4 acres). It's a maze of courtyards and palaces on several levels, all connected by an intricate system of passageways. Some of the palaces had five floors, connected by exterior stairways, and each floor had as many as nine rooms arranged like a maze.

Before you leave the Great Plaza, be sure to examine some of the 70 beautiful stelae and altars right in the plaza. You can see the full development of Maya art in them, for they date from the Early Classic period right through to the Late Classic period. There are three major stylistic groups: the stelae with wrap-around carving on the front and sides and text on the back; those with a figure carved on the front and text in glyphs on the back; and those with a simple carved figure on the front, hieroglyphs on the sides, and a plain back. The oldest stela, no. 29 (now in the Tikal Museum), dates from A.D. 292; the most recent is no. 11 in the Great Plaza, which dates from A.D. 869.

If you head southwest from Temple II, you'll come to the area known as:

5 El Mundo Perdido (the Lost World)

This plaza contains the **Great Pyramid,** which stands 34m (114 ft.) high and is the oldest excavated building in Tikal. This pyramid is one of the most popular spots for watching the sunset. If you've timed it right, you might be able to hang out here and watch the show; otherwise, make a mental note to get your bearings and come back later. Directly east of the Great Pyramid is the **Plaza of the Seven Temples,** which dates to the Late Classic period. Bordering this plaza on the east side is an unexcavated pyramid, and behind this is **Temple V.** This entire area is known as the **South Acropolis.** You can climb Temple V, but be forewarned: While the view from above is beautiful, the climb, both up and down, is on a very steep and rather rickety wood stairway, which can be scary.

If you cross through the South Acropolis to the east and then turn north in the general direction of the Great Plaza, you'll come to the East Plaza. From here you can walk southeast on the Méndez Causeway to **Temple VI (Temple of the Inscriptions),** which contains the most extensive hieroglyphics in Tikal, although they are nearly illegible. It's worth coming out this way just for the chance to spot some wild animals, which seem to be fairly common in this remote corner of the park.

THE MUSEUMS

The most formal museum here has been officially christened the **Sylvanus G. Morely Museum,** but is also known as the **Tikal** or **Ceramic Museum.** This museum, located between the Jungle Lodge and the Jaguar Inn, has a good collection of pottery, mosaic masks, incense burners, etched bone, and stelae that are chronologically displayed. Of note are the delicate 7.6-to-13-centimeter (3-to-5-in.) mosaic masks made of jade, turquoise, shell, and stucco. There's a beautiful cylindrical jar from about A.D. 700 depicting a male and female seated in a typical Maya pose. Also on exhibit are a number of jade pendants, beads, and earplugs, as well as the famous **stela no. 31,** which is carved on all four sides. Two sides show spear throwers, each wearing a large feathered headdress and carrying a shield in his left hand; on the front is a complicated carving of an individual carrying a head in his left arm and a chair in his right. This Early Classic–period stela is considered one of the finest. Be sure to check out the reconstruction of the tomb of Hasaw Chan K'awil, who was also known as Ah Cacao, or "Lord Chocolate."

The second museum is known as the **Lithic** or **Stelae Museum,** and is in the large visitor center, which is on your left as you arrive at the parking area coming from Flores. The spacious display area contains a superb collection of stelae from around the ruins. Just outside the front door of the museum is the scaled relief map (mentioned above) that will give you an excellent perspective on the relationships between the different ruins at Tikal. Both museums are open daily from 8am to 5pm, and a Q80 will get you into both.

Tip: Visit the museums only if you have extra time or a very specific interest in either the stelae or ceramic works. The ruins themselves are by far much more interesting and interactive.

SUNRISE, sunset

Tikal is a magical and mystical place. Many claim that this magic and mystique is only heightened around sunrise and sunset. Sunsets are easier to catch and a more dependable show. Sunrises tend to be more a case of the sun eventually burning through the morning mist than of any impressive orb emerging. However, afternoons can often be clear, especially during the dry season, allowing for excellent sunset viewing from the tops of the main temples here. In either case, much of the attraction can be found all around you, as the bird and animal life of the jungle are much more active around sunrise and sunset. If you're staying right at the ruins, your chances are better of catching either or both of these occasions.

If you're not staying inside the national park, minivans and collective taxis leave Flores and El Remate early enough to get you to the Tikal entrance gate at 6am when it opens. This will generally enable you to get to the top of one of the main temples by 6:30am, which is usually still early enough to catch the sun burning through the mist just over the rainforest canopy.

If you plan on staying for sunset, be absolutely positive that your return transportation will wait for you. The park officially closes at 6pm. Depending upon the season, the sun will set below the treetops anywhere between 5 and 6pm, allowing just enough time to watch the spectacle and get out of the park in time.

Tip: If you're planning on catching either the sunrise or sunset, it's a very good idea to bring along a flashlight, just in case.

Where to Stay

There are only three hotels and a campground in the little Tikal village near the entrance to the ruins. Unless you have more than 2 days to spend exploring the region, I recommend staying near the ruins, as it allows you to enter early and stay late, and helps you avoid the Great Plaza and North Acropolis during the peak period when they are swarmed with day-trippers.

Although the ruins are officially open from 6am to 6pm, those staying at the site can sometimes finagle their way in earlier. Better yet, those staying at the site can have their admission ticket stamped, allowing them to stay inside the park until 8pm and a chance to catch both the sunset and moonrise from the top of one of the temples.

Note: Rooms are often difficult to get at the park, and making reservations is essential during the high season. However, communication with the hotels here is difficult and undependable, and many reserve all of their high-season bookings for groups and prepaid package tours. Overbooking on behalf of these hotels is also not uncommon. Demand is high, and rooms are very limited here. If you're just going for a couple of nights, go with an organized tour to save yourself some hassle; if you plan to spend more time in the area or don't mind spending a night in Flores or Santa Elena if necessary, you can probably make your arrangements in Tikal.

Note: All of the hotels below get their electricity from generators, and some only run these generators for limited periods throughout the day. None have air-conditioning, and even though most have fans, these fans will do you little good on a hot night when the generator isn't running.

EXPENSIVE

Jungle Lodge Also known as Posada de la Selva, this is the biggest and most upscale hotel right at the park. However, that's not saying much. At times there can be a cattle-car feel to the operation, and service can be lax. The majority of the rooms are housed in duplex bungalows, with high ceilings, white-tile floors, two double beds with mosquito netting, and a ceiling fan. Each has its own little porch with a couple of chairs, which are great places to sit and read a book, or do some bird-watching. The bungalows are connected by stone paths through lush gardens. Two junior suites feature king-size beds, a large Jacuzzi-style tub (but without jets), and private patios in both the front and back of the room. There are also 12 older rooms with polished cement floors and shared bathroom facilities.

Tikal village, Petén. ⓒ502/7861-0447 or 502/2476-8775. Fax 502/2476-0294. www.junglelodgetikal. com. 50 units (40 w/private bathroom). $150 bungalow; $40 double w/shared bathroom. MC, V. **Amenities:** Restaurant; bar; small outdoor pool. *In room:* No phone.

MODERATE

Jaguar Inn 🗡 This is the most humble and economical of the hotels right at the park. Still, the rooms are all quite clean, spacious, and well kept. Most come with two queen beds and a small veranda strung with a hammock. The best rooms are a couple of large, second-floor affairs. However, I also like bungalow no. 10, with its king-size bed and private veranda. If you're on a tight budget, you can also camp here, or rent one of their hammocks with mosquito netting and a locker for Q40 per person. These folks offer electricity 24-hours per day.

Tikal village, Petén. ⓒ502/7926-0002 reservations in Santa Elena, or 502/7783-3647 at the lodge. Fax 502/7926-2413. www.jaguartikal.com. 14 units. $61 double. AE, MC, V (5% surcharge). **Amenities:** Restaurant; small outdoor pool; Wi-Fi. *In room:* No phone.

Tikal Inn Set back amid the trees, the Tikal Inn is the farthest hotel from the entrance to the ruins as you walk down the old airstrip. The best rooms here are the individual bungalows, which feature high thatch roofs, tile floors, local furniture and textiles, and rustic wood trim. The smaller rooms in the main building have cement floors. All of the rooms are airy and cool, but feel pretty spartan. As at the Jungle Lodge, there's a refreshing pool here, and these folks even have a small Internet cafe. Meals are served family-style, and the food is a definite step up from the fare served at the *comedores* near the campground.

📷 Seeing the Forest from the Trees

Just outside the entrance to Tikal National Park is the **Canopy Tour Tikal** (ⓒ 502/7926-4270; www.canopytikal. com). A series of treetop platforms are connected by heavy wire cables, so that more adventurous travelers can zip from platform to platform via a harness-and-pulley system. Canopy Tour Tikal actually has two separate zip-line tours to choose from, a somewhat slower tour for wary souls and a faster system for adrenaline junkies. They also have a series of trails and hanging suspension bridges through the thick rainforest here. This attraction is open daily from 7am to 5pm, and the cost is Q240 per person, including shuttle transportation to or from Tikal or El Remate. For transport to and from Santa Elena or Flores, add on an extra Q40.

PLAY ball!

Imagine a game that combines the ball and hoop of basketball, the protective pads and jarring contact of American football, and the no-hands policy of soccer.

This is the 3,000-year-old Maya ball-game of Pak-a-Tuk ("Juego de Pelota" in Spanish, "Uluma" in the indigenous Nuahtl language of Mexico). It is depicted in one form or another on thousands of artifacts, murals, and descriptive carved stelae found at archaeological sites.

Experts think the sport's primary purpose was ritualistic, or that it was a metaphor for the Maya dialectic cosmology. Perhaps it was just pure entertainment.

Other questions remain. Was it a game played by two nobles from different kingdoms, or by two teams of various numbers? Did the match last for hours or for days? And when the game was finally over, was the losing team sacrificed to the gods for its failure, or did the winning team lose their heads as a reward for pleasing the gods with their skill?

There are numerous ball courts to be found in Guatemala. They can be found at the archaeological sites of Cancuen, Nakbe, Naranjo, and Quiriguá. At Tikal, in the jungles of the Petén, there are seven, and several more are found throughout the rest of the country. Nearly every pre-Columbian city of any significant size appears to have had at least one, and more than 700 ball courts are found as far north as Arizona. The ball courts vary in size; some have open ends, while others have closed ends.

Despite the extensive findings by hundreds of archaeologists and the score of competing theories, there is no universal agreement as to the reasons, rules, regulation sizes, or results of this mysterious game.

Tikal village, Petén. ⓒ **502/7861-2444,** or ⓒ /fax 502/7861-2445. www.tikalinn.com. 32 units. $70–$80 double. Rate includes breakfast. MC, V. **Amenities:** Restaurant; bar; small outdoor pool. *In room:* No phone.

CAMPING

Just off the main parking lot at the site is a nice lawn with some trees for shade, marked and designated as the camping area. You can also set up your tent on some concrete pads, under an open-air thatch palapa roof. The camping area has simple shared shower and toilet facilities, and a communal cooking area. The campground (no phone) charges Q80 for the privilege of putting up a tent and using the facilities. You can also rent hammocks and pitch them under open-air palapas for an additional Q40.

Tip: If you plan on sleeping in a hammock, or even taking an afternoon siesta, you should really try to get a mosquito net that fits over the hammock. Most of the places that rent and sell hammocks in this area have these nets.

Where to Dine

Most folks who stay near the ruins take all their meals at their hotel. If you're looking for variety or staying at the campsite, there are several little restaurants (*comedores*) between the main camping area and parking lot and the gate at the beginning of the road to Flores. As you arrive at Tikal from Flores, you'll see them on the right side; **Comedor Imperio Maya, Comedor La Jungla,** and **Comedor Tikal** are the best of the bunch. All are rustic and pleasant, and all serve hefty plates of fairly tasty food at low prices. You can get a large serving of roast chicken, with rice, beans, and fresh tortillas, along with a drink, for around Q40.

Within the area of the ruins, you'll find picnic tables beneath shelters and itinerant soft-drink peddlers, but no snack stands. If you want to spend all day at the ruins without having to walk back to the parking area for lunch, take sandwiches. Most of the hotels here and in Flores, as well as the *comedores,* will make you a bag lunch to take into the park.

Tikal After Dark

While you could hang out at your hotel or spend the evening swinging on a hammock, the best nighttime activity here is to visit the ruins by moonlight. Those staying near the entrance can have their admission ticket validated to allow them to roam the park until 8pm, and in some cases even later, depending on the disposition of the guards. If the moon is waxing, full, or just beyond full, you're in for a real treat. *Tip:* Before venturing into the park at night, be sure to ask about the current level of safety.

FLORES & SANTA ELENA ★

488km (303 miles) NE of Guatemala City; 65km (40 miles) SW of Tikal; 136km (84 miles) NW of the Belizean border

Since accommodations in Tikal are limited, most travelers choose to (or must) overnight in the sister cities of Flores and Santa Elena, which are connected by a narrow causeway. This is not necessarily such a bad thing, since there's a lot more to do and see in these towns, plus a far wider range of hotels and restaurants.

Seen from the air, Flores appears almost perfectly round. This quiet town, with its colonial-style buildings and cobblestone streets, is one of the most fascinating in Guatemala. Though most people spend time here only en route to or from the Tikal ruins, Flores is well worth exploring for a day or two. A walk around the circumference of the island presents a sort of Venetian experience. Buildings come right down to the water's edge. In fact, since the lake's water level has risen over the years, some of the outlying streets and alleys are flooded. Dugout canoes, kayaks, and motor launches sit at makeshift docks all around the circumference of the island.

Santa Elena, Flores's mainland counterpart, on the other hand, is a ramshackle, modern boomtown with little at all to recommend it. However, Santa Elena is where you'll find the airport, bus stations, a host of hotels, and a good view of Flores. The name Flores is often used as an umbrella term encompassing Flores, Santa Elena, and San Benito, a small town to the west of Santa Elena.

Flores is the unofficial capital of Guatemala's Petén region. El Petén has always been a remote region, and it was here, on the banks of Lake Petén Itzá, that the Itzá people, descendants of the Mayas, resisted Spanish conquest until the end of the 17th century. Conquistador Hernán Cortés visited the Itzá city of Tayasal, which once stood on the far side of the lake, in 1525, but had not tried to conquer the Itzás, who had a reputation for being fierce warriors. However, in 1697, the Spanish finally conquered the Itzás, and Tayasal became the last Indian city to fall under Spanish rule. Two years after taking Tayasal, the Spanish moved to Flores, an island that could easily be defended. They renamed this island Nuestra Señora de los Remedios y San Pablo de los Itzaes, and built a fort here between 1700 and 1701. In 1831, the island was once

> ### Horsing Around
>
> One of the most curious pieces of local history revolves around a sick horse that was left in Tayasal by Hernán Cortés when he passed through the area. The Itzás had never seen horses before, and as soon as Cortés left, they began worshiping it. When the horse died, a stone statue of it was made, and the worship continued until Spanish missionaries arrived in Tayasal 100 years later. The missionaries, appalled by this idolatry, proceeded to pitch the blasphemous statue into the lake. To this day the legendary horse statue has never been discovered, though searches continue to be launched from time to time.

again renamed, this time being given the name Flores in honor of a Guatemalan patriot.

9 | Essentials

GETTING THERE

BY PLANE   See "By Plane" under "Essentials" in "Tikal," earlier in this chapter.

BY CAR   To get here from Guatemala City, see "By Car" under "Essentials" in "Tikal," earlier in this chapter.

The road between Tikal and Flores is well paved, and the trip takes around an hour by car. To get to either of the sister towns from Tikal, head south out of the ruins, and turn right at Ixlú (El Cruce). Continue on past the airport, and you'll come to Santa Elena first. Stay on the main avenue into town and head toward the lake, where you'll find the causeway to Flores.

BY BUS   For information on getting to Flores and Santa Elena by bus from Guatemala City, see "By Bus" under "Essentials" in "Tikal," earlier in this chapter.

GETTING AROUND

Those in Santa Elena or Flores will most likely want to go to Tikal or explore the region around Lake Petén.

BY MINIVAN   If you don't have a car, the best way to get around this area is by minivan. Minivans from Flores and Santa Elena to Tikal leave roughly every hour between 5 and 10am, and less frequently thereafter. These minivans leave from Tikal for the return trip roughly every hour from noon to 6pm. Every hotel in Flores and Santa Elena can arrange a minivan pickup for you. The trip usually takes an hour and costs Q50 to Q60 per person each way. You can buy a round-trip fare at a slight savings; however, this commits you to a specific minivan company, and I've found I prefer paying a little extra to have more flexibility in grabbing my return ride when I'm ready to leave.

BY TAXI   A private cab (which is usually a minivan) from Tikal to Santa Elena/Flores will run around Q350 to Q450 each way. Between Tikal and El Remate (later in this chapter), the fare is about Q100 to Q150. The higher rate is usually for a minivan that can hold anywhere from six to eight passengers. A taxi is your best option if you decide to explore the area around the lake. Be sure to bargain, as the first price you are quoted is almost certainly above the going rate and subject to some negotiation.

Flores & Santa Elena

ACCOMMODATIONS ■
Hotel Casa Elena
  de las Flores **15**
Hotel Del Patio **16**
Hotel Isla de Flores **7**
Hotel Maya Internacional **17**
Hotel Petén **3**
Hotel Petén Espléndido **14**
Hotel Santana **2**
La Casona de la Isla **5**
La Casona del Lago **13**

DINING ◆
Café Archeologico
  Yaxhá **9**
Capitán Tortuga **4**
El Mirador **14**
La Luna **6**
Pizzería Picasso **10**

NIGHTLIFE ★
AAdictos **12**
Bar Raices **1**
Cool Beans **8**
Las Puertas **11**

See inset above

✝ Church
ⓘ Information
✉ Post office

9

TIKAL & THE PETÉN | Flores & Santa Elena

205

BY BUS Very inexpensive local bus service connects Flores and Santa Elena to Tikal and several neighboring communities. However, this service is infrequent, slow, and often uncomfortably overcrowded. **Línea Dorado** (see earlier) has three daily buses from Santa Elena to Tikal leaving at 5 and 8:30am and 3:30pm. The return buses leave Tikal at 2 and 5pm. Ask at your hotel or around town for current schedules, as they change periodically. The trip takes 2 hours; the one-way fare is Q50.

BY CAR The road between Santa Elena and Flores and Tikal is paved, well marked, and heavily traveled. It's about 32km (20 miles) from Flores to Ixlú, and another 32km (20 miles) on to the park and ruins of Tikal.

For information on renting a car, see "Getting Around" under "Tikal," earlier in this chapter.

ORIENTATION

The town primarily known as Flores actually consists of three smaller towns that have merged. Flores proper sits on a small island out in Lake Petén Itzá, and is connected to the mainland by a long causeway. On the mainland are Santa Elena (nearest the airport) and San Benito (closer to the bus terminal and market). Whether you arrive by air or bus from Guatemala City or Belize, you'll come into town from the east. The road in from the airport leads straight through Santa Elena to the market and bus terminal, while the causeway to Flores is a right turn in the middle of Santa Elena.

FAST FACTS There is an information booth run by the Guatemalan Tourist Board, **INGUAT** (✆ **502/7926-0533;** www.visitguatemala.com), at the Flores airport, and another one in downtown Flores (✆ **502/7867-5334**) on Avenida Flores, on the north side of the Central Park. Both can help provide basic maps to the region and ruins, as well as brochures for local hotels and tour agencies. To contact the **local police,** dial ✆ **502/7926-1365.**

You'll find several banks in downtown Santa Elena. Most have ATMs, and many of these will work with your debit or credit card. There are also a couple of ATMs on the island of Flores. Check with your home bank and the PLUS or Cirrus systems in advance to confirm. All will exchange money. Most of the hotels and restaurants in Flores and Santa Elena will also exchange dollars for *quetzales,* although they may give you a slightly less favorable rate than you would get at a bank.

The **Flores post office** is on the Avenida Barrios, 1 block south of the Parque Central, or Central Park, which is in front of the church. **Santa Elena's post office** is on Calle 4 and Avenida 7. Both are open Monday through Friday from 8am to 5pm. To contact the **local police,** dial ✆ **502/7926-1365.** There are a host of Internet cafes around Flores and Santa Elena.

What to See & Do

Flores is a town for walking, and the whole island is only about 5 blocks wide in any direction. At the center is a small central park or plaza, anchored by the town's Catholic church. Be sure to check out its beautiful stained-glass windows.

One of the most popular things to do in Flores is take a **tour of the lake ★**. You will be inundated with offers for boat tours. Ask at your hotel or one of the local tour agencies, or talk to the numerous freelancers approaching you on the street. Be sure to inspect the craft beforehand, if possible, and make sure you feel comfortable with its lake-worthiness. Also, make sure your guide is bilingual. These tours last anywhere from 1 to 3 hours, and usually include stops at **La Guitarra Island** (Guitar Island), which features a picnic and swimming area, as well as at the mostly unexcavated

Holy Bats . . . Man!

Located some 24km (15 miles) west of Tikal is another small and relatively unexcavated Maya site, **El Zotz ★**. *Zotz* means "bat" in the local Mayan dialect, and that's exactly what you'll find here. Each night around sunset, tens of thousands of bats exit en masse from several caves, creating a spectacular sight. You might even see a bat falcon dive into the mass and pluck out dinner. Most of the tour agencies in Flores and Santa Elena can arrange trips to El Zotz, although these tend to be hardy overnight affairs with a fair amount of hiking involved. Rates run between $250 and $300 per person for a 3-day, 2-night excursion.

ruins of Tayasal. Here, be sure to climb **El Mirador ★**, a lakeside pyramid that offers a fabulous view of Flores. Many of these tours also stop at the small **Petencito Zoo** and **ARCAS** (www.arcasguatemala.com), a conservation organization and animal rehabilitation center, that has some interpretive trails and displays of rescued animals either in recuperation, or unable to be released. These tours cost between Q80 and Q160 per person, depending on the length of the tour and the size of your group. Don't be afraid to bargain. Entrance to the zoo is an extra Q20.

You can also **explore the lake** on your own in a kayak or canoe. While you can do this out of Flores, I find the lakeshore near El Remate a better place to take out a kayak or canoe. Rates run around Q15 per hour. To find a worthy craft, ask at your hotel or at one of the local tour agencies. Be careful paddling around the lake; when the winds pick up, especially in the afternoons, it can get quite choppy and challenging.

If you're a spelunker, you might want to explore **Aktun Kan (Cave of the Serpent),** a large cavern just outside Santa Elena. The cave takes its name from a legend about a giant snake living there. (Don't worry, it's only a legend.) Yet another legend has it that this cave is connected to a cave beneath the church on Flores. To reach Aktun Kan, either walk south out of Santa Elena on the road that crosses the causeway from Flores, or ask a taxi to take you there. The fare should be around Q15 round-trip. Although there are lights in the cave, be sure to bring a flashlight for a little extra illumination.

There are a host of local tour operators that can arrange any of the tours listed above, as well as guided tours to Tikal and the ruins listed below. The best of these are **Martsam Travel ★★** (✆ 866/832-2776 in the U.S. and Canada, or 502/7867-5093 in Guatemala; www.martsam.com) and **San Juan Travel** (✆ 502/5847-4738). Martsam is a particularly well-run, local operation that consciously works to implement sustainable and responsible tourism practices that broadly benefit the local community, while educating and enlightening the foreign traveler.

STUDYING SPANISH

Eco Escuela de Español ★ (✆ 502/5940-1235; www.ecoescuelaespanol.org) runs a community-based language school program in the small village of San Andrés, on the shore of Lake Petén Itzá. The program costs just $150 per week, including lodging and three meals daily with a local family, as well as 4 hours of daily class time, usually one-on-one. The setting allows for intensive language instruction, as well as many chances to really interact with the local culture and natural surroundings.

If you want to stick closer to the action in town, check in with the **Dos Mundos Spanish Academy** (☏ **502/5830-2060;** www.flores-spanish.com), which offers a wide range of course and accommodations options.

OTHER NEARBY RUINS

If the Tikal ruins in El Petén piqued your interest in Maya history, visit some of the more remote ruins of the region, which will have you traveling through uninhabited jungles and encountering a great deal of wildlife including coatimundis, howler and spider monkeys, anteaters, tapirs, and possibly even jaguars. **Martsam Travel ★★** (☏ **866/832-2776** in the U.S. and Canada, or **502/7867-5093** in Guatemala; www.martsam.com) is my favorite local tour operator, and they run trips to all of the sites mentioned below.

YAXHÁ ★★ Thanks to the publicity bestowed upon this site by the TV show *Survivor: Guatemala,* **Yaxhá** is now one of the prime archaeological sites to visit in Guatemala. In fact, this is the third-largest Maya ceremonial city in Guatemala—behind Tikal and El Mirador. At one point, Yaxhá supported a population of more than 20,000, and more than 400 buildings, five acropolises, and three ball courts have been discovered here. Be sure to climb **Temple 216 ★★★,** located in the East Acropolis. This is the tallest structure here, and provides excellent views of lakes Yaxhá and Sacnab, as well as the surrounding rainforests. The sunsets here rival those in Tikal. Yaxhá is one of the few Maya cities to retain its traditional Maya name, which translates as "green waters."

You can combine a visit to Yaxhá with a trip to the ruins of **Topoxté,** which are located on a small island in Lake Yaxhá. This small yet intriguing site is thought to have been a residential city for local elites. However, it was also a fortified city, where Maya warriors put up a valiant defense against Spanish forces. **Note:** You'll probably be warned and see the signs, but just in case, do not swim in Lake Yaxhá, as it is home to a robust population of crocodiles. Many organized tours here also include a stop at the nearby minor ruins of Nakum, which are currently being excavated. However, this makes for a long day. The turnoff for the 11km (7-mile) dirt road into the site is located about 32km (20 miles) east of Ixlú, or El Cruce. The Q80 admission grants you access to Yaxhá, Topoxté, and Nakum. If you want to stay at Yaxhá, camping is allowed at a well-tended campsite down by the lakeshore.

If you want to stay right on the lake at Yaxhá and just a stone's throw away from the archaeological site, check out **Campamento Ecológico El Sombrero** (☏ **502/4147-6380;** www.ecosombrero.com), which has comfortable but basic rooms in thatch-roof bungalows. About half of the bungalows come with private bathrooms, the rest with shared bathrooms. They also allow camping, and even rent out hammocks with mosquito netting under a common shelter. The park itself also has several very comfortable and well-located lakeside campsites.

EL CEIBAL This is another popular ruins site, and offers one of the most scenic routes along the way. To reach **El Ceibal ★,** head from Flores to Sayaxché (about 65km/40 miles), which is a good-size town with a few basic hotels. From Sayaxché, you must hire a boat to take you 18km (11 miles) up the Río de la Pasión. The Late Classic–era ruins here are known for having the only circular temple in all of El Petén. There are also several well-preserved stelae arranged around one small temple structure on the central plaza, as well as a ball court. Many of the designs at El Ceibal indicate that the city had extensive contact with cities in the Yucatán, but whether this contact was due to trade or warfare is unclear. Your best bet for visiting El Ceibal is to book an excursion with one of the tour agencies in Flores or Santa Elena. Full-day trips run around $75 to $100. Overnight trips can also be arranged, combining a visit to El Ceibal to even more obscure Maya sites such as **Aguateca** and **Petexbatún.** These trips are around $100 to $250 per day.

If you get to Sayaxché on your own, look for **Viajes Don Pedro** (℡ 502/7928-6109). These folks run regular boats to El Ceibal and charge around Q500 per person round-trip. However, if you have a group, be sure to try and negotiate a flat rate for the boat, which should carry anywhere from four to eight people. If you want to stay in the area, check out **Chiminos Island Lodge ★★** (℡ 502/2335-3506; www.chiminosisland.com), which has six (almost) luxurious cabins in the rainforest on a small island in the waters of the Petexbatún Lagoon.

UAXACTÚN Uaxactún (pronounced "Wah-shahk-*toon*") is yet another Maya ceremonial center, located 24km (15 miles) north of Tikal. Though many of the pyramids and temples here have been uncovered, they have not been restored as extensively as those at Tikal. Uaxactún also hosts what is believed to be the oldest known astrological observatory yet discovered in the Maya world. Watch the sunset from the observatory temple, located in Group E on the eastern side of the ruins, and see the sun line up precisely with other temples on the equinoxes and solstices.

Your best bet for visiting Uaxactún is to book the excursion with one of the tour agencies in Flores or Santa Elena. Full-day trips cost about $75 to $100, and can be combined with a stop at Tikal, although I think that's trying to cram too much into a single day. If you have your own 4WD vehicle, you can drive here yourself. The ruins at Uaxactún are open daily from 6am to 6pm, and no admission is charged. However, you must pass through Tikal National Park, therefore incurring the Tikal entrance fee of Q150. Keep in mind that the dirt road to Uaxactún is sometimes not passable during the rainy season, so be sure to ask locally about current conditions before heading off.

EL MIRADOR ★★ Finally, truly adventurous travelers can book a multiday jungle trek to El Mirador, the largest Maya ceremonial city in Guatemala. Barely excavated, El Mirador features the tallest pyramidal structure in the known Maya world, **La Danta,** which reaches some 79m (260 ft.) in height. The trip here involves at least 5 days of hiking and jungle camping. **Martsam Travel** (p. 207) is the best operator to contact for a trip to El Mirador.

Where to Stay

There are a host of budget lodgings in San Benito, especially around the bus terminal, but I strongly advise travelers to stick to Santa Elena and Flores proper.

EXPENSIVE

Hotel Maya Internacional Built on the banks of Lake Petén Itzá, on the Santa Elena side of the bridge, this long-standing hotel has well-kept and comfortable rooms, with tile floors and plenty of space. The best rooms have beautiful lake-view balconies—my favorites are nos. 49 through 52. The small pool has been built with an infinity effect that makes it appear to blend into the lake. The hotel's restaurant features a large dining area with a high thatch roof, as well as open-air lakefront seating.

Calle 1 and Av. 8, Santa Elena. ℡502/7926-1276 at the hotel, or 2223-5000 reservations in Guatemala City. Fax 502/2334-8134. www.villasdeguatemala.com. 26 units. $122 double. AE, DC, MC, V. **Amenities:** Restaurant; small exercise room; pool; free Wi-Fi. *In room:* A/C, TV, no phone.

Hotel Villa Maya ★   Hotel Villa Maya is located about 5 minutes from the airport, on the shores of Lake Petén Itzá, but away from the twin cities and toward Tikal. The setting and surrounding forests are lovely. Peace and quiet, if that's what you're looking for, are an added bonus, on top of the slightly reduced travel time to the ruins. However, if you want access to the restaurants and shops in Flores, you'll need either your own car or a taxi. Most of the rooms are found in a series of two-story buildings, set on the edge of the lake. Local hardwoods are used generously to trim details and furnish the place. The rooms are simple, spacious, and clean, and each comes with a small triangular balcony overlooking the lake. The hotel also has a pool with a cascading waterfall, as well as a wonderful dock and deck area over the lake.

15 min. from Santa Elena Internacional Airport on Lake Petenchel, 4km (2½ miles) north of the well-marked turnoff on the road from Santa Elena to Tikal. ✆ **502/2223-5000** reservations in Guatemala City, or 5410-1592 at the hotel. Fax 502/2334-8134. www.villasdeguatemala.com. 56 units. $125 double. AE, MC, V. **Amenities:** Restaurant; bike rental; Jacuzzi; pool; room service; watersports equipment rental; free Wi-Fi. *In room:* A/C, minibar.

MODERATE

Hotel Del Patio   This hotel's central courtyard, with its tall fountain flowing into a cloverleaf pool, is classic colonial Guatemala. The rooms are simple, clean, and comfortable, although the decor is definitely dated and you can find better deals around town. I'd opt for a second-floor unit, just so you can admire the courtyard from above as you enter and exit your room. A midsize kidney-shaped pool and tiny gym, as well as a good international restaurant, round out the amenities.

Calle 8 and Av. 2, Santa Elena, Petén. ✆ **502/7926-0104** or 502/7926-1229. Fax 502/7926-3030. www. caminoreal.com.gt. 21 units. $61 double. AE, MC, V. **Amenities:** Restaurant; bar; small gym; pool; room service. *In room:* A/C, TV.

Hotel Petén Espléndido   This modern upscale hotel is located in Santa Elena just off the causeway on the shore of Lake Petén Itzá, with a great view of Flores. The rooms feature contemporary decor and more modern amenities than you'll find anywhere else in town. The bathrooms are even equipped with telephones, and four rooms are designed for travelers with disabilities. The best rooms are the second-floor rooms with balconies directly fronting the lake. If you don't get one of these, the hotel's waterfront restaurant has a great view and serves good international and local cuisine. There's a relaxing and refreshing pool area, with a separate Jacuzzi. This place offers a free airport shuttle, as well as free paddleboats for use on the lake, and has a helpful tour desk and concierge. They are also actively involved in efforts to clean up the lake, sort their hotel waste, and are recognized as a sustainable operation by Great Green Deal and the Rainforest Alliance.

1a Calle 5-01, Zona 1, Santa Elena, Flores, Petén. ✆ **502/2360-8140** reservations number in Guatemala City, or 502/7926-0880 at the hotel. Fax 502/7926-0866. www.petenesplendido.com. 62 units. $90–$150 double. AE, DC, MC, V. **Amenities:** Restaurant; bar; concierge; outdoor pool; room service. *In room:* A/C, TV, hair dryer, safe.

La Casona de la Isla   La Casona de la Isla shows the same attention to service as the other properties run by this local hotel group. The guest rooms here are all fairly small and lack much in the way of style, but they do have tile floors, ceiling fans, and air-conditioning—although some of these A/C units can be rather old and noisy. Most come with a private balcony, and almost all of these have good views of the lake. The hotel is built in an L-shape around a stone terrace with lush gardens and a small swimming pool featuring a sculpted stone waterfall and separate Jacuzzi.

Its restaurant serves good Guatemalan and international fare in a small dining room off the lobby, and there's a back patio bar with an excellent view overlooking the lake.

Calle 30 de Junio, Flores, Petén. © **502/7867-5163.** www.hotelesdepeten.com. 26 units. $52–$57 double. Rates include taxes. AE, DC, MC, V. **Amenities:** Restaurant; bar; outdoor pool and Jacuzzi; free Wi-Fi. *In room:* A/C, TV.

La Casona del Lago ★★ This is the most luxurious hotel of a group run by a small local chain, although it's also the only one not on the island of Flores proper. (Don't confuse this with La Casona de la Isla, which is part of the same chain and in Flores.) Still, this hotel is located right on the shores of the lake, with excellent views of its waters and picturesque island city. The three-story building is built in an L-shape, around a central pool and Jacuzzi area, and painted a bright primary blue, with sparkling white trim. Rooms are spacious, with two double beds, white-tile floors, a couple of sitting chairs, and a separate desk area, and they feature a host of modern amenities, including 21-inch televisions.

Calle Litoral, Zona 1, Santa Elena, Flores, Petén. ©/fax **502/7952-8700.** www.hotelesdepeten.com. 32 units. $88–$98 double. Rates include full breakfast and taxes. AE, DC, MC, V. **Amenities:** Restaurant; outdoor pool and Jacuzzi; free Wi-Fi. *In room:* A/C, TV, hair dryer.

INEXPENSIVE

Hotel Casa Elena de las Flores ☺ This neat little hotel in downtown Santa Elena offers well-kept rooms at a fair price. Still, most of the rooms are on the small side, and their televisions are tiny. At the center of the hotel is a pretty little pool and lovely interior courtyard with shady palm trees. The pool even has a water slide, which is a hit with children. The hotel is kept immaculate, and there's a friendly air to the whole operation. You'll find a simple restaurant on the grounds, as well as an inviting second-floor bar. For a good view, head up to the unfinished rooftop terrace.

Av. 6 and Calle 2, Santa Elena, Petén. © **502/7926-2235.** Fax 502/7926-0097. www.casaelenadelas flores.com. 28 units. $45–$52 double. AE, MC, V. **Amenities:** Restaurant; small outdoor pool; room service; free Wi-Fi. *In room:* A/C, TV.

Hotel Petén From the street, this hotel looks very modest. Walk through the doorway, though, and you'll find an attractive small courtyard with tropical plants, a tiny semi-indoor pool, and a nice brick-and-stucco building of several floors. The rooms are all well-kept. The best rooms are those on the top two floors with private balconies and an excellent view of the lake. In fact, only five rooms here don't have a lake view, so when you reserve or check in, be sure you get one that does. There's a popular restaurant on the ground floor. These folks also have an in-house tour company, and are owned by the same company as a couple of other nearby hotels, in case this one is full.

Calle 30 de Junio, Flores, Petén. ©/fax **502/7867-5203.** www.hotelesdepeten.com. 21 units. $48–$52 double. Rates include taxes. AE, DC, MC, V. **Amenities:** Restaurant; Jacuzzi; pool. *In room:* A/C, TV.

Hotel Santana ★ 🐟 This is a great choice if you're looking to snag a lakefront room with a balcony and a view, all at a very good price. Most of the rooms here fit the criteria I just mentioned, and those on the third and fourth floors have the best views—still, be sure you get a lake-view room, and not one of the less desirable interior affairs. The rooms here are all cool, clean, and fairly spacious, and a definite cut above the rest of the options on the island of Flores in this price range. The large open-air dining room is a delightful place to sit and enjoy the lakeside setting as well.

There's a small kidney-shaped pool, with a built-in waterfall and swim-up bar, in a little courtyard to the side.

Calle 30 de Junio, Flores, Petén. ✆/fax **502/7867-5123** or 502/7867-5193. www.santanapeten.com. 35 units. $40–$60 double. AE, MC, V. **Amenities:** Restaurant; outdoor pool; free Wi-Fi. *In room:* A/C, TV.

Where to Dine

There are tons of places to eat around Flores and Santa Elena. Most are simple, serving local and Mexican cuisine and geared toward locals and the backpacking crowd.

In addition to the places listed below, **Pizzeria Picasso,** Calle 15 de Septiembre, across from El Tucán (✆ **502/7867-5198**), serves pretty good wood-oven pizza and a variety of pastas, while **El Mirador Restaurant** at the Hotel Petén Espléndido (p. 210) serves good but far from spectacular international fare; however, the setting is certainly the most elegant you'll find in this neck of the woods.

Café Arqueológico Yaxhá ★ 🏛 GUATEMALAN/MAYAN This is a relaxed and welcoming spot that serves excellent local fare, including dishes based on pre-Colombian recipes and ingredients. I recommend the *Pollo Xni Pec,* which is chicken in a spicy tomato sauce, served with yucca. The German owner is an archeologist, and photos of archeological sites adorn the walls, books on the subject matter are available to browse, and talks, slide-shows, and guided tours are often offered. This is also a good place to come for coffee drinks and fresh fruit smoothies. If interested in contributing to the local community, you can ask here about volunteer opportunities.

Calle 15 de Setiembre, across from El Tucán, Flores. ✆ **502/5830-2060.** www.cafeyaxha.com. Main courses Q30–Q90. AE, MC, V. Daily 7am–9pm.

Capitán Tortuga ★ INTERNATIONAL This popular restaurant has a long and wide-ranging menu. You can get everything from pizzas to barbecue ribs to vegetarian shish kabobs. They also have a wide range of coffee and espresso drinks, as well as ice creams and freshly baked desserts. The large main dining room sits under a high thatch room. However, I prefer the tables on the small outdoor patio that fronts the lake, or those in the second-floor, open-air dining room reached from a stairway out back. Service can be slow at times, but if you're with a group or sharing a drink with fellow travelers, you might not mind.

Calle 30 de Junio, next to La Casona de la Isla, Flores. ✆ **502/7867-5089.** Main courses Q32–Q120. AE, MC, V. Daily 11:30am–11pm.

La Luna ★★ INTERNATIONAL This hip little restaurant is the most creative and refined option in Flores. The menu ranges from steak in pepper sauce to lobster tails, with a host of fish and chicken—and even some vegetarian—options in between. I recommend starting with some stuffed peppers or a falafel side. There are three separate dining areas, and all are artistically decorated. My favorite room features a faux ceiba tree (Guatemala's national tree) in the center and a wild sculpture on one wall made of wood and mirrors.

Calle 30 de Junio, across from La Casona de la Isla, Flores. ✆ **502/7867-5443.** Main courses Q40–Q130. MC, V. Mon–Sat noon–11pm.

Flores & Santa Elena After Dark

There are several bars along Calle Sur fronting the lake just over the bridge as you enter Flores. Of these, **AAdictos** (no phone) is one of the liveliest. For a view of the lake and a happening dance, DJ, and party scene, you can head to **Bar Raíces**

(© 502/5521-1843), at the far western end of Calle Sur. Another good option, near the center of the island, is **Las Puertas ★** (© 502/7867-5242; corner of Calle Centroamérica and Avenida Santa Ana), which is a popular bar/restaurant that has nightly DVD movie showings, and occasionally live music. Finally, for a mellow scene, try **Cool Beans ★** (© 502/5571-9240; Calle 15 de Septiembre), a popular place for tourists and itinerant backpackers, with a convivial, laid-back vibe, free Wi-Fi, plenty of board games, and a view of the lake to boot.

EL REMATE ★★

32km (20 miles) E of Flores; 32km (20 miles) S of Tikal; 60km (37 miles) W of Melchor de Mencos

The small village of El Remate, located on the eastern shores of Lake Petén Itzá, is another popular spot to stay while visiting Tikal. Its midway location between Flores and Tikal keeps you closer to the ruins but also in a much more tranquil and pristine environment than Flores or Santa Elena. Currently, a handful of budget lodgings can be found in the tiny village here, while more upscale options can be found on the shores of the lake heading north out of the village.

Essentials

GETTING THERE

BY PLANE See "By Plane" under "Essentials" in "Tikal," earlier in this chapter.

BY MINIVAN Scheduled and independent minivans ply the route between Santa Elena/Flores and Tikal throughout the day. Any of these will drop you off in El Remate. For more information, see "Getting Around" under "Tikal," earlier in this chapter, and below. Fares from Flores to El Remate run around Q20 and Q40 per person.

BY CAR El Remate is located about a mile north of Ixlú on the road between Santa Elena and Tikal. The road is well paved from Flores and Santa Elena, as well as to Tikal and the Belize-Guatemala border, 60km (37 miles) to the east.

GETTING AROUND

El Remate is tiny, and you can easily walk anywhere in town. Some of the hotels listed below are located a mile or so north of the village, on the road that circles Lake Petén Itzá. If you're in El Remate, you'll most likely want to go to Tikal, visit Santa Elena and Flores, or explore the region.

BY TAXI Taxis charge between Q150 to Q200 for the one-way trip between El Remate and Tikal, and between Q100 to Q150 for the trip between El Remate and Santa Elena or Flores. The higher rates are for a minivan that can hold anywhere from six to eight passengers. A taxi is your best option if you decide to explore the area around the lake. There are often taxis hanging around town. If not, your hotel can call one for you. Be sure to have your hotel set a fair price, or be prepared to bargain, as the first price you are quoted is likely to be above the going rate and subject to some negotiation.

BY MINIVAN If you don't have a car, the best way to get around is by minivan. Scheduled and unscheduled minivans ply the route between Flores and Tikal throughout the day. All of these pass through El Remate, dropping off and picking up passengers. You can get a minivan at almost any hotel in El Remate, or walk a few hundred yards out to the main road to Tikal and flag one down. The ride takes about a half-hour to either Tikal or Flores, and the one-way fare is Q20 to Q40 per person.

If you're out on the lake during the daytime, scan the shoreline northwest of El Remate, and try to pick out the "Sleeping Crocodile," a silhouette formed by the shape of the forested hills as they descend toward the lake. If you can't find it, ask a local for help.

What to See & Do

Most people use El Remate as a base for trips to the ruins at Tikal. However, as small lodges and isolated resorts start to pop up here, so do the many tour and activity options.

Just west of El Remate is the **Biotopo Cerro Cahuí,** a small nature reserve with some trails and good wildlife-viewing opportunities. More than 180 species of birds have been spotted here. A couple of loop trails climb uphill from the entrance and offer excellent views of the lake. I recommend you visit this park with a guide, as incidents of violence against tourists closed it for a period a few years ago. Ask at your hotel's desk or hire a guide through **Martsam Travel ★★** (✆ **866/832-2776** in the U.S. and Canada, or 502/7867-5093 in Guatemala; www.martsam.com). The reserve is open daily from 8am to 4pm, and admission is Q40.

One of the most popular activities in El Remate is **renting a canoe or kayak** for paddling around on the lake. Most of the hotels in town either rent kayaks or canoes, or can arrange one for you. Rates run around Q35 per hour, or around Q120 per day.

Similarly, most of the hotels in town either rent or provide **mountain bikes** for their guests, or can arrange for their rental. The dirt road that circles Lake Petén Itzá is excellent for a mountain bike ride. Rates are about Q60 per day.

El Remate is also gaining some local renown for its woodcarving. You'll see several roadside stands set up on the route between Ixlú and El Remate, and onward to Tikal. If you ask around El Remate, you might even be able to visit one or more of the artisans.

Where to Stay & Dine

Most visitors take their meals at their hotels, but you'll find some simple restaurants (*comedores*) in the center of the village. The best of these is **El Muelle** (✆ **502/5514-9785;** www.elmuellehotel.com), which has a great view of the lake, as well as a swimming pool, which you can use if you eat here. If you're looking for something more exotic, try the restaurant at the **Hotel Mon Ami** (✆ **502/7928-8413;** www.hotelmonami.com), which features a mix of Guatemalan, French, and Italian fare.

On the route between the Petén Province and Río Dulce lies a wonderful isolated ecolodge, **Finca Ixobel ★** (✆ **502/5410-4307;** www.fincaixobel.com), which is about 100km (62 miles) away from both Flores and Río Dulce. Accommodations include a campground, dorm rooms, and private thatch-roof bungalows. Plus, there's an inviting lake for swimming and plenty of nearby rainforests, caves, and rivers to explore.

VERY EXPENSIVE

La Lancha Resort ★★ This is filmmaker Francis Ford Coppola's Guatemalan piece of his mini-hotel chain in the Mundo Maya. The main lodge has a commanding view of the lake and features a soaring, open-air, A-frame thatch roof oriented towards the view. Below the lodge is a kidney-shaped pool. A steep trail leads down to the shore of the lake, where you'll find a swimming area and some canoes and kayaks. The rooms are all duplex bungalows. The "lake view" units are quite spacious, while the "jungle view" rooms are more compact. All are tastefully and artistically decorated and very comfortable. All feature a shared wooden veranda, and you can probably figure out the view from the room names.

Lago Petén Itzá, Petén. ✆ **800/746-3743** in the U.S., or ✆/fax 502/7928-8331 in Guatemala. www. lalanchavillage.com. 10 units. $210–$280 double. Rates lower in the off season; higher during peak periods. AE, MC, V. **Amenities:** Restaurant; bar; bike rental; outdoor pool. *In room:* A/C, minifridge, no phone, free Wi-Fi.

EXPENSIVE

In addition to the place listed below, the folks at Gringo Perdido (see below) have just opened a neighboring project, **Piramide Paraiso** (www.hotelgringoperdido.com), which features large luxury villas ($200 double, including 3 meals), with all the modern amenities, including two Jacuzzi tubs, in each unit, one inside and one on the balcony.

Camino Real Tikal ★   Although nowhere near as intimate or artistic as **La Lancha Resort** (see above), this modern resort, set on a hillside above the lake, is still a good choice. The bungalows are set in a long line along a ridge over the lake, and all have wonderful lake views. Inside, the rooms are spacious and feature contemporary and tasteful decor. Every room has a private balcony or porch; the third-floor units have the best views. There are two restaurants and a lovely outdoor pool area, while down by the water there's a dock out into the lake, a sandy beach area for swimming, and a wood-fired sauna. The hotel offers a free shuttle to the park and the airport in Flores.

5km (3 miles) west of El Remate. ✆ **502/7926-0204.** Fax 502/7926-3030. www.caminorealtikal.com. gt. 72 units. $140–$160 double. AE, MC, V. **Amenities:** 2 restaurants; 2 bars; bike rental; pool; room service; sauna; watersports equipment rental. *In room:* A/C, TV, hairdryer, minifridge, Wi-Fi ($10 per day).

MODERATE

Hotel Gringo Perdido   Three kilometers (1¾ miles) north of El Remate on the dirt road that circles Lake Petén Itzá, you'll find one of Guatemala's original jungle lodges. This little offbeat paradise is arranged along the lakeshore, with shady rustic hillside gardens, a restaurant, a quiet camping area, and rooms ranging from a rustic dormitory to some almost plush private bungalows. The whole thing seems to blend into and get swallowed up by the rainforest. In fact, this hotel is located within the boundaries of the Biotopo Cerro Cahui Plant and Wildlife Preserve. Throughout their long history here, the owners have worked hard to lessen their environmental impact, while aiding local conservation causes. The Gringo Perdido, which means "the lost American," offers good swimming in the lake, 3.2km (2 miles) of nature trails, and tranquility.

3.2km (2 miles) west of El Remate, Petén. ✆ **502/2334-2305** or 502/4899-4615. www.hotelgringo perdido.com. 13 units (2 w/shared bathroom). $70 double with shared bath; $90 double with private bath. Rates include breakfast and dinner. $5 per person to camp, with meals extra. V only (with 8% surcharge). **Amenities:** Restaurant. *In room:* No phone.

INEXPENSIVE

In addition to the places listed below, a few very inexpensive options, catering to the backpacking crowd, are right in El Remate. I recommend simply walking around to

see which one best fits your fancy and budget. One good option is **Hotel Mon Ami**
(ⓒ **502/7928-8413;** www.hotelmonami.com).

La Casa de Don David Hotel ☙ This hotel's rooms are located in a series of
buildings arrayed around a large and lush garden area. All are clean and simple.
There's an open-air octagonal hammock hut for reading and resting, and you can
catch a glimpse of Lake Petén from here. Most of the rooms have air-conditioning,
and you'll pay slightly more for these. My favorite room is no. 13, which is a corner
unit with a private hammock on its front porch. The hotel offers bicycles free for
guest use. The hotel has an extensive recycling program, uses grey-water for irriga-
tion, and has installed energy-saving light bulbs and water heaters. David Kuhn and
his wife Rosita have lived in this area for more than 30 years, and they are a wealth
of information and advice. David was the original *gringo perdido* of the nearby nature
lodge (see above), but left there to open this delightful little place.

El Remate, Petén. ⓒ**502/7928-8469** or 502/5306-2190. www.lacasadedondavid.com. 15 units. $40–
$52 double. Rates include 1 meal (breakfast, lunch, or dinner). MC, V. **Amenities:** Restaurant. *In room:*
No phone.

La Mansión del Pájaro Serpiente ★ ⛫ Set off the main road to Tikal, on a
hillside overlooking the lake, this place has both standard and deluxe bungalows,
beautiful gardens, and a friendly atmosphere. The bungalows feature beautiful stone
and woodworking details, with local textile and crafts filling out the decor. The deluxe
rooms feature televisions and air-conditioning. Several rooms are quite large and
should be classified as junior suites, as they also have a separate sitting area just off
the bedroom. The "honeymoon suite" comes with its own plunge pool and is high on
the hill, with a great view. The midsize free-form pool is set amidst lush gardens, and
almost feels like a natural pond in the jungle. The open-air restaurant has a great view
of the lake and specializes in local cuisine. The owners raise peacocks, and there are
always several wandering around the grounds.

El Remate, Petén. ⓒ/fax **502/7926-8498** or 502/5702-9434. 11 units. $45 double; $55 deluxe double.
No credit cards. **Amenities:** Restaurant; outdoor pool. *In room:* No phone.

El Remate After Dark

El Remate is a quiet village, and most visitors head to the small bar at their hotel or
hostel to chat with fellow travelers. Some, however, head out to the lake to see the
crocodiles by the light of a high-powered flashlight or headlamp. Two-hour tours,
which can be arranged through your hotel, are headed by a guide, who will scan the
shore and inlets for the red reflection of the crocodiles' eyes. If you're lucky, they
won't submerge as you slowly approach. The cost is Q150–Q240.

CENTRAL GUATEMALA: LAS VERAPACES, EL ORIENTE & COPÁN

Verapaz translates to "true peace," but its history reveals a path of destruction blazed by the Spanish conquistadors who met unprecedented resistance in the high mountains of this region. The fierce resistance was such that the Spaniards dubbed the area Tierra de Guerra (Land of War). In the early 16th century, a groundbreaking human-rights activist, the Dominican priest Fray Bartolomé de las Casas, proposed the use of gentle persuasion, "evangelical love," and religious conversion instead of outright suppression of the indigenous people. De las Casas's tactic was so successful that by 1545, Prince Phillip of Spain renamed the region Verapaz, and prohibited the use of the name Tierra de Guerra.

Today, the high mountains, dense forest, and rugged terrain offer a sense of peaceful respite from the more hectic and crowded destinations of Guatemala's Western Highlands. The Verapaz region is actually divided into two, hence Las Verapaces. This is a heavily indigenous region, and the Mayan languages of Q'eqchi and Pocomchí are dominant rather than Spanish.

Cobán, which is an adventure tourism hot spot, is the most important city in the Verapaz region, and makes an excellent base from which to explore Las Verapaces. The region south and east of Las Verapaces is known as **El Oriente,** or "the East." While it has no significant draw for tourists, it's home to the historic city of **Esquipulas,** near the southeastern border by Honduras. The magnificent Basílica and famous ***Black Christ*** (p. 230) are revered by Roman Catholics who travel throughout Guatemala and the world on pilgrimage. Just over the border, in Honduras, lay the Maya ruins of **Copán,** one of the most important Classic

Maya archaeological sites yet discovered, with perhaps the best preserved and displayed collection of stone carvings and stelae.

COBAN ★

213km (132 miles) E of Guatemala City; 583km (362 miles) S of Tikal

Cobán is the most important city in the Verapaz region, and serves as the social and commercial hub for all the surrounding towns, villages, and tourist destinations. Cobán is still known as the "Ciudad Imperial," as it was dubbed by the Spanish crown when it was founded in 1538. The city sits at more than 1,300m (4,000 ft.) and enjoys a cool, yet wet, climate. (Cool mist or outright rain are common here.) Cobán is also the gateway for some of Guatemala's best eco- and adventure-tourism destinations and activities.

Essentials

GETTING THERE

BY BUS Monja Blanca (© 502/2251-1878 in Guatemala City, or 7951-3571 in Cobán) has buses leaving every hour between 4am and 5pm. Its station in Guatemala City is at 8a Av. 15-16, Zona 1. In Cobán, the buses leave from 2a Calle 2-77, Zona 4. The fare is Q45 each way.

The tourist shuttle companies, including **Atitrans** ★ (© 502/7832-3371 24-hr. reservation number; www.atitrans.net) and **Turansa** (© 502/2390-5757; www.turansa.com), all have daily routes from Guatemala City to Cobán and Semuc Champay. The fare is around Q240 to Q360.

You can also use Cobán as a midway point between Guatemala City and Tikal and the Petén, or Lago Izabal, Río Dulce, and the Caribbean coast.

BY CAR If you have a car, take the Carretera al Atlántico (CA-9) out of Guatemala City to the crossroads at El Rancho. The exit and road to Cobán is well marked.

Coffee & Cardamom

While Guatemala was one of United Fruit Company's quintessential banana republics and is now most famous for its shade-grown, volcanic mountain coffee, it's also the world's principal exporter of another agricultural product—cardamom.

Grown primarily in the Alta Verapaz mountains near Cobán, cardamom was brought to the region as a cash crop by German immigrants in the mid-20th century. Like coffee, this aromatic spice thrives in the area's cool, moist mountain climate. Today, cardamom is Guatemala's fourth-most-important cash crop behind coffee, bananas, and sugar. Small producers—farmers with less than 4 hectares (10 acres) of land—grow 70% of the country's cardamom crop.

Cardamom is an important ingredient in the curries and cuisine of India, where it's also believed to be a medicinal herb and an antidote for snake and scorpion venom. In Scandinavia, the spice is used to flavor bread and pastries, and across the Middle East, it's often added to coffee and thought to be a powerful aphrodisiac. In Guatemala, keep your eye out for cardamom-flavored chewing gum, *chicle de cardamomo*. It's sold in convenience stores and supermarkets across the country.

Las Verapaces

GETTING AROUND

Cobán is very compact, though the very center of the city sits atop a plateau with steep hills on all sides, making walking strenuous at times. Taxis are plentiful and inexpensive. If you can't flag one down, have your hotel call you one.

If you're going to any of the nearby attractions such as Semuc Champey or the Candelaria Caves, your best bet is to join a tour. Alternately, you can get to most of these places on a local bus. Ask your hotel for current times and departure locations.

Renting a car once you arrive in Cobán is also a good option. Check out **Tabarini Rent A Car** (© 502/7952-1504; www.tabarini.com). Rates run around Q320 to Q960 per day depending on whether you opt for a compact sedan or small SUV.

ORIENTATION

Cobán's central plaza is a long, thin trapezoid, with the Catholic church, Catedral de Santo Domingo, at the widest, eastern end. This spot has the highest elevation in town, and is also the busiest.

FAST FACTS The **post office** is located at 2a Calle 2-02, Zona 3 (© 502/7951-4476). Most hotels have their own Internet cafes, and there are many around downtown

As you drive into Cobán, keep your eye out around Km 199. You'll see a sign for Aldea Chitul, and there on your left are a couple of small caves that are actively used as sights for Maya ritual prayers and ceremonies. If you choose to stop and observe, be respectful, and do not take photos.

Cobán, such as the ones at **Café Fantasia** and **Hostal Doña Victoria.** (See later in this chapter.)

There are several **banks** and **ATMs** within a block or two of the city's central plaza. Dial ℂ **502/7952-1225** for the **police,** ℂ **502/7952-1459** for the **Red Cross.** If you need medical attention, head to the **Centro de Salud,** 7a Calle 6-24, Zona 11 (ℂ **502/7951-4155**).

What to See & Do

While many of this region's principal attractions are outside of Cobán, the city and its immediate environs have a lot to offer visitors.

On a hill overlooking the city sits the **Templo El Calvario** ★, an 1810 church with a beautifully restored facade. You'll have to climb a flight of steep and broad steps before reaching the commanding view, and on the way you'll pass a series of altars used for specific prayers—health, love, wealth, success. It's believed that this site has been sacred to the local Maya for millennia, and the ongoing prayers here still bear the Maya influence. El Calvario is located at the north end of 7a Avenida. **Warning:** Avoid this area after dark or when there are few other people around, as attacks and robberies have occurred.

The city's main Catholic church, the **Catedral de Santo Domingo,** was built in the mid–16th century under the direction of Fray Melchor del los Reyes. It underwent subsequent modifications in 1741, 1792, and 1965. Today, the most interesting feature of this church is its massive whitewashed facade, which is rather plain and lacking ornamentation, but impressive in its size and antiquity. Inside you'll find a decent collection of colonial-era religious art and sculpture.

Just north of the Templo El Calvario is the **Parque Nacional Las Victorias,** a nature reserve that's a good place for a walk, jog, or bird-watching. The park has a few trails, as well as picnic tables and open-air shelters. Camping is permitted, but I don't recommend it as it's dangerous, and there have been attacks and robberies. If you want to camp, head toward Lanquin or Semuc Champey (see below). Las Victorias park is open daily from 8am to 4pm. Admission is Q5.

In the heart of Cobán sits the small, but rewarding, **Príncipe Maya Museum** ★★, 6a Av. 4-26, Zona 3 (ℂ **502/7952-1541**). This private museum has an extensive collection of pieces ranging from utilitarian pottery and ornamental burial urns to musical instruments and elegant jewelry. There are jade inlaid teeth, a full burial reconstruction, and a panel from the Cancuen archaeological site with intricate bas-relief hieroglyphics. One of my favorite pieces here is a miniature Olmec man. The museum is open Monday through Saturday from 9am to 5pm. Admission is Q15.

Plant enthusiasts will want to visit **Vivero Verapaz** (ℂ **502/7952-1133**), which claims to have more than 35,000 plants, including more than 650 species of orchids. You'll also be able to check out Guatemala's national flower, Monja Blanca (White

Cobán

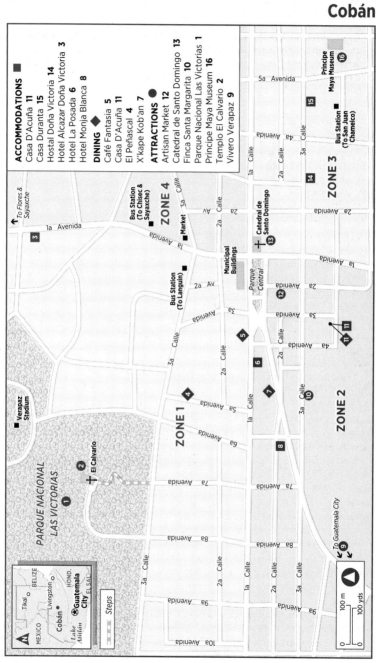

ACCOMMODATIONS ■
Casa D'Acuña **11**
Casa Duranta **15**
Hostal Doña Victoria **14**
Hotel Alcazar Doña Victoria **3**
Hotel La Posada **6**
Hotel Monja Blanca **8**

DINING ◆
Café Fantasia **5**
Casa D'Acuña **11**
El Peñascal **4**
X'kape Kob'an **7**

ATTRACTIONS ●
Artisan Market **12**
Catedral de Santo Domingo **13**
Finca Santa Margarita **10**
Parque Nacional Las Victorias **1**
Principe Maya Museum **16**
Templo El Calvario **2**
Vivero Verapaz **9**

Cobán is the site of one of Mesoamerica's greatest celebrations of Maya culture. For 2 weeks in late July and early August, the city of Cobán and other towns around Las Verapaces celebrate La Fiesta Nacional Indígena de Guatemala (National Indigenous Folkloric Festival). One of the highlights of the celebrations is the selection of Rabin Ajua, the local "queen" of the festivities, chosen from representatives of the various communities around Las Verapaces. The selection of Rabin Ajua is made on July 21, and is the centerpiece of the celebrations, which include traditional local cuisine, music, and dance.

Nun). This nursery–cum–botanical garden is open daily from 9am to noon and 2 to 5pm. Admission is Q15 and includes a guided tour in English and Spanish.

If coffee is the only species of tropical flora that interests you, you're in luck. **Finca Santa Margarita** ★, 3a Calle 4-12, Zona 2 (✆ 502/7951-3067), is a working coffee plantation in the heart of downtown Cobán. These folks offer a 1½-hour guided tour in English and Spanish on the history, technique, and culture of coffee growing and processing, with a tasting afterward. Tours are available Monday through Friday from 8 to 11am and 2 to 3pm, and Saturday 8am to 10:30am. The cost for both admission and a tour is Q30.

Shopping

Cobán isn't a great shopping town, but there is a small, local **artisan market** (✆ 502/4145-8722), located in the Parque Navidad, behind the city's government buildings, just downhill from the central park. However, the offerings here are pretty standard tourist fare. I prefer the small craft shop at **X'kape Kob'an** ★ (see later), which focuses on locally produced arts and craft works. It also sells locally produced organic coffee and chocolate bars.

Attractions & Activities Farther Afield

Candelaria Caves ★★ This impressive cave system is sacred to the Q'eqchi Maya, and stretches continuously for some 29km (18 miles). The main gallery, **Tzul Tacca,** is almost 60m (200 ft.) high, 30m (100 ft.) wide, and 200m (650 ft.) long, and features massive stalagmites and roof windows that let in light. Side galleries hold evidence of ancient Maya rituals, and the entire system is traversed by the Candelaria River. (You can even float through the caves in an inner tube.)

You can visit the Candelaria Caves on a day trip out of Cobán, but to really enjoy them, you should stay overnight at the **Complejo Cultural y Ecológico Cuevas de Candelaria** ★ (✆ 502/4035-0566; www.cuevasdecandelaria.com). All of the tour operations in Cobán offer guided multiday trips here.

10km (6 miles) west of the village of Raxrujá, which is north of the town of Chisec. Admission Q30. Daily 8am–4pm.

Grutas del Rey Marcos and Balneario Cecilinda About 8km (5 miles) south of Cobán sits the town of San Juan Chamelco, home to a colonial-era church and gateway to two popular local attractions: Grutas del Rey Marcos, a small cave system, and Balneario Cecilinda, a complex of natural spring–fed pools.

The **Gruta del Rey Marcos ★** features beautiful stalagmite and stalactite formations. Some of these are very large; one has even been dubbed the Leaning Tower of Pisa. At one point you'll have to ford a small river to get to the more impressive cave galleries.

If the weather's nice, you'll definitely enjoy a dip in the pools at the **Balneario Cecilinda,** which are very popular with locals, so expect to meet many if you come on a sunny weekend.

If you want to stay in the area, check out **Don Jerónimo's** (✆ 502/5301-3191; http://dearbrutus.com/donjeronimo), a delightful and rustic joint with a gregarious owner who knows the area well. This place specializes in ecological and spiritual vacations or retreats, and serves up tasty vegetarian cuisine. Don Jerónimo's is located 1km (less than a mile) before the Gruta del Rey Marcos.

About 8km (5 miles) south of Cobán in the town of San Juan Chamelco. Grutas del Rey Marcos ✆ **502/7951-2756.** Balneario Cecilinda ✆ **502/5308-9307.** www.grutasdelreymarcos.com Admission Q10 for each attraction. Both open weekends 8am–6pm. The caves will open with prior reservation during the week if you come with a semi-sizable group. It's possible, but slightly complicated, to get here by public transportation. Your best bet is to take a taxi, which should cost around Q75. Alternatively, you could sign up for a day tour.

Kan' Ba ★★ The entrance to this cave attraction (near the entrance to Semuc Champey) sits above the Cahabón River and features a smaller river that emerges from the cave mouth and cascades in a waterfall to the Cahabón below. Visitors see the cave in an unusual way; first by wading/swimming up to it, and second by candlelight. Candles are provided, but I recommend bringing a waterproof headlamp. The trip to the cave takes about 20 minutes each way, and at the end you can take a 15-minute inner-tube ride on the Cahabón River, which ends at the Hostal Las Marías (see below), which happens to own and run this attraction.

Near entrance to Semuc Champey, 9km (5½ miles) beyond Lanquin, a 2-hr. drive from Cobán. ✆ **502/7861-2209.** Tour Q50 per person. Daily 9am–5pm, but subject to change.

Lanquin The Lanquin cave is a popular destination, and while it's worth visiting if you have some extra time on a trip to Semuc Champey, I find it a little disappointing. The geological formations are more interesting at the Grutas del Rey Marcos and the Candelaria Caves, while the adventure is much greater at Kan' Ba. A lighted trail leads about 400 meters (1,312 feet) into the depths of the cave. Leaving little to the imagination, the locals have named many of the Lanquin stalactite and stalagmite formations after the animals they vaguely resemble.

The best time to visit Lanquin is in the late afternoon, when thousands of bats exit the cave to feed. There's good swimming in the river near the mouth of the cave, and

---

 Take a Break

Touring the town can take its toll, and a coffee break is the perfect way to recharge your battery. If you want to keep your eye on the action, grab a seat at the side-street cafe at **Hotel La Posada,** 1a Calle 4-12, Zona 2 (✆ 502/7952-1495), which overlooks the west end of the central plaza. For a wide selection of exotic coffee drinks and the chance to check your e-mail, head to **Café Fantasia ★,** 1a Calle 3-13, Zona 2 (✆ 502/5001-0003), which is also just off the plaza but set back a bit from the action.

You can camp at both Semuc Champey and Lanquin. However, if you're looking for a little more comfort and an on-site restaurant, I recommend the **Hostal Las Marías** (📞 502/7861-2209; www.posadalasmarias.com), located just before the entrance to Semuc Champey,

or **Hotel El Recreo Lanquin Champey** (📞 502/7983-0056), which is located just outside of Lanquin on the way to Semuc Champey. Both are simple, clean, and comfortable, and good places to meet other travelers.

you can even camp here. The small town of Lanquin (which I prefer over the cave) has a number of churches, including one that dates to the 1500s.

About 64km (40 miles) from Cobán; the cave is located another half-mile outside of town, along the road to Semuc Champey. 📞**502/7983-0061.** Admission Q30. Daily 8am–6pm.

Parque Nacional Laguna de Lachuá ★★ Located in the northwest corner of the Alta Verapaz, this 9,712-hectare (24,000-acre) national park has a stunningly beautiful turquoise lake as its centerpiece. The lake, more than 5km (3 miles) across at its widest point and more than 219m (720 ft.) deep, gets its majestic blue hue from its high sulfur content and is surrounded by lush forests of tropical flora and fauna.

Camping is available, and while there are bathrooms, showers, and basic cooking facilities, you'll have to bring your own food and drinking water. All of the tour operations in Cobán offer guided multiday trips here.

Entrance to Lachuá National Park at the town of San Marcos. 📞 **502/4084-1706.** www.lachua.org. Admission Q50. Camping Q25 per person in a tent, with a few basic dorm beds with mosquito netting available for Q70. Daily 7:30am–4:30pm.

Semuc Champey ★★★ Widely advertised as the most beautiful spot in Guatemala, this place lives up to expectations. A geological oddity, Semuc Champey consists of a series of limestone pools and gentle waterfalls set in a narrow rainforest canyon. Aside from the stunningly beautiful waters and surroundings, what makes this spot special is the fact that these pools and waterfalls are actually a bridge of land (about 300m/984 ft. long) resting atop the raging Cahabón River. Visitors can watch the river disappear in a torrent at one end of the bridge and then, after enjoying a swim and leisurely hike, see it emerge downstream.

There are a couple of hiking trails here, including one loop trail, El Mirador, which brings you to a spectacular lookout above Semuc Champey. This loop trail takes about 45 minutes, but can take longer if you decide to hang out at the lookout. If you walk directly to the pools and falls, it's just a 15-minute hike from the parking lot and entrance.

The best way to visit is on an organized tour, which usually includes transportation, lunch, and a visit to one or more other attractions in the area, such as the town and caves of Lanquin, and/or the Kan' Ba cave. Ask your hotel, or contact **Aventuras Turísticas ★** (📞 502/7951-4213; www.aventurasturisticas.com).

Some guides will take you to the cave where the river emerges, which involves free climbing down the crack of the last waterfall. The reward is the sound and fury of the water as you stand underneath Semuc Champey while the Cahabón River shoots out. *Warning:* When I did this, there were no ropes or protection of any kind. A slip or fall can be fatal. Moreover, your family will have absolutely no chance of successfully suing anybody on your behalf. While I count the experience of standing in this cave as one of the most amazing experiences of my time in Guatemala, keep in mind that there is very serious risk involved.

9km (5½ miles) beyond Lanquin, a 2-hr. drive from Cobán. © **502/7983-0061.** www.semucchampey. com. Admission Q50 adults, Q10 children 5–12. Daily 8am–6pm. Parking additional Q10; camping allowed for Q35 per person.

ORGANIZED TOURS

The best way to see and experience the various attractions and activities around Cobán is by organized tour. While it's possible to do so via public transportation or in your own vehicle, this can be a tricky way to go for many visitors, as it's confusing, and the route is not well marked. It's much easier and hassle-free to go on a tour. Most of the tours are small-scale operations that are reasonably priced. The guides know the area, and many of the organized tours combine two or more attractions or activities into a single day, which would be fairly impossible to do via public transportation. The best local tour operator is **Aventuras Turísticas ★** (© **502/7951-4213;** www.aventurasturisticas.com). These folks offer a wide range of tour options from half-day city tours and **white-water rafting ★** to bird-watching and guided visits to all of the attractions listed in this chapter. Rafting trips on the Cahabón River—which has class III and class IV rapids—are available out of·Cobán for 1 or more days. In addition, they can arrange multiday trips to some farther-flung regions, including the Petén and Caribbean coast. Most day tours cost Q240 to Q480 per person per day, and include lunch, transportation, and entrance fees. Prices may vary according to group size. The tour desk at the **Casa D'Acuña** (© **502/7951-0482)** is also very good, and can organize just about any tour or adventure in the regionIn addition to the tour operators mentioned above, **Proyecto Ecológico Quetzal ★** (© **502/7952-1047;** www.ecoquetzal.org) is a nonprofit, non-governmental initiative working to promote ecologically, socially, and culturally sensitive tourism in the Alta Verapaz region. They offer a number of different multiday tour options that will get you close to the people and ecosystems of this rich region. These are also the best folks to contact if you want to spot a resplendent quetzal in the wild.

Where to Stay

MODERATE

Casa Duranta ★★   The large rooms in this colonial-era home are spread around a very large interior garden. Most are furnished with two queen-size beds, a large bathroom, and a television—most of which are large flatscreen sets. Intricate iron work is spread around the hotel, ranging from headboards and luggage racks to wall-size candle holders. The restaurant serves a mix of Guatemalan and international fare.

   The Underworld

The ancient Maya believed that caves were a mystical portal between the world of the living and the underworld of spirits and the dead, which they called **Xibalba.** From their earliest days, there is evidence that the Mayas made extensive use of caves for ritual purposes, as well as for the daily tasks of keeping dry, storing grains, and gathering water.

3a Calle 4-46, Zona 3. ℂ**502/7951-4188.** Fax 502/7951-4716. www.casaduranta.com. 10 units. Q427 double. AE, DC, MC, V. **Amenities:** Restaurant; bar. *In room:* TV, no phone, free Wi-Fi.

Hotel La Posada ★   This atmospheric hotel is just off the city's central plaza, and parts of the building are more than 400 years old (the place has been in the same family since colonial times). The rooms are simple, but rather distinct (one is housed in the residence's former chapel), and can have fireplaces, wooden floors, or antique four-poster beds. The newer annex across the street is stylistically similar, and I recommend the large and comfortable room no. 15 for couples and honeymooners, as it comes with a queen-size bed facing a beautiful built-in fireplace under a high exposed-beam ceiling. The old building has beautiful gardens and common areas, and a broad shared interior veranda with massive terra-cotta tiles. There's a good restaurant, as well as a separate street-side cafe.

1a Calle 4-12, Zona 2. ℂ**502/7952-1495.** Fax 502/7951-0646. www.laposadacoban.com. 17 units. Q500 double. Lower rates in the off season. AE, DC, MC, V. **Amenities:** Restaurant; bar; free Wi-Fi. *In room:* No phone.

INEXPENSIVE

In addition to the places listed below, **Hotel Monja Blanca** (ℂ **502/7952-1712;** 2a Calle 6-30, Zona 2) is another excellent centrally located downtown budget option.

Casa D'Acuña ⚐   This place's popularity is disproportionate to the comfort of its rooms, which are very basic. Only one has a double bed (the rest have either one or two bunk beds), and all rooms share a couple of communal bathrooms and showers, which are kept nearly immaculate. The convivial hostel atmosphere here is a big draw, as is the large courtyard garden and the hotel's restaurant, which is one of the best in town. They also have an excellent tour operation.

4a Calle 3-11, Zona 2. ℂ**502/7951-0482.** Fax 502/7952-1547. www.casadeacuna.com. 7 units, all with shared bathroom. $13 double. AE, DC, MC, V. **Amenities:** Restaurant; bar. *In room:* No phone.

Hostal Doña Victoria ⚐   A former nunnery, this centrally located building is more than 400 years old and oozes character. The rooms are quite basic, but most are spacious (except the bathrooms, which are quite small), with antique tile floors, wood ceilings, carved-wood headboards, and 13-inch TVs. The central garden and surrounding courtyards offer several good spots to sit and read a book or talk with fellow travelers. There's a good restaurant and popular Internet cafe as well. These folks also run the somewhat more upscale **Hotel Alcazar Doña Victoria** (below) and the excellent tour company **Aventuras Turísticas** (p. 224).

3a Av. 2-38, Zona 3. ℂ**502/7951-4213.** Fax 502/7952-1389. www.hotelescoban.com. 9 units. $19–$30 double. AE, DC, MC, V. **Amenities:** Restaurant; bar. *In room:* TV, no phone.

Hotel Alcazar Doña Victoria ★   Located on the outskirts of town, this hotel has comfortable rooms in a beautifully decorated and restored old home. There's a large tiled courtyard at the center of the building, and one interior wall is the recreation of a church altar, with various niches occupied by antique carved religious figures. Rooms vary considerably. My favorites are nos. 12 through 15, which are large, second-floor rooms in a quiet part of the main building, and have a shared veranda in front. Be careful of room nos. 31 to 35, which back on to a busy street and can be noisy. The restaurant here is excellent, and these folks have a top-notch tour operation.

1a Calle 5-34, Zona 1. ✆ **502/7952-1143.** Fax 502/7951-4265. www.hotelescoban.com. 50 units. $33–$38 double. AE, DC, MC, V. **Amenities:** Restaurant; bar. *In room:* TV, no phone.

Where to Dine

When in Las Verapaces, be sure to sample the local specialty *kac ik,* a savory turkey soup served with enough turkey, vegetables, tubers, and tamales to make a meal. *Kac ik* is either spicy or served with extra chili on the side. It's spelled a number of ways on menus across the country, so don't be surprised if you see it written as "cack ick" or a similar variation.

In addition to the places listed below, the restaurant at **Hotel La Posada ★** (see above) is an excellent choice. For lunch or a lighter meal, try **Café Fantasia,** 1a Calle 3-13, Zona 2 (✆ **502/5001-0003**).

MODERATE

Casa D'Acuña ★★ 🏫 GUATEMALAN/INTERNATIONAL   The restaurant in this budget hotel is easily the best and most popular in Cobán. The menu here is quite varied. The budget clientele tend to stick to the pizzas, pastas, and Mexican fare, but there's a raging wood-fired grill, which churns out well-prepared steaks, chicken, seafood, and grilled vegetables, all of which go well with the selections from their rather extensive wine list. Lunches feature excellent salads and sandwiches. For dessert, save room for the homemade chocolate brownies.

Inside Casa D'Acuña, 4a Calle 3-11, Zona 2. ✆ **502/7951-0482.** Reservations recommended. Main courses Q40–Q120. AE, MC, V. Daily 6:30am–10pm.

INEXPENSIVE

El Peñascal GUATEMALAN   This long-standing local favorite is still one of the best places in town to get good regional food. In addition to standard Chapin fare, you can get turtle soup, *tepesquintle* (a large wild rodent), and *kac ik.* The large L-shaped dining room features red tile floors and glass-topped wooden tables, while a second-floor dining area offers more seats and a view of the main dining room, where there's often live marimba music on weekends.

5a Av. 2-61, Zona 1. ✆ **502/7951-2102.** Main courses Q40–Q96. MC, V. Daily 7am–10pm.

X'kape Kob'an ★★ GUATEMALAN   It's worth searching out this cozy little coffee shop and restaurant. The owners are deeply involved in local environmental and cultural conservation efforts. The menu features the almost ubiquitous local *kac ik,* as well as *kakaw-ik,* a traditional Maya soup flavored with local chocolate and honey. There are also seven different types of tamales, and some international dishes, including crepes, lasagna, and chiles rellenos. The restaurant has a lovely and lush garden, and when it's not raining, I recommend sitting out here.

4a Diagonal, 5-13, Zona 2. ✆ **502/7951-4152.** Main courses Q20–Q60. AE, MC, V. Mon–Fri 7am–9pm; Sat 9am–8:40pm.

Coban After Dark

Cobán is a quiet mountain town and shuts down early most nights. The best bar in town, **Bok'atas,** 4a Calle 3-34, Zona 2 (✆ **502/5906-6564**), has a relaxed vibe with both indoor and open-air seating, and serves sandwiches, tapas, and full meals. For dancing, try **Keops,** 3a Calle 4-71, Zona 3, a popular local disco open weekend nights. Relatively late-run movies are shown at the theater in the **Magdalena Mall** (✆ **502/7952-2127**) at the entrance to Cobán.

En Route to Coban: Baja Verapaz & Biotopo del Quetzal

South of Cobán spreads the region known as Baja Verapaz, which gets its name from its slightly lower (*"baja"*) elevation. The principal attraction in this region is the **Biotopo del Quetzal,** a small natural reserve protecting an area of tropical cloud forest that's one of the few remaining habitats of the resplendent quetzal, the national bird of Guatemala.

Biotopo del Quetzal ★ Founded in 1976, the Biotopo del Quetzal covers an area of approximately 1,000 hectares (2,470 acres) of mountainous tropical cloud forest. In addition to its namesake resident (the quetzal), the Biotopo is home to an abundance of tropical flora and fauna. Sadly, due to surrounding deforestation and fragmentation, it's becoming increasingly difficult to spot a quetzal here, but you will see a wealth of epiphytic orchids, bromeliads, and mosses, as well as a host of other bird species, including the Emerald Toucanet and highland guan. If you're lucky, you might spot a howler monkey. The best time to see a quetzal in the Biotopo is March through June.

There are two different loop trails here, one marked *corto* (short); the other *largo* (long). They are about 2km (1.25 miles) and 4km (2.5 miles) in length, respectively. The short loop will take about 45 minutes to an hour, the long trail about twice as along. Several small waterfalls line the trails. Be sure to check out the information hut near the entrance to the trails, as well as the small collection of orchids and bromeliads.

At Km 160.5 on the road btw. Guatemala City and Cobán. (C)**502/5333-6947** or 5216-5855. Admission Q40. Daily 7am–4pm. Any bus to or from Cobán (see "Getting There: By Bus," earlier in this chapter) can drop you here.

SALAMÁ & RABINAL

Baja Verapaz is also home to a few small towns and villages renowned for their art and craftworks. Most notable of these are **Salamá** and **Rabinal.** For tours around Salamá or Rabinal, contact **Ecocenter Tours** (C) 502/7940-0459) or **Ecoverapaz** (C) 502/7940-0146), two long-standing, local guide companies.

Salamá is the provincial capital and largest city in the Baja Verapaces. At the center of Salamá is a beautiful colonial-era church with an ornately carved altar adorned with 18-karat gold. The city also has an interesting temple dedicated to the Roman goddess Minerva. This temple, built in 1916, is perhaps partly responsible for the region's renown in the realm of arts and craftworks. Salamá's market day on Monday is the biggest and best in the Verapaces.

Guatemala's National Bird: The Resplendent Quetzal

Revered by pre-Columbian cultures throughout Central America, the resplendent quetzal has been called the most beautiful bird on earth. Ancient Aztec and Maya Indians believed that the robin-size quetzal protected them in battle. The males of this species have brilliant red breasts; iridescent emerald green heads, backs, and wings; and white tail feathers complemented by a pair of iridescent green tail feathers that are more than .5m (1¾ ft.) long. The females look similar, but lack the long tail feathers.

The smaller village of **Rabinal** is named after the Rabinaleb' Maya of this region. It was founded as a Spanish colonial town by Fray Bartolomé de las Casas in 1537. The market here is held on Sunday, and in addition to beautiful *huipiles* and wood-carvings, the artisans of this town are famous for their low-fired pottery.

If you do visit Rabinal, be sure to stop in at the **Museo Rabinal Achí,** 2a Calle and 4a Avenida, Zona 3 (② 502/7938-8721; www.museorabinal.org), a small museum with a collection of Maya historical and cultural displays. The museum is open daily from 8am to 5pm. There's no entrance fee, but donations are encouraged.

There are no hotels or *posadas* of note in Salamá or Rabinal. If you find yourself needing or wanting to stay here, try the **Hotel Real Legendario,** 8a Av. 3-57, Zona 1 (② 502/7940-0501), a simple and tidy option in the heart of Salamá.

Salamá and Rabinal are located off the main Ruta Las Verapaces, which runs from El Rancho north to Cobán. Marked as both CA-14 and CA-17 at El Rancho cross-roads, it forks at Km 47, where CA-17 heads toward Salamá and Rabinal, while CA-14 continues on to Cobán. Salamá is another 17km (10 miles) from the fork, Rabinal another 8km (5 miles) west of Salamá.

WHERE TO STAY & DINE

Posada Montaña de Quetzal   This mountain lodge is popular with Guatemalan weekenders, and while the rooms are certainly acceptable, I find them slightly over-priced for the region. The rooms feature red brick floors, faux-stucco walls, and simple decor. The individual cabañas are spread along a path leading down from the main lodge and rooms, and come with a separate sitting room and either one or two bedrooms. Each has a fireplace and stockpile of wood in the living room. There's a midsize pool with a diving board and a separate children's pool, though it's often too cool and cloudy to make use of them. The restaurant serves excellent local cuisine at very reasonable prices.

Km 156 Ruta Las Verapaces. ② **502/6620-0709** or 5800-0454. www.hposadaquetzal.com. 26 units. $31 double room; $44 double cabaña. AE, DC, MC, V. **Amenities:** Restaurant; pool. *In room:* No phone.

Ram Tzul 🏮   This is by far the best choice in the area. The rooms are very spa-cious, with floors made from the cross section of tree trunks set in concrete. The second-floor rooms are the better bet, with large picture windows and a pitched roof with several gables. The main lobby building and restaurant are housed in a massive three-level structure with a high ceiling supported by bamboo posts and beams. The name of this place translates to "mountain heart, mountain spirit" in the Mayan Q'eqchi language. The hotel sits on its own 100 hectare (247 acre) private reserve, with a trail down to a lovely waterfall. The reserve was created to help protect fragile habitat used by the endangered Resplendent Quetzal. In fact, the hotel is an out-growth of the reserve initiative. Nonguests can hike the trail for Q40.

Km 158.5 Ruta Las Verapaces. ② **502/5908-4066** at the lodge, or 2335-1805 in Guatemala City. Fax 502/2335-1802. www.m-y-c.com.ar/ramtzul. 12 units. $45 double. AE, DC, MC, V. **Amenities:** Restaurant; bar. *In room:* No phone.

ESQUIPULAS

222km (137 miles) SE of Guatemala City

Esquipulas may be a relatively nondescript city along the remote eastern border of the country, but it happens to be Guatemala's most important Roman Catholic pil-grimage site. The main church in Esquipulas was upgraded to the status of basilica in 1968, and houses the city's prime treasure: *El Cristo Negro (The Black Christ),* a dark-skinned statue of Christ that's believed to have healing powers. The Basílica and *Black Christ* have been visited by Pope John Paul II, Mother Teresa, and Che Guevara, among others, and it's estimated that more than one million people make the pilgrimage each year.

Essentials

GETTING THERE

BY CAR   To reach Esquipulas by car, take the Carretera al Atlántico (CA-9) out of Guatemala City to the crossroads at Río Hondo. Turn south here onto CA-10. The exit will be marked for Zacapa, Chiquimula, and Esquipulas. The trip should take 3 to 3½ hours. There's a wonderful lookout located on the road into Esquipulas, about a mile before you hit the center of town. It will be on your left as you arrive, and it's worth a stop for the panoramic view of the city below.

BY BUS   **Rutas Orientales,** 19a Calle 8-18, Zona 1 (© **502/2220-9188** or 2251-2160; www. rutasorientales.com), buses depart from Guatemala City's Zona 1 terminal every half-hour between 4:30am and 6pm. The fare is Q50. Return buses leave Esquipulas from 11a Calle, just south of the Basílica, every half-hour between 2:30am and 5pm. The bus ride takes roughly 4 hours.

GETTING AROUND

There are scores of taxis, motor taxis, and tuk tuks in Esquipulas. Most rides around town cost Q5 to Q15.

ORIENTATION

The city, and nearly all activity in it, is centered around the Basílica. The church, fronted by a park that's nearly 2 square blocks in size, sits on 11a Calle, the main road into and out of Esquipulas. All of the hotels and restaurants of interest to tourists are located within a 4-block radius of the Basílica. The north and south sides of the Basílica are packed with souvenir stands selling religious memorabilia, votive candles, and creative kitsch. There are several banks within a block or two of the Basílica, and the police station, post office, and town hall are located at the western end of 6a Avenida.

What to See & Do

La Basílica & El Cristo Negro ★★   Sculpted by Quirio Cataño in Antigua, the *Black Christ* dates back to 1595. By 1603, it already had a miracle attributed to it, but it wasn't until 1735, when Father Pedro Pardo de Figueroa was miraculously cured while praying in front of the statue, that things really began to happen. Father Pedro was eventually elected Archbishop of Guatemala, and he used the power of this position to order the construction of a cathedral worthy of this miraculous icon. The current Basílica was finished in 1758, and is a beautiful and grand church that has withstood Guatemala's regular cycle of massive earthquakes, a miracle in itself.

The *Black Christ* is currently exhibited in a glass case set at the back of the Basílica's main altar. The entrance to see it is along the left side of the church. At peak periods, this line can be quite long, and it might take more than an hour to get your chance to walk around the enclosed display case.

During Holy Week, July 21 to July 27, and around January 15 (the official festival day of the *Black Christ*), the town is packed with religious pilgrims, including a large number of Guatemalans who bring their cars to be blessed by the priests. You'll spot

Walk Backward

Believing it an offense to turn your back on the *Black Christ,* pilgrims exit the viewing area by walking backward.

The going is slow at times, but the narrow pathway has no steps or railings on either side, making the task rather easy.

these cars, decked out in colored ribbons and religious trinkets, in a specially designated parking lot and on the road on their way out of town.

Doble Vía and 3a Av. Basílica. © **502/7943-1108.** Free admission. Daily 6am–8pm. Mass is observed 6:30 and 11am, and 5pm Mon–Sat; 6:30, 8, 9:30, and 11am, and 12:30 and 5pm on Sun.

La Cueva de las Minas   Not far from the Basílica is the Cueva de las Minas, a natural cave that's been used for centuries for Maya ritual ceremonies. Some claim the *Black Christ* actually emerged from these caves, while others say that its sculptor, Quirio Cataño, got his inspiration here. The cave is about 46m (150 ft.) deep, and you'll often see local devotees lighting candles and praying.

A small zoo here holds a modest collection of local animals. I find the enclosures and displays rather inadequate and sad, particularly those for the crocodile and ocelot. There's also a restaurant, some picnic tables, and even a basketball and volleyball court.

1km (⅔ mile) outside of town, off the route to the Honduran border, which heads out from behind the south side of the Basílica. Admission Q10. Daily 7am–5pm.

OTHER ATTRACTIONS

Most visitors to Esquipulas come solely to visit the *Black Christ.* However, there are a few other nearby attractions. Families with children should head to **Chatun** (© **502/7873-0909;** www.parquechatun.com), a family-style recreation complex with a swimming pool, sports facilities (including a zip-line attraction), climbing wall, and children's petting zoo. Admission is Q65 for adults, Q55 for children 12 and under, with an extra fee Q40 for the zip-line. Chatun is located 3km (2 miles) outside of Esquipulas on the road to Honduras.

If you're looking for a day trip, the Ipala Volcano is a popular tourist spot. The crater of this 1,650m (5,400-ft.) volcano forms a beautiful blue lake and makes a great hike. If you want to visit the volcano, ask your hotel for a reputable guide, as you shouldn't visit this remote site unaccompanied.

Where To Stay

EXPENSIVE

Porta Hotel Legendario ★   This is the largest and most resortlike hotel in Esquipulas. However, I don't think they can justify the rates they charge, especially when compared with the competition. Still, if you want a large swimming pool and some of the trappings of a modern business-class hotel, this is the place for you. The rooms are relatively simple with plenty of space, clean tile floors, and somewhat dated decor. The large pool is clearly the best feature here. The Legendario is located about 3 blocks from the Basílica.

9a Calle 3-00, Zona 1. © **502/7943-1824** in Esquipulas, or 2361-9683 reservations in Guatemala City. Fax 502/7943-1022. www.portahotels.com. 45 units. $140–$150 double room. Lower rates available weekdays and off season. Rates highest on weekends and holy days. AE, DC, MC, V. **Amenities:** Restaurant; piscine; 2 bars. *In room:* A/C, TV.

MODERATE

Portal de la Fe ★   This hotel is on the main drag in Esquipulas, just 2 blocks from the Basílica. The rooms, spread throughout three floors, are modern and somewhat stylish, with ornate iron headboards and very firm beds. The rooms come in different sizes with various bed distributions, but all have private bathrooms and 13-inch TVs. Six of the rooms have air-conditioning, while those on the third floor have small balconies. (Room nos. 302–304 actually have views of the Basílica from their balconies.) For those who don't get these rooms, there's a rooftop terrace with good views. There's no restaurant here, but there are plenty nearby. The hotel has one computer available with free Internet usage and free Wi-Fi throughout the hotel.

11a Calle 1-70, Zona 1. © **502/7943-4124.** 36 units. $56–$85 double. Lower rates available weekdays and off season. Rates highest on weekends and holy days. AE, DC, MC, V. **Amenities:** Pool; free Wi-Fi. *In room:* TV, no phone.

INEXPENSIVE

Hotel El Peregrino 🗡   While you could save a little by going with a basic room (a twin bed is all you'll get), I heartily recommend the slight splurge for one of the more "deluxe" rooms, which are more spacious and come with a wider bed, which they call semi-matrimonial, and cable television. By far the best feature at this hotel is the pool, which has a patio with good views of the Basílica and the surrounding hills. There's also a separate children's pool and a small jungle gym. The hotel's popular restaurant serves good Guatemalan fare, and is right in the center of the action on the side street fronting the church.

2a Av. 11-94, Zona 1. © **502/7943-1054.** Fax 502/7943-1474. www.elperegrinoesquipulas.com. 33 units. $19–$41 double. Lower rates available weekdays and off season. Rates highest on weekends and holy days. AE, DC, MC, V. **Amenities:** Restaurant; pool; free Wi-Fi. *In room:* TV, no phone.

Where To Dine

MODERATE

La Hacienda ★ ☺ GUATEMALAN/STEAKHOUSE   This is the fanciest and most upscale restaurant in Esquipulas. The food here is far more expensive than you'll find at any other place in town, but it's well prepared and filling, and includes steak, grilled chicken, and a children's menu with smaller portions. Pair your entree with a bottle of French, Chilean, Italian, or Argentine wine; the restaurant has the best wine list in Esquipulas. The dimly lit dining rooms have wooden tables and chairs, and there are even a few tables on an open-air patio in front.

2a Av. and 10a Calle. © **502/7943-1748.** Main courses Q60–Q150. AE, MC, V. Daily 7am–10pm.

INEXPENSIVE

La Rotunda GUATEMALAN/INTERNATIONAL   This place rises slightly above the rest of the *comedores* and other basic restaurants in town, with its menu of Guatemalan fare, Mexican burritos and tacos, and long list of pizzas, which are actually not bad. Breakfasts are filling and a bargain. A typical Guatemalan breakfast of eggs, tortillas, refried beans, and plantains is the forte here, but you can get an omelet or even a breakfast burrito. The second-floor dining room is shaped in a half-circle with large picture windows all around, giving you a view of the traffic, motorized and pedestrian, on the main street below.

1a Av. and 11a Calle. © **502/7943-2038.** Main courses Q30–Q90. V. Daily 7am–10pm.

COPAN ★★

239km (148 miles) E of Guatemala City; 110km (68 miles) S of Río Hondo; 12km (7½ miles) S of the Honduran border

Just past the Guatemalan border in Honduras lies **Copán,** one of the most spectacular Maya ceremonial cities of Mesoamerica. The town is a small picturesque city with rough cobblestone streets and a buzzing central plaza that's the heart and soul of the place. Copán is surrounded by beautiful forests with waterfalls, hot springs, and excellent bird-watching and adventure-tourism possibilities. *Note:* The currency used in Copán is the *lempira,* which at press time was about L18.5 to $1. In this section, prices are quoted in *lempiras* rather than *quetzales,* as *quetzales* are not accepted.

Essentials

GETTING THERE

BY CAR If you're driving to Copán, take the Carretera al Atlántico (CA-9) out of Guatemala City to the crossroads at Río Hondo. Turn south here on to CA-10. The exit will be marked for Zacapa, Chiquimula, and Esquipulas. About 10km (6 miles) south of the city of Chiquimula you'll see the turnoff for El Florido and Copán Ruinas on your left. From here it's about 38km (24 miles) to the border crossing at El Florido, and from there another 12km (7½ miles) to Copán Ruinas. The road is paved the entire way, and on a good day the journey can take about 4½ hours.

BY BUS Hedman Alas (**②** 504/651-4037 in Copán Ruinas, or 502/2362-5072 in Guatemala City; www.hedmanalas.com) offers daily bus service from Guatemala City, leaving at 5 and 9am from their terminal at 2a Av. 8-73, Zona 10. Return buses leave Copán Ruinas at 2:20 and 6:30pm. The fare is $45 one-way, $80 round-trip. The one-way trip takes about 5 hours.

GETTING AROUND

You can easily walk anywhere in Copán Ruinas, including the archaeological site. However, if you need a taxi, they are plentiful and inexpensive. Most of the taxis are small motor taxis or tuk tuks, which circulate around town and gather on the north and south sides of the central plaza. A taxi ride between town and the archaeological site should cost L20 to L40 per person.

ORIENTATION

It may be confusing, but the actual Maya ruins here are called Copán, while the little town is officially known as Copán Ruinas. Most folks refer to it generically as Copán

---

Crossing the Border

Crossing the border at El Florido on your way to Copán is relatively easy and cheap. Theoretically, Guatemala and Honduras are part of the same CA-4 immigration agreement, and your original 90-day tourist visa should be good in each country. In practice you will have to pay around $5 in official border fees, and may be hit up for more depending upon the mood of the border agents. If you're driving a rental car, be sure to have all your papers in order and clear the trip with the rental-car agency in advance.

Copán Ruinas

ACCOMMODATIONS ■
Casa Rosada **2**
Hacienda San Lucas **21**
Hotel Brisas
  de Copán **9**
Hotel La Posada **7**
Hotel Marina Copán **6**
La Casa de Café **5**
Plaza Copán Hotel **13**
Yat B'alam **17**

DINING ◆
Carnitas N'ia Lola **20**
Hacienda San Lucas **21**
Llama del Bosque **3**
Momo's **16**
Pizza Copán **15**
Pizza Italia **11**
Twisted Tanya's **19**
Vamos A Ver **18**
Via Via Café **4**

ATTRACTIONS ●
Alas Encantadas **1**
Casa K'inich **8**
Los Sapos **21**
Macaw
  Mountain **10**
Museo Regional
  de Arqueología **14**
Museum of Maya
  Sculpture **12**

or make the appropriate distinction when necessary. The town is very compact, and everything of importance is located within a 4-block radius of the central plaza. No official street names are actually used, and directions are given in relation to the central plaza or some other known landmark.

FAST FACTS   **Banco Atlántida** and **BAC** both front the central plaza and are fast and safe places to exchange money or use an ATM. To contact the local police, dial ☏ **504/651-4060.** The post office (☏ **504/651-4447**) is located just west of the Copán Museum. There are a half-dozen or so Internet cafes around town; most charge around L20 to L40 per hour. For medical emergencies, ask your hotel, or call Dr. Boqui at the **Clínica Handal** (☏ **504/651-4408**). **Hondutel,** a half-block south of the central plaza, is the best place for international phone calls.

What to See & Do
COPÁN ★★★
Copán is one of the grandest and most magnificently preserved of all Maya ceremonial cities. Surrounded by thick jungle and set beside the gentle Copán River, the ruins are famous for their raw stone-carved hieroglyphics, massive stelae, and the

impressive Hieroglyphic Stairway. Your visit here should include the extensive archaeological ruins, the excavated tunnels, and Museum of Maya Sculpture.

The current area around Copán has been inhabited since at least 1400 B.C., and some of the earlier discoveries here show Olmec influences. The Great Sun Lord Quetzal Macaw, who ruled from A.D. 426 to 435, was the first of 16 consecutive kings who saw the rise and fall of this Classic Maya city. Some of Copán's great kings included Smoke Jaguar, 18 Rabbit, and Smoke Shell. The history of these kings is meticulously carved into the stones at the ruins.

Copán was famously "discovered" in 1839 and bought for just $50 by the adventurer John L. Stephens, who documented the story in his wonderful book, *Incidents of Travel in Central America, Chiapas and Yucatan* (1841). The book is beautifully illustrated by Stephens's companion Frederick Catherwood.

Visitor Information

The entrance to the Copán archaeological site is located along a well-marked highway about a half-mile from the town of Copán Ruinas. The visitor center and ticket booth are at one end of the parking lot; the Museum of Maya Sculpture is at the other. The **Copán Guides Association** has a booth at the entrance to the parking area. Here, you can hire a bilingual guide for a 2-hour tour of the site for L925, no matter the size of your group. These guides are extremely knowledgeable, and I highly recommend hiring one for your first visit. Admission to the archaeological site, which includes the main Copán ruins and the Sepulturas, is L280. Admission does not include a guide. Visits to the tunnels and Museum of Maya Sculpture are extra (see below).

Museum of Maya Sculpture

I recommend you begin your visit at the Museum of Maya Sculpture, which is located across from the entrance, a few hundred yards from the small visitor center where you pay your entrance fee. This large, two-story structure was built to protect some of Copán's more impressive pieces from the elements. Inside you'll see beautifully displayed and well-documented examples of a broad range of stone carvings and hieroglyphics. At the center of the museum is a full-scale replica of the Rosalia Temple, which lies well preserved inside the core of Temple 16 (which you'll see later at the ruins). The museum also contains the reconstructed original facade of one of the site's ball courts. Admission to the museum is L95.

The Ruins

The ruins are at the end of a relatively short path from the museum exit. I recommend starting at the western plaza of **Temple 16.** As you face Temple 16, the **Acropolis** will be to your left. A trail and steps lead around the back, where you can

Cash Flow

The *lempira* is the official currency of Honduras. At press time, there were 18.5 *lempira* to the U.S. dollar, and approximately 2.27 *lempira* to 1 Guatemalan *quetzal*. Numerous money-changers hang around the border crossing, but they often offer bad exchange rates. It's safe to change your money with them, but you'll have to bargain hard to get a good rate. Alternatively, you can wait until you reach Copán Ruinas and get better rates at any bank or hotel.

Copán Archaeological Site

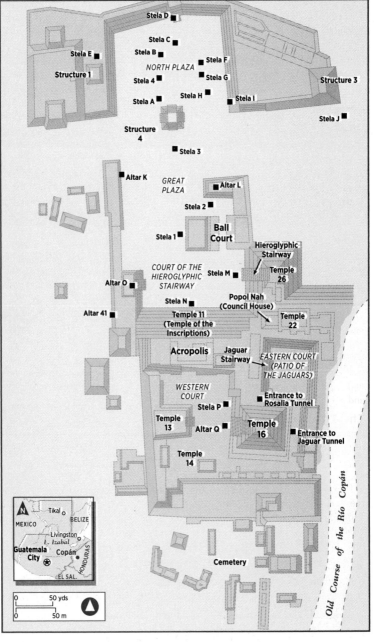

Stela D

Stela C

Stela E

Stela B

Stela F

NORTH PLAZA

Structure 1

Stela 4

Stela G

Structure 3

Stela A

Stela H

Stela I

Stela J

Structure 4

Stela 3

Altar K

GREAT PLAZA

Altar L

Stela 2

Stela 1

Ball Court

Hieroglyphic Stairway

COURT OF THE HIEROGLYPHIC STAIRWAY

Stela M

Temple 26

Altar O

Popol Nah (Council House)

Stela N

Temple 22

Altar 41

Temple 11 (Temple of the Inscriptions)

Acropolis

Jaguar Stairway

EASTERN COURT (PATIO OF THE JAGUARS)

WESTERN COURT

Stela P

Entrance to Rosalia Tunnel

Temple 13

Altar Q

Temple 16

Entrance to Jaguar Tunnel

Temple 14

Cemetery

Old Course of the Rio Copán

Tikal
BELIZE
MEXICO
Livingston
L. Izabal
Guatemala City
Copán
HONDURAS
EL SAL.

0 — 50 yds
0 — 50 m

enjoy a view over the Copán River to the surrounding mountains. Follow the path to the **Patio of the Jaguars,** where you'll find the entrances to the **Rosalia** and **Jaguar** tunnels (see below). Continue on over the top of the **Acropolis** and the **Temple of Inscriptions,** and then down into the **Great Plaza,** where Copán's greatest hieroglyphic treasures were found.

The Temple of Inscriptions anchors the south end of the Great Plaza. To its east is the **Hieroglyphic Stairway.** This stairway, built by **King Smoke Shell,** rises up some 64 steps, each of which is carved or faced with hieroglyphs, telling the history of Copán's kings and their line of succession. To those literate in the language, the stairs once read as a giant book. Today, many of the carved stairs have fallen or faded, but enough remain to give a sense of the scale of this amazing achievement. The stairway is currently under cover, which makes it difficult to see. The lighting is poor, especially on cloudy days, but the trade-off in terms of preservation makes this necessary.

 Rodent Royalty

Though Copán's illustrious 13th ruler is known in English as King 18 Rabbit, it would be more accurate to refer to him as King 18 Agouti, the rodent which is depicted in his hieroglyph.

At the foot of the Hieroglyphic Stairway, and all around the Great Plaza, are examples of Copán's carved stelae. Many of these are carved on all four sides with detailed depictions of rulers, animals, and mythic beasts, as well as glyphs that tell their stories. Some of the stelae are originals, while others are replicas.

Las Sepulturas

Located about 2km (1½ miles) from the Great Plaza, Las Sepulturas is believed to have been a major residential neighborhood reserved for Copán's elite. The site gives you a sense of what the day-to-day living arrangements of an upper-crust Maya may have been like. Las Sepulturas was once connected to the Great Plaza by a broad, well-worn causeway (which has been identified by NASA with digital satellite imaging), but today it's reached via a gentle path through lush forests with excellent bird- and animal-watching opportunities.

The Rosalia & Jaguar Tunnels

Opened to the public in 1999, these two tunnels give visitors a firsthand look at the historical layering technique of the Maya builders, who would construct subsequent temples around and over existing ones, no matter how beautiful and intricate the original.

Entrance to the two tunnels is an extra L185 above the general admission, though these are well-lit modern excavations and not tunnels left by the ancient Maya, so it's a toss-up whether or not it's really worth the extra money. However, the tunnels are fascinating and do give you a further sense of the massive scale of the archaeological undertaking.

ATTRACTIONS IN & AROUND TOWN

Alas Encantadas   This is a small butterfly garden and breeding project with loads of winged creatures, exhibits illustrating the various stages of metamorphosis, and a botanical garden with more than 200 species of orchids.

300m (¼ mile) outside of town on the road to the Guatemalan border. ✆ **504/651-4133.** Admission $6 for adults, $2.50 for children 12 and under. Daily 8am–4:30pm.

Café Welchez Coffee Plantation ★ 🎒 Finca Santa Isabel is where the Café Welchez brand of shade-grown coffee is produced. The tour, which leaves by bus from Copán, begins in the mountain nursery and takes you through the entire processing method with the occasional chance to spot birds and butterflies in the surrounding rainforest.

Outside Copán. ✆**504/651-4200.** www.cafehonduras.com. Tours are given daily with **Yaragua Tours** (✆**504/651-4147;** www.yaragua.com), which includes transportation, $25 per person.

Casa K'inich ☺ The Casa K'inich, or the Maya Children's Museum, has interactive and educational exhibits that teach kids (and adults) how to count and add in different Mayan dialects and how to play the ancient ballgame of the Maya. This place is run by a local non-profit organization actively working to conserve, protect and promote the local cultural and natural heritage. The museum is located in the rear of the public library building, which fronts the north side of the central plaza.

Fuerte Cabañas. ✆**504/651-4105.** www.asociacioncopan.org. Free admission. Mon–Sat 8am–noon and 1–4pm.

Los Sapos The small ceremonial site of Los Sapos, located across the river from Copán, is believed to be tied to ancient Maya birthing and fertility practices. This is a very small and minimally excavated site. You can see some stone carvings of *sapos,* or frogs, and the carved figure of a pregnant woman. In addition, the site features the exposed foundations of a few large structures. Several tour agencies in town offer horseback riding tours that include a visit here.

5km (3 miles) from Copán Ruinas, on the grounds of Hacienda San Lucas. Admission L40. Open daily by appointment.

Macaw Mountain ★ ☺ Macaw Mountain features an extensive collection of tropical birds, primarily parrots and macaws, and some local raptors. The way the birds are displayed makes this place special. (The enclosures are quite large and well done, and you can even walk through some of them.) This attraction is spread out over a lush setting of a tropical forest and coffee plantation, with a beautiful river and well-designed trails. There's an excellent riverside restaurant and a separate coffee shop with home-roasted beans.

4.8km (3 miles) west of the central plaza up a dirt road. ✆**504/651-4245.** www.macawmountain.com. Admission L185. Daily 9am–5pm.

Museo Regional de Arqueología ★ Also known simply as the Copán Museum, this museum holds a small collection of pottery and artifacts from the ruins, as well as a series of interpretive and explanatory displays. Perhaps the most interesting exhibit here is the complete burial niche of an ancient Copán scribe. If you're going to the ruins and the museum there, there's no need to visit this place. However, if you're hanging around town, it will only take you about 30 to 45 minutes to tour all the exhibits.

West side of central plaza. Admission L40. Daily 9am–5pm.

OUTDOOR ACTIVITIES

If you want to do some bird-watching, take a horseback ride, soak in a nearby hot spring, explore some caves, or tube on the Copán River, contact a local tour agency such as **McTours** (✆ **504/651-4453;** www.mctours-honduras.com), **Yaragua** (✆ **504/651-4147;** www.yaragua.com), or **Xukpi** (✆ **504/651-4684;** www.xukpitourscopan.com).

read ALL ABOUT IT

Even after more than 150 years, *Incidents of Travel in Central America, Chiapas and Yucatan,* Vols. 1 and 2, and *Incidents of Travel in Yucatan,* Vols. 1 and 2, are still gripping reads. These fascinating tomes were penned by American explorer, writer, diplomat, and business scout John L. Stephens, and illustrated by his British travel companion, Fredrick Catherwood. They include detailed accounts of the pair's rugged travels, a glimpse into mid-19th-century Guatemalan life, and descriptions of some of the Maya ruins of this region.

In 1839, Stephens was appointed Special Ambassador to Central America by U.S. President Martin Van Buren. During this time, the government of the United States of Central America disintegrated into civil war. *Incidents of Travel in Central America, Chiapas and Yucatan* describes some of the events that Stephens witnessed. Of even greater importance, it provides descriptions of either the discovery or early exploration of several major ancient Maya cities, including Tikal and Copán. Stephens actually bought the ruins of Copán from a local farmer for around $50.

The books are beautifully illustrated with the extremely accurate and detailed drawings of Catherwood, an architect and draftsman. In an odd twist, these groundbreaking books were used by the Church of Latter Day Saints founder Joseph Smith as proof of the accuracy of the Book of Mormon.

Originally a lawyer, Stephens became known as the father of American archaeology. His additional writings—*Incidents of Travel in Egypt, Arabia Petraea, and the Holy Land,* and *Incidents of Travel in Greece, Turkey, Russia and Poland*—earned him the top rank in his genre. In 1850, Stephens traveled to Panama to work on the construction of a trans-isthmus railroad, but died from malaria in 1852, before the railway's completion. Stephens is immortalized in *Maya Explorer,* a detailed biography by Victor Wolfgang Von Hagan.

For his part, Catherwood published the beautiful *Views of Ancient Monuments in Central America,* with 25 watercolor lithographs he made at various ruins. While this rare book is out of print, you can see fabulous examples of his work in large format in the biography *The Lost Cities of the Mayas: The Life, Art and Discoveries of Frederick Catherwood* by Fabio Bourbon.

Shopping

The streets of Copán Ruinas are often lined with young artisans selling handmade jewelry and carvings. The town is also brimming with simple souvenir shops selling T-shirts, jade carvings, and Guatemalan crafts and textiles. (However, if you're coming from or going to Guatemala, you'll want to save your purchases of Guatemalan goods for your time there.)

The **Casa de Todo ★**, 1 block downhill from the Banco de Occidente corner of the central plaza (℃ **504/651-4185**), is an excellent gift shop with unique local crafts, a coffee shop, an Internet cafe, and a simple restaurant serving Guatemalan fare; they even have a couple of rooms for overnight stays. **Casa del Jade** (℃ **504/651-4185;** www.casavillamil.com), 1 block north of the plaza, is part of a Guatemalan chain that sells a wide variety of jewelry and collectibles that contain the Maya's preferred stone. The boutique gift shops beneath the hotel **Yat B'alam**

(p. 241), on Calle la Independencia, have one of the most unique and upscale selections of Honduran-made crafts, accessories, and home furnishings

Where to Stay

EXPENSIVE

Hacienda San Lucas ★★ 🏨 This is my favorite hotel in the area, set on a hillside across the river from and overlooking the Copán archaeological site. The rustic elegance of the rooms is a throwback to its former life as a farm and ranch, as are the high wood-beam and plank ceilings. The large rooms each are outfitted with two queen-size beds, a large shared veranda with hammocks, and a beautiful stone shower. However, TV and Internet are not available. In fact, the only light in the rooms is provided by candles and a few solar-powered lamps. The hotel restaurant has excellent meals, and uses locally grown organic produce whenever possible. In 2009, owner Flavia Cueva was awarded the Copán Prize for her work in the community and in promoting sustainable tourism. The hotel abuts the **Los Sapos ruins** (see above), and has several excellent hiking trails on its grounds. Sunsets are taken in on a long lawn off of the main lodge building.

5km (3 miles) south of Copán Ruinas on the road to Los Sapos ruins. ✆ **504/651-4495.** Fax 504/651-4106. www.haciendasanlucas.com. 8 units. $125 double. Rates include full breakfast. AE, MC, V. **Amenities:** Restaurant; bar. *In room:* No phone.

Hotel Marina Copán ★ This hotel spans an entire city block facing the central plaza. The rooms are all tastefully decorated and come with large TVs, while the suites have tons of space and other nice touches, such as a Jacuzzi, a kitchenette, and a view. My favorite is no. 331, a third-floor corner suite with a large balcony and a great view of town. Many of the standard rooms come with a balcony, so it's worth requesting one when you make a reservation. There's a pool in the center of the hotel and plenty of areas to relax among plants and fountains.

Parque Central. ✆ **504/651-4070.** Fax 504/651-4477. www.hotelmarinacopan.com. 52 units. $104–$145 double; $209–$290 suite. AE, MC, V. **Amenities:** Restaurant; bar; small gym w/sauna; midsize pool; room service; free Wi-Fi. *In room:* A/C, TV.

MODERATE

Casa Rosada ★★ 🍴 Elegance and romance are two words that come to mind when trying to describe this charming Spanish colonial–style inn with just a few rooms. They don't overdo anything. Hand-carved wooden mirror frames and hand-woven accent rugs have been chosen with care. Rooms are appointed with brick floors and Honduran art on the walls. The bathrooms are the finest in Copán, with a

10

CENTRAL GUATEMALA | Copan

shower featuring dual showerheads and speakers so you can listen to the radio while bathing. There's even a bidet. There are several great little nooks and patios amid gardens and plants where you can steal away with a good book. Casa Rosada is also one of the few hotels in the entire country that go out of their way to accommodate travelers with disabilities.

One block west and one block north of the NW corner of the park. ☎ **504/651-4321.** www.lacasa rosada.com. 5 units. $87 double, rates include breakfast. MC, V. *In room:* A/C, TV/DVD, CD player, hair dryer, free Wi-Fi.

La Casa de Café ★ 🗲 This house-turned-bed-and-breakfast, located a few blocks outside the center of town, has a good view of the Copán valley and the mountains of neighboring Guatemala. The rooms are all cheery, bright, and comfortable. Those occupying the higher ground are a little older and smaller, but they have the aforementioned view from their shared veranda. The newer rooms have exposed beam ceilings and beautiful mosaic tile sinks, with a veranda that lets out onto a small garden. The owners are extremely knowledgeable about the area, and they also rent out a few fully equipped apartments nearby.

1 block south and 4 blocks west of the central plaza. ☎ **504/651-4620.** Fax 504/651-4623. www. casadecafecopan.com. 10 units. $55 double. Rates include full breakfast. AE, MC, V. *In room:* No phone.

Plaza Copán Hotel ★ This hotel has a good location on the corner of the central plaza with a good deal to boot. All of the rooms are spacious and feature red tile floors and high ceilings. I like no. 213, which comes with a king-size bed and a private corner balcony overlooking the central plaza. There's a small pool in the central courtyard and a popular restaurant. The hotel also has a helpful tour desk.

Parque Central. ☎ **504/651-4508.** Fax 504/651-4039. www.plazacopanhotel.com. 20 units. $58 double. Rates lower in the off season, higher during peak periods. AE, MC, V. **Amenities:** Restaurant; bar; small pool. *In room:* A/C, TV.

Yat B'alam ★★ This charming hotel is one of the best values in Western Honduras, and is an excellent choice and value in downtown Copan Ruinas. The ground floor is laid out like a cobblestone colonial street lined with craft shops and a cafe. There are just a handful of rooms, all on the second level with tiled floors, dark-wood contemporary furniture, and deep red decor. Several have particularly high ceilings, and rooms near the street have the best views. Common areas with couches are sprinkled throughout, and some boast good views as well.

Calle la Independencia. ☎ **504/651-4338.** Fax 504/651-3517. www.yatbalam.com. 4 units. $65 double. MC, V. Amenities: Cafe. *In room:* A/C, TV, fridge, Wi-Fi.

INEXPENSIVE

There are a score of budget options in Copán, and the competition for the backpacker crowd is fierce. If you have the time, you can always just walk around and see who's got the best room for the best price. My choices for real budget hounds are **Hotel La Posada,** a half-block north of the western edge of Parque Central (☎ **504/651-4059;** www.laposadacopan.com), and **Hotel Brisas de Copán,** 1 block north of the eastern edge of Parque Central (☎ **504/651-4566**).

Where to Dine

EXPENSIVE

Hacienda San Lucas ★★ 🏛 INTERNATIONAL/HONDURAN   The in-house restaurant at this lovely hotel is probably the best restaurant in Copán, and certainly the most atmospheric. Meals are served in an open-air patio in front of the old haci-enda building. The five-course candlelit dinners are my favorite, with the choice of main courses including the house specialty of fire-roasted chicken with *adobo* sauce, a mole based on the herbs, spices, and nuts used by the ancient Maya of this area. Lunches are a bit more casual and range from homemade tamales to a salad-and-sandwich combination. The dinner hours listed below are for seatings; you can then stay and enjoy the meal, which often takes around 2 hours. A taxi here from town should run you L75 each way.

5km (3 miles) south of Copán Ruinas on the road to Los Sapos ruins. ©/fax **504/651-4495.** www.haciendasanlucas.com. Reservations required. Lunch main courses L189–L378; prix-fixe dinner L555. AE, MC, V. Daily 8:30am–3pm and 7–8:30pm.

MODERATE

Carnitas N'ia Lola ★★ HONDURAN   Grilled and barbecued meats are the specialty of this bi-level restaurant, located literally on the edge of town. N'ia's is one of the most consistently popular restaurants in Copán, partly because of the delicious food and partly because of the waitresses who carry drinks and dishes from the kitchen on their heads. Brochettes, typical dishes, tacos, and steaks are all good. *Anafre,* a bean fondue eaten with tortilla chips, is served in place of bread. Happy hour is from 6:30 to 8:30pm.

2 blocks south of the central plaza. ©**504/651-4196.** Main courses L110–L275. MC, V. Daily 10am–10pm.

Twisted Tanya's ★ 🏠 INTERNATIONAL   Part upscale fusion restaurant and part itinerant party central, this place mixes together elegance and extravagance in equal doses. The lovely open-air, second-floor corner dining room has white muslin curtains and fancy table settings. The white-board menu changes daily, and may include anything from homemade curries with coconut rice to salmon in a Jack Dan-iel's glaze. There are always a couple of vegetarian items to choose from. Twisted Tanya's offers a $22 prix-fixe menu of soup or salad, entree, and dessert. An early-bird backpacker special will get you soup, pasta, and dessert for around $8–$10. The des-serts here are all homemade, decadent, and deservedly renowned. Their popular 2x1 happy hour is from 4 to 6pm.

1 block south and 1 block west of the central plaza. ©**504/651-4182.** www.twistedtanya.com. Reserva-tions recommended. Main courses $6–$15. AE, MC, V. Mon–Sat 3–10pm.

INEXPENSIVE

In addition to the places listed below, you can't go wrong at **Vamos A Ver** (© **504/651-4627**) or **Momo's** (© **504/651-3692**), both serving international fare, with the latter specializing in steak. For pizza and Italian fare, try **Pizza Italia** (© **504/651-4172**) or **Pizza Copán** (© **504/651-4381**).

Llama del Bosque 🍴 HONDURAN   This is the place to come for simple, local fare served fast and at rock-bottom prices. Start with black-bean soup and a hard-boiled egg, and then opt for any of the grilled meat plates. For lighter meals, there are sandwiches and burritos. This is also a great choice for breakfast.

1½ blocks west of the central plaza. ©**504/651-4431.** Main courses L35–L95. MC, V. Daily 7am–10pm.

Vía Vía Cafe INTERNATIONAL/VEGETARIAN   I find the food at this popular spot a bit disappointing, but you can't beat it as a meeting place for locals and tourists alike. There are a few tables on a small, street-side porch, and more in a lush open-air interior courtyard. While there are some chicken dishes on the menu, this place really caters to vegetarians. One of the best dishes here is the *capela*, a homemade carrot-and-pesto lasagna. There are a host of other options, including Thai curries, Indian *pakoras*, and hearty sandwiches and veggie burgers. I'd steer clear of the pad Thai, which is a poor imitation of the real thing. This place is actually part of an extensive international chain that caters specifically to itinerant backpackers.

1½ blocks west of the central plaza.© **504/651-4652.** www.viaviacafe.com. Main courses L65–L95. MC, V. Daily 6:30am–midnight.

Copan After Dark

Copán Ruinas is a relatively quiet town. Aside from the hotel and restaurant bars (of which Twisted Tanya's is always a good call), the most happening spot seems to be **Café Xibalba** (© **504/651-4182**). In addition, you might try the **Tunkul Bar** (© **504/651-4410**), or head to the **Vía Vía Cafe** (see above) for a more relaxed vibe. **Wine Barcito** (Calle Independencia 1 block south of Parque Central), in a tiny room beside the Pabellon Maya souvenir shop, is tops for wine. **Papa Chango's** down the hill from the center (and near the Hedman-Alas bus station) is the only real spot for a very late night, as a noise ordinance in the center forces restaurants and bars in Copán to close by midnight.

IZABAL & THE ATLANTIC LOWLANDS

Although Guatemalans, tourists, and guidebooks all refer to Guatemala's Atlantic Highway and Atlantic coast, these are misnomers—Guatemala's eastern coast actually fronts the Caribbean Sea. Nonetheless, this chapter deals with the area running northeast, east, and south of Guatemala City, which is reached via the Carretera al Atlántico (Atlantic Hwy.). With the notable exception of the Maya ruins of Quiriguá, there's not much to see along the highway itself until you reach the area around Lago Izabal, Río Dulce (Fronteras), and the coastal settlements of Puerto Barrios and Livingston. Once there, you'll find a lush, tropical region favored by boaters and those looking for something truly out of the ordinary in Guatemala.

LIVINGSTON ★

318km (197 miles) NE of Guatemala City; 23km (14 miles) NW of Puerto Barrios; 40km (25 miles) NE of Río Dulce

The small, hillside, coastal town of Livingston is the main Garífuna settlement in Guatemala. The Garífuna are a unique race (see the box, below) with a language, culture, and cuisine all their own, so it should come as no surprise that Livingston, a laid-back burg on the Caribbean coast, is worlds apart from the rest of Guatemala. In fact, once in Livingston, you're just as likely to hear a mix of English and Garifuna, as Spanish. And you'll often hear the town referred to as **La Buga,** its Garífuna name. The town's geographical isolation has helped it maintain its mellow image and lifestyle, as well as its appeal to those looking to truly get away from it all.

Essentials

GETTING THERE

There are no roads into or out of Livingston, though the town itself does have some paved streets and a few cars. You must arrive by boat, either from Río Dulce or Puerto Barrios. For directions on how to reach either Río Dulce or Puerto Barrios by bus or car, see the appropriate sections below. If arriving by car, you can find secure parking at several public lots near the boat docks, or at one of the hotels. I recommend **Bruno's** (see later in this chapter). Rates run around Q30 ($3.75) per day.

BY BOAT Livingston can be reached by regular boat-taxi service from both Río Dulce and Puerto Barrios. **ASOTRANSLALI** (Asociación de

Lancheros de Livingston; ℭ **502/7947-0870**) is in charge of boat taxis in Livingston. The boat dock and ASOTRANSLALI office are at the end of Calle Principal, at the bottom of the steep hill leading up to the center of town.

Scheduled boats run regularly in both directions from Puerto Barrios to Livingston at 6:30, 7:30, 9 and 11am. These cost Q35 and take about 30 minutes. In the afternoon, boats leave each port as they fill up, which is roughly every 2 hours with the last boat leaving Puerto Barrios around 7pm and Livingston at 5pm.

Collective boats leave for Livingston from the main dock in Río Dulce daily at 9:30am and 2:30pm. The fare is Q125 one-way; Q180 round-trip. Other boats will run throughout the day once they fill to capacity, or you can rent a boat that will hold up to 10 people for around Q1,250. Some of the boats arriving from Río Dulce will dock at a separate pier just upriver from the main dock in front of the restaurant Bugamama.

GETTING AROUND
Livingston is so small it's nearly a village, and everything is within walking distance. The town, however, is set on a very steep hill, so you have to hoof it up or down to get where you're going. There are actually now a couple of taxis and tuk tuks, which charge Q10 for a ride anywhere in town.

THE garífuna

Throughout the 18th century, escaped and shipwrecked slaves assimilated into the native Caribbean Indian populations on several islands in the Lesser Antilles, predominantly on St. Vincent. The West Africans were a mixed lot, including members of the Fon, Yoruba, Ewe, and Nago tribes. Over the years, the West African and indigenous elements blended into a new people, known first as Black Caribs and today as Garífuna or Garinagu. The Garífuna have their own language, traditions, history, and rituals, which celebrate the group's two primary cultural sources. For example, ritual possession ceremonies spoken in a language whose etymological roots are predominantly Arawak are accompanied by African-style drumming and call-and-response singing.

The Black Caribs were fierce warriors and frequently fought the larger colonial powers to maintain their freedom. In 1796, despite the celebrated leadership of Joseph Chatoyer, the Garífuna were soundly defeated by the British forces, who subsequently shipped several thousand of the survivors off to exile on the island of Roatán, in then British Honduras. The Garífuna began migrating and eventually settled along the coasts of what are present-day Honduras, Nicaragua, Guatemala, and Belize. The local Garífuna first settled Livingston in 1802, arriving from Roatan, Honduras. For nearly 2 centuries now, the Garífuna have lived quiet lives of farming, fishing, and light trading with their neighbors, while steadfastly maintaining their language, heritage, and traditions. Each year on November 26 (and for several days around the date), Livingston comes alive to celebrate **National Garífuna Day.** For an in-depth look at Garífuna history and culture, check out www.labuga.com.

ORIENTATION

Livingston sits on a point of land where the Río Dulce meets the **Bahía de Amatique,** which is part of the Caribbean Sea. The principal boat dock, or *muelle municipal,* lies at the bottom of Calle Principal. The center of town is straight up the steep hill leading away from the *muelle municipal,* and is where most of the hotels, restaurants, bars, banks, and shops are. Calle Principal actually runs up the hill to its crest and then back down on the other side to the sea, where you'll find the town's main beach, a few more hotels and restaurants, and the path to Los Siete Altares and Playa Blanca.

FAST FACTS   There is only one bank in Livingston, **Banrural,** which is located on Calle Principal. To contact the local **police,** dial ☏ **502/5314-3219.** There's a small, local health clinic (☏ **502/7947-0143**) near the center of town.

What to See & Do

There are several reputable tour agencies in Livingston that can organize tours, including those to the destinations listed below. In addition, every hotel in town can set you up. If you're looking for a reputable outfit, try **Exotic Travel** (☏ **502/7947-0049;** www.bluecaribbeanbay.com) or **Happy Fish** (☏ **502/7947-0661;** www. happyfishtravel.com.)

Los Siete Altares ★★   No trip to Livingston is complete without a visit to Los Siete Altares, a series of seven waterfalls connected by a lazy jungle creek. The whole

ACCOMMODATIONS ■
La Casa Rosada **15**
Hotel Gil Resort **9**
Hotel Río Dulce **8**
Hotel Rios Tropicales **10**
Hotel Salvador Gaviota **2**
Hotel Villa Caribe **11**
Posada El Delfín **16**

DINING ◆
Bahia Azul **5**
Bugamama **13**
El Malecón **12**
Happy Fish **7**
La Casa Rosada **15**
McTropic **6**

ATTRACTIONS ●
Los Siete Altares **1**
Municipal Museum **14**

NIGHTLIFE ★
Hotel Villa Caribe **11**
Tropicool Disco **3**
Ubafu **4**

thing is set amid lush rainforest, and while it's a pretty spot year-round, it's best to visit during the rainy season, when the creek and waterfalls are running at their strongest. All of the local hotels and tour agencies offer guided hikes or boat trips here. The falls are located just off the beach, some 5km (3 miles) north, and it's easy to walk here by following the simple path that parallels the beach heading out of Livingston. Whether you come by yourself or with a guide, make sure you go all the way to the top and final waterfall. (Some bored or rushed guides will only bring their group to the first waterfall or two.)

There's a fabulous pool for swimming by the final waterfall—and several others along the way—and the adventurous can dive off the top of the falls into the pool. Sadly, the natural beauty is offset by graffiti, which covers the rocks.

If you go on a guided hike, it will almost certainly begin with a walk through the village of Livingston, giving you an intimate look into the daily lives of some of the locals. From here you'll climb to a promontory with a good panoramic view of the town and the Caribbean, then continue on to a small river, where a waiting canoe will take you on a short ride through the mangroves to the beach. These tours cost around Q80 per person, and include a simple lunch. A boat trip can replace the hike (a

While I highly recommend hiking to Los Siete Altares, I'd be remiss if I didn't warn you of two serious problems. First, despite the fact that it's easy to walk by yourself, be sure to ask your hotel about the current security situation. Over the years, tourists have been attacked and robbed along this walk. Don't do it alone or in a very small group, and make sure to do the hike in the busy part of the day, between 9am and 4pm, when there will be other groups and tourists around. Second, no matter whom you go with, be forewarned that the beach between Livingston and Los Siete Altares can be, depending upon tides and weather conditions, perhaps the most garbage-strewn stretch of sand I've ever seen. On one hike there I encountered a solid band of plastic bottles, old shoes, and other assorted refuse at least 1m (3½ ft.) wide running the entire 5km (3 miles) between the town and the waterfalls, just beyond the high-tide line. Local industry leaders always claim it is a seasonal phenomenon that is caused by a mix of heavy river runoff, coastal currents, and tidal conditions. However, it's an all too common phenomenon, no matter what the cause.

positive for some), and cost around Q104 per person. If you sign up for a guided tour, find out whether or not this entrance fee is included in the price. There's a small *comedor* at the entrance to the waterfalls where you can get a lunch or something cold to drink.

Just off the beach, some 5km (3 miles) north. ℂ **502/5731-1312.** Admission Q15. Daily 8am–4pm.

Playa Blanca ★ Playa Blanca is the best beach in the area, partly due to its distance from the outflow of the Río Dulce and the heavy pollution generated by the residents of Livingston. The sand here is a bit whiter and softer, and the water a bit bluer than you'll find closer to town. This is actually a private beach (hence the admission charge), and to get here, you need to sign up for a guided tour or hire a boat through ASOTRANSLALI (ℂ **502/7947-0870**). I recommend going with a guided tour with one of the local tour agencies for around Q110. These tours usually include lunch and a visit to Los Siete Altares.

Located about 12km (7½ miles) northwest of Livingston. Admission Q15.

Río Dulce ★★ A boat trip up the Río Dulce is one of the most popular area attractions. Just upriver from Livingston, the Río Dulce enters a narrow canyon known as **La Cueva de la Vaca,** which features steep walls some 92m (300 ft.) tall. One section, **La Pintada,** is made up of sheer, bright white-rock cliffs. Unfortunately, near the waterline, much of this white rock is marred by graffiti. However, beyond the graffiti is lush tropical rainforest. There are a few hot springs along the river, which form different heated pools and swimming areas. As you exit the canyon, the river broadens out into **El Golfete.** This long, wide section continues on until the river once again narrows near the town of Río Dulce.

Off El Golfete lies the **Biotopo Chocón Machacas** ★, a protected area of mangroves and rainforest canals that's home to a healthy population of manatees. Often called "sea cows," manatees are massive aquatic mammals that can reach more than 3m (10 ft.) in length and weigh more than 454 kilograms (1,000 lb.). Many tours take a trip through the Biotopo, although sightings of manatees are far from guaranteed. Nonetheless, the area is quite beautiful, and the bird-watching is excellent.

Finally, some tours go all the way to the town of Fronteras, which is also simply known as Río Dulce. Fronteras sits at the demarcation point between Río Dulce and Lago Izabal. A visit here usually includes a tour of the **Castillo de San Felipe ★** (see later in this chapter). All of the tour agencies in town offer trips up the Río Dulce. Prices range from $15–$30 depending upon the specific tour. Try **Happy Fish** (see below).

Attractions in town are limited to a small **municipal museum** (© 502/7947-0944) with a few interpretive and written displays detailing the Garífuna culture and history, and a small park just outside the museum, where you'll see a few crocodiles in a round enclosure. The large reptiles are impressive in size and menacing, but the unkempt and small pens they are kept in make this quite a sad display. The museum is open Monday through Saturday from 8am to 5pm. Admission is Q15.

While the local population lives largely off the sea, there are no major sportfishing operations in Livingston. If you're interested in a fishing outing, contact a tour agency or ask around the docks for a local fisherman who's willing to take you out. Contact **Happy Fish** (© 502/7947-0661; www.happyfishtravel.com) about day trips. Rates are a flat $400 for a boat holding up to seven people or around $50 per person for a group outing put together by the agency. Snorkelers will need to travel out of Livingston to the nearby cays of Belize.

Shopping

Aside from street vendors hawking handmade jewelry and simple trinkets, there's not much of a shopping scene in Livingston. One major exception, however, is the **Q'eqchi' women's craft cooperative ★★**, run by **Ak' Tenamit** (www.aktenamit. org), a community development project that does major educational, health, and social work with the Q'eqchi' Maya of the area. Offerings include woven baskets, various textile projects, and artisanal papers made from banana and corn byproducts. They are located about a 15-minute boat ride upriver from Livingston; however, their wares are also sold at the gift shop at Bugamama (see below). Still, if you want to visit them directly, you can hire a boat at the docks to take you there for around Q80 round-trip.

The local music is percussion-based with roots in West Africa. In some cases, modern electric instruments are added, and a rock or reggae influence can be heard. CDs are available in gift shops around town, and from street vendors, but be sure to take a listen first to make sure it's of reasonable quality.

Where to Stay

When you arrive in Livingston, your boat will invariably be met by aggressive touts trying to steer you to a hotel where they'll get a commission. Some will even claim that the hotel you are asking about is full, or has recently closed. In general, I wouldn't believe them, especially if you have a confirmed reservation.

EXPENSIVE

Hotel Villa Caribe ★★ ☺ This is easily the most luxurious hotel in Livingston, and it almost qualifies as a resort with its hillside location and views over the Río Dulce and Caribbean Sea. Rooms are large and comfortable, and all come with a private balcony. The best rooms in the house are the five individual bungalows, which are classified as junior suites. These all come with air-conditioning, a minifridge, and TV. My favorite of these is Punta Palma, which practically hangs off the side of the hill and has a private deck to take advantage of the view. There's a large pool and plenty of lounge chairs, which you'll appreciate given the hot and humid climate. The restaurant serves good international and local cuisine in a semi-elegant setting, often featuring live Garífuna music and dancing. There's a small beach in front of the hotel, but you'd be much better off heading to their "private" section of Playa Blanca, a 20-minute boat ride away. The hotel used to be called Tucán Dugú, and some locals still refer to it this way.

1 block up from the municipal dock. *C* **502/2223-5000** central reservation number in Guatemala City, or 7947-0072. www.villasdeguatemala.com. 42 units. $125 double; $140 junior suite. AE, DC, MC, V. **Amenities:** Restaurant; bar; large outdoor pool. *In room:* No phone.

MODERATE

Hotel Gil Resort ★   This hotel offers up simple, cozy rooms with air-conditioning at very reasonable rates. I prefer the second-floor rooms, which have wooden floors and higher ceilings. Rooms no. 8 and no. 9 are oceanfront end units with a shared balcony. Set on a steep hillside, the best feature here is the cascading multilevel deck and balcony structure built facing the ocean, with several different sitting areas and private nooks. At the bottom of the hill you'll find a shade-covered dock and swimming area. There's also a tiny plunge pool here.

5 blocks west of the municipal dock. *C* **502/7947-0039** or 5206-8124. www.gilresorthotel.com. 14 units. $50 double. AE, DC, MC, V. **Amenities:** Restaurant; free Wi-Fi. *In room:* A/C, no phone.

Posada El Delfín ★   Set on the waterfront west of the municipal dock, this is an alternative to Villa Caribe in Livingston's high-end market. However, I think Villa Caribe has this place beat in terms of service, comfort, and amenities. That said, the rooms here are spacious and have air-conditioning (which is not the case at Villa Caribe). Those on the first floor have checkerboard tile floors, which I prefer to the carpeted second-floor units, which can get a bit musty. There's a tiny pool—or giant tepid Jacuzzi—in the covered ground-floor patio. The best room by far, and one of the best in Livingston, is the honeymoon suite located at the end of a pier jutting into the bay. This second-floor room has a wraparound deck, a giant living area, a king-size bed, and a large-screen TV.

3 blocks west of the municipal dock. *C* **502/7947-0694.** Fax 502/7947-0077. www.posadaeldelfin. com. 24 units. $50 double; $65 suite; $125 honeymoon suite. Rates lower midweek and off season; slightly higher during peak periods. AE, DC, MC, V. **Amenities:** Restaurant; tiny pool. *In room:* A/C.

INEXPENSIVE

There are a host of budget options in Livingston. Many are quite stuffy, moldy, and uncomfortable, so I'd stick to **Casa Rosada** (below). However, real budget hounds can try either **Hotel Ríos Tropicales** (*C* **502/7947-0158;** www.mctropic.com) or **Hotel Río Dulce** (*C* **502/7947-0764**), both of which are located on Calle Principal, near the center of town.

If you want to stay right on the beach close to Los Siete Altares, check out **Hotel Salvador Gaviota** (*C* **502/5514-3275** or 7947-0874; www.hotelsalvadorgaviota. es.tl), a very basic operation that boasts a decent beach for swimming and easy access to the waterfalls.

Finca Tatín ★★   This place is a low impact riverside ecolodge located 20 minutes by boat outside of Livingston. Accommodations range from dorm rooms and private rooms with shared bathroom facilities to a few private bungalows and cabins with their own bathrooms. All are basic, with minimal amenities, but they're very well kept. Most of the beds are made of soft foam, but at least they have mosquito netting. There's a relaxed, collegial vibe to the whole place, and you couldn't pick a better spot to get away from it all and explore the tropical rainforests. Kayak tours through the rainforest rivers are the specialty here, but you'll also have the chance to visit some local indigenous communities. These folks are also founding members of Eco-Rio, a local organization working to protect the Rio Dulce ecosytem and promote sustainable tourism. A full meal plan runs around Q100 per day.

Río Tatin, Río Dulce. ✆ **502/5902-0831** or 4148-3332. www.fincatatin.centramerica.com. Q160 private bathroom bungalow; Q65 shared bathroom; Q45 dorm. These rates are per person. No credit cards. **Amenities:** Restaurant. *In room:* No phone.

La Casa Rosada 🏠 This is my favorite budget option in Livingston. The individual wooden bungalows all share several well-maintained common bathrooms and showers. Each comes with two twin beds, each of which is set under a fan and mosquito net. Colorful decor livens up the rooms, and the walls are mostly made of screened mesh to encourage cross ventilation. The hotel is set on the waterfront and has a thatch-roof *palapa* built out over the water. The owners, a Belgian-and-Guatemalan couple, also run an excellent tour operation, which visits all the major tourist destinations mentioned above, as well as one of the best restaurants in town (see below).

5 blocks west of the municipal dock. ✆ **502/7947-0303.** Fax 502/7947-0304. www.hotelcasarosada.com. 10 units, all with shared bathroom. $20 double. Rates include taxes. No credit cards. **Amenities:** Restaurant. *In room:* No phone.

Where to Dine

In addition to the places listed below, **El Malecón** (✆ **502/7947-0063**), **McTropic** (✆ **502/4138-1899**), and **Bahía Azul** (✆ **502/7947-0133**) are all good options.

INEXPENSIVE

Bugamama ★ 🏠 INTERNATIONAL This is my favorite restaurant in Livingston. Part of the Ak' Tenamit community development project, the restaurant is a training school for local youth, and profits go to support various local community health and education projects. Often bustling, this is one of the best and most popular joints in town, and serves up a mean *tapado* and other local specialties, plus more exotic dishes, such as tempura vegetables and spicy shrimp fettuccine. The rambling wooden building is painted in bright colors, and tables are spread through a couple of rooms and open-air decks. Visitors and locals alike spend time here nursing a coffee, reading a book, or playing cards or backgammon. There's an attached Internet cafe and gift shop, and a separate coffee shop located across the street.

> **Eat Like a Local**
>
> A local specialty, *tapado* is a seafood stew made with coconut milk, featuring the freshest catch of both fish and shellfish, as well as a mix of vegetables that might include potatoes, sweet potatoes, yucca and/or plantains.

1 block west of the municipal dock. ✆ **502/7947-0891.** www.bugamama.org. Main courses Q45–Q110. AE, DC, MC, V. Daily noon–10pm.

Happy Fish ★ INTERNATIONAL/SEAFOOD This open-air, street-side restaurant is one of the most popular spots in town for breakfast, lunch, and dinner. Most of the tables are set in the front dining room, where a thatch roof and slow-turning ceiling fans battle the heat. However, there are a few tables right on the street under large beach umbrellas. The menu features a mix of local fare, seafood, and some international dishes. The *tapado* here is good, but a little sweet. I'd stick to the fresh fish or seafood options. They have an espresso machine, making this a top choice for breakfast or a midday break. The restaurant also has an excellent tour agency, an Internet cafe, and a bar.

Calle Principal. ✆ **502/7947-0661.** Main courses Q40–Q240. AE, DC, MC, V. Daily 7:30am–10pm.

La Casa Rosada ★★ 🎁 INTERNATIONAL/SEAFOOD The food, service, and selection are consistently excellent at the intimate restaurant of this budget hotel, where subdued lighting and shell and bamboo curtains add to the ambience. The menu changes regularly, but always features a broad selection of dishes including several vegetarian options, fresh seafood, and an excellent *tapado*. Other options might include curried shrimp, a Thai-influenced special, or a spicy pasta with mixed seafood. All dinners, no matter what main dish you choose, start with a fresh salad and bread, and finish with dessert. Reservations, including your choice of a main dish, must be made by 6pm.

5 blocks west of the municipal dock, Livingston. ✆ **502/7947-0303.** www.hotelcasarosada.com. Reservations required. Main courses Q55–Q130. No credit cards. Daily 6:30am–9pm.

Livingston After Dark

For years, the most happening bar in Livingston has been **Ubafu** ★★, 2 blocks west of Calle Principal, on the road to the cemetery (no phone), which has live Garífuna, punta, or reggae music most nights. Traditional Garífuna drum ensembles feature a variety of conga-style wooden drums with skin heads, but one of their more interesting percussion instruments is made from several turtle shells, which are strung together and worn by the drummer like a personal trap set. This is still my favorite bar; however, it's getting a run for its money from the waterfront nightspot, **Tropicool Disco** ★ (no phone). For a more formal presentation of Garífuna drumming and dancing, head to the **Hotel Villa Caribe** (✆ **502/2334-1818**), which has presentations to accompany their dinner service several nights a week.

RIO DULCE, FRONTERAS & LAGO IZABAL ★★

308km (191 miles) E of Guatemala City; 84km (52 miles) W of Puerto Barrios

Guatemala's largest lake, **Lago Izabal,** is located in an isolated, stunningly beautiful, forested section of the country, which is largely ignored by tourists. The river port town of Fronteras, commonly called Río Dulce, is the only major settlement in the area, and is located at the narrow section where Lago Izabal becomes the Río Dulce, which flows northeast toward Livingston and the sea.

Essentials

GETTING THERE

BY CAR To reach Río Dulce by car, take the Carretera al Atlántico (CA-9) out of Guatemala City to La Ruidosa crossroads at Km 245. From here it's another 34km

(21 miles) north on highway CA-13 to Río Dulce. Highway CA-13 also connects Río Dulce with Flores, Tikal, and El Petén.

BY BUS Litegua (© **502/7930-5251** in Río Dulce, 2220-8840 in Guatemala City; www.litegua.com), **Autobuses del Norte** (**ADN;** © **502/2251-0050;** www.adnautobusesdelnorte.com), and **Línea Dorada** (© **502/7767-5198;** www.linea dorada.info) all have direct daily service between Guatemala City and Fronteras, Río Dulce. All have terminals within a couple of blocks of each other in Zona 1. Between the three lines, buses begin leaving around 5am and leave at least once every hour, with the last departure around 2pm. The trip from Guatemala City takes about 5½ hours, and fares run between Q80 and Q180 one-way. Splurge for one of the "executive" or "deluxe" buses, which are more modern, comfortable, and faster. Alternatively, you can take any bus to Puerto Barrios, get off in La Ruidosa, and wait for a local bus to pass on its way to Río Dulce. Or, if you're coming from Antigua or Panajachel, all of the local tour agencies can arrange a scheduled minivan transfer to Río Dulce for Q100 to Q360.

There's also regular bus service between Río Dulce and Flores, Petén. **Línea Dorada** and **ADN** both run this route, which takes about 3½ hours each way.

BY BOAT Río Dulce is serviced by regular boat-taxi service from both Livingston and Puerto Barrios. The main boat dock is located at the base of the bridge on the Fronteras side. Collective boats leave Río Dulce for Livingston from the main dock at 9:30am and 2:30pm every day. The fare is Q125 one-way; Q180 round-trip. Other boats will run throughout the day once they fill to capacity, or you can rent a boat that will hold up to 10 people for around Q1,250.

GETTING AROUND

For many purposes, boats are the preferred means of travel. Head to the main boat dock in Río Dulce, where you can catch regular service to Livingston and El Castillo San Felipe. You can also hire a small motor launch to take you around for Q800 for a half-day.

For land travel, taxis are readily available on the main road through Fronteras. If you can't flag one down, have your hotel call one for you.

ORIENTATION

There are hotels and restaurants clustered around the shores of Río Dulce, on both sides of the bridge, and farther afield. While the whole area is most commonly referred to as Río Dulce, there are more specific designations here. Approaching from Puerto Barrios or Guatemala City, the area around the base of the bridge is known as El Relleno. After crossing the bridge, you'll come to Fronteras, the larger and more important settlement.

FAST FACTS Banco Agromercantil (© **502/7948-1235**), **Banco Industrial** (© **502/5514-0889**), and **Banrural** (© **502/7930-5159**) can all be found on the

Shelter from the Storm

Río Dulce is a major "hurricane hole," which means it's a safe and secure anchorage during hurricane season. Between July and October of each year, the marinas and anchorages, as well as the bars and restaurants, are packed with sailors seeking safe harbor during the Caribbean hurricane season.

main road in the center of Fronteras. The **Centro de Salud** health center (*(C)* **502/ 7930-5209**) is also in this area. The number for the local **police** is *(C)* **502/7930- 5406.**

What to Do In & Around Rio Dulce

Everything in this area revolves around its biggest attraction, Lago Izabal. Most hotels and tour agencies in town offer boat tours of the lake. Almost all of these make a stop at **Castillo de San Felipe,** and many also head to **Finca El Paraíso** (see below). Some tours head down the Río Dulce to Livingston, passing through **El Golfete** and **Cueva de la Vaca,** often making a side trip to **Biotopo Chocón Machacas.** For more details on these destinations and attractions, see the Livingston section earlier in this chapter. Your best bet for lining up a tour is to contact the folks at **Tijax Express** (*(C)* **502/7930-5505;** www.tijax.com), which has an office just off the main street in Fronteras.

Since Río Dulce is such a popular destination with cruising yachts, there are almost always a couple of sailboats working the charter business. Ask your hotel or around the dock at **Bruno's** or the **Restaurante Río Bravo.**

Castillo de San Felipe ★ In 1652, Spanish colonists built this stone fort at the narrowest point of Lago Izabal, where it begins its life at the Río Dulce and flows down to Livingston. The fort was built here to dominate the waterway access into the lake and defend the Spanish from British, French, and Dutch raiders. While the stone battlements and cannons offered good protection from a water-launched attack, land attacks were a different story, and the fort was destroyed in 1686 and subsequently rebuilt.

A bilingual guide will be on hand when you enter to give you a quick 20-minute tour. The cost is included in the admission price, but be sure to tip a little. In addition to tours of the fort, there are picnic tables on the grounds and even a swimming area on the lake. The easiest way to get here is by boat. Boats leave throughout the day from the main dock and charge Q15 each way.

On the shore of the Río Dulce, 3.2km (2 miles) west of the main bridge in Fronteras. No phone. Admission Q20. Daily 8am–5pm.

EL ESTOR

El Estor is a beautiful community on the north shore of Lago Izabal, with forested mountains that appear to cascade into the lake. There are a couple of natural attractions of note, and many of the boat tours from Río Dulce stop here.

El Boquerón ★ This is a stunning natural river canyon cut by the Río Sauce a few miles east of El Estor. The best way to get here is on an organized tour out of Río Dulce. The trip includes a ride up the canyon in a boat or kayak to a small riverside beach, where the swimming is excellent. Contact **Tijax Express** (*(C)* **502/7930- 5505;** www.tijax.com).

No phone. Free admission. No official hours.

Finca El Paraíso ★ A beautiful jungle waterfall of thermally heated water is the prime attraction at this working farm and ecotourism project. At the base of the fall you can bathe in both hot and cold water pools. These folks have a pleasant restaurant by the lakeshore, and several simple bungalows for staying overnight.

At Km 299 on the road around the lake. No phone. Admission Q20.

Where to Stay

In addition to the places listed below, **Hotel Nana Juana** (✆ **502/7930-5230;** www.hotelmarinananajuana.com) is a relatively upscale hotel and marina, while **Casa Perico** (✆ **502/7930-5666**) is a good budget option.

MODERATE

Banana Palms ★ ☺ This is a good resort-style option, popular with Guatemalan families. The hotel is actually several miles outside of Fronteras, set on a lovely section of the lakeshore and very close to El Castillo de San Felipe. Each room, all very large suites, is equipped with a kitchenette, sitting room, and spacious bedroom with two queen-size beds. The second-floor deluxe units each have an outdoor Jacuzzi on their open-air deck, and some of these have excellent views of the lake. The grounds are beautiful, with lush gardens and a pretty walkway along the lakeshore. The large pool features a volleyball net and a separate children's pool. There's also a game room by the lake with a Ping-Pong table, pool table, and foosball; an outdoor basketball court; and private marina with motor boats and kayaks for hire.

Just beyond El Castillo de San Felipe. ✆ **502/7930-5041** or 2334-2598 reservation number in Guatemala City. www.bananapalms.com.gt. 33 units. $82–$129 double. Rates higher during peak periods. AE, DC, MC, V. **Amenities:** Restaurant; bar; midsize pool. *In room:* A/C, TV.

Catamaran Island Hotel ★ 🏨 This is my favorite hotel in Río Dulce, and although it's not technically an island, you can really only get here by boat. The individual wooden cabins are relatively simple and bare-bones, but feature air-conditioning and a private porch or deck area. The best ones are either right on the edge or out over the water. At the over-water main lodge, you'll find a dark and stately, yet decidedly tropical, bar; a computer with Internet connection; and a large TV with satellite feed. The restaurant is massive, and there's a daytime bar near the pool at the center of the compound. These folks are popular with itinerant cruising sailors, and they even have a tennis court.

Fronteras. ✆ **502/7930-5494.** Fax 502/7930-2492. www.catamaranisland.com. 36 units. $92 double. Rates include full breakfast. Rates higher during peak periods. AE, DC, MC, V. **Amenities:** Restaurant; 2 bars; midsize outdoor pool; unlit outdoor tennis court. *In room:* A/C, no phone.

INEXPENSIVE

Bruno's There are a variety of room choices here, but the best are found in a three-story concrete building facing the river. All of the rooms come with a shared balcony, and those on the top floor have the best views. However, even the best rooms here, which come with air-conditioning and TVs, feel a bit bare and basic. If you're on a budget, you can opt for a less expensive dorm room. Still, the hotel is well located and offers good value, plus it has a pool near the river and one of the most popular restaurants in town, which serves as one of Río Dulce's principal social hubs.

Fronteras. ✆ **502/7930-5721** or 5692-7292. www.mayaparadise.com. 14 units. $4.40 per person dorm room; $63 double room with private bathroom. AE, DC, MC, V. **Amenities:** Restaurant; bar; small outdoor pool. *In room:* No phone.

Hacienda Tijax While I find the rooms a bit rough around the edges, you can't beat the setting and amenities. Located a short boat ride away from the main docks in Río Dulce, Tijax features a mix of accommodations ranging from basic rooms and individual cabins with shared bathrooms to private cabins with air-conditioning and large two-story family-style bungalows. The rooms are fairly Spartan, and in some cases show the effects of the harsh and extremely humid climate. All come with mosquito netting over each bed. I recommend splurging on one of the air-conditioned cabins. The best things about this place are its pool, common areas, and the surrounding jungle. Travelers from around the world seem to converge at Tijax, and there's a friendly, hostel-like vibe to the place. The pool, which is almost always busy during the day, features two separate unheated Jacuzzis. The owners here take sustainable tourism and sustainable farming seriously, and the hotel is certified by the Green Deal sustainable tourism program.

Fronteras. ℂ **502/7930-5505.** www.tijax.com. 28 units. $29 double cabin with shared bathroom; $47 double cabin with private bathroom; $84 double bungalow. AE, DC, MC, V. **Amenities:** Restaurant; 2 bars; 2 Jacuzzis; small outdoor pool; free Wi-Fi. *In room:* No phone.

Where to Dine

In addition to the places listed below, the **Restaurante Vista Rio** (ℂ **502/7930-5665**) is another excellent and popular local joint, with a lovely riverfront location, wood-fired pizza oven, and delectable barbeque.

INEXPENSIVE

Bruno's INTERNATIONAL   This popular hotel/restaurant is Río Dulce's prime meeting ground for itinerant sailors, land-based travelers, assorted expatriates, and other lost souls. There's a crowded bulletin board listing everything from tours, boat cruises, and available rooms to boats for sale, boats looking for crew, and massage therapists. The food here is well prepared, fairly priced, and copious, so the wood tables and chairs can fill up quickly. Their fried *mojara*—a local freshwater fish—is excellent. Barbecue nights on Wednesday and Sunday feature ribs, burgers, and chicken, while the great breakfasts include Guatemalan dishes and American fare such as pancakes, omelets, and home fries.

Under the bridge, Río Dulce. ℂ **502/7930-5174** or 7930-5721. Main courses Q48–Q96. AE, DC, MC, V. Daily 7am–9:30pm.

Restaurante Río Bravo ★ INTERNATIONAL/GUATEMALAN   The food here is good and served in big portions, and you can't beat the setting, built on a wooden deck jutting into the river. The menu features a mix of local Guatemalan fare alongside a long list of pizzas and pastas. This place—and its attached Internet cafe—is almost always bustling and the tables closest to the water are a hot commodity.

Under the bridge, Río Dulce. ℂ **502/7930-5167.** Main courses Q60–Q90. AE, DC, MC, V. Daily 7am–10pm.

PUERTO BARRIOS

297km (184 miles) NE of Guatemala City; 23km (14 miles) SE of Livingston; 41km (25 miles) NE of Río Dulce

Founded in 1884 by President Rufino Barrios, Puerto Barrios is literally the end of the road—CA-9 dead ends in the city. Puerto Barrios (joined at the hip with its neighboring sister port city Santo Tomás de Castilla) is a busy, industrial port city with virtually no appeal to tourists. For years this was the main shipping center for United Fruit Company's operations in Guatemala. Puerto Barrios is, however, a principal transit point for coming from, or heading to Livingston, Belize, or the Honduran Bay Islands. Almost all major bus lines and boats connecting Guatemala's Atlantic coast with the rest of the country and with popular tourist destinations in Belize and the Honduran Bay Islands make connections in Puerto Barrios. Because of the difficulty of coordinating boats and buses, some tourists end up spending the night in Puerto Barrios. Just outside of Puerto Barrios, there are a few nice beaches and some wonderful tropical rainforests. You'll see some vacation homes of wealthy Guatemalans all along the waterfront heading out of Puerto Barrios.

Essentials

GETTING THERE

BY CAR To reach Puerto Barrios by car, take the Carretera al Atlántico (CA-9) out of Guatemala City. Puerto Barrios is the end of the line some 295km (183 miles) to the northeast.

BY BUS **Litegua** (© 502/7948-1002 in Puerto Barrios, 2220-8840 in Guatemala City; www.litegua.com) has direct daily service between Guatemala City and Puerto Barrios. The Litegua terminal in Guatemala City is at 6a Calle and 9a Avenida, Zona 1. The first bus leaves for Puerto Barrios at 4:30am, and they run at least every hour, often on the hour and half-hour, until 6pm. Return buses have a similar frequency, but between the hours of 1am and 4pm. The bus station in Puerto Barrios is at the corner of 6a Avenida and 9a Calle. The trip takes about 5 hours each way. Fares are between Q60 and Q96 one-way. Splurge for one of the "executive" or "deluxe" buses, which are more modern, comfortable, and faster.

BY BOAT Scheduled boats run from Puerto Barrios to Livingston at 6:30, 7:30, 9 and 11am. The 30-minute trip costs Q35. Boats leave in the afternoon, roughly every 2 hours or, when demand is high, as they fill to capacity.

   Transportes El Chato (© 502/7948-5525) runs a daily boat to Punta Gorda, Belize, at 10am. The return boat leaves Punta Gorda at 2pm. The one-way ride takes around 1 hour and costs Q200. Before heading to Punta Gorda, you must have your passport stamped at the **Immigration Office,** 9a Calle and 2a Avenida (© 502/7948-7773) which is located just 1 block from the dock.

   Boats to and from Livingston, as well as to Punta Gorda, Belize, use the municipal dock at the end of 12a Calle.

GETTING AROUND

Taxis are plentiful in Puerto Barrios, and cabs are always waiting to meet incoming boats from Livingston and Punta Gorda, as well as all incoming buses. Given the seediness and relative insecurity of the city, I'd recommend taking a taxi most places. If none are readily available, have your hotel call you one, or try **Pedro at Gretaxmitur** (© 502/5194-7704).

ORIENTATION

While Puerto Barrios remains a busy port, much of the commercial traffic was shifted just down the bay to Santo Tomás de Castillo after a 1976 earthquake damaged many of the port facilities. Several banks, shops, and services are located in the compact downtown area. In the case of a medical emergency, contact the local **hospital** (© 502/7947-5846).

What to Do In & Around Puerto Barrios

Most tourists use Puerto Barrios as a gateway to Livingston or Belize since there's not much to see here, but just out of town a very pretty waterfall, **Las Escobas,** has a good swimming hole at its base. You might also want to visit **Punta Manabique,** a long point of land with mangroves and swamps jutting out into Amatique Bay, or hike in the rainforests of Cerro Gil. All around this area, there's good bird-watching and nature-viewing, which you can enjoy on hikes or boat rides. For tours or other information, ask at your hotel.

Fishing, snorkeling, and scuba diving are popular at the nearby Belizean cays. If you want to do any tours or activities while you're in the city, ask at your hotel, or check in with the folks at **Amatique Bay Resort and Marina** (below).

Where to Stay

Hotel options right in town are rather limited and desultory. Although you can't beat it for atmosphere and location, the **Hotel del Norte,** 7a Calle and 1a Avenida (© 502/7948-2116), has definitely seen better days. The sea, salt air, and heavy humidity have all taken their toll on this classic waterfront hotel. Another option close to the center of the city is **Hotel Valle Tropical** (© 502/7948-7084), which is a rather dreary concrete block building painted an awful pale green and getting a little long in the tooth.

In addition to the places listed below, **Hotel Marbrissa** (© 502/7948-1450; www.marbrissa.com) is a good, cozy, midrange resort-style hotel on the outskirts of town.

VERY EXPENSIVE

Amatique Bay Resort and Marina ☺ This the biggest and most complete beach resort on Guatemala's Caribbean coast. Set on expansive grounds on its namesake bay, the resort boasts a small patch of white-sand beach and sea, as well as a full-service marina with scuba diving and fishing operations. The hotel was built on and around the ruins of a colonial-era port, and they even have an old Catholic church, lighthouse, and small fort. The rooms are modern, spacious, and tastefully decorated. Many are suites or apartments with fully equipped kitchens. A wide range of tours and activities are available here, and on-site attractions include a butterfly farm and turtle hatchery. Service can be spotty here, and most of the clientele are timeshare owners or local vacationers.

4km (2½ miles) east of Puerto Barrios, on the Bahia de Amatique. © **502/7948-1820.** Fax 502/7948-1823. 61 units. $150 double; $210–$320 suite. AE, DC, MC, V. **Amenities:** 2 restaurants; 2 bars; children's program; full-service dive shop; large outdoor pool; free Wi-Fi. *In room:* A/C, TV, hair dryer.

INEXPENSIVE

Hotel Puerto Libre Although it's located on the outskirts just off the busy Carretera al Atlántico's crossroads into the city, this is still a safe bet in Puerto Barrios. The rooms here are comfortable and well maintained, and there's a midsize pool. The hotel also does brisk business as a local conference center, with five separate conference rooms and facilities.

Km 292 Carretera al Atlántico. © **502/7979-9188** or 7979-9189. www.hotelpuertolibre.com. 41 units. $36–$41 double. Rates almost double during Easter week. AE, DC, MC, V. **Amenities:** Restaurant; bar; small pool. *In room:* A/C, TV.

Where to Dine

In addition to the place listed below, the restaurant at the **Hotel Puerto Libre** (© 502/7979-9188) serves up a mix of international and Guatemalan fare, with an emphasis on seafood.

INEXPENSIVE

Restaurante Safari ★ INTERNATIONAL/SEAFOOD   The best restaurant in Puerto Barrios, Restaurante Safari has a great space jutting over the water. The open-air dining room is quite large, and can get very busy on Fridays and Saturdays, so arrive early if you want a waterfront table. Fresh fish and seafood are the best choices, although the long menu features a wide range of other options. If you're not going to make it to Livingston, be sure to try the *tapado*.

5a Av. and 1a Calle. ✆ **502/7948-0563.** Main courses Q45–Q125. AE, DC, MC, V. Daily 9am–9pm.

Puerto Barrios After Dark

As a port city, Puerto Barrios has its fair share of dingy bars and strip joints. Most are centered around 6a and 7a avenidas, and 6a and 7a calles. Personally, I'd recommend most tourists avoid this area, as it can be pretty dangerous, especially for foreigners. Your best bet is to head to the Restaurante Safari for some mellow drinks overlooking the water, or stick to your hotel facilities.

Side Trip: Quirigua ★

Quiriguá is a small yet important Maya archaeological site, located just off the Carretera al Atlántico some 94km (58 miles) from Puerto Barrios. Set close to the banks of the Motagua River, this UNESCO World Heritage Site was predominantly a trading city with close ties to Copán. The Late Classic city thrived from A.D. 692 to 900, during which Quiriguá's greatest leader, Cauac Sky (A.D. 724–784), reigned. Quiriguá was visited in 1841 by John L. Stephens, who tried to buy the site for as much as he'd paid for Copán. In the end he failed, or was too cheap, and the site was purchased by the United Fruit Company in 1910. The company built banana plantations everywhere, but fortunately spared and protected the area's Maya ruins.

To get to Quiriguá, you'll either have to come as part of an organized tour, or drive yourself. If you're driving, take the well-marked exit off the Carretera al Atlántico, 1.5km (1 mile) east of the town of Los Amates. From here, it's another 3km (2 miles) on a well-graded dirt road, through working banana plantations, to the park's entrance.

When you enter Quiriguá, your first stop should be the small museum and visitor center, which features some historical information, photos, and a scale model of the site. Even though all of the written material is in Spanish, the displays will help you get a grasp of the content. The main attraction at Quiriguá is its massive carved stelae. The tallest of these, and in the Maya world, is **stela E,** which is more than 10m (35 ft.) tall and weighs more than 65 tons. In addition to the stelae, there are massive carved stones in various shapes including frogs, serpents, turtles, and mythical beasts, all covered with hieroglyphs. Most of the stelae are found in Quiriguá's **Great Plaza,** which is surrounded by low temple buildings. At the north end of the Great Plaza lies the **Acropolis,** which occupies the highest ground on the site and offers a good panoramic view of the plaza and surrounding forests. *Note:* Because of the landscape, bird-watching is excellent, but it also means that mosquitoes are a problem, so bring repellent.

Most of Quiriguá's stelae were erected during the reign of Cauac Sky, and his face graces seven of the nine carved stelae at the site. In A.D. 738, Cauac Sky apparently conquered Copán, captured King 18 Rabbit, and had him decapitated in the Great

Plaza. This event is depicted on **zoomorph G.** After this victory, Quiriguá began converting itself from a vassal trade city into a more classic ceremonial center. Grand new stelae were erected on the Great Plaza roughly every 5 years, beginning in A.D. 751 and continuing on until A.D. 806.

While Quiriguá's stelae and zoomorphic stones are somewhat protected under tall thatch roofs, many have already been severely damaged by the ravages of time, and, more recently, by graffiti.

Quiriguá (© **502/5550-6586**) is open daily from 8am to 4:30pm; admission is Q80. You can easily tour the whole site in a couple of hours or less. If you end up needing to spend the night near Quiriguá, check into the **Hotel Royal** (© **502/ 7947-3639** or 502/7947-3348), a very basic option located right on the main highway (Carretera al Atlantico) near the turn off to the ruins.

PACIFIC COAST

W hile the country's Pacific coast is popular with Guatemalans, it's often neglected—or outright avoided—by most tourists. Part of this is for good reason. Guatemala's Pacific beaches pale in comparison to those found in Mexico, the Caribbean, and most of the rest of Central America, and they also take a back seat to the country's cultural, historic, architectural, and natural attractions. This region is almost uniformly hot and humid, and the beaches are overwhelmingly made up of dark, volcanic sand. The waters are often too rough for swimming, and the shores are unfortunately often strewn with garbage and other bits of jetsam. There are virtually no beach resorts and very few hotels of real comfort along the entire coast.

So why go? The beach towns of **Monterrico** and **Puerto San José** are fast and easy shots from Guatemala City and Antigua, and brim with Guatemalan revelers and families on weekends. This area has also earned international renown for its excellent **deep-sea fishing,** with record numbers of billfish being raised. And, while they are trying to keep the word from getting out, more and more surfers are heading this way to ride the many miles of beach breaks found here, especially those at **Sipacate** and **Iztapa.**

The Pacific coast can be easily included in a loop trip either to or from the highland city of Quetzaltenango, passing through the towns of **Retalhuleu** and **Santa Lucía Cotzumalguapa.** The latter has several interesting archaeological sites nearby and a good museum. For its part, Retalhuleu serves as a base for visiting one of several nearby amusement parks, which are seeking to make the place a sort of mini-Orlando, at least in the minds of Guatemalans and other Central American visitors.

MONTERRICO

124km (77 miles) S of Guatemala City; 70km (43 miles) SW of Escuintla

Monterrico is Guatemala's top beach destination, but the town is tiny and accommodations are limited. The beach here is a broad swath of dark volcanic sand backed by coconut palms and mangrove. Perhaps the town's biggest draw is its other natural charms. While often inhospitable to most sunbathers, Monterrico's beaches are prime nesting grounds for several species of **sea turtles,** and the beach's backing mangrove forests have been protected as part of the **Reserva Natural Monterrico** and are home to a wide range of tropical flora and fauna.

Essentials

GETTING THERE

BY BUS & BOAT   Because there are no direct public buses to Monterrico, most travelers book travel with a shuttle company. From Guatemala City, Antigua, or Panajachel, any tour agency or hotel in town can book you a minibus shuttle for around Q80 to Q240. Given the convenience, I think it's well worth the splurge.

There are no direct buses to Monterrico from Guatemala City. To get here head to the southern bus terminal at 4a Calle and 8a Avenida, Zona 12, and take a bus to Iztapa. In Iztapa, pick up a minibus to Monterrico. The whole trip will run you around Q32.

Alternately, you can take any bus from the main Zona 4 bus terminal heading to the El Salvador border, and get off in Taxisco. Several lines service this route, and buses leave at least every half-hour between 5am and 9pm. In Taxisco you can transfer to a local bus or taxi to La Avillana, where you'll pick up the ferry, or *lanchón,* to Monterrico. Buses from Taxisco to La Avillana are usually waiting and leave roughly every hour. Ferries run almost constantly during daylight hours between La Avillana and Monterrico, and tend to leave whenever full. The entire fare, including the ferry, should run you around Q40, slightly more if you take a cab from Taxisco to La Avillana.

BY CAR   If you're coming by car, you can take one of two routes. In either case, you'll head south out of Guatemala City on CA-9 toward Escuintla. I recommend heading straight from Escuintla to Puerto Quetzal, and then on to Iztapa. At the end of the road in Iztapa, you'll cross the bridge to Pueblo Viejo, where the road picks up again for Monterrico. From Pueblo Viejo it's 26km (16 miles) on a well-paved road to Monterrico. There's a Q20 toll each way on this bridge.

The most direct, yet more complicated, route is to drive from Escuintla over to Taxisco and then down to La Avillana. In La Avillana, a car ferry should be waiting to take you across to Monterrico. The 20-minute ferry ride costs around Q80 each way, and tends to run during daylight hours, with the occasional cushion of an hour or so on either end. These leave according to demand.

GETTING AROUND

Monterrico is small enough that you can easily walk anywhere in town. There are no official taxi companies in town, but your hotel will probably be able to find someone who works as a freelance taxi driver if you need one.

ORIENTATION

Both routes into Monterrico will land you on the Calle Principal, which runs perpendicular to, and dead-ends at, the beach. Most of the hotels are located on dirt roads

---

   Watching Over You

If you're driving, it's worth keeping an eye out around Km 54.5 of the highway between Guatemala City and Escuintla. As you head south, look to the right, and you should be able to pick out what locals claim to be the face of an ancient Maya in the rock and mountain formation in the distance. The lore is that he's looking toward and watching over Guatemala City.

Pacific Coast

running parallel to the beach in each direction off of Calle Principal. There are a host of cut-rate budget hotels and simple *comedores* all along Calle Principal.

FAST FACTS   There are no banks, ATMs, hospitals, or major services in Monterrico. Be sure to bring as much cash as you think you'll need, as very few establishments here accept credit cards. There is an Internet cafe on Calle Principal.

Fun On & Off the Beach

Monterrico is the textbook definition of a laid-back beach town. Given that the surf here is often too rough for most casual bathers, the prime activities are hanging out in a hammock and reading a book. If you do decide to swim, make sure you feel very comfortable with your abilities and ask your hotel if the current surf conditions are safe. It's often best to choose a spot where you see others already swimming. Also, be sure to bring sandals, as the sand can get extremely hot under the bright sun.

A good way to stay off your feet is to take a horseback ride along the beach. Your hotel should be able to arrange a ride for around Q20 to Q40 per hour. They can also arrange a fishing excursion with a local boat captain, which should run you Q600 to Q1,600 for a half-day depending on the size and comfort level of the boat and the type of tackle provided.

If you want to brush up on your Spanish, check in with **El Proyecto Lingüístico Monterrico** (*©* **502/5558-9039**) on the Calle Principal. Rates run $90 for 20 hours of study over a 5-day week. For an extra $50 per week, they can arrange room and board with a local family.

Parque Hawaii (Hawaii Park)   Similar to but less touristy than the Reserva Natural de Monterrico (Monterrico Nature Reserve), this project is run by the **Asociación de Rescate y Conservación de Vida Silvestre** (**ARCAS;** www.arcas guatemala.com). ARCAS is actively involved in environmental protection and education, and runs several excellent volunteer programs. This protected zone is comprised of ecosystems similar to those found at the reserve. All of the hotels and tour agencies can arrange for a guided tour of Parque Hawaii. Tours usually last around 4 to 5 hours, and run between Q40 and Q80 per person, depending upon the size of your group. On the trip, you'll see a wide range of bird fauna, as well as the chance to see caiman and iguanas in the wild. For more information, ask your hotel.

About 7km (4⅓ miles) east of Reserva Natural de Monterrico.

Reserva Natural de Monterrico (Monterrico Nature Reserve) ★   Sometimes referred to as the Biotopo Monterrico–Hawaii, this protected area covers some 28 sq. km (11 sq. miles), more than 70% of which are aquatic, including mangroves, canals, or estuaries. The reserve is home to a wide range of fauna, which are best seen by taking a boat tour through the canals. The visitor center on Calle Principal provides basic information and can arrange for a guide. All of the local hotels can arrange a boat tour through the reserve. Nighttime tours to watch the turtles lay their eggs, generally between July and October, are also available.

Visitor center on Calle Principal, just east of the village center. *©* **502/7885-0688.** Admission Q10. Daily 8am–5pm.

Tortuguerio Monterrico ★★   The main purpose of this facility is to protect and release turtle hatchlings. Volunteers collect turtle eggs just after nesting to save them from poachers and natural predators. They then care for them and release them to

ACCOMMODATIONS ■
Café del Sol **4**
Dos Mundos
　Pacific Resort **12**
Dulce y Salado **13**
Hotel Atelie del Mar **3**
Hotel Pez de Oro **10**
Hotel Utz Tzaba **1**
Johnny's Place **9**

DINING ◆
Hotel El Kaiman **7**
Johnny's Place **9**
Taberna El Pelícano **8**

ATTRACTIONS ●
El Proyecto Linguistico
　Monterrico **2**
Parque Hawaii **14**
Reserva Natural de
　Monterrico **15**
Tortuguerio Monterrico **11**

NIGHTLIFE ★
El Animal Desconocido **6**
El Caracol **5**

sea once they've hatched, allowing a greater percentage of hatchlings to reach the sea. In addition to the turtle project, they raise and care for iguanas and caimans, have a short interpretive trail through the surrounding forest, and arrange boat tours through the area's mangrove canals.

A few blocks east of Calle Principal. Admission Q10; Q30 with a 45-min. guided tour. Daily 8am–5pm.

Where to Stay
EXPENSIVE

Dos Mundos Pacific Resort ★★　This hotel has brought a touch of class and plush comfort to Monterrico. All of the individual bungalows feature thatch roofs and high ceilings, Mexican tile floors, hand-painted sinks, and luscious rainwater shower heads. All have a private veranda or patio, some of which are quite large. There are pools, one in the center of the complex, and the other fronting the beach. The restaurant, like so many in the area due to its high concentration of Italian expats, specializes in Italian cuisine, and is quite good. These folks take particular care in keeping the beach right in front of the hotel clean of detritus and debris—a nice touch.

On the beach, about a half-mile east of Calle Principal. ©/fax **502/7848-1407.** www.dosmundos pacific.com. 14 units. $98–$120 double. AE, DC, MC, V. **Amenities:** Restaurant; bar; 2 outdoor pools. *In room:* A/C, no phone, free Wi-Fi.

MODERATE

In addition to the place listed below, the **Hotel Utz Tzaba** (© **502/5318-9452;** www.utz-tzaba.com) is another good beachfront option, a few miles west of Monterrico, while **Hotel Atelie del Mar** (© **502/5752-5528;** hotelateliedelmar.com) is a pretty, well-run spot just across from the beach, with a large, welcoming pool, and quiet, relaxed vibe.

Hotel Isleta de Gaia ★★   Located on the far eastern end of the country close to the El Salvador border, this is a very isolated beach getaway. The piece of coastline that hosts the hotel is only reachable by boat after crossing the Chiquimula lagoon, hence they call themselves an island. The thatch-roof bungalows are some of the best designed, decorated, and equipped resort rooms to be found on the coast. Most are simple, single-story units good for a couple or small family, although there are also a few two-story suites, that can hold up to six people. If you're looking for a semi-luxurious and isolated beach vacation in this neck of the woods, this is an excellent choice.

Las Lisas. ©/fax **502/7885-0044.** www.isleta-de-gaia.com. 12 units. $70–$77 bungalow; $129 2-floor bungalow; $162 VIP bungalow. AE, DC, MC, V. **Amenities:** Restaurant; bar; outdoor pool; watersports equipment rental. *In room:* No phone, free Wi-Fi.

Hotel Pez de Oro ★   Although the hotel lacks any major amenities, the individual bungalows are cozy and atmospheric. The spacious bungalows feature high thatch roofs, tile or polished and painted concrete floors, overhead ceiling fans, and carved-wood furniture. Each comes with a private balcony or porch. My favorite is no. 13, which is set on raised stilts, and has a good view of the ocean and more breeze thanks to the elevation.

On the beach, about 3 blocks east of the Calle Principal. © **502/5232-9534** or 2368-3684 for reservations in Guatemala City. www.pezdeoro.com. 18 units. $50–$60 double. These are weekend rack rates, including tax. Rates lower midweek; slightly higher during peak periods. No credit cards. **Amenities:** Restaurant; bar; 2 small outdoor pools. *In room:* No phone.

INEXPENSIVE

In addition to the place listed below, two other good choices are **Café del Sol,** on the beach about 2 blocks west of Calle Principal (© **502/5810-0821;** www.cafe-del-sol.com); and **Dulce y Salado,** on the beach about 500 yards east of Calle Principal (© **502/4154-0252;** www.dulceysaladoguatemala.com).

Johnny's Place   One of the most popular places in Monterrico, this Canadian-owned joint has a variety of accommodations including dorm rooms, rustic two-bedroom bungalows, and a semi-luxurious three-bedroom "villa." The bungalows are the most common option, and feature polished concrete floors, concrete block walls, and a large, screened-in common area with basic kitchenette. The wood-frame beds all come with mosquito netting. The best rooms in the house are found in the villa, with air-conditioning, television, and a hot-water shower—the rest of the rooms have cold-water showers. Everything here is pretty worn and pretty rustic. There are four small, mostly shallow, pools spread around the sandy grounds. A thatch-roof *palapa* on the beach is equipped with a line of hammocks, and the hotel's beach volleyball court often has a pickup game going.

On the beach, about 2 blocks east of the Calle Principal. ✆ **502/4170-8345** or 5812-0409. www.monterrico-guatemala.com/johnnys-place.htm. 12 units, 1 dorm. $6 dorm bed; $25–$50 double room; $63 2-bedroom bungalow; $120 villa. These are weekend rack rates; rates lower midweek, slightly higher during peak periods. AE, DC, MC, V. **Amenities:** Restaurant; bar; 4 small outdoor pools. *In room:* No phone.

Where to Dine

In addition to the place listed below, the restaurants at aforementioned **Dos Mundos Pacific Resort, Hotel Pez de Oro,** and **Dulce y Salado** all have respectable Italian fare, while the restaurant at **Johnny's Place** serves up good American bar food mixed with Mexican and Italian options. For Guatemalan cooking and simple seafood, try any of the *comedores* on the main road leading toward the beach.

Taberna El Pelícano ★ 🏠 INTERNATIONAL/SEAFOOD   This is easily the best and most interesting restaurant in Monterrico. The menu is longer and more creative than anything else in town, and features a variety of pastas, entrees, vegetarian dishes (including an eggplant "steak"), desserts, and a list of daily specials. A small garden fronting the wooden tables hosts a fountain and a pair of large, almost tame, pelicans, the restaurant's namesake mascots.

Across from Johnny's. ✆ **502/5584-2400.** Main courses Q60–Q160. MC, V (5% surcharge). Wed–Sat noon–2pm and 5–10pm; Sun noon–3pm.

Monterrico After Dark

Monterrico is a mellow beach town, but things do pick up on Friday and Saturday nights. The most consistently popular bars in town are on or around Calle Principal, and include **El Caracol, El Animal Desconocido ★**, and **Johnny's Place** (see above). On most Saturday evenings, the **Hotel El Kaiman** has a raging disco.

PUERTO SAN JOSE

108km (67 miles) S of Guatemala City; 52km (32 miles) S of Escuintla

Puerto San José is the quickest and easiest beach to reach from Guatemala City or Antigua, and therefore it's also the most popular and developed. Still, the beach and its chaotic downtown hold little appeal for most foreign visitors. Puerto San José was once Guatemala's principal industrial and trade port, but that role has been entirely taken over by Puerto Quetzal, a few miles to the east. Perhaps the greatest draw to Puerto San José and vicinity is the ripe fishing grounds found just offshore. This area is developing a reputation as a major destination for **sportfishing,** with record numbers of marlin and sailfish being raised.

The beach right in front of Puerto San José is particularly unappealing. The best beach in the area is **Chulamar,** several miles to the west, where you'll find the Villas del Pacífico resort (below). Just east of Puerto San José is the beachfront residential community of **Likin,** and just beyond that the beach towns of **Puerto Quetzal** and **Iztapa.**

Essentials

GETTING THERE

BY BUS   **Transportes Esmeralda** (℃ **502/2471-0327**) buses leave for Puerto San José roughly every half-hour between 6am and 9pm from Guatemala City's main Terminal de Autobuses in Zona 4. The fare is Q20. The ride takes about 2 hours each way. Return buses follow roughly the same schedule.

BY CAR   If you're coming by car, head south out of Guatemala City on CA-9, the Pacific Coast Highway, toward Escuintla. From Escuintla it's a straight shot on a paved highway to Puerto Quetzal, where the highway ends. Follow the signs and flow of traffic for the last few miles to Puerto San José. The drive takes about 90 minutes, not including Guatemala City traffic.

GETTING AROUND

Taxis and tuk tuks are plentiful around Puerto San José, and most rides cost just Q10 to Q15. You can walk around the small downtown area, but it's a bit seedy, and most of the hotels listed here are quite a bit outside of the downtown hub.

ORIENTATION

Puerto San José is busy and chaotic, especially considering its size. Several banks, pharmacies, Internet cafes, and *comedores* can be found in the downtown area, which is only about 6 blocks long by 4 blocks wide. The closest modern hospital, **Hospital Génesis,** 3a Av. 2-68, Zona 1 (℃ **502/788-0187**), is located in Escuintla. If you need to contact the local police, dial ℃ **502/7881-1333.**

Fun On & Off the Beach

As I said above, the beach here is rather unappealing. In fact, the beach is separated from the town by a broad canal. Small boats will take you across the canal throughout the day for around Q5. If you want to do some swimming or just hang on the beach, you're better off heading west out of town to the nearby beach of **Chulamar.**

If you're looking to try your hand at landing a sailfish, marlin, or mahimahi, check in at the **Marina Pez Vela** (℃ **502/2379-5778;** www.marinaguate.com) which, in addition to serving as the cruise ship terminal, is also home to the area's main fishing fleet. You can ask around the docks for a boat and captain. If you prefer to line things up in advance, I recommend two dedicated fishing lodges below, or you can contact

---

 Party Time

The town hosts rowdy *fiestas* in honor of the city's Patron Saint, San José (Saint Joseph) from March 16 to March 22, when hotels are packed with revelers, and a town fair and carnival takes over the area. Live concerts, carnival rides and games, and scores of food booths and souvenir stands are part of the festivities.

the **Great Sailfishing Company** (© **877/763-0851** in the U.S. and Canada, or 502/7832-1991; www.greatsailfishing.com) or **Parlama Sport Fishing ★** (© **502/ 5704-4254;** www.parlama.com). Both of these operations run day trips for folks staying in this area, as well as in Antigua or Guatemala City. Rates run around $400 to $1,200 per day, depending on the type of boat and number of people fishing. The best fishing season runs from November to May, when the sails are plentiful and the seas relatively calm. However, locals swear that the fishing is superb year-round.

Where to Stay & Dine

Of the hotels listed below, only Hotel Martita is actually *in* Puerto San José. The others are several miles outside of the city. I've yet to find a restaurant of note in Puerto San José, and most folks, myself included, are content to dine at the various hotel restaurants.

If you want a beachfront hotel, right in Puerto San José, that's very reasonable and reasonably clean and well kept, check out **Posada Quetzal** (© **502/7832-9858;** www.posadadelquetzal.com).

VERY EXPENSIVE

Hotel Soleil Pacífico ☺   This large, all-inclusive resort hotel is the best option right in Puerto San José, and it's equally sought after by Guatemalan weekenders and international sportfishers. The rooms have all the basic amenities you need, contemporary decor, firm beds, and plenty of space. All have a private balcony or patio, although none have ocean views. The rooms are set back from the beach, which is reached by a broad, arching pedestrian bridge over a mangrove canal. There is a mix of room types with various suites and deluxe suites, all of which are really family units with more sleeping options and often a full kitchenette. The hotel's main pool is very large, and on weekends and holidays there's a nightly cabaret-style show in their massive open-air amphitheater, which is followed by a lively disco. Meals at the property restaurant are adequate, but the best thing about eating here is the ocean view from the second-floor *mirador.*

Chulamar. © **502/7879-3131.** Fax 502/7930-3935. www.gruposoleil.com. 128 units. $145 per person; $280–$420 per person in a suite. Rates are all-inclusive. These are weekend rates. Rates lower midweek; slightly higher during peak periods. AE, DC, MC, V. **Amenities:** 2 restaurants; 3 bars; children's program; 2 outdoor pools; watersports equipment. *In room:* A/C, TV, hair dryer.

Pacific Fins ★★   This place boasts the plushest accommodations, and the best food, service, boats, and gear on Guatemala's Pacific coast. My only complaint is that the location lacks beach access, and that means you're rather confined to the hotel compound when not out on the water. Still, most fishermen and visitors here spend a very large part of their waking hours out on the sea. When not out on the waves, you can entertain yourself with in-room amenities such as large flatscreen televisions. There's free Wi-Fi throughout the complex, as well as a couple of complimentary computers for guest use, and free international phone calls with their VoIP connection.

Iztapa. ℂ **888/700-3467** in the U.S. or Canada, or 502/7881-4788 in Guatemala. www.pacificfins.com. 10 units. $2,650–$4,900 per person for a 3-day/4-night package. The wide range in prices are dependent upon group size. Rates include round-trip transportation from Guatemala City, all meals and drinks, full-day fishing, and all tackle. Lower rates available in the off season. AE, DC, MC, V. **Amenities:** Restaurant; bar; Jacuzzi; outdoor pool. *In room:* A/C, TV, free Wi-Fi.

Sailfish Bay Lodge ★   If you're coming to this area to fish, this dedicated fishing lodge has an enviable location on the ocean side of the canal just outside of the inlet and harbor of Iztapa. The accommodations are modern and comfortable, and the focus on fishing is apparent. In fact, all of the tours and packages offered here are for anglers, and the fishing starts early and is taken seriously. Still, when you're not on the water, there's plenty to enjoy at this plush beachfront resort, which happens to front one of the country's top surf breaks. If you want to enjoy the waves without riding them, the pool, Jacuzzi, restaurant, and bar are all set on the edge of the beach with excellent views of the water.

Iztapa. ℂ **800/638-7405** in the U.S. or Canada, or 502/4079-5710 in Guatemala. www.sailfishbay.com. 8 units. $2,606 double for a 2-day/3-night package; $3,800 for a 3-day/4-night package. Prices per person. Rates include round-trip transportation from Guatemala City, all meals and drinks, full-day fishing, and all tackle. Lower rates available in the off season. AE, DC, MC, V. **Amenities:** Restaurant; bar; Jacuzzi; outdoor pool. *In room:* A/C, TV.

MODERATE
Hotel Martita 🏄   This modern, downtown hotel is your best bet in this price range, and a good option for folks here just for the fishing. This two-story place has the cleanest and most comfortable rooms in Puerto San José, and truly feels like an oasis in the midst of the clutter and clamor of this busy port town. There's a popular pool in the center of the complex, which is reserved for hotel guests, while another pool is open daily to locals and those staying at other hotels. You'll find this place just beside the train tracks that head toward the sea.

Av. de Comercio. ℂ **502/7888-4848** at the hotel, or 2366-9492 in Guatemala City. Fax 502/7888-4846. www.hotelmartita.com. 38 units. $75 double. Rates include breakfast buffet. These are weekend rates. Rates lower midweek; slightly higher during peak periods. AE, DC, MC, V. **Amenities:** Restaurant; bar; 2 midsize pools, each w/children's pool. *In room:* A/C, TV.

RETALHULEU

192km (119 miles) W of Guatemala City; 58km (36 miles) S of Quetzaltenango; 133km (83 miles) W of Escuintla

For some inexplicable reason, the denizens of Retalhuleu have dubbed their city the "Capital of the World," which is more than a bit presumptuous. Founded in 1877, **Reu,** as it's commonly known, *is* the capital of Suchitepéquez, a rich and important

Tongue Twister

> Retalhuleu is a bit of a tongue twister, even for native Guatemalans. This is probably why it's almost universally called Reu, which is pronounced "Reh-ooh."

agricultural region. It also makes a reasonable base for exploring some nearby archaeological sites, a couple of beaches, and IRTRA, Guatemala's large amusement and theme park complex.

The city is compact, with a pretty colonial-era church and active central plaza. **Takalik Abaj ★★**, an important archaeological site, is just 30km (18 miles) from the city center, and several other popular sites are just outside the easily reachable town of **Santa Lucía Cotzumalguapa ★** (see below).

Essentials

GETTING THERE

BY BUS Retalhuleu is serviced by regular bus service between Guatemala City and the Mexican border at Tecún Umán, as well as from Quetzaltenango. From Guatemala City, **Transportes Fortaleza del Sur** (✆ 502/5900-8026; www.fds tours.com) buses leave roughly every 30 minutes between 2am and 7pm from 19 Calle 8-70, Zona 1. The one-way trip takes around 6 hours and costs Q50. Return buses run at the same frequency during roughly the same hours. The Reu bus station is located on the northern outskirts of town.

BY CAR Retalhuleu can be reached either from Quetzaltenango or Escuintla. If you're coming from Guatemala City, the quickest route is to take CA-9, the Pacific Coast Highway, to Escuintla, and from there head west on CA-2, the coastal highway, toward Mazatenango and the Mexican border. If you're driving from Quetzaltenango, head south via Zunil to Reu.

GETTING AROUND

You can easily walk the entire downtown area of Retalhuleu. If you're too tired, or night has fallen, taxis and tuk tuks are plentiful, and most rides cost just Q10 to Q15. A trip to Xocomil or Xetulul should run around Q50. If you're having trouble flagging down a cab, have your hotel call you one.

ORIENTATION

Retalhuleu is about 4km (2½ miles) south of the coastal highway. Upon entering you're greeted by a beautiful avenue—*la calzada de las palmas*—lined with tall Royal palm trees. The entire city is centered around its popular central plaza, and just about every hotel, restaurant, attraction, and service is within a 2-block radius of this plaza.

FAST FACTS There are several banks within a block of the central plaza, including **Banco G&T Continental** (✆ 502/7771-3849) and **Banco Industrial** (✆ 502/7771-0684). The **post office** (✆ 502/7771-0909) fronts the central plaza. There are also a host of Internet cafes around Reu. One of the best, **Café Internet Antigua** (✆ 502/7771-4421), has two separate storefronts in downtown.

The **Hospital Nacional de Retalhuleu** (✆ 502/7771-0116) is located on Boulevard Centenario 3a Avenida, Zona 2.

What to See & Do

My favorite thing to do in Reu is to grab a seat somewhere on the central plaza and people-watch. If you're not into sitting still, you can tour the church. Like the colonial-era churches around Guatemala, **La Iglesia de San Antonio de Padua** has undergone successive rebuilding following various earthquakes. Nonetheless, it's a pretty and well-kept church with a beautiful whitewashed facade.

The city's main attraction, **Museo de Arqueología y Etnología** (© 502/7771-0557), is quite small and relatively unimpressive. Located cater-cornered to the church and facing the central plaza, the museum has a small collection of ceramic, stone, jade, and obsidian artifacts, as well as a finely done scale model of the city's church. There's also a room with historical photographs. The museum is open Tuesday through Saturday from 8:30am to 5pm, Sunday 9am to 12:30pm. Admission is Q10.

If you want to do any tours in the area, I recommend you contact **Reuxtreme ★★** (© 502/5202-8180; www.reuxtreme.com). These folks offer a whole host of adventure, soft-adventure, and cultural tour options. Their strong suit is mountain biking, hiking, kayaking, and canopy tour adventures, but they can also hook you up with a guided tour to **Takalik Abaj** (see below), or a dude-ranch type experience on a local cattle farm.

Where to Stay & Dine

If the hotels listed below are full, try **Hotel Astor,** 5ta Calle 4-60, Zona 1 (© 502/7771-2559; hotelastor@intelnett.com). If you want to eat someplace beside the Don José, try **Restaurante La Luna** (© 502/7771-0194), which fronts the plaza.

MODERATE

Hotel Posada de Don José ★ If you end up spending the night in Retalhuleu, this should be your first choice. The two-story downtown hotel is built around a relaxing central courtyard and pool. The rooms are well kept and comfortable, although the decor and furnishings are dated. Some rooms come with a small balcony overlooking the street, which may be a plus or minus, depending upon whether you're more interested in local character or peace and quiet. There are a handful of suites, which come with separate sitting areas. The restaurant here is one of the best and most dependable in town.

5ta Calle 3-67, Zona 1. © **502/7771-0180.** Fax 502/7771-4176. www.hotelposadadedonjose.com. 23 units. $60 double; $70 suite. Rates include breakfast and taxes. AE, DC, MC, V. **Amenities:** Restaurant; bar; small outdoor pool; room service. In room: A/C, TV, hair dryer.

INEXPENSIVE

Hostal Casa Santa Maria Run by the folks at **Reuxtreme** (see above), this cozy little hotel is located in a converted old downtown home. The rooms are simply done, but most have high ceilings and queen-size beds. There's no restaurant here, but breakfasts and snacks are served. There's a tiny, postage stamp–size pool in one of the interior courtyards. Service is friendly, and the excellent in-house tour agency is a real plus.

4ta Calle 4-23, Zona 1. © **502/7771-6136.** www.hostalcasasantamaria.com. 6 units. $32–$50 double. Rates include continental breakfast Mon–Fri. V. **Amenities:** Tiny outdoor pool; free Wi-Fi. In room: A/C, TV, no phone.

Retalhuleu After Dark

There is very little in the way of nightlife in Reu.

Side Trips from Retalhuleu

Retalhuleu serves as an excellent gateway to the following attractions. Alternately, you can visit any of these as a day trip out of Quetzaltenango, or as part of a route connecting Quetzaltenango to the Pacific beaches or Guatemala City.

RUINS OF TAKALIK ABAJ ★★

This remarkable and often neglected Maya site dates from the pre-Classic period. Its name translates to "Standing Stone" in the modern K'iche dialect, and is often referred to as Abaj Takalik. So far, more than 85 structures built around some dozen different plazas have been discovered. Takalik Abaj contains a wealth of carved stone sculptures and monuments, many showing clear influence of the Mexican Olmec tribes combined with prototypical and archaic Maya traits. It's even speculated that Olmec and Maya peoples may have coexisted at this site. Takalik Abaj thrived as a ceremonial and trade center from the 8th century B.C. through the 2nd century A.D., with close ties to Kaminaljuyú (present day Guatemala City). There are various well-preserved stelae here, as well as anthropomorphic carved stones. Be sure to check out the unique *barrigón,* or "fat-bellied," sculptures. One of the more remarkable finds at Takalik Abaj is the unlooted grave of an early Maya king who was buried in full regalia. There's also an early ball court, which is built in an uncommon "T" shape. However, the ball court has been reburied to protect it from the elements.

Takalik Abaj also contains a minizoo of sorts, with allegedly rescued and rehabilitating animals either found wounded or saved from poor living conditions, although I'm not sure I find their current digs all that appealing.

The archaeological site is open daily from 7am to 5pm, and admission is Q50. A guide is included with the price of admission and will accompany your group no matter what size. These guides are volunteers, and I recommend you leave a little tip of about Q8 to Q16 per person, even if he speaks only rudimentary English. All of the signage here is in Spanish only.

It's possible, yet complicated, to get to Takalik Abaj by public transportation. Your best bet is to either sign on for a guided tour or hire a taxi. Any hotel in town (or in Quetzaltenango, for that matter), can arrange a half-day tour for around Q120 to Q240. The folks at **Takalik Maya Lodge** (see below) offer a day tour that visits the archaeological site and their coffee plantation, and also includes lunch, for Q240 per person. If you're driving, head west out of Reu on CA-2 toward the Mexican border to the town of El Astinal. From here there are signs directly to the site.

Where to Stay

Takalik Maya Lodge ★　If you want to stay close to Takalik Abaj, you'll definitely want to check out this lodge. Taking over parts of a working coffee plantation that's also directly part of the archaeological site, this is one of the more unique hotels in Guatemala. The lodge has two types of rooms, those in the old coffee plantation, or El Paseo del Café Estancia, and Kacike Maya. I prefer the latter. The two large suites here are very liberal interpretations of the rooms previously occupied by Maya royalty. In either case, the rooms are comfortable, with firm beds and tasteful decor, and minimal amenities. There's also a restaurant and a swimming pool, and in addition to touring the Maya ruins and coffee plantation, activity options include horseback riding, hiking, and bird-watching. The hotel has dedicated 10 hectares (25 acres) of local forest and archeological sites as part of its own private reserve, and has another 11 hectares under regeneration, turning cleared farmland back into wild forest. They are also verified as part of the Rainforest Alliance's Sustainable Trip program.

Takalik Abaj Archaeological Park, Terrace 9. ℭ **502/2334-7693** or 4055-9831. www.takalik.com. 10 units. $38 per person in El Paseo del Café Estancia; $58 per person in Kacike Maya. Rates include breakfast and taxes. AE, DC, MC, V. **Amenities:** Restaurant; bar; small pool. *In room:* No phone.

GUATEMALA'S DISNEYLAND

Xocomil and Xetulul—the first a water-themed park, the latter similar to Disney's Epcot Center–are two of the country's biggest theme parks. If you're traveling with children and the theme parks are your primary destination, you might want to stay at either **La Ranchería,** which has spacious, spread-out bungalows, or the **Palajuno,** which continues the Epcot-like theme with units taking their design and decor from various tropical countries around the world. Both of these can be booked directly through **IRTRA** (ℭ **502/2423-9000**). Both theme parks, as well as the IRTRA hotels, are located about 12km (7½ miles) north of Retalhuleu, on the road to Quetzaltenango.

Xetulul ★ ☺   The local version of Epcot, this park is divided into several areas devoted to the architecture of the Maya world, plus those devoted to countries such as Guatemala, France, Italy, and Spain. Amusement park rides and adventures are interspersed with, or integrated into, miniature versions of a Maya temple, a Guatemalan colonial-era town, el Palazzio Vecchio, and the Moulin Rouge. The park is remarkably well done and admirably maintained. The re-creation of the Trevi fountain is particularly impressive.

ℭ **502/7722-9450.** Admission $25 adults; $13 children, students, and seniors. Thurs–Sun and major holidays 10am–6pm.

Xocomil ★★ ☺   This is a large and well-designed water park featuring several high, fast, and exhilarating water slides, two wave pools, a "lazy river" float ride, several children's play pools, and everything else you might want or expect from a water park. I especially like some of the local touches, including the re-creations of Maya temples that are integrated into the rides and surroundings. I also like the Nido de Serpientes, a complex of seven simultaneous and intertwined water slides that let out into one common pool. There are several restaurants and snack stands on-site, which is a good thing, since the hot and humid clime of this area is quite conducive to a full day here.

ℭ **502/7729-4000.** Admission Q80 adults; Q50 children, students, and seniors. Thurs–Sun, plus major holidays, 9am–5pm.

THE COASTAL HIGHWAY & SANTA LUCÍA COTZUMALGUAPA ★

As you drive from Retalhuleu toward Guatemala City or the Pacific beaches, you'll pass by the town of Santa Lucía Cotzumalguapa. While there's not much in town, there are a couple of interesting archaeological sites nearby, and one very good museum just outside of town. Perhaps feeling the pressure of Reu's naming itself "the Capital of the World," Santa Lucía calls itself "the World Capital of Happiness." However, Santa Lucía may have more of a leg to stand on. My Guatemalan friends

Big Trees

If you're driving along the road between Retalhuleu and Escuintla, keep an eye out for the many giant ceiba trees that dot the roadside, particularly around Santa Lucía. Revered by the ancient Maya, these towering trees have long, broad, and smooth trunks, and some of the specimens you'll see along this highway are more than 200 years old.

say the town will throw a party at the drop of a hat, and quite often you'll find marimba bands playing at night in the town's central plaza.

If you decide to stay in Santa Lucía, your first choice should be the **Hotel Santiaguito** (📞 **502/7882-5435**). Located on the old Carretera al Pacifico at Km 90.4, this miniresort has a popular restaurant, spacious modern rooms, and a large, refreshing pool.

Note: Several years ago a beltway, or *circumvalación,* was built to bypass the town of Santa Lucía Cotzumalguapa. If you want to visit any of the sites listed below or the hotel mentioned above, you'll want to get off the coastal highway and head toward the center of town.

Finca el Baúl   Even farther outside of the town sits Finca el Baúl. Set on a high hill in the midst of a working sugar-cane plantation, this place remains an active site of Maya ritual and worship. Still believing the site sacred, local Maya often come to a hilltop clearing here to make offerings, light candles, and perform ceremonies. Regardless of whether or not there are any practitioners on hand, you can visit the small museum and see a collection of the carved stones and stelae found on the surrounding grounds. The large stones have been carved into anthropomorphic images of crocodiles, serpents, and Maya gods. It's sort of a misnomer to call this collection a museum, as most are displayed simply in a broad open-air cleared area.

About 6km (4 miles) north of Santa Lucía. Free admission. Mon–Fri 8am–4pm; Sat 8am–1pm. Hilltop prayer site located off the main road to the Finca, about 2.5km (1½ miles) before the museum. Your best bet for getting here is to hire a taxi for around Q120 round-trip with stops in Bilbao and prayer site, as well as time to explore.

Las Piedras (Bilbao Stones)   Just on the northern edge of Santa Lucía sits a collection of massive carved stones. The largest and most impressive of these, Monument 21, has been copied in fiberglass and is on display at the **Museo de Cultura Cotzumalguapa** (below). The others have been severely damaged by time, the elements, and vandals. Although it's a short and easy walk from town, you should only visit this site with a reputable guide and after checking on the current safety status, as there have been attacks on tourists here.

Just north of downtown. Free admission. There are no official operating hours.

Museo de Cultura Cotzumalguapa (Cotzumalguapa Cultural Museum) ★
Set just a few blocks inland from the highway on the eastern edge of town, this small museum houses an interesting collection of stelae and stone carvings gathered from nearby archaeological sites, including **Bilbao** (see above). The museum features an excellent replica of the massive carved anthropomorphic stone, Monument 21, from Bilbao. There are also a half-dozen or so carved stelae on the grounds outside the

museum. Some of these are originals, while others are copies. It will only take you around 20 to 30 minutes to tour the museum.

The ticket booth and administration are found in a small house just beyond the museum. You may have to wake up, or shout to find, the caretaker, who will then collect your admission. The museum and its collection are part of the **Finca Las Ilusiones,** a former sugar-cane estate. If you ask politely, the caretaker may give you a quick tour of the old church across from the museum and the large manor or estate house next door.

ⓒ **502/5736-0403.** Admission Q10. Daily 7am–noon and 2–4pm.

FAST FACTS

FAST FACTS: GUATEMALA

Area Codes There are no regional area codes in Guatemala. Most phone numbers are eight digits. However, there are some anomalies. Some toll-free or public service numbers may be three-, four-, or six-digit numbers.

Business Hours Banks are usually open Monday through Friday from 9am to 4pm, although many have begun to offer extended hours. Offices are open Monday through Friday from 8am to 5pm (many close for 1 hr. at lunch). Stores are generally open Monday through Saturday from 9am to 6pm (many close for 1 hr. at lunch). Stores in modern malls generally stay open until 8 or 9pm and don't close for lunch. Most bars are open until 1 or 2am.

Cellphones (Mobile Phones) See "Staying Connected," p. 58.

Drinking Laws The legal drinking age in Guatemala is 18, although it's almost never enforced. Liquor, everything from beer to hard spirits, is sold in specific liquor stores, as well as at most supermarkets and even convenience stores.

Driving Rules See "Getting There & Getting Around," p. 36.

Electricity Guatemala uses standard U.S.-style two- and three-prong electric outlets with 110-volt AC current. Wherever you go, bring a **connection kit** of the right power and phone adapters, a spare phone cord, and a spare Ethernet network cable—or find out whether your hotel supplies them to guests.

Embassies & Consulates All major consulates and embassies, where present, are in Guatemala City. **Canada,** 13a Calle 8-44, Zona 10 (© 502/ 2365-1250; www.canadainternational.gc.ca); **United Kingdom,** Avenida de la Reforma and 16a Calle, Torre Internacional, Zona 10 (© 502/2380-7300; www.ukinguatemala.fco.gov.uk); and the **United States,** Av. de la Reforma 7-01, Zona 10 (© 502/2326-4000; http://guatemala.usembassy.gov).

Emergencies In case of any emergency, dial © **1500** from anywhere in Guatemala. This will connect you to **Asistur,** which will have a bilingual operator, who in turn can put you in contact with the police, fire department, or ambulance service, as necessary. Alternately, you can dial © **110** for the National Police; and © **125** for the Red Cross (Cruz Roja, in Spanish). Moreover, © **911** works as an emergency number from most phones in Guatemala.

Gasoline (Petrol) Gasoline, or *gasolina* in Spanish, is sold as *normal* and *premium;* both are unleaded. Premium is just higher octane. Diesel is available at almost every gas station as well. Most rental cars run on premium, but always ask your rental agent what type of gas your car takes. Gas stations are widely available along the highways, and in all major cities, towns, and tourist destinations. When going off to remote places, try to leave with a full tank of gas because gas stations can be harder to find. At press time, premium cost Q28 per gallon.

Holidays   Official holidays in Guatemala include **January 1** (New Year's Day), Thursday and Friday of Holy Week, **June 30** (Armed Forces Day), **July 1** (Day of Celebration), **August 15** (Virgen de la Asunción), **September 15** (Independence Day), **October 20** (Commemoration of the 1944 Revolution), **November 1** (All Saints' Day), **December 24** and **25** (Christmas), and **December 31** (New Year's Eve).

For more information on holidays see "Guatemala Calendar of Events," in chapter 3.

Hospitals   The country's best hospitals are in Guatemala City. **Hospital Centro Médico,** 6a Av. 3-47, Zona 10 (© 502/2279-4949; www.centromedico.com.gt), is an excellent private hospital, with English-speaking doctors on staff.

Insurance   **Medical Insurance**   For foreign travel, most U.S. health plans (including Medicare and Medicaid) do not provide coverage, and the ones that do often require you to pay for services upfront and reimburse you only after you return home.

As a safety net, you may want to buy travel medical insurance, particularly if you're traveling to a remote or high-risk area where emergency evacuation might be necessary. If you require additional medical insurance, try **MEDEX Assistance** (© 410/453-6300; www.medexassist.com) or **Travel Assistance International** (© 800/821-2828; www.travelassistance.com; for general information on services, call the company's **Worldwide Assistance Services, Inc.,** at © 800/777-8710).

Canadians should check with their provincial health plan offices or call **Health Canada** (© 866/225-0709; www.hc-sc.gc.ca) to find out the extent of their coverage and what documentation and receipts they must take home in case they are treated overseas.

Travelers from the U.K. should carry their European Health Insurance Card (EHIC), which replaced the E111 form as proof of entitlement to free/reduced cost medical treatment abroad (© 0845/606-2030; www.ehic.org.uk). Note, however, that the EHIC only covers "necessary medical treatment," and for repatriation costs, lost money, baggage, or cancellation, travel insurance from a reputable company should always be sought (www.travelinsuranceweb.com).

Internet Access   Internet cafes are very common in all the major cities and tourist destinations around Guatemala. Rates run between Q4 and Q12 per hour.

Language   Spanish is the official language of Guatemala. English is spoken at most tourist hotels, restaurants, and attractions. Outside of the tourist orbit, English is not widely spoken, and some rudimentary Spanish will go a long way. Some 23 Mayan dialects are also widely spoken around the country. In many rural areas, many residents speak their local dialect as their primary language, and a certain segment of the population may speak little or no Spanish.

Legal Aid   If you need legal help, your best bet is to first contact your local embassy or consulate. See "Embassies & Consulates" above for contact details. Alternately, you can ask at your hotel, or at a local tour agency that works frequently with foreign visitors.

Mail   A post office is called *correo* in Spanish. Most towns have a main *correo,* usually right near the central square. In addition, most hotels will post letters and postcards for you. It costs around Q7 to send a letter to the U.S. or Europe. Postcards to the same destinations cost Q5. However, it's best to send anything of any value via an established international courier service. **DHL,** 12a Calle 5-12, Zona 10 (© 502/2379-1111; www.dhl.com), and **Fed Ex,** 14a Calle 3-51, Zona 10 (© 1801/0033339 www.fedex.com), both have offices in Guatemala City, with nationwide coverage for pickup and delivery. DHL also has offices in Antigua and Panajachel.

Newspapers & Magazines   *La Prensa Libre* is the country's most highly regarded daily newspaper, with an outstanding investigative reporting staff. The lower-brow *Nuestro Diario* has the highest circulation. There are several other daily papers, including

Siglo XXI. There are currently no English-language newspapers. The free, monthly, English-language **Revue Magazine** (www.revuemag.com) is the most valuable information source for most tourists, with museum, art gallery, and theater listings. It is widely available at hotels and other tourist haunts around the country.

Passports   **For Residents of Australia**   Contact the **Australian Passport Information Service** at ✆ **131-232,** or visit www.passports.gov.au.

For Residents of Canada   Contact the central **Passport Office,** Department of Foreign Affairs and International Trade, Ottawa, ON K1A 0G3 (✆ **800/567-6868;** www.ppt.gc.ca).

For Residents of Ireland   Contact the **Passport Office,** Setanta Centre, Molesworth Street, Dublin 2 (✆ **01/671-1633;** www.foreignaffairs.gov.ie).

For Residents of New Zealand   Contact the **Passports Office,** Department of Internal Affairs, 47 Boulcott Street, Wellington, 6011 (✆ **0800/225-050** in New Zealand or 04/474-8100; www.passports.govt.nz).

For Residents of the United Kingdom   Visit your nearest passport office, major post office, or travel agency or contact the **Identity and Passport Service (IPS),** 89 Eccleston Square, London, SW1V 1PN (✆ **0300/222-0000;** www.ips.gov.uk).

For Residents of the United States   To find your regional passport office, check the U.S. State Department website (http://travel.state.gov/passport) or call the **National Passport Information Center** (✆ **877/487-2778**) for automated information.

Police   In case of an emergency, dial ✆ **1500** from anywhere in Guatemala. This will connect you to a bilingual operator at Asistur who can put you in contact with the police, fire department, or ambulance service. Dial ✆ **110** or **120** for the **National Police,** and ✆ **125** for the **Red Cross** (**Cruz Roja,** in Spanish). As in the U.S., ✆ **911** works as an emergency number from most phones in Guatemala.

Smoking   While not as bad as most of Europe, a large number of Guatemalans smoke, and public smoking regulations and smoke-free zones have yet to take hold. Restaurants are required by law to have nonsmoking areas, but enforcement is often lax, air circulation poor, and the separation almost nonexistent. Bars, discos, and clubs, on the whole, are often very smoke-filled in Guatemala.

Taxes   There is a Q240 tax that must be paid upon departure. This is often included in your airline ticket price. Be sure to check in advance. If not, you will have to pay the fee in cash at the airport. There is an additional airport security fee of Q20.

A 12% IVA (value added) tax is tacked on to the purchase of all goods and services. An additional 10% tax, on top of the 12% IVA, is added to all hotel rooms and lodgings.

Telephones   **To call Guatemala:** If you're calling Guatemala from the United States:

1. Dial the international access code: 011.
2. Dial the country code 502.
3. Dial the number. The whole number you'd dial for a number in Guatemala would be 011-502-XXXX-XXXX.

To make international calls: To make international calls from Guatemala, first dial 00 and then the country code (U.S. or Canada 1, U.K. 44, Ireland 353, Australia 61, New Zealand 64). Next, dial the area code and number. For example, if you want to call the British Embassy in Washington, D.C., dial 00-1-202-588-7800.

Toll-free numbers: There's no hard and fast rule about toll-free numbers in Guatemala. Numbers beginning with 0800 and 800 are almost always toll-free. However, some toll-free numbers are anomalies. Three-, four-, and six-digit phone numbers are also often toll-free. Calling a 1-800 number in the U.S. from Guatemala is not toll-free. In fact, it costs the same as an overseas call.

Time   Guatemala is 6 hours behind Greenwich Mean Time, which is equivalent to Central Standard Time in the United States. Daylight saving time is observed by setting clocks ahead 1 hour from the last Sunday in March to the last Sunday in October.

Tipping   While there is a 12% IVA tax on all goods and services, none of this counts as a tip. In restaurants, a minimum tip of 10% is common and expected. Tip more if the service was exemplary. Taxi drivers do not expect, and are rarely given, a tip.

Toilets   Public restrooms are hard to come by in Guatemala. You must usually count on the generosity of some hotel or restaurant, or duck into a museum or other attraction. Although it's rare that a tourist would be denied the use of the facilities, you should always ask first.

Water   Drink only bottled water within Guatemala City and be especially careful to do so when traveling outside the capital, as waterborne diseases are very common in this country.

AIRLINE AND RENTAL WEBSITES

MAJOR AIRLINES

Aeroméxico
www.aeromexico.com

Air France
www.airfrance.com

Air New Zealand
www.airnewzealand.com

Alitalia
www.alitalia.com

American Airlines
www.aa.com

British Airways
www.british-airways.com

Continental Airlines
www.continental.com

Delta Air Lines
www.delta.com

Iberia Airlines
www.iberia.com

Japan Airlines
www.jal.co.jp

Korean Air
www.koreanair.com

Lan Airlines
www.lanchile.com

Lufthansa
www.lufthansa.com

Philippine Airlines
www.philippineairlines.com

Qantas Airways
www.qantas.com

South African Airways
www.flysaa.com

Swiss Air
www.swiss.com

TACA
www.taca.com

United Airlines
www.united.com

US Airways
www.usairways.com

CAR-RENTAL AGENCIES

Alamo
www.alamo.com

Avis
www.avis.com

Budget
www.budget.com

Dollar
www.dollar.com

Hertz
www.hertz.com

National
www.nationalcar.com

Thrifty
www.thrifty.com

MAJOR HOTEL & MOTEL CHAINS

Barceló
www.barcelo.com

Best Western International
www.bestwestern.com

Clarion Hotels
www.choicehotels.com

Crowne Plaza Hotels
www.ichotelsgroup.com/
crowneplaza

Holiday Inn
www.holidayinn.com

Howard Johnson
www.hojo.com

InterContinental Hotels & Resorts
www.ichotelsgroup.com

Radisson Hotels & Resorts
www.radisson.com

Westin Hotels & Resorts
www.starwoodhotels.com/westin

USEFUL TERMS & PHRASES

Spanish is the official language of Guatemala and the most widely spoken. In fact almost every Guatemalan speaks Spanish, although sometimes it's as a second language. Each of the country's 23 indigenous groups has its own language, and these groups comprise almost half of the country's population.

Around Lake Atitlán you'll find speakers of Ki'che (the largest language group, making up about 10% of the population), Cakchiquel, and Tz'utujil. Mam is spoken in the Cuchumatanes Mountains near the Mexican border, while the Alta Verapaz and Petén regions are home to many speakers of Kekchi. The Garífuna people (descendants of former slaves and Carib Indians) along the Caribbean coast have a language all their own. Many speak English as well.

Those who speak Spanish as their primary language, known as *ladinos,* are concentrated in urban areas, along the Pacific coast, and in the Petén.

Following the Peace Accords of 1996, Guatemala's constitution was amended to "recognize, respect, and promote" indigenous languages. Children now receive instruction in their native language in school, bilingual judges and interpreters staff courtrooms, and government employees use indigenous languages when providing social services at the community level.

Guatemalan Spanish is considered one of the most pure, in terms of clarity and pronunciation, to be found in the Americas. Compared to the Spanish spoken in Mexico and the Caribbean, Guatemalan Spanish tends to be more clearly enunciated and slightly slower. It feels almost languid in comparison to, say, Puerto Rican or Cuban Spanish. This is one of the reasons language schools are so popular throughout the country. Many language schools now offer classes in Mayan languages as well as Spanish, especially in the more remote regions of the country. For a list of these schools, see chapter 3.

Below is a list of common Spanish terms and phrases. A note on pronunciation: The Spanish letter *ñ* is pronounced *ny* as in "ca*ny*on." In Guatemala, when the letter *x* appears in words of Maya origin (like "Xela"), it's pronounced *sh* as in "*sh*ell."

BASIC VOCABULARY
English-Spanish Phrases

English	Spanish	Pronunciation
Hello	**Buenos días**	*bweh*-nohss *dee*-ahss
How are you?	**¿Cómo está usted?**	*koh*-moh ehss-*tah* oo-*stehd*

English	Spanish	Pronunciation
Very well	**Muy bien**	mwee byehn
Thank you	**Gracias**	*grah*-syahss
Goodbye	**Adiós**	ad-*dyohss*
Please	**Por favor**	pohr fah-*vohr*
Yes	**Sí**	see
No	**No**	noh
Excuse me (to get by someone)	**Perdóneme**	pehr-*doh*-neh-meh
Excuse me (to begin a question)	**Disculpe**	dees-*kool*-peh
Give me	**Deme**	*deh*-meh
Where is . . . ?	**¿Dónde está . . . ?**	*dohn*-deh ehss-*tah*
the station	**la estación**	la ehss-*tah*-syohn
the bus stop	**la parada**	la pah-*rah*-dah
a hotel	**un hotel**	oon oh-*tehl*
a restaurant	**un restaurante**	oon res-tow-*rahn*-teh
the toilet	**el servicio**	el ser-*vee*-syoh
a good doctor	**un buen médico**	oon bwehn *meh*-dee-coh
the road to . . .	**el camino a/hacia**	el cah-*mee*-noh ah/ *ah*-syah
To the right	**A la derecha**	ah lah deh-*reh*-chah
To the left	**A la izquierda**	ah lah ees-*kyehr*-dah
Straight ahead	**Adelante**	ah-deh-*lahn*-teh
I would like . . .	**Quiero . . .**	*kyeh*-roh
to eat	**comer**	ko-*mehr*
a room	**una habitación**	*oo*-nah ah-bee-tah-*syohn*
Do you have . . . ?	**¿Tiene usted . . . ?**	Tyeh-neh oo-*sted*
a book	**un libro**	oon *lee*-broh
a dictionary	**un diccionario**	oon deek-syoh-*nah*-ryoh
How much is it?	**¿Cuánto?**	*kwahn*-toh
The check	**La cuenta**	la *kwen*-tah
When?	**¿Cuándo?**	*kwan*-doh
What?	**¿Qué?**	keh
What time is it?	**¿Qué hora es?**	keh *oh*-rah ehss
Yesterday	**Ayer**	ah-*yehr*
Today	**Hoy**	oy
Tomorrow	**Mañana**	mah-*nyah*-nah
Good	**Bueno**	*Bweh*-noh
Bad	**Malo**	*Mah*-loh
Better (best)	**(Lo) Mejor**	(Loh) Meh-*hohr*
More	**Más**	Mahs
Less	**Menos**	*Meh*-nohs
No smoking	**Se prohibe fumar**	Seh proh-*ee*-beh foo-*mahr*

English	Spanish	Pronunciation
Postcard	**Tarjeta postal**	Tar-*heh*-tah poh-*stahl*
Insect repellent	**Repelente contra insectos**	Reh-peh-*lehn*-teh *cohn*-trah een-*sehk*-tohs
Breakfast	**Desayuno**	deh-sah-*yoo*-noh
Lunch	**Almuerzo**	ahl-*mwehr*-soh
Dinner	**Cena**	*seh*-nah
Do you speak English?	**¿Habla usted inglés?**	ah-blah oo-*stehd* een-*glehss*
Is there anyone here who speaks English?	**¿Hay alguien aquí que hable inglés?**	eye *ahl*-gyehn ah-*kee* keh ah-bleh een-*glehss*
I speak a little Spanish.	**Hablo un poco de español.**	ah-*bloh* oon *poh*-koh deh ehss-pah-*nyohl*
I don't understand Spanish very well.	**No (lo) entiendo muy bien el español.**	noh (loh) ehn-*tyehn*-do mwee byehn el ehss-pah-*nyohl*

MORE USEFUL PHRASES

English	French	Pronunciation
The meal is good.	**Me gusta la comida.**	Meh *goo*-stah lah koh-*mee*-dah
May I see your menu?	**¿Puedo ver el menú (la carta)?**	*Pweh*-doh vehr el meh-*noo* (lah *car*-tah)
The check, please.	**La cuenta, por favor.**	Lah *kwehn*-tah pohr fa-*borh*
What do I owe you?	**¿Cuánto le debo?**	*Kwahn*-toh leh *deh*-boh
What did you say?	**¿Mande?** (formal)	*Mahn*-deh
	¿Cómo? (informal)	*Koh*-moh
I want (to see) . . .	**Quiero (ver) . . .**	*kyeh*-roh (vehr)
a room	**un cuarto** or **una habitación**	oon *kwar*-toh, *oo*-nah ah-bee-tah-*syohn*
for two persons	**para dos personas**	*pah*-rah dohs pehr-*soh*-nahs
with (without) bathroom	**con (sin) baño**	kohn (seen) *bah*-nyoh
We are staying here only . . .	**Nos quedamos aquí solamente. . .**	Nohs keh-*dah*-mohs ah-*kee* soh-lah-*mehn*-teh
one night.	**una noche.**	*oo*-nah *noh*-cheh
one week.	**una semana.**	*oo*-nah seh-*mah*-nah
We are leaving . . .	**Partimos (Salimos) . . .**	Pahr-*tee*-mohs (Sah-*lee*-mohs)
tomorrow.	**mañana.**	mah-*nya*-nah
Do you accept . . . ?	**¿Acepta usted . . . ?**	Ah-*sehp*-tah oo-*sted*
credit cards?	tarjetas de crédito?	tahr-HEH-tahs deh KREH-dee-toh
bills?	billetes?	bee-YEH-tehs
coins?	monedas?	moh-NEH-dahs
Is there a laundromat . . . ?	**¿Hay una lavandería . . . ?**	Eye *oo*-nah lah-*bahn*-deh-*ree*-ah

Mayan Languages

1. TACANEC
2. KANJOBEL
3. SIPACAPENSE
4. AGUATECO
5. SACAPULTECO
6. USPANTECO
7. TZ'UTUJIL
8. POKOMAM

MEXICO

Lacandón

ITZÁ
Flores

Tikal

Belmopan

BELIZE

Sayaxché

Poptún

San Luis

MOPÁN

CARIBBEAN
SEA

Livingston

Puerto
Barrios

CHUJ

JACALTECO

POKOMAM

IXIL

Cobán

KEKCHI

El Estor

Lago
Izabal

POKOMCHI

MAM

K'ICHE

ACHI

ACHI

Lake
Atitlán

CAKCHIQUEL

Guatemala
City

Antigua

POKOMCHI

HONDURAS

Champerico

Escuintla

Monterrico

EL SALVADOR

PACIFIC
OCEAN

English	Spanish	Pronunciation
near here?	**cerca de aquí?**	*sehr*-kah deh ah-*kee*
Please send these clothes to the laundry.	**Hágame el favor de mandar esta ropa a la lavandería.**	*Ah*-gah-meh el fah-*bohr* deh mahn-*dahr* eh-stah *roh*-pah a lah lah-*bahn*-deh-*ree*-ah

MARKET TIPS

English	French	Pronunciation
Where is the craft / artisan market?	¿Donde Esta el mercado de artesanías?	*dohn*-deh eh-stah ehl mehr-*kah*-doh deh ahr-teh-*sah*-nee-ahs
That's beautiful. May I look at it?	**¡Eso es hermoso! ¿Puedo verlo?**	eh-soh ehs ehr-*moh*-soh *pweh*-doh *vehr*-loh
When is the market open?	¿Cuándo está abierto el mercado de granjeros?	*kwahn*-doh ehs-*tah* ah-*byehr*-toh ehl mehr-*kah*-doh deh grahn-*heh*-rohs

English	French	Pronunciation
Is that open every day of the week?	¿Eso está abierto todos los días de la semana?	*eh*-soh ehs-*tah* ah-*byehr*-toh *toh*-doh lohs *dee*-ahs deh lah seh-*mah*-nah
How much does that cost?	¿Cuánto cuesta eso?	*kwahn*-toh *kwehs*-tah *eh*-soh
That's too expensive.	Eso es muy caro.	*eh*-soh ehs *moo*-ee *kah*-roh
How much for two?	¿Cuánto por los / las dos?	*kwahn*-doh pohr lohs / lahs dohs

NUMBERS

1	uno (oo-noh)		16	dieciséis (dyeh-see-sayss)
2	dos (dohss)		17	diecisiete (dyeh-see-syeh-teh)
3	tres (trehss)		18	dieciocho (dyeh-syoh-choh)
4	cuatro (kwah-troh)		19	diecinueve (dyeh-see-nweh-beh)
5	cinco (seen-koh)		20	veinte (bayn-teh)
6	seis (sayss)		30	treinta (trayn-tah)
7	siete (syeh-teh)		40	cuarenta (kwah-rehn-tah)
8	ocho (oh-choh)		50	cincuenta (seen-kwehn-tah)
9	nueve (nweh-beh)		60	sesenta (seh-sehn-tah)
10	diez (dyehss)		70	setenta (seh-tehn-tah)
11	once (ohn-seh)		80	ochenta (oh-chehn-tah)
12	doce (doh-seh)		90	noventa (noh-behn-tah)
13	trece (treh-seh)		100	cien (syehn)
14	catorce (kah-tohr-seh)		1,000	mil (meel)
15	quince (keen-seh)			

QUANTITY

English	Spanish	Pronunciation
some	algún -a / algunos -as	ahl-*goon* / ahl-*goo*-nah / ahl-*goo*-nohs / ahl-*goo*-nahs
none	nada / ninguno -a / ningunos -as	*nah*-dah / neeng-*goo*-noh / neeng-*goo*-nah / neeng-*goo*-nohs / neeng-*goo*-nahs
all	todo -a / todos -as	*toh*-doh / *toh*-dah / *toh*-dohs/ *toh*-dahs
many / much	mucho -a / muchos -as	*moo*-cho / *moo*-cha / *moo*-chohs / *moo*-chas
a little bit (can be used for quantity or for time)	un poco / una poca	oon *poh*-koh / oo-nah *poh*-kah
dozen	una docena	doh-*seh*-na

SIZE

English	Spanish	Pronunciation
small	pequeño -a	peh-*keh*-nyoh / peh-*keh*-nyah
the smallest (literally "the most small")	el / la / lo más pequeño -a	ehl / lah / loh mahs peh-*keh*-nyoh / peh-*keh*-nyah

English	Spanish	Pronunciation
medium	mediano -a	meh-*dyah*-no / meh-*dyah*-na
big	grande	*grahn*-deh
fat	gordo -a	*gohr*-doh / *gohr*-dah
wide	ancho -a	*ahn*-cho / *ahn*-cha
narrow	estrecho-a/angosto -a	(add pronunciation)ahng-*goh*-stoh / ahng-*goh*-stah

TIME

Time in Spanish is referred to, literally, by the hour. "What time is it?" translates literally as "What hour is it? / What hours are they?"

For full coverage of number terms, see p 286.

HOURS OF THE DAY

English	Spanish	Pronunciation
What time is it?	¿Qué hora es?	keh *oh*-ra ehs
At what time?	¿A qué hora?	ah keh *oh*-rah
For how long?	¿Por cuánto tiempo?	pohr *kwahn*-toh *tyehm*-poh
It's one o'clock.	Es la una.	ehs lah *oo*-nah ehn *poon*-toh
It's two o'clock.	Son las dos.	sohn lahs *dohs* ehn *poon*-toh
It's two thirty.	Son las dos y media.	sohn lahs *dohs* ee meh-dyah
It's two fifteen.	Son las dos y cuarto.	sohn lahs *dohs* ee *kwahr*-toh

WEATHER

What's the weather like?   Cómo está el tiempo?

What's the temperature?   Cuántos grados hace?

What's the forecast?   Cuál es el pronósotico (del tiemop)?

DAYS OF THE WEEK

English	Spanish	Pronunciation
Monday	lunes	(*loo*-nehss)
Tuesday	martes	(*mahr*-tehss)
Wednesday	miércoles	(*myehr*-koh-lehs)
Thursday	jueves	(*wheh*-behss)
Friday	viernes	(*byehr*-nehss)
Saturday	sábado	(*sah*-bah-doh)
Sunday	domingo	(doh-*meen*-goh)

MONTHS OF THE YEAR

English	Spanish	Pronunciation
January	enero	eh-*neh*-roh
February	febrero	feh-*breh*-roh
March	marzo	*mahr*-soh

English	Spanish	Pronunciation
April	abril	ah-*breel*
May	mayo	*mah*-yoh
June	junio	*hoo*-nee-oh
July	julio	*hoo*-lee-oh
August	agosto	ah-*gohs*-toh
September	septiembre	sehp-*tyehm*-breh
October	octubre	ohk-*too*-breh
November	noviembre	noh-*vyehm*-breh
December	diciembre	dee-*syehm*-breh
next month	el mes entrante	ehl *mehs* ehn-*trahn*-teh
	el próximo mes	ehl *prohk*-see-moh *mehs*
last month	el mes pasado	ehl *mehs* pah-*sah*-doh

SEASONS OF THE YEAR

English	French	Pronunciation
spring	la primavera	lah pree-mah-*veh*-rah
summer	el verano	ehl veh-*rah*-noh
autumn	el otoño	ehl oh-*toh*-nyoh
winter	el invierno	ehl een-*vyehr*-noh

MENU TERMS

FISH

atún   tuna
calamares   squid
camarones   shrimp
cangrejo   crab
ceviche   marinated seafood salad
dorado   mahimahi
langosta   lobster
langostinos   prawns

lenguado   sole
mejillones   mussels
mero   grouper
ostras   oysters
pargo   snapper
pulpo   octopus
tiburón   shark

MEATS

bistec   beefsteak
cerdo   pork
chicharrones   fried pork rinds
chuleta   cutlet
conejo   rabbit
cordero   lamb

costillas   ribs
jamón   ham
lengua   tongue
pato   duck
pavo   turkey
pollo   chicken

VEGETABLES

aceitunas   olives
alcachofa   artichoke
berenjena   eggplant
cebolla   onion
elote   corn on the cob

ensalada   salad
espárragos   asparagus
espinacas   spinach
frijoles   beans
palmito   heart of palm

VEGETABLES

papa   potato
pepino   cucumber
remolacha   beet
repollo   cabbage

tomate   tomato
vainica   string beans
yuca   cassava, or manioc
zanahoria   carrot

FRUITS

aguacate   avocado
carambola   star fruit
cereza   cherry
ciruela   plum
fresa   strawberry
limón   lemon or lime
mango   mango
manzana   apple
melocotón   peach

mora   raspberry
naranja   orange
pera   pear
piña   pineapple
plátano   banana
sandía   watermelon
toronja   grapefruit
uvas   grapes

BASICS

aceite   oil
ajo   garlic
arroz   rice
azúcar   sugar
huevo   egg
huevos estrellados   sunny-side up eggs
huevos revueltos   scrambled eggs
mantequilla   butter
miel   honey

mostaza   mustard
natilla   sour cream
pan   bread
pimienta   pepper
queso   cheese
sal   salt
tamal   filled cornmeal pastry
tortilla   flat corn pancake
tostadas   toast

DRINKS

agua pura   purified water
aguas   soft drinks
batido   milkshake
bebida   drink

cerveza   beer
leche   milk
licuado   shake
ron   rum

OTHER RESTAURANT TERMS

asado   roasted
caliente   hot
cambio   change
comida   food
congelado   frozen
cuchara   spoon
cuchillo   knife
la cuenta   the bill
frío   cold
frito   fried
grande   big

la cuenta   the bill
medio   medium
muy cocido   well-done
pequeño   small
plato   plate
plato hondo   bowl
poco cocido   rare
propina   tip
servilleta   napkin
tenedor   fork
vaso   glass

TRAVEL TERMS

HOTEL TERMS

Aire acondicionado air-conditioning
almohada pillow
baño bathroom
calefacción heating
cama bed
cerradura de puerta door lock
colchón mattress
cuarto room

escritorio desk
hospedaje hotel or inn
manta blanket
mosquitero mosquito net
posada hotel or inn
sabanas sheets
ventilador fan

TRANSPORTATION TERMS

Aduana Customs
aeropuerto airport
avenida avenue
avión airplane
aviso warning
bus bus
calle street
correo mail or post office
cuadra city block
dinero money
embajada embassy
entrada entrance
este east
frontera border
lancha boat

norte north
oeste west
occidente west
oriente east
pasaporte passport
piloto chauffeur or driver
pinchazo literally, flat tire, but used to indicate tire repair shop
rebasar to pass while driving
no rebasar do not pass
salida exit
sur south
tumulo speed bump
vuelo flight

EMERGENCY TERMS

emergencia emergency
enfermo sick
farmacia pharmacy
hospital hospital

ladrón thief
peligroso dangerous
policía police
médico doctor

TYPICAL GUATEMALAN WORDS & PHRASES

camioneta	chicken bus (You might also hear, "*cheecken boos.*")
chapín	Guatemalan
campesino	Rural farmer, or peasant farmer
chino	Literally "Chinese," but used to refer to any Asian, or anyone who looks vaguely Asian.
chulo	beautiful
codo	cheap
comedor	basic restaurant
corte	Native-style skirt
gringo	North American/European/white person

huipil	Native-style woman's top
jalón	a ride
parrandear	to party
pinchazo	Literally a flat tire, but also seen on roadside signs throughout the country to advertise tire repair operations.
¡Púchica!	excited exclamation
¿Qué onda vos?	What's up?
típico	Native-style
tumulo	speed bump
vos	you

Index

Accommodations